Sandoval

THEORIZING REVOLUTIONS

"The authors have produced our best available guide to contemporary studies of revolution."
Charles Tilly, Columbia University

Is the era of revolution over? Did it end in 1989? It doesn't seem so in places like the West Bank, Peru, Mexico and Algeria and it may be just around the corner in many other locations. While the discourse and the locations of revolution may change, revolutions themselves will be with us for some time to come.

In *Theorizing Revolutions*, some of the most exciting thinkers in the study of revolutions today look critically at the many theoretical frameworks through which revolutions can be understood and apply them to specific revolutionary cases. The theoretical approaches considered in this way include state- and agent-centered perspectives, structural theory, elite models, demographic theories, ethnic/race studies, cultural studies, and feminism, and the revolutions covered range in time from the French Revolution to Eastern Europe in 1989 and in place from Russia to Vietnam and Nicaragua. Throughout, the authors identify and test new and emergent theoretical approaches and attend to the fruitful crossing and blurring of the boundaries of disciplines, including sociology, history, politics, ethnic studies, gender studies, cultural studies, and demography which the study of revolutions encourages.

John Foran is Associate Professor of Sociology at the University of California, Santa Barbara.

THEORIZING
REVOLUTIONS

Edited by John Foran

London and New York

First published 1997
by Routledge
11 New Fetter Lane, London EC4P 4EE

Simultaneously published in the USA and Canada
by Routledge
29 West 35th Street, New York, NY 10001

Typeset in Baskerville by
BC Typesetting, Bristol

Printed and bound in Great Britain by
Clays Ltd, Bungay, Suffolk

British Library Cataloguing in Publication Data
A catalogue record for this book is available from the British Library

Library of Congress Cataloging in Publication Data
Theorizing revolutions:
edited by John Foran.
p.   cm.
Includes bibliographical references and index.
1. Revolutions.
HM281.T44   1996
303.6′4–dc21   96-40838
                                                CIP

ISBN 0–415–13567–2 (hbk)
ISBN 0–415–13568–0 (pbk)

CONTENTS

CONTENTS

vi

FIGURES AND TABLES

FIGURES

TABLES

CONTRIBUTORS

John Foran, Associate Professor of Sociology and Director of the Program in Latin American and Iberian Studies at the University of California, Santa Barbara, is author of *Fragile Resistance: Social Transformation in Iran from 1500 to the Revolution* (1993). He is working on a book on the origins of revolutions in the Third World.

Jack A. Goldstone is Professor of Sociology at University of California, Davis, and former director of the Center for Comparative Research in History, Society, and Culture. He is the author of *Revolution and Rebellion in the Early Modern World* (1991), co-editor of *Revolutions of the Late Twentieth Century* (1991), and editor of the *Encyclopedia of Political Revolutions* (1998).

Jeff Goodwin, an Associate Professor of Sociology at New York University, has written a number of articles on revolutions and revolutionary movements. He is completing a book entitled *State and Revolution, 1945–1991* (1998).

Richard Lachmann teaches sociology at SUNY-Albany. He is the author of *From Manor to Market: Structural Change in England, 1536–1640* (1987) and *Capitalists in Spite of Themselves: Elite Conflict and European Transitions* (1997).

Christopher McAuley teaches political economy in the Department of Black Studies at the University of California, Santa Barbara. His dissertation dealt with the racial origins of world capitalism, and he is currently undertaking a study of the work of Oliver C. Cox.

Valentine M. Moghadam has been Senior Research Fellow at the United Nations University in Helsinki. She is the author of *Modernizing Women: Gender and Social Change in the Middle East* (1993), the editor of five other books as well as many articles on the Middle East. She is currently Director of Women's Studies and Associate Professor of Sociology at Illinois State University.

Eric Selbin is Assistant Professor of Political Science at Southwestern University in Georgetown, Texas and the author of *Modern Latin American Revolution* (1993). He received his Ph.D. in political science from the University of Minnesota.

Timothy P. Wickham-Crowley is Associate Professor of Sociology and Associate Director of the Center for Latin American Studies at Georgetown University. He has authored *Exploring Revolution: Essays on Latin American Insurgency and Revolutionary Theory* (1991) and *Guerrillas and Revolution in Latin America: A Comparative Study of Insurgents and Regimes Since 1956* (1992). His current projects include a socio-political analysis of development and underdevelopment throughout the New World since 1492 and an attempt to show the structured parallels between sociological theories and various Marxisms and feminisms.

ACKNOWLEDGEMENTS

I would like to thank first and foremost the contributors to this collection, who have been through a long process (or does it feel long only to me?) to create something that I am very excited about. It is obvious but worth saying that without you this volume would not exist, and I am very grateful for your labor on it. That the pieces are all original essays, and that their authors could have published them elsewhere, but did not, is a source of considerable satisfaction for an editor working with such a wonderful group of scholars.

I would like also to thank the several readers of each chapter, who are acknowledged in the first note to most contributions – the time you have taken with these pieces has enriched them. An even larger thanks to the reviewer of the whole manuscript for Routledge, whose comments have improved the final result, and above all, the introduction.

At Routledge in London, appreciation is due to our editor, Mari Shullaw, who had the vision to support this project before it was completed, and to her assistant, Joanne Mattingly. I hope that the book comes close to the vision!

Closer to home, I am very grateful for the tireless efforts of my research assistant Joe Bandy, of the Department of Sociology at the University of California, Santa Barbara, who tracked down every missing reference. What remains missing cannot be found by human effort.

Finally, this book is dedicated to its readers, the next generation of scholars of revolution. I hope that some of them will make revolutions as well, in their own ways. And in the end, to the constant revolutionary in my life, Kum-Kum Bhavnani, and to Cerina, the new one.

INTRODUCTION

John Foran

Is the era of revolution over? Did it end in 1989? And was that such a long time ago, in any case? It doesn't seem to be necessarily over in places like the West Bank and Gaza, Mexico (Chiapas), Algeria or Peru, and may be just around the corner in many other locations (Egypt? Zaire?). The discourse of revolution may be changing; the international loci and foci may be moving (with the demise of the Soviet Union and the consolidation of democracies in Latin America); the actors may be changing (with more women and ethnic minorities active; though, as this volume notes, both have long histories of revolutionary activism) – all of this may be (arguably) true. But revolutions are going to be with us to the end of history, and – *pace* Francis Fukiyama – that is not in sight.

Only a long historical and wide geographic optic can shed light on the future of revolutions. And that is why we have taken disparate theoretical and disciplinary approaches here as well. Our title indicates our purposes in this volume: to attend to the recent upsurge in the academic study of revolutions by careful attention to theoretical innovation, to identify new and emergent approaches and push them further conceptually and empirically, and to attend to the crossing and blurring of the boundaries of the disciplines. While most of us work as sociologists, we still feel that this is the social science with the most interdisciplinary sweep. Further, a careful study of the literature on revolutions since the mid-1970s cannot fail to note the accomplishments of sociologists and their journals (this is where the action is, and has been for some time, covering wide interdisciplinary ground, as evidenced in this collection). In the less narrow sense a wide range of disciplines are covered in these pages: sociology, history, politics, ethnic studies, gender studies, cultural studies, and demography. The distinct theoretical approaches systematically scrutinized along the way include state-centered perspectives, structural theories, world-system analysis, elite models, demographic theories, and feminism.

Each of the chapters that follow reviews debates in one of these disciplines and/or perspectives, advances an original theory, and does as much empirical analysis of cases as space and expertise permit. It is our feeling that

1

theoretical and empirical work cannot advance separately: historically and comparatively grounded studies are the best way to explore and exploit the gains of theory, just as theory must be used to illuminate the particularities of individual cases. I have divided the book into two parts, one emphasizing the strengths of structural approaches, and the other insisting on the irreducible contributions of culture and agency. We are well aware of the somewhat artificial nature of this divide, and many of us seek to explode this duality in interesting ways (e.g., Wickham-Crowley's process approach to structure, Goodwin's acknowledgement of culture alongside states, Lachmann's structural approach to agency, my own attempts to blend culture and political economy). Yet it still seems a useful distinction, or at least one with which any student of revolution must come to terms. In the end, if the next generation of students finds new syntheses that acknowledge the independent weight of the various contending approaches, while yet knitting them better together, they will have realized and extended a project identified by many of the contributors to this volume.

Our intended audience is this future generation: sociologists, historians, political scientists, social theorists, policy-makers(?), and revolutionaries(!) among them – people wanting to know the frontiers and horizons of the study of revolutions and social movements; thus people curious about and interested in knowing what's on the cutting edge and wanting to take it further. The literature reviews should be accessible to advanced undergraduates; the original theories should be of interest to specialists at the graduate and postgraduate level; it is hoped that the examples will make the theories more understandable to beginners and more convincing to the adept. Finally, we draw the reader's attention to the bibliography to this volume, which as a collective project represents one of the most comprehensive, up-to-date such resources ever compiled. We hope that this diverse audience reads us with pleasure and engages in moving these debates into new and fruitful directions toward the ever-receding horizon of theorizing revolutions.

The first part of this book traces the contours of structural theorizing about revolution. Ever since Theda Skocpol's path-breaking study, *States and Social Revolutions* (1979), structural theories have been the approach of choice, whether taking off from or criticizing her work. Both theoretical and empirical gains have been registered, notably in the works of some of the contributors to this section of the book. Allow me to provide the first "review" of each chapter of this volume (my biases, as editor, should be evident, compensated, one hopes, by my familiarity with these pieces).

Jeff Goodwin opens the dialogue with a spirited and bracing brief for state-centered approaches to revolution. After skillfully disentangling several variants – theories of state-autonomy, the state-capacity approach, the political-opportunity perspective, and the state-constructionist view – he acutely assesses their strengths. Effectively dismissing certain critiques and

2

openly acknowledging the validity of others, he proposes solutions to the weaknesses of this set of approaches by significantly expanding the domain and angle of the "state" to include its relations with and effects upon a range of other relevant structures and actors: the international arena, civil society, and political culture. In so doing he enters a claim against post-structural and postmodern theorists about the nature of *power*, which he argues goes far beyond the local setting to the center of the state and polity. He also suggests solutions to a number of key puzzles in the study of revolutions: Why are social revolutions "modern" phenomena? Why are they so concerned with state power? Why is state breakdown so important for success? What explains the time and place of revolutions? And why do risky revolutionary ideologies sometimes succeed in mobilizing large numbers of people? At the end of the chapter, these questions are taken up in the context of the case of Cuba. The result is perhaps the best map ever drawn of the *multiple* roles of the state in the making, and analysis, of revolutions.

Timothy Wickham-Crowley performs a similar *tour de horizon* for structural perspectives on revolutions. Like Goodwin, he argues trenchantly for structuralism rather than *post*-structuralism in theorizing revolution and in social theory more generally. Also analogously to Goodwin, he expands and redefines his domain to include social processes, thus dissolving a standard and troubling dichotomy in social theory. Instead, he contrasts social structural theories with cultural and agency-based theories in providing another fresh "map" of the terrain. He observes that structuralists and culturalists have been largely talking past one another, the former focused on exploring the causes of revolution, the latter preoccupied with outcomes. He concludes judiciously that neither pure structuralism nor culturalism (or alteratively, voluntarism versus contingency theories) will do; rather, theories must specify the mechanisms by which their causes operate, or are "mediated" by social and historical processes. Another way to interpret these debates, which Wickham-Crowley hints at, is to see that both structuralists and culturalists have important – but quite distinct – things to say about the revolutions they do study (compare, for example, the narratives of Lynn Hunt and William Sewell on the French Revolution with Theda Skocpol's macrocausal account). A final intriguing point raised is that theorists may be quite close in the terms adopted by Wickham-Crowley, yet very different in their actual causal theories (cf., Jeffery Paige, Theda Skocpol, and world-system theory; or myself and Forrest Colburn). This calls for further attempts to map the terrain as Wickham-Crowley has, along different axes.

Richard Lachmann's chapter on elites and masses cuts into the problem of revolutions in some unique ways, focused neither on classes nor on states. His argument concerns agency, but a highly *structured* form of agency (see Wickham-Crowley in Part I or Eric Selbin and my own two chapters in Part II for contrasts). Using striking paired comparisons, Lachmann makes a bold argument for the importance of elites alongside masses as actors, working out the patterns of revolutionary outbreak and success in terms of varying combinations of elite unity or conflict, and mass participation or quiescence. He finds that single, unified elites are immune to mass revolutionary challenges, which may occur, but will fail as in Eastern Europe in 1956 and 1968. The argument that mass mobilization succeeds only in the presence of elite divisions is advanced through a look at the civil wars and revolutions of England and France. This revises our understanding of the events of 1789–95 in France as determined by the internal divisions among old and new financial, commercial, and landed elites, propelled forward by successful mass mobilization by the new elites. Lachmann's elite-centered structural theory of revolutions paradoxically accords the state a reduced role in the causes and consequences of revolutions, at least for the pre-twentieth-century period. Like the work of Charles Tilly, these comparative materials are all drawn from European examples, although across a very great time period; the Third World looks different, one might imagine. There is also an argument here about the limits of revolutionary action, whether in fourteenth-century Italy or England in 1649. The result is a theory of actors' success or failure in taking power, and of the long-term structural effects of "success." Finally, he makes useful points on the *varied* effects of wars in the struggles between and among revolutionaries and the *status quo*.

Jack Goldstone's contribution extends his earlier work based on rebellion and revolution in the early modern world to the twentieth century, especially the Third World. He takes pains to distinguish his approach from demographic determinism; rather, his focus is on the impact of demography on social movements, mediated through social, political, and economic *institutions*. Demography, like geography and communication, has remained largely undertheorized in the study of revolutions. Goldstone ranges over diverse cases from around the world to specify the links between population growth and political crisis, through a series of key effects: a decline in state capacity to manage society, the alienation of elite actors, and the mobilization of mass movements in which urban people and youth generally come to play significant roles in shaping revolutionary outcomes. Goldstone's work has clear policy implications for governments, while at the same time avoiding the usual traps in talking about population, and thus offers illuminating insights as well for the radicals of the late twentieth century.

The second part of this volume shifts attention to issues of agency and culture. Its contributors argue that these are the cutting edge of the study of revolutions, as they are in the study of social movements more generally, and social theory broadly. In the field of revolutions, recent contributions by Eric Selbin and Forrest Colburn may be noted as briefs for this new work, and Eric Selbin here opens Part II with a statement of the problem and his case. The two chapters by the editor also attempt to take this up. Two other relatively new but rapidly growing areas of inquiry in the social sciences are ethnicity and gender. Now increasingly established counterparts and correctives to the long-standing disciplines, they are beginning to enter the literature on revolutions as well.

Eric Selbin issues an impassioned – and important – call for the return of agency and ideas, or actors and their conceptions, to center stage in the study of revolution. He goes beyond an "add and stir" approach to focus on agency, although stopping short (if just) of an "actor-determinism." He asks us *how* to bring people back in, further advancing this new thread in the literature. His answer lies in the ideas articulated by revolutionary leaders and their reception (or not) by the population. Taken together, these consti-tute "idea streams" capable of animating rebellions across time and space. The looseness of the term "culture," moreover, is interrogated and refracted into the more manageable notions of "collective memories," "symbolic poli-tics," and "popular political culture." Turning Theda Skocpol's celebrated invocation of Wendell Phillips on its head, he asserts: "without people articu-lating compelling stories with engaging and empowering plots, revolutions will not come." The sum effect of this short but highly suggestive chapter is to re-open considerations of the options people perceive as available to them as they attempt to bring about deep social transformation.

Next, Val Moghadam expands the disciplinary scope of revolutions to take into account the burgeoning literature on women and revolutions, noting the continued absence of gender in theories of revolution (a critique the rest of us are subject to!). She elaborates a distinctive argument about the existence of two models of gender relations pursued by revolutionaries across time and space: a women-in-the-family model that has striven to assimilate women's aspirations to patriarchal cultural and social positions, and a women's emancipation project accompanying the great socialist revo-lutions, beginning with Russia, in which sexual and gender equality – rather than difference – were propounded. Paradoxically, it was the French Revo-lution that pioneered the women-in-the-family model, followed in the twen-tieth century by Mexico, Algeria, Iran, and Eastern Europe, among others. In all of these cases the strong roles played by women in making revolutions were rolled back by new regimes stressing ideologies of gender difference. In Russia, China, Cuba, South Yemen, Vietnam, Nicaragua, and elsewhere, by contrast, women gained more formal and actual rights despite the recup-eration of their autonomous organizations by the states that emerged. Moghadam's discernment of these patterns and her argument that revolu-tions necessarily possess a gender dimension open up a space for future analy-sis of the relations among gender, class, state, and the global context in understanding the causes, course, and outcomes of revolutions.

Chris McAuley breaks new ground as well with an insightful journey into the relationships among underdevelopment, race, and revolution over a 200-year span of the history of the Americas, from the early-nineteenth-century wars of liberation through the upheavals in Mexico, Cuba, and Nicaragua across the twentieth. The indisputable participation of diverse racial groups in these cases is contrasted with the disappointing outcomes of so many of these experiments in change, and is linked, moreover, to the racist realities of the societies in question. Just as patriarchy has proven an Achilles" heel for real social transformation, racism has plagued revolutionaries" attempts to remake their world in a more egalitarian vein. The uncanny reflections of both these structured inequalities in the academy, moreover, have only just begun to be undone, and equally imperfectly. McAuley, along with Moghadam, provide hints of a future synthesis of race, class, and gender as interlocked domains of struggle and reflection.

Another major shift in theorizing revolutions has come in the area of cultural studies. Complementary to the cases made by Goodwin and Wickham-Crowley in Part I for nuanced state-centered and structural approaches, I argue in Chapter 8 that culture is not the sole explanation either. Indeed, where they include culture, social networks, and class as key independent variables, I include state, social structure, and international relations. Do we meet in the same place? Almost. Goodwin is most impressed by the "framing" approach to culture; I more by the insights of cultural studies. Wickham-Crowley sees culture as specific to given societies, and thus incapable of broad general significance; I attempt to find a workable balance between the unique and the abstract qualities of culture, or more precisely, political *cultures* of opposition. This chapter ranges across causes and outcomes, and includes brief discussions of the cases of France, Cuba, Nicaragua, El Salvador, Iran, and Eastern Europe. All three of us agree that culture does not float free of social conditions, that structure and process are equally important, and that resources and organizations loom large in understanding the effectivity of political cultures in the revolutionary process.

In the concluding chapter to the volume, I attempt to draw together a multi-causal model of the origins of Third World social revolutions. This model embraces much of what my fellow contributors to this project have highlighted, including a role for the state, for structure as well as culture and agency, for the world-system as well as the domestic setting. It insists that class (with race and gender) remains a central key to understanding social structure, that Third World revolutions have significant economic causes, that political culture is indispensable for making and understanding revolutions. It uses the fairly new technique of Boolean analysis pioneered by Charles Ragin and brought into the study of revolution by Tim Wickham-Crowley to assess the reasons for the success of a few revolutions in the Third World and the failures of many others to come to power. Like the work of Wickham-Crowley, Goldstone, and others, it aims for a theory or model capable of explaining a wide range of cases, and thus takes us another step on the road to an ever-elusive comprehensive theory of revolution.

It will become apparent to the careful reader of this introduction and the pages to follow that the contributors to this volume do not agree on many of the issues involved in understanding revolutions. Indeed, no comprehensive theory of any aspect of revolutions – origins, processes and actors, or outcomes – has stood the test of time and comparative research. The study of revolutions has entered a period in which older certainties have been partly undone, and no consensus yet exists about the shape of a new paradigm. Clearly, debates continue about the relative importance of agency versus structure, culture versus political economy, class versus elites and masses, or how race and gender figure in the picture. That these issues are being raised increasingly by the present generation of scholars is in itself a positive sign of intellectual ferment, however. It is at the same time a call for synthesis, or at least a challenge for more sophisticated integration of diverse analytic elements.

Have we achieved such a synthesis here? Undoubtedly not. But I believe we have charted many of the themes that the next generation will grapple with. To theorize revolutions is a collective enterprise, more so than most, given the complexities of the debates and the diversity of the historical material. No theoretical unity can be imposed on this territory, yet our hope is that we have presented the cutting edge of the state of the art, located somewhere in an intellectual field where the perennial theoretical debates intersect with the increasing blurring of disciplinary boundaries.

You, the readers, will be the ultimate judges of the success of these steps toward that horizon, and of our volume as a whole. We look forward to your reactions and continued dialogue on all the issues raised herein. Let many (a thousand?) interpretations blossom, but let us engage in conversations with each other, attending to the insights of each.

Part I

THE FRONTIERS OF STRUCTURES

1

STATE-CENTERED APPROACHES TO SOCIAL REVOLUTIONS

Strengths and limitations of a theoretical tradition

Jeff Goodwin

I argue in this chapter that state-centered theoretical approaches comprise some of the most powerful analytic tools that are currently available to analysts of social revolutions. By contrast, fashionable post-structuralist conceptions of power simply beg too many fundamental questions. Certain types of cultural analyses, as we shall see, as well as the recent turn to "civil society," are somewhat more useful. But state-centered approaches are even more helpful for resolving the key puzzles that are distinctive to the study of social revolutions.[1] (Throughout, I refer to state-centered *approaches* in the plural, because – as I shall detail – there is no single statist perspective or argument, but several overlapping ones.) Of course, state-centered analysis, like any theoretical tradition, has its blindspots and limitations, which I shall also address. Fortunately, these limitations point the way toward a more powerful synthetic perspective on revolutions and collective action.

What is the statist theoretical tradition all about? All of the state-centered approaches that I shall review emphasize or "center" a particular set of causal mechanisms – namely, those processes whereby states (foreign as well as domestic) shape, enable, or constrain economic, associational, cultural, and even social-psychological phenomena. State-centered theorists argue that these mechanisms are, for certain purposes, more powerful or causally important than (or at least complementary to) a range of alternative causal processes – for example, those emphasizing social class, civil society, culture, or social psychology. Statist perspectives, then, are intentionally one-sided.

And yet partly *because* of this one-sidedness, state-centered approaches are exceptionally valuable for understanding social revolutions. This follows, at least in part, from the fact that revolutions themselves are unusually state-centered phenomena. As Charles Tilly notes, "whatever else they involve, revolutions include forcible transfers of power over states, and therefore any useful account of revolutions must concern, among other things, how states and uses of force vary in time, space and social setting."[2]

I should note at the outset that I do not write as an unbiased observer. My own empirical investigations into insurgencies and social revolutions have been resolutely state-centered.[3] I must obviously believe, then, that statist approaches to social revolutions are especially powerful! At the same time, I shall try to clarify the various limitations of this perspective.[4] After discussing the considerable strengths of state-centered approaches to social revolutions, accordingly, I shall review the main weaknesses of statist analysis and suggest some of the theoretical resources that are available for redressing them.[5] I also examine how certain strengths and limitations of state-centered approaches are exemplified in a case study of the Cuban Revolution.

Before discussing the analytic strengths of state-centered approaches to social revolutions, let me begin by distinguishing the distinctive forms of state-centered analysis. Understanding the *variety* of statist perspectives is important for appreciating both the strengths and limitations of this theoretical tradition.

FOUR TYPES OF STATE-CENTERED ANALYSIS

A good deal of confusion has resulted from the failure of proponents and critics alike to distinguish among – or even to note the existence of – four distinctive versions of statist analysis, namely, the state-autonomy, state-capacity, political-opportunity, and state-constructionist approaches. Because individual states exist within an international state system, furthermore, each of these approaches has geopolitical as well as domestic dimensions.

The *state-autonomy perspective*, with which the others are most often conflated, emphasizes the variable autonomy of state officials or "state managers" from the dominant social class, civil society more generally, or other states.[6] According to this perspective – which derives from Max Weber's political sociology – politicians, bureaucrats, and military officers may develop identities, interests, ideologies, and (ultimately) lines of action that are very different from those of organized groups in civil society or the officials of other states; they may not be usefully conceptualized, accordingly, as representatives of powerful capitalists, interest groups, the "popular will," or foreign potentates. In fact, the interests of state officials in accumulating resources (through taxes, for example) and mobilizing the population (for war against other states, for example) may sometimes conflict with the interests of powerful social groups (including the dominant class), not to mention external actors. Overt conflicts between state officials, on the one hand, and economic elites or mobilized groups, on the other, are typically adduced as evidence for this perspective.

A second statist approach – which may also be traced to Weber – emphasizes the actual material and organizational capacity (or lack thereof) of state officials to implement successfully their political agenda, even in the face of opposition from powerful actors in civil society or from other states. This perspective focuses on variations in states' fiscal resources, military power, and organizational reach (or "penetration") into civil society – what Michael Mann has termed the "infrastructural power" of states.[7] Key determinants of such variations include the organizational or bureaucratic rationality of state institutions as well as the extent to which states confront threats from other states that require war preparation. (Some states also receive large infusions of resources from other states; a state's position in the international state system, in other words, may strongly shape its capacities.)[8] While this second, *state-capacity approach* is typically utilized alongside the state-autonomy perspective, the two are analytically distinct; state officials, after all, may have very different aims than economic elites or other states and yet lack the capacity actually to implement their preferred policies. State autonomy, in other words, does not necessarily imply state capacity, or vice versa.

A third state-centered approach emphasizes how the apparent responsiveness or permeability of states or "polities" influences the ability of mobilized social groups to act collectively or substantively influence state policies.[9] More specifically, "political opportunities" (which mobilized groups themselves usually attempt to create or manipulate) are deemed necessary – in addition to (for example) grievances and organization – for people to act collectively or to shape the agenda of state officials.[10] At the very least, according to this *political-opportunity perspective*, the state must either lack the means (infrastructurally speaking) or simply be unwilling to violently suppress such groups; it also helps if these groups can find powerful allies within a divided state or polity.[11] And geopolitics is again important here. Some social groups, for example, may form alliances with, and receive significant resources from, foreign states; and international wars and imperial overextension have often produced political crises that have created unprecedented opportunities for political mobilization.[12]

There exists, finally, what Theda Skocpol calls a "Tocquevillian" approach, which emphasizes how states shape the very identities, social ties, ideas, and even emotions of actors in civil society.[13] To my mind, this is perhaps the most interesting statist approach of all, yet it is often elided in discussions of state-centered theory or else conflated with the political-opportunity perspective. I propose that we label this approach the *state-constructionist perspective*,[14] because it examines the ways in which states help to construct or constitute various aspects of civil society that are (falsely) conceptualized as wholly exterior to states.[15] In other words, the focus here – as against a political-opportunity approach – is not so much on whether a state or polity provides incentives or opportunities to act for already existing networks of like-minded people; rather, state constructionism emphasizes how the actions of foreign as well as domestic states help to make cognitively plausible and morally justifiable certain sorts of collective grievances, emotions, identities, ideologies, and associational activities (but not others) in the first place.[16]

ANALYTIC STRENGTHS OF STATE-CENTERED APPROACHES TO REVOLUTIONS

How are these various theoretical approaches useful for understanding social revolutions in particular? In what follows, I emphasize how statist approaches help to resolve a series of key problems that are distinctive to the study of social revolutions.

The centrality of state power and state breakdowns

To begin with, consider this puzzle: *Why is social revolution, unlike many other forms of social conflict, a peculiarly "modern" phenomenon?* Why, in other words, have social revolutions occurred with considerable frequency during the nineteenth and twentieth centuries, yet seem not to have occurred at all before the seventeenth? This puzzle concerns the "conditions of existence" of revolutions – that is, the background conditions (which have widely existed, evidently, for only the past century or two) that are necessary for social revolutions to occur. A state-centered perspective offers a compelling solution to this puzzle: the international state system itself. In other words, *no states, no revolutions.* This basic proposition, frequently reiterated by Charles Tilly, is usually overlooked by analysts of revolutions; it is taken for granted by virtually all scholars of revolutions, including Marxists, culturalists, and state-centered analysts themselves.

From a state-centered approach, in other words, it is much more than a convention or a mere matter of convenience that scholars write books and articles about, for example, the "French," "Russian," and "Cuban" revolutions. In fact (as a state-capacity approach would suggest), prior to the emergence of consolidated national states,[17] social revolutions as we now understand them – whether as radically transformative processes, a distinctive political repertoire, or a moral ideal – were simply impossible. Until the modern era, that is, there existed no institution with sufficient infrastructural power to remake extensive social arrangements in fundamental ways; the consolidated national state, however, made it possible to do – and to think of doing – just that. (Revolutionaries themselves, in fact, have often consolidated states precisely in order to remake societies.) Thus, while social conflict may be as old as humanity itself, the reality and ideal of radically transforming a "society," "nation," or "people" – the economic, political, and cultural arrangements of a large population – are coeval with the modern state system as it originated in Europe and was then transported and emulated around the globe.

14

This analysis immediately suggests a solution to another puzzle: *Why are revolutionary movements, unlike other types of social movements, concerned with "seizing" or "smashing" state power?* If the preceding analysis is correct, those who would radically transform modern societies must obviously concern themselves with the state. (If they do not, the state will certainly concern itself with them!) In other words, because the state enforces (through violence if necessary) the most fundamental "rules" of a society (whether these are codified as laws or not) by virtue of its control of the principal means of coercion, any radical recasting of these rules requires access to, and indeed a fundamental reorganization of, state power itself. Because of their actual and potential infrastructural power, in other words, states are necessarily the target (although not the *only* target) of revolutionary movements.

This view of revolutions, I should note, is shared by state-centered and Marxist analysts alike, even though the latter are otherwise keen to emphasize how class struggles are supposedly the driving force behind them. "The basic question of every revolution," wrote Lenin, "is that of state power."[18] The task of revolutionaries, in his view, was not simply to change laws or to replace government officials, but rather to change the structural characteristics of the state – to create "an entirely different kind of power" with which society as a whole could then be recast.[19] Perry Anderson similarly notes that

> one of the basic axioms of historical materialism [is] that secular struggle between classes is ultimately resolved at the *political* – not at the economic or cultural – level of society. In other words, it is the construction and destruction of States which seal the basic shifts in the relations of production, so long as classes subsist.[20]

It follows that successful revolutionary movements must, at the very least, secure or "seize" state power. And this implies, by definition, that the old state must collapse; for if it persists in the face of a revolutionary challenge, then the revolutionaries have obviously failed to attain the sort of power that they need in order to change society as a whole in a more or less radical fashion.[21]

We now possess the solution to yet another conundrum: *Why must the state break down, collapse, or capitulate for a revolution, unlike many other forms of social protest, to succeed?* That state breakdowns create the sort of political opportunities necessary for full-fledged revolutionary change is perhaps the best-known idea to emerge from statist analyses of revolution; it is a point that is central, for example, to Theda Skocpol's influential state-centered study, *States and Social Revolutions*.[22] In fact, Skocpol not only utilizes a political-opportunity approach in order to explain why transformative, class-based revolts from below could occur in France, Russia, and China, but also employs a state-autonomy perspective in order to explain the political crises that created such opportunities in the first place. Indeed, one of the more interesting claims of Skocpol's study is that the political crises that made revolutions possible in France, Russia, and China were *not* brought about by revolutionaries; rather, conflicts between dominant classes and autonomous state officials – conflicts, Skocpol emphasizes, that were produced or exacerbated by geopolitical competition – directly or indirectly brought about such crises, thereby opening up opportunities that rebellious lower classes and self-conscious revolutionaries seized, sometimes years later.

By illuminating the origins of, and the political opportunities created by, these sorts of state crises and breakdowns, state-centered approaches help to resolve yet another classic puzzle: *Why do social revolutions occur when and where they do?* It has become virtually obligatory for scholars to note that people are not often rebellious in the poorest of societies or during the hardest of times; and even where and when people are rebellious, and strong revolutionary movements form, they may not always be able to seize state power – *unless*, that is, they are able to exploit the political opportunities opened up by state breakdowns.

The limited utility of post-structuralist conceptions of power, at least for the analysis of revolutions, should now be apparent.[23] In fact, any view of power as "decentered," largely nonviolent, local, mobile, and ubiquitous fails to grasp the crucial difference that centralized state power (and its breakdown) makes for a variety of social processes, including social revolutions. Furthermore, the notion that the state itself is simply the "institutional crystallization" or "institutional integration of power relationships" that are fundamentally "local" in nature fails to grasp the potential autonomy and distinctive capacities of states; it also underestimates the role of state power in constructing, or reconstructing, localized power relationships in the first place.[24]

The formation of revolutionary movements

And yet, of course, state power and its breakdown cannot alone explain (or predict) social revolutions; analysts also need to explain why and how specifically revolutionary movements are able to take advantage of these crises and actually seize power.[25] After all, an organized revolutionary movement simply may not exist or possess the sufficient leverage or "hegemony" within civil society that is necessary to take advantage of extant political opportunities. In such cases, state power will be reconsolidated – if it is reconsolidated at all – by surviving factions of the old regime or by political moderates who eschew any radical transformation of the state or society.

Here again, I would propose, a state-centered perspective provides us with some indispensable analytic tools. For although statist approaches (as we shall see) do not adequately theorize collective action as such, they are particularly helpful in resolving the following puzzle: *Why are groups with a*

16

specifically revolutionary agenda or ideology, as well as a radical or high-risk strategic repertoire, sometimes able to attract broad popular support?[26] State-centered approaches point to at least five distinctive state practices or characteristics that help to engender hegemonic revolutionary movements; these are causally "cumulative," in the sense that a hegemonic revolutionary movement is more likely to develop the more they characterize a given state.

1. *State sponsorship or protection of unpopular economic and social arrangements.* In certain societies, economic and social arrangements – particularly those involving people's work or livelihood – may be widely viewed as unjust (that is, as not simply unfortunate or inevitable). Yet unless state officials are seen to sponsor or protect those arrangements – through legal codes, surveillance, taxation, conscription, and, ultimately, force – specifically *revolutionary* collective action is unlikely. People may blame their particular bosses or superiors for their plight, for example, or even whole classes of bosses, yet the state itself may not be challenged (even when the aggrieved are well organized and the political context is opportune) unless there exists a palpable symbiotic relationship between the state and these elites. (Of course, the fact that a despised state must actively protect certain institutions will itself serve, in many instances, to delegitimize them.)

For this reason, "ruling classes" that do not directly rule may be safer than those that do; other things being equal, that is, some measure of state autonomy from the dominant economic class may act as a bulwark against revolution. In such contexts, contentious, anti-elite actions may be chronic, in such forms as pilfering, malingering, sabotage, riots, strikes, and demonstrations; yet such actions are unlikely to escalate beyond a local or, at most, regional level in a way that would seriously and directly threaten a strong state.[27] And yet rebels are not revolutionaries, we have seen, unless they seriously contend for state power.

It follows that states that regulate or abolish perceived economic and social injustices are less likely to become the target of political demands (revolutionary or otherwise) than those that are seen to cause or reproduce such injustices. On the other hand, a state that suddenly attempts to reform unpopular institutions that it has long protected may not be able to preempt thereby a revolutionary challenge; on the contrary, such reforms, or even attempted reforms, may be perceived as signs of the state's weakness and, accordingly, will simply serve to accelerate revolutionary mobilization. We might term this the "too-little-too-late syndrome." As Tocqueville argued, "the most perilous moment for a bad government is one when it seeks to mend its ways. . . . Patiently endured so long as it seemed beyond redress, a grievance comes to appear intolerable once the possibility of removing it crosses men's minds."[28]

In sum, grievances may become "politicized" (that is, framed as resolvable only at the level of the state), and thereby a basis for specifically revolutionary collective action, only when the state sponsors or protects economic and social conditions that are viewed as grievous. Note that this is a state-constructionist argument: state practices, in this case, help to constitute a distinctive strategic orientation among aggrieved groups in civil society.

2. *Exclusion of mobilized groups from state power or resources.* Even if aggrieved groups direct their claims at the state, they are unlikely to seek its overthrow (or radical reorganization) if they manage to attain some significant share – or believe they *can* attain such a share – of state power or influence. Indeed, even if such groups view their political influence as unfairly limited, their access to state resources or inclusion in policy-making deliberations – unless palpably cosmetic – will likely prevent any radicalization of their strategic repertoire or guiding ideology. In fact, the political "incorporation" of mobilized groups – including the putatively revolutionary proletariat – has typically served to *deradicalize* them.[29] For such groups often view this sort of inclusion as the first step in the accumulation of greater influence and resources; in any event, they are unlikely to jeopardize their relatively low-cost access to the state – unless that state itself is in deep crisis – by engaging in "disloyal" or illegal activities.

Political inclusion also discourages the sense that the state is unreformable or an instrument of a narrow class or clique and (accordingly) needs to be fundamentally overhauled. Tocqueville emphasized how the exclusionary nature of French absolutism bred, by contrast, a political culture character-ized by a utopian longing for total revolution – even though French social conditions were comparatively benign by European standards of the time.[30]

Accordingly, neither open, democratic polities nor authoritarian yet inclu-sionary (for example, "populist") regimes have generally been challenged by powerful revolutionary movements. By contrast, chronic exclusion of mobilized groups from access to state power is likely to push them toward a specifically revolutionary strategy or repertoire – that is, militant, extralegal, and even armed struggle aimed at overthrowing the state. Such exclusion, after all, serves as an object lesson in the futility of legalistic or constitutional politics (i.e., "playing by the rules"). Exclusionary authoritarian regimes, in other words, tend to "incubate" radical collective-action: those who special-ize in it tend to prosper, because they come to be viewed by many people as more realistic and potentially effective than political moderates, who them-selves come to be viewed as hopelessly ineffectual.[31] Partly for this reason, virtually every powerful revolutionary movement of the present century developed under an exclusionary regime, including the Bolsheviks in Russia, the Communists in China and Vietnam, Castro's July 26 Movement in Cuba, the broad coalition that opposed the Shah in Iran, and the guerrilla movements of Central America.

Note that this argument has both political-opportunity and state-constructionist aspects. In the former sense, it emphasizes how the *lack* of routine opportunities to influence state policy tends to push certain groups and individuals towards radical politics; in the latter sense, emphasis falls on the ways in which exclusionary state practices reinforce the plausibility and justifiability of a radical political orientation or collective identity.

3. *Indiscriminate, but not overwhelming, state violence against mobilized groups and oppositional political figures.* Like political exclusion, indiscriminate state violence against mobilized groups and oppositional figures is likely to reinforce the plausibility, justifiability, and (hence) diffusion of the idea that the state needs to be violently "smashed" and radically reorganized. For reasons of simple self-defense, in fact, people who are literally targeted by the state may arm themselves or join groups that have access to arms. Unless state violence is simply overwhelming (see below), indiscriminate coercion tends to back-fire, producing an ever-growing popular mobilization by armed movements and an even larger body of sympathizers.[32] Revolutionary groups may thus prosper not so much because of their ideology *per se*, but simply because they can offer people some sort of protection from certain sorts of states. Many studies of revolutions emphasize that groups have turned to militant strate-gies or armed struggle only after their previous efforts to secure change through legal means were violently repressed.[33]

Like political exclusion, indiscriminate state violence also reinforces the plausibility and diffusion of specifically revolutionary ideologies, that is, ideologies that envisage a radical reorganization not only of the state, but of society as well. After all, a society in which aggrieved people are routinely denied an opportunity to redress perceived injustices, and even murdered on the mere suspicion of political disloyalty, is unlikely to be viewed as requiring a few minor reforms; those people are more likely to view such a society as in need of a fundamental reorganization. In other words, violent, exclusionary regimes often unintentionally foster the hegemony of their most radical social critics – religious zealots, virtuous ascetics, socialist militants, and radical nationalists, for example, who view society as more or less totally cor-rupted, incapable of reform, and thus requiring a thorough and necessarily violent reconstruction.[34]

4. *Weak policing capacities and infrastructural power.* Of course, as the political-opportunity approach emphasizes, no matter how iniquitous or authoritar-ian a state may be – or the society which it rules – it can always retain power so long as it is capable of ruthlessly repressing its enemies. Such a state may in fact have many enemies – including revolutionary foes – yet they will prove quite ineffective so long as the state's coercive might remains over-whelming.

Long before a state breakdown, however, revolutionaries may become numerous and well organized if the state's policing capacities and infrastruc-tural power more generally are chronically weak or geographically uneven. Guerrilla movements, for example, have typically prospered in peripheral and especially mountainous areas where state control is weak or nonexistent: the Communist movement in China grew strong in the northwest periphery, Castro's movement in Cuba's Sierra Maestra, and El Salvador's guerrilla armies in that country's mountainous northern departments.[35] And revolutionaries are doubly fortunate if they confront states and armies that are ineffectual due to corruption or bureaucratic incoherence, which are often purposively fostered by ruling cliques or autocrats who fear palace coups.[36] In such situations, revolutionaries themselves may bring about or accelerate state breakdowns not only through direct military pressure, but also by exacerbating conflicts between states (especially personalistic dictatorships) and dominant classes, and between states and their foreign supporters. These sorts of conflicts, in addition to the general insecurity that revolutionary situations engender, may also accelerate state breakdowns by creating economic downturns that bring on fiscal crises for states.[37]

5. *Corrupt and arbitrary personalistic rule that alienates, weakens, or divides counterrevolutionary elites.* As these last remarks suggest, autocratic and so-called neopatrimonial dictatorships are especially vulnerable to revolution. In fact, such regimes not only tend to facilitate the formation of hegemonic revolutionary movements, but they cannot easily defeat such movements once they have formed; examples include the absolutist monarchies in France, Russia, and Iran, and the dictatorships of Díaz in Mexico, Chiang in China, Batista in Cuba, Somoza in Nicaragua, and Ceauşescu in Romania.[38] As especially narrow and autonomous regimes, such dictatorships tend to have few fervid supporters; they also possess the discretionary power that may alienate certain state officials and military officers as well as vast sectors of society – including middle strata and even elites in addition to lower classes. In fact, because dictators often view economic and military elites as their chief foes, they may attempt to weaken and divide them in various ways, even though such groups share with dictators a counterrevolutionary orientation. By weakening counterrevolutionary elites, however, dictators may unwittingly play into the hands of revolutionaries, since such elites thereby become too weak either to effectively oppose the revolutionaries or to oust the dictator and reform the regime, thereby preempting revolution.

Of course, not all dictators are equally adept at controlling their armed forces and rival elites; their incompetence or incapacity in this regard does not bode well for them personally, but it may prove decisive in preempting social revolution. For if civilian and military elites can remove corrupt and repressive dictators, and perhaps institute democratic reforms, they thereby undermine much of the appeal of revolutionaries. (In fact, this is precisely what happened in the Philippines with the ouster of Ferdinand Marcos.)[39]

In sum, not only are certain types of states liable to break down and thereby create the sort of political opportunities that strong revolutionary movements can exploit, but also certain states unintentionally foster the very formation and indeed hegemony of radical movements by politicizing popular grievances, foreclosing possibilities for peaceful reform, compelling people to take up arms in order to defend themselves, making radical ideologies and identities plausible, providing the minimal political space that revolutionaries require to organize disgruntled people, and weakening counterrevolutionary elites, including their own officer corps. By thus illuminating both state breakdowns and processes of revolutionary mobilization I hope to have shown that state-centered approaches provide us with some powerful tools for explaining social revolutions.

SOME COMMON CRITICISMS OF STATE-CENTERED APPROACHES

Of course, like any theoretical tradition, the statist perspective has its share of critics. However, the various complaints that have been directed against this tradition are very uneven in their persuasiveness. Before turning to some of the more potent criticisms of statist analysis, I want to examine several that either rest upon unfounded assumptions or are simply unconvincing. Four such criticisms merit a brief response.

1. *"Societies affect states as much as, or possibly more than, states affect societies."*[40] This broad and rather imprecise generalization challenges one combination of the state-autonomy and state-capacity approaches, namely, the view that all states are autonomous from civil society and actually have the capacity to impose their preferred policies.[41] This is certainly a view worth challenging, but it is not clear that many state-centered theorists would defend it. In fact, state-centered theorists have generally emphasized that state autonomy and capacities are *potential* and *variable* rather than "given" a priori. As we have seen, moreover, statist analysts have emphasized precisely how state *breakdowns*, as well as infrastructurally *weak* states, have encouraged important social processes, including the formation of revolutionary movements.

This criticism also seems to confuse state-centered analysis with a sort of sweeping *political determinism* that robs "society" of any analytic autonomy whatsoever.[42] But a state-centered perspective hardly implies that states are the *only* institutions that matter or that states themselves are not potentially shaped and constrained by a variety of social factors. In fact, it is possible and sometimes desirable to combine or complement a state-centered analysis with, for example, class analysis.[43]

2. *State officials are usually not autonomous actors; instead, they typically respond to the demands of the dominant class or (occasionally) of militant lower classes.* This criticism – the principal one expressed, of course, by Marxists – is a narrower version of the preceding one, emphasizing how specifically *class*-based demands determine state policies.[44] Like the previous criticism, this one also challenges one extreme version of the state-autonomy approach, namely, the idea that all states are autonomous from the demands of social classes (and, accordingly, are never influenced by such classes). Again, this is a claim that few if any statists would wish to make; it seems more reasonable, in fact, to assume that the relationship between states and classes is in fact quite variable over space and time.

Two other points about this criticism also need to be made. First, it has usually been raised in the context of complex, detailed debates about the relative importance of class and state actors in formulating specific state policies.[45] These debates, whichever side one finds most convincing, hinge upon the marshalling and interpretation of particular facts and sequences of events. Neither side, including those who emphasize the importance of class actors, has suggested that their opponents *must* be wrong a priori, irrespective of the actual historical record. The *theoretical* grounds for believing that states *may* be autonomous from class forces, in other words, have not been seriously challenged in these debates; what is disputed is the relative autonomy of particular state actors in specific times and places (such as Democratic politicians in the US Congress during the 1930s).

Second, even in those cases in which the class-biased character of state policies has been convincingly established, it would be quite unfortunate to dismiss or ignore state-centered perspectives on that account. In fact, state autonomy may very well explain why such policies were adopted in the first place. (For example, certain state officials may be in a better position than particular capitalists to assess the interests of the capitalist class as a whole.)[46] The state-capacity approach, moreover, may be helpful for understanding which, if any, class-based policies can actually be implemented. The political-opportunity perspective, furthermore, may be helpful for understanding whether other classes or groups can successfully mobilize *against* such policies. (In this regard, it may make a great deal of difference whether individual capitalists are simply acting in similar ways or the state is enforcing – with violence, if necessary – certain laws or policies at their behest.) And a state-constructionist analysis may be helpful for understanding why specifically *class*-based actors are politically organized and influential.

3. *As a type of "structuralism," state-centered analysis necessarily neglects the purposive (including strategic) and cultural dimensions of social action.* The conflation of state-centered analysis with the sort of "structuralism" that denies the importance of purposive human agency would seem to rest upon an elementary confusion.[47] In fact, statist analysis may emphasize the actions and policies of state actors just as much as the impersonal "structural" characteristics of states (and both are undoubtedly important). For example, rationally calculating (and acting) state officials are the analytic pivot in some types of state-centered studies.[48]

The criticism that state-centered analysis fails to treat culture seriously is only partially correct.[49] (I discuss the sense in which it *is* accurate in the next section.) While most statist analyses have in fact been "structuralist" or "instrumentalist" in the sense of neglecting the shared beliefs of politicians and state officials, this quality seems fortuitous rather than inevitable. So, for example, one important state-centered study, James M. Jasper's *Nuclear Politics: Energy and the State in the United States, Sweden, and France* (1990),[50] emphasizes precisely the ways in which the ideologies and "policy styles" of state officials shape state policies. Jasper's study is no less state-centered for treating such officials as cultural actors rather than as rational calculators or as puppets of external forces. As Jasper emphasizes, moreover, state practices are "always already" cultural practices.[51]

It is also possible, as Robert Wuthnow has convincingly shown, to explain the diffusion and institutionalization of ideologies from a state-centered perspective.[52] As we have seen, in fact, a state-constructionist approach is indispensable for understanding how radical ideologies and strategic repertoires sometimes resonate with and diffuse among broad masses of people.

4. *Because they interpenetrate one another, the very distinction between "states" and "societies" is untenable and should be scrapped.* This criticism, which is perhaps the most radical that has been raised against statist approaches, has been elaborated most fully in a much discussed article by Timothy Mitchell.[53] Mitchell notes that "the edges of the state are uncertain; social elements seem to penetrate it on all sides, and the resulting boundary between state and society is difficult to determine."[54] Mitchell terms this the "boundary problem." He points out, for example, that upper classes have sometimes controlled certain state institutions, making it difficult if not impossible to distinguish state power from the class or economic power of such groups. Mitchell concludes that "The state should not be taken as . . . an agent, instrument, organization or structure, located apart from and opposed to another entity called society."[55] Even more, he questions the *analytic* utility of the conceptual distinction between states and societies.

This is a problematic argument. To begin with, upper-class control of certain state institutions does not destroy the statist character of those institutions – the fact, that is, that they are backed (unlike other organizations) by a monopoly of legitimate violence. Indeed, this situation would seem to be one in which state institutions are an "instrument" of the upper classes; yet Mitchell concludes that such a formulation is somehow impermissible.

In my view, Mitchell's argument exemplifies what Margaret Archer has termed, in a different context, the fallacy of "central conflation."[56] Archer uses the term to characterize studies that, striving mightily to avoid either cultural or "structural" determinism, posit that ideas and social structure are so closely connected that "there is no way of 'untying' the constitutive elements. The intimacy of their interconnection denies even relative autonomy to the components involved."[57] Mitchell, analogously, seems to assume that because states and societies are so closely bound together, it is impossible to examine their interaction.

The "boundary problem" that Mitchell discusses is real enough, and social analysts do often reify the concepts of state and society in problematic ways. Yet it seems more helpful (and interesting) to recognize that concrete institutions may sometimes share certain analytic characteristics of both states *and* societies rather than to jettison these concepts completely.

Throughout his article, in fact, Mitchell himself refers quite unselfconsciously to such things as "the French state," "state practices," and "state–society relations." His own language, in other words, would seem to testify to the unavoidable importance of the *conceptual* distinction between states and societies.[58]

LIMITATIONS OF STATE-CENTERED APPROACHES

Although these general criticisms of state-centered perspectives are ultimately unhelpful, statist approaches do have their limitations. In this section, I examine some of the more serious theoretical gaps in state-centered analysis and point to some theoretical resources than can help to bridge them. A proper recognition of these gaps not only reveals the limits of what state-centered analyses can reasonably hope to explain, but also helps to highlight more clearly what statist approaches to social revolutions *can* explain.

For analysts of revolutionary movements (or collective action in any of its forms), the fundamental problem with statist analysis is that it does not theorize the nonstate or nonpolitical sources – or the *independent* explanatory weight – of three general factors: *associational networks* (including class formations and "civil society" more generally), *material resources*, and *collective beliefs and discourses* (including grievances, strategies, and identities).[59] Needless to say, this is a significant problem indeed given the potentially crucial connection between social organization, resources, and culture, on the one hand, and collective action (revolutionary or otherwise), on the other. Fortunately, there are some powerful theoretical resources at hand that can help to make that connection.

For example, the role of social organization and interpersonal ties in mobilization processes has been powerfully addressed by so-called "social network analysts."[60] These scholars emphasize the crucial role of networks of social ties in recruiting people into, and then sustaining their collective identification with and commitment to, social movements and perhaps even larger political communities (thereby obviating a need, in some cases, for substantial material resources). Network analysts also stress how such social ties, sometimes in the shape of formal organizations, provide the relational infrastructure of actual collective actions. These insights have also been underscored by those who emphasize the importance of "civil society" – that is, voluntary associational activities – as a mechanism for democratic dialogue and as a bulwark against state oppression; these insights may also be found in the work of Marxists who emphasize the importance of class-based collective action in particular.[61]

From all these perspectives, in fact, individuals with a strong inclination to pursue reformist or even revolutionary change, and who also find themselves in a political context that allows or even encourages such pursuits, will still be unable to act effectively unless they are connected to a sufficiently large social network of like-minded people. Seemingly "appropriate" political opportunity structures, in other words, will not give rise to collective action if such networks do not exist.

Of course, state-centered analysts can justly counter that these associational networks are often politicized and radicalized, and even built up in the first place, as a result of specific state structures and policies. Social networks, after all, do not simply fall from the sky. Network analysts, proponents of "civil society," and Marxists, unfortunately, often neglect the ways in which state actions shape the very formation (or prevent the formation) of voluntary organizations and revolutionary associations in particular. Still, these associations are also typically rooted in class or ethnic relations, extended kinship networks, religious communities, urban neighborhoods, or rural villages – still other social networks, that is, that do not derive wholly or even in part from state practices. And associational networks and practices have their own dynamics and emergent properties that need to be taken seriously and analyzed in their own right. Revolutionaries themselves, for example, may act in ways that expand or corrode their ties to other people. For these reasons, a state-centered perspective on the associational networks of civil society is inherently limited.

The potentially autonomous influence of material resources on collective action, for its part, has been most carefully theorized by resource-mobilization and political-process theorists,[62] as well as by certain rational-choice theorists.[63] All of these analysts point out (albeit in somewhat different ways) that even tightly knit groups may not be able to act collectively – at least not for long or with much effectiveness – if they do not have steady access to the money and various sorts of infrastructure and technology – means of communication and transportation, weapons, safehouses, etc. – that are necessary to sustain their activities and (perhaps) motivate people to contribute to their cause. In other words, even tightly knit groups that would seem to have the opportunity as well as an interest in acting collectively may not be able to do so effectively without substantial material resources. So again, collective action (whether revolutionary or not) may depend on much more than an encouraging political context.

Of course, a group's access to material resources generally depends on how it is inserted into specific social networks and institutions; the class composition of such groups is of particular importance in this regard. Nonetheless, access to specifically *state* resources may also be quite important for political mobilization – even for would-be revolutionaries who are violently excluded from the state. Defectors from the state's armed forces, for example, often bring along their guns. Guerrilla armies, furthermore, usually build up their arsenals through raids on peripheral army garrisons or ambushes of government troops. And some revolutionary groups, of course, have had access to the resources of *foreign* states – which is one of the ways in which the international state system (and geopolitical competition in particular) matters for revolutionary conflicts. While the extent of external aid to revolutionaries has often been exaggerated by their opponents,[64] such aid figured prominently (which is not to say decisively) in the revolutionary conflicts in Mexico, Vietnam, Algeria, and Afghanistan.[65]

Finally, the potentially independent role of beliefs, identities, and strategic repertoires in collective action has been powerfully underscored recently by theorists of so-called "framing processes," especially David Snow and Robert Benford and their collaborators.[66] These theorists, drawing on Goffman's important study,[67] argue that "objective" reality is recognized (or indeed recognizable) as unjust *and* alterable only when it is interpreted or "framed" as such by means of specific cultural systems or discourses. When extant collective frames do not allow such an interpretation – even of a reality that an external observer might find both unconscionable and easily rectified – then collective action aimed at altering that reality is obviously impossible. In fact, even resourceful groups that would seem to have the opportunity as well as a rational interest in changing their predicament will not (indeed, cannot) do so in the absence of an appropriate cognitive frame.

Of course, as we have seen, a state-centered perspective would emphasize that the plausibility, justifiability, and diffusion of a militant collective-action repertoire or a specifically revolutionary ideology or identity may be strongly shaped by specific state practices. Revolutionary "frames," ideologies, strategies, and cultures, that is, no more drop from the sky than do social networks or material resources. Unfortunately, framing theory and other forms of cultural analysis often overlook the specifically political processes by which collective beliefs and discourses are formulated and broadly diffused – typically as quite unintended outcomes of states practices.

Still, like associational networks, revolutionary ideologies and strategic repertoires are also rooted in a variety of social relations and cultural systems that may not derive wholly or much at all from state practices. And such ideologies have their own substantive properties that demand to be taken seriously and analyzed in their own right. (Revolutionary Marxism and Islamic "fundamentalism," for example, envisage the radical reconstruction of societies in very different and distinctive ways.) For these reasons, a state-centered perspective on culture and ideology – like that on networks and resources – is inherently limited.

THE CASE OF THE CUBAN REVOLUTION

The strengths and limitations of a statist perspective are exemplified in several recent comparative studies of Latin American social revolutions, including works by Robert Dix, Timothy Wickham-Crowley, and John Booth and Thomas Walker.[68] All of these studies explicitly engage and often endorse different strands of state-centered theory (as well as other theoretical approaches) in their attempt to explain why radical movements in the region have seized power only in Cuba and Nicaragua in recent decades. More interestingly, I think, the strengths and limitations of statism are also evident in a recent case study of the Cuban Revolution – a nonpolemical analysis that does not in any way explicitly draw upon or attempt to criticize a state-centered (or any other) theoretical perspective.

Marifeli Pérez-Stable's *The Cuban Revolution: Origins, Course, and Legacy* (1993) develops a generally persuasive multi-causal account of the revolution, albeit one that "highlights the importance of social classes in the breakdown of the old Cuba and the making of the revolution."[69] (Pérez-Stable notes that while she has been influenced by both Theda Skocpol and Charles Tilly, she has "refrained from engaging the literature on revolutions.")[70] In fact, two of the factors that, according to Pérez-Stable, "interacted to render Cuba susceptible to radical revolution" were the weakness of Cuba's *clases económicas* (the bourgeoisie) and the relative strength of the *clases populares* (popular sectors), influenced in part by the ideology of radical nationalism.[71] However, Pérez-Stable also draws attention to two other causal factors that refer, at least in part, to characteristics of the Cuban state, namely, what she terms "mediated sovereignty" (i.e., the Cuban state's lack of autonomy from the US government and US corporations) and a near-chronic "crisis of political authority" that deepened with the dictatorship of General Fulgencio Batista during the 1950s.[72]

Pérez-Stable's account would thus seem to demonstrate both the necessity and the insufficiency of treating the prerevolutionary Cuban state as an independent causal factor in the revolution. She implies that the geopolitical subservience and weakness of that state, as well as the serious legitimation crisis that developed following Batista's coup of 1952, created a political opportunity for some sort of revolution; at the same time, she suggests that analysts also need to take into account the strength (and ideology) of Cuba's social classes in order to understand why a radical revolution actually occurred. Indeed, Pérez-Stable strongly suggests that the political crisis of the 1950s would not have resulted in social revolution were it not for the weakness of the Cuban bourgeoisie and the strength of the radicalized popular sectors.

And yet the story is even more interesting than this. For Pérez-Stable's account also suggests that the very weakness of conservative and moderate political forces in Cuba on the eve of the revolution, as well as the gradual attachment of the popular sectors to Fidel, the July 26 Movement, and the rebel army, were themselves primarily a result of actions taken by the Batista dictatorship. In other words, Pérez-Stable makes a number of state-constructionist arguments in her account of the *fidelistas*' rise to power.

Pérez-Stable repeatedly suggests, for example, that "Batista's resistance to calling elections undermined the moderate opposition and bolstered the July 26th Movement" and, more generally, "bolstered those who argued that armed struggle was the only way to challenge his rule."[73] Indeed, both the moderate opposition and the Communist Party – which at first viewed Fidel as a "putschist" and "adventurist" – positively "endorsed armed rebellion when other avenues of struggle against Batista had all but disappeared."[74] Pérez-Stable further notes how broad sectors of the popular classes and even members of the *clases económicas* were disgusted by the harsh repression and undisguised corruption of the *batistato*. She notes that many wealthy Cubans supported the insurrection, contributing 5 million to 10 million pesos to the rebels; indeed, Pérez-Stable suggests that "virtually all Cubans" backed Fidel and the rebel army by January 1, 1959: "the *clases económicas* . . . joined in celebrating the revolution."[75]

At the same time, Pérez-Stable emphasizes that Batista might have pre-empted social revolution had he simply been less intransigent: "The general might have consented to free and honest elections and ushered in a pro-visional government in late 1955 when Cosme de la Torriente led the civic dialogue movement or early in 1958 when the Catholic church revived it."[76] Unfortunately, "Batista became more intransigent as momentum gathered against his rule."[77]

Revolution might also have been averted had the Cuban military replaced Batista with some sort of provisional government – as the United States came to hope and scheme[78] – or had the armed forces simply contained the guerrillas in the Sierra Maestra. But the corruption and politicization of the Cuban military under Batista divided and fatally weakened that institution. Pérez-Stable notes the unsuccessful *coup* attempt led by Colonel Ramón Barquín and the much more serious naval uprising against Batista at Cienfuegos.[79] She also refers to the failed government offensive against the rebels during the summer of 1958, although she might have said more about the reasons for this crucial failure. This offensive, after all, clearly demon-strated that the Cuban armed forces as a whole had neither the will nor the capacity to fight an effective counterinsurgency war, thereby sealing Batista's fate. Pérez-Stable might have noted, for example, that the com-manding officer in northern Oriente province – a political appointee whose promotion rankled many professional officers – simply refused to engage the rebels.[80] "By the end of the summer," Luis Pérez has noted,

> The army simply ceased to fight. Desertions and defections reached epidemic proportions. Retreating units became easy prey for advan-cing guerrilla columns. . . . Local military commands surrendered, often without firing a shot. Some defected and joined the opposition.[81]

"Military prowess," Pérez-Stable concludes, "did not ultimately defeat Batista."[82] In sum, the fact that the rebels could not be geographically con-tained, nor popular support for them preempted, was itself primarily a consequence of the character and decisions of the Batista dictatorship and of the Cuban armed forces.

Pérez-Stable's analysis thus clearly demonstrates the utility of a state-centered perspective for understanding the Cuban Revolution. The Batista regime, she shows, not only created a political opportunity for some sort of revolution in Cuba, but also positively weakened the civilian and military enemies of a radical revolution and unwittingly enhanced the popular appeal of the *fidelistas*. The alignment (and ideology) of class forces in Cuba that Pérez-Stable highlights, in other words, was itself very strongly shaped by the nature of the *batistato*.

On the other hand, Pérez-Stable's account of the causes of the Cuban Revolution also points to some of the limitations of a purely statist perspective. The weakness of the Cuban bourgeoisie, for example, was not simply a result of state policies, but also was rooted in (among other factors) the historic division of interests between nascent industrialists and the sugar industry.[83] The oppositional hegemony of the fidelistas, moreover, while certainly bolstered by the character of the *batistato*, was also a result of the astute political maneuvering of the rebels themselves and of their unswerving commitment to armed struggle and Cuban self-determination.[84] Fidel himself first "captured the popular imagination," as Pérez-Stable puts it, with his "integrity, compassion, and dignity, and . . . a political program of nationalist reform."[85] Radical nationalism itself, in fact, appealed to many Cubans not simply because their state was historically subservient to the United States, but also because the Cuban economy and class relations – which were strongly but of course not wholly shaped by that state – were widely viewed as exploitative and unjust.[86] Pérez-Stable's study suggests, in sum, that an adequate explanation of the Cuban Revolution requires an examination not only of the prerevolutionary Cuban state and its effects on civil society; it also demands an analysis of the independent role of class relations, popular culture, and the nature and actions of the revolutionaries themselves as they built a vast network of active supporters and sympathizers.

CONCLUSIONS

Due to its various theoretical shortcomings, a state-centered perspective alone will not completely explain (nor accurately predict) the emergence or character of collective action, including revolutionary movements. These very shortcomings, however, point the way toward a more powerful synthetic perspective on social revolutions and collective action. Clearly, such a perspective will necessarily highlight the role of social networks, resource mobilization, and framing processes in addition to state structures and practices. Of course, networks, resources, and culture cannot be simply "tacked on" to a state-centered analysis in the guise of "independent variables." For, as the state-constructionist approach in particular emphasizes, all these factors are themselves more or less strongly influenced by state-centered processes.

In my view, we still await the formulation of the sort of synthetic perspective on revolutions and collective action that we clearly need.[87] Until that theory materializes, however, state-centered approaches will remain perhaps our single most powerful theoretical perspective on social revolutions, and any superior perspective will need to incorporate the insights of this theoretical tradition. Indeed, this tradition's insights into both state breakdowns and revolutionary mobilization tell us much, if not everything, that we need to know about social revolutions, and they help to resolve some of the key puzzles that revolutions have raised for social analysts.

NOTES

1. By social revolution, I mean a relatively rapid and fundamental change not only of state institutions, but also of the economic, cultural, and associational arrangements among the population governed by those institutions. A revolutionary movement, as I use the term, is a social movement with self-consciously social-revolutionary goals.
2. Charles Tilly, *European Revolutions, 1492–1992* (Oxford: Blackwell, 1993), 5.
3. See my "Old Regimes and Revolutions in the Second and Third Worlds: A Comparative Perspective," pp. 575–604 in *Social Science History*, volume 18, number 4 (Winter 1994); "Why Guerrilla Insurgencies Persist, or the Perversity of Indiscriminate State Violence," paper presented at the 1993 annual meetings of the American Sociological Association, Miami Beach; "Colonialism and Revolution in Southeast Asia: A Comparative Analysis," pp. 59–78 in Terry Boswell, editor, *Revolution in the World–System* (Westport: Greenwood Press, 1989); *State and Revolution, 1945–1991* (Cambridge: Cambridge University Press, 1998); Jeff Goodwin and Theda Skocpol, "Explaining Revolutions in the Contemporary Third World," pp. 489–507 in *Politics and Society*, volume 17, number 4 (December 1989); and John Foran and Jeff Goodwin, "Revolutionary Outcomes in Iran and Nicaragua: Coalition Fragmentation, War, and the Limits of Social Transformation," pp. 209–47 in *Theory and Society*, volume 22, number 2 (April 1993).
4. In this regard, see my "Toward a New Sociology of Revolutions," pp. 731–66 in *Theory and Society*, volume 23 (1994); and Mustafa Emirbayer and Jeff Goodwin, "Network Analysis, Culture, and the Problem of Agency," pp. 1411–54 in *American Journal of Sociology*, volume 99, number 6 (May 1994).
5. This chapter discusses the relevance of state-centered analysis only for understanding the origins or causes of social revolutions, including the formation of strong revolutionary movements. I should note, however, that statist perspectives have also been employed to explain the long-term outcomes of revolutions. See, for example, Theda Skocpol, *States and Social Revolutions: A Comparative Study of France, Russia, and China* (Cambridge: Cambridge University Press, 1979), part two; and Foran and Goodwin, "Revolutionary Outcomes in Iran and Nicaragua."
6. See Peter Evans, *Embedded Autonomy: States and Industrial Transformation* (Princeton: Princeton University Press, 1995); Michael Mann, *The Sources of Social Power*, volume two: *The Rise of Classes and Nation-States, 1760–1914* (Cambridge: Cambridge University Press, 1993); Skocpol, *States and Social Revolutions*; Ellen Kay Trimberger, *Revolution from Above: Military Bureaucrats and Development in Japan, Turkey, Egypt, and Peru* (New Brunswick: Transaction, 1978); Otto Hintze,

The Historical Essays of Otto Hintze, edited by Felix Gilbert (New York: Oxford University Press, 1975); and Katharine Chorley, *Armies and the Art of Revolution* (Boston: Beacon Press, 1973 [1943]).

7. Mann, *The Sources of Social Power*, volume two. Infrastructural power refers, more specifically, to "the institutional capacity of a central state, despotic or not, to penetrate its territories and logistically implement decisions:" ibid., 59. See also Evans, *Embedded Autonomy*; and Joel S. Migdal, *Strong Societies and Weak States: State–Society Relations and State Capabilities in the Third World* (Princeton: Princeton University Press, 1988).

8. See Randall Collins, "Prediction in Macrosociology: The Case of the Soviet Collapse," pp. 1552–93 in *American Journal of Sociology*, volume 100, number 6 (May 1995); Charles Tilly, *Coercion, Capital, and European States, AD 990–1992*, revised edition (Cambridge: Blackwell, 1992); and Hintze, *Historical Essays*.

9. This approach rests upon two important distinctions made by Charles Tilly: the distinction between "states" on the one hand (i.e., organizations that control the principal means of coercion within a bounded population) and "polities" on the other (i.e., the state plus those "member" groups with routine access to it), and the distinction between the capacity to act collectively, which Tilly terms "mobilization" (the quantity of resources, including labor and skills, collectively controlled by a group) and actual collective action. See Tilly, *From Mobilization to Revolution* (Reading, MA: Addison-Wesley, 1978), chapter three.

10. Sidney Tarrow defines "political opportunity structure" as those "dimensions of the political environment that provide incentives for people to undertake collective action by affecting their expectations for success or failure:" *Power in Movement: Social Movements, Collective Action and Politics* (Cambridge: Cambridge University Press, 1994), 85. The notion of "structure" here seems problematic; after all, short-term or even ephemeral state actions can be as consequential as the long-term "structural" characteristics of a state.

11. See Tarrow, *Power in Movement*; and Herbert P. Kitschelt, "Political Opportunity Structures and Political Protest: Anti-Nuclear Movements in Four Democracies," pp. 57–85 in *British Journal of Political Science*, volume 16 (January 1986).

12. See Collins, "Prediction in Macrosociology;" Tilly, *European Revolutions*; Paul Kennedy, *The Rise and Fall of the Great Powers: Economic Change and Military Conflict from 1500 to 2000* (New York: Random House, 1987); Skocpol, *States and Social Revolutions*; and Chorley, *Armies and the Art of Revolution*.

13. This approach is so named, of course, for Alexis de Tocqueville's masterful use of it in *The Old Regime and the French Revolution*, translated by Stuart Gilbert (New York: Doubleday, 1955), and in *Democracy in America* (New York: Modern Library, 1981). See Skocpol, "Bringing the State Back In: Strategies of Analysis in Current Research," in Peter B. Evans, Dietrich Rueschemeyer, and Theda Skocpol, editors, *Bringing the State Back In* (Cambridge: Cambridge University Press, 1985), 21.

14. This label is modelled on the well-known idea of "social constructionism," that is, the notion that certain social phenomena are recognized, defined, or even produced (in whole or in part) through cultural and discursive symbols (e.g., political grievances, social problems, and collective identities). I do not limit the idea of state constructionism, however, to the cultural or discursive effects of states; as I suggest below, the organization and practices of states – which are only partially discursive in nature – are equally if not more consequential.

15. A "private" corporation, for example, cannot logically or temporally exist outside of a state-enforced legal order; the corporate form itself is legally defined and enforced, as are the property rights that attach to it.

16. See Pierre Birnbaum, *States and Collective Action: The European Experience* (Cambridge: Cambridge University Press, 1988); Ira Katznelson, "Working-Class Formation and the State: Nineteenth-Century England in American Perspective," pp. 257–84 in Evans, Rueschemeyer, and Skocpol, *Bringing the State Back In*; and Robert Wuthnow, "State Structures and Ideological Outcomes," pp. 799–821 in *American Sociological Review*, volume 50 (1985).

17. Tilly differentiates "consolidated" national states ("large, differentiated, [and] ruling heterogeneous territories directly, claiming to impose a unitary fiscal, monetary, judicial, legislative, military and cultural system on its citizens") from "segmented" states (for example, "a city-based bishopric and its immediate hinterland, or . . . a composite of different sorts of unit, each enjoying considerable distinctness and autonomy"). See Tilly, *European Revolutions*, 35, 31. Note that "national" states in this sense are *not* necessarily "nation-states," which rule peoples who share a homogeneous ethnic or religious identity (and which are, in fact, quite rare). See Tilly, *Coercion, Capital, and European States*, 2–3.

18. Lenin, "The Dual Power" [1917], in Robert C. Tucker, editor, *The Lenin Anthology* (New York: Norton, 1975), 301.

19. Ibid., 301–302.

20. Anderson, *Lineages of the Absolutist State* (London: Verso, 1974), 11; emphasis in original.

21. This does not rule out the possibility, on the other hand, that revolutionaries may institute radical changes in those parts of a country that they effectively control, even if the central government has not been toppled.

22. See also Skocpol, *Social Revolutions in the Modern World* (Cambridge: Cambridge University Press, 1994). State breakdowns are also emphasized in Jack Goldstone's *Revolution and Rebellion in the Early Modern World* (Berkeley and Los Angeles: University of California Press, 1991). Although Goldstone presents an explanation of these breakdowns that is very different from Skocpol's (one that emphasizes demographic pressures), he shares her view that revolts from below cannot succeed so long as states remain fiscally and militarily strong. See Randall Collins, "Maturation of the State-Centered Theory of Revolution and Ideology," pp. 117–28 in *Sociological Theory*, volume 11, number 1 (March 1993). See also Chorley's classic study, *Armies and the Art of Revolution*.

23. See especially Michel Foucault, *Discipline and Punish: The Birth of the Prison* (New York: Vintage, 1979), and *The History of Sexuality*, volume one: *An Introduction* (New York: Vintage, 1990) and Timothy Mitchell, "The Limits of the State: Beyond Statist Approaches and their Critics," pp. 77–96 in *American Political Science Review*, volume 85, number 1 (March 1991).

24. Foucault, *History of Sexuality*, volume one: 93, 96.

25. I thus disagree with Randall Collins to the extent that his writings sometimes seem to imply that state breakdowns themselves automatically induce revolutionary movements or popular mobilizations: see Collins, "Prediction in Macrosociology," 1561; "Maturation of the State-Centered Theory," 119, and "The Romanticism of Agency/Structure Versus the Analysis of Micro/Macro," *Current Sociology*, volume 40, number 1 (Spring 1992), 82.

26. I borrow the notion of a collective-action repertoire from Tilly, *From Mobilization to Revolution*, chapter five. The concept of high-risk activism is borrowed from Doug McAdam, "Recruitment to High-Risk Activism: The Case of Freedom Summer," pp. 64–90 in *American Journal of Sociology*, volume 92 (1986).

27. As James C. Scott has emphasized, class struggles "from below" only very rarely break out of their localistic and necessarily disguised forms, even when inequalities, class identities, and oppositional subcultures are quite salient. See Scott,

Domination and the Arts of Resistance: Hidden Transcripts (New Haven: Yale University Press, 1990).

28. Tocqueville, *The Old Regime*, 177.

29. See Mann, *The Sources of Social Power*, volume two, chapter eighteen; Reinhard Bendix, *Nation-Building and Citizenship* (Berkeley and Los Angeles: University of California Press, 1977); and Selig Perlman, *A Theory of the Labor Movement* (Philadelphia: Porcupine Press, 1979 [1928]).

30. Tocqueville, *The Old Regime*, especially part three, chapter one. I have elsewhere argued that Tocqueville sheds considerable light on the gradual rejection by Eastern European dissidents of a reformed socialism or "socialism with a human face;" by 1989 these dissidents generally rejected Communism in toto and were proponents of a Western-style, democratic capitalism. See my "Old Regimes and Revolutions in the Second and Third Worlds."

31. See Goodwin and Skocpol, "Explaining Revolutions in the Contemporary Third World;" Seymour Martin Lipset, "Radicalism or Reformism: The Sources of Working-Class Politics," pp. 1–18 in *American Political Science Review*, volume 77 (1983); and Samuel P. Huntington, *Political Order in Changing Societies* (New Haven: Yale University Press, 1968).

32. See Goodwin, "Why Guerrilla Insurgencies Persist;" T. David Mason and Dale A. Krane, "The Political Economy of Death Squads: Toward a Theory of the Impact of State-Sanctioned Terror," pp. 175–98 in *International Studies Quarterly*, volume 33 (1989); and Ted Robert Gurr, "Persisting Patterns of Repression and Rebellion: Foundations for a General Theory of Political Coercion," pp. 149–68 in Margaret P. Karns, editor, *Persistent Patterns and Emergent Structures in a Waning Century* (New York: Praeger, 1986).

33. See Marifeli Pérez-Stable, *The Cuban Revolution: Origins, Course, and Legacy* (New York: Oxford University Press, 1993); John A. Booth and Thomas W. Walker, *Understanding Central America*, second edition (Boulder: Westview Press, 1993); John Walton, *Reluctant Rebels: Comparative Studies of Revolution and Underdevelopment* (New York: Columbia University Press, 1984); and Benedict J. Kerkvliet, *The Huk Rebellion: A Study of Peasant Revolt in the Philippines* (Berkeley and Los Angeles: University of California Press, 1977).

34. This argument is nicely developed in Tim McDaniel, *Autocracy, Modernization, and Revolution in Russia and Iran* (Princeton: Princeton University Press, 1991), chapter seven.

35. See Eric R. Wolf, *Peasant Wars of the Twentieth Century* (New York: Harper & Row, 1969); and Jenny Pearce, *Promised Land: Peasant Rebellion in Chalatenango, El Salvador* (London: Latin America Bureau, 1985).

36. See McDaniel, *Autocracy, Modernization, and Revolution*, chapter two; and Timothy P. Wickham-Crowley, *Guerrillas and Revolutions in Latin America: A Comparative Study of Insurgents and Regimes Since 1956* (Princeton: Princeton University Press, 1992), chapters eight and eleven.

37. See John Foran's Chapter 9 in this volume on the comparative-historical sociology of Third World social revolutions.

38. See Goodwin, "Old Regimes and Revolutions in the Second and Third Worlds;" John Foran, "A Theory of Third World Social Revolutions: Iran, Nicaragua, and El Salvador Compared," pp. 3–27 in *Critical Sociology*, volume 19 (1992); Wickham-Crowley, *Guerrillas and Revolution*; McDaniel, *Autocracy, Modernization, and Revolution*; Farideh Farhi, *States and Urban-Based Revolutions* (Urbana and Chicago: University of Illinois Press, 1990); Goodwin and Skocpol, "Explaining Revolutions in the Contemporary Third World;" Jack A. Goldstone, "Revolutions and Superpowers," pp. 34–48 in Jonathan R. Adelman, editor, *Superpowers*

and Revolutions (New York: Praeger, 1986); and Robert H. Dix, "Why Revolutions Succeed and Fail," pp. 423–46 in *Polity*, volume 16, number 3 (Spring 1984).

39. See Richard Snyder, "Explaining Transitions from Neopatrimonial Dictatorships," pp. 379–99 in *Comparative Politics*, volume 24 (July 1992).

40. Joel S. Migdal, Atul Kohli, and Vivienne Shue, "Introduction: Developing a State-in-Society Perspective," in their jointly edited *State Power and Social Forces: Domination and Transformation in the Third World* (Cambridge: Cambridge University Press, 1994), 2.

41. Migdal, for example, emphasizes how state-centered theories "encounter . . . difficulties when they assume that the state organization is powerful and cohesive enough to drive society." This assumption, he notes, is especially problematic for students of African societies, such as Senegal, which has a conspicuously "weak" state: Migdal, "The State in Society: An Approach to Struggles for Domination," in *State Power and Social Forces*, 20.

42. See Kohli and Shue, "State Power and Social Forces: On Political Contention and Accommodation in the Third World," in *State Power and Social Forces*, 303. To be sure, a few state-centered theorists (such as Birnbaum and Kitschelt) sometimes lapse into a sort of political determinism, but this is hardly a logical requirement of statist analysis as such!

43. See Skocpol, *States and Social Revolutions*; and Wickham-Crowley, *Guerrillas and Revolution*.

44. See Paul Cammack, "Bringing the State Back In?" pp. 261–90 in *British Journal of Political Science*, volume 19 (1989).

45. See, for example, Michael Goldfield, "Worker Insurgency, Radical Organization, and New Deal Labor Legislation," pp. 1257–82 in *American Political Science Review*, volume 83, number 4 (December 1989), and Theda Skocpol and Kenneth Finegold's response, "Explaining New Deal Labor Legislation," pp. 1297–304 in *American Political Science Review*, volume 84, number 4 (December 1990).

46. This was Nicos Poulantzas's position in his famous debate with Ralph Miliband.

47. See Youssef Cohen, *Radicals, Reformers, and Reactionaries: The Prisoner's Dilemma and the Collapse of Democracy in Latin America* (Chicago: University of Chicago Press, 1994), chapters two and three. The confusion probably derives from Skocpol's polemic against "voluntaristic" accounts of revolutionary political crises. See her *States and Social Revolutions*, chapter one. But this polemic was clearly directed against the view that such crises, as they arose in France, Russia, and China, were caused by the actions of self-conscious revolutionaries and/or revolts from below; for Skocpol, that argument (as we have seen) stood the actual historical record on its head. Nowhere, in any event, did she question the potential importance of human agency as such.

48. See Margaret Levi, *Of Rule and Revenue* (Berkeley and Los Angeles: University of California Press, 1988).

49. See Roger Friedland and Robert R. Alford, "Bringing Society Back In: Symbols, Practices, and Institutional Contradictions," in Walter W. Powell and Paul J. DiMaggio, editors, *The New Institutionalism in Organizational Analysis* (Chicago: University of Chicago Press, 1991), especially 235–8.

50. James M. Jasper, *Nuclear Politics: Energy and the State in the United States, Sweden, and France* (Princeton: Princeton University Press, 1990).

51. See also Peter A. Hall, *Governing the Economy: The Politics of State Intervention in Britain and France* (New York: Oxford University Press, 1986); and Frank Dobbin, *Forging Industrial Policy: The United States, Britain, and France in the Railway Age* (New York: Cambridge University Press, 1994). The idea that culture stands opposed to structure can also be faulted for a too narrow understanding of "structural-

ism." Cultures, after all, can themselves be treated as persistent, supraindividual "systems" or "structures" that enable and constrain social behavior as much as "social" structures. See Clifford Geertz, *The Interpretation of Cultures* (New York: Basic Books, 1973); and Emirbayer and Goodwin, "Network Analysis, Culture, and the Problem of Agency."

52. Wuthnow, "State Structures and Ideological Outcomes," and *Communities of Discourse: Ideology and Social Structure in the Reformation, the Enlightenment, and European Socialism* (Cambridge, MA: Harvard University Press, 1989).

53. Mitchell, "The Limits of the State."

54. Ibid., 88.

55. Ibid., 95.

56. Archer, *Culture and Agency* (Cambridge: Cambridge University Press, 1988).

57. Ibid., 80.

58. Mitchell would apparently have us focus on "disciplinary power," which he argues has produced the state–society distinction as a "metaphysical effect:" "The Limits of the State," 94. Yet this would simply recreate the "boundary problem" in a new form, since it is often difficult to distinguish disciplinary from nondisciplinary practices. Here again, it seems to me, he is talking about an *analytic* distinction that is often blurred in the real world.

59. State-centered approaches also neglect autonomous social-psychological processes, including the role of collective emotions. In this respect, however, they are no different than most other theoretical traditions in sociology, including the dominant perspectives in social movement research. See Mustafa Emirbayer and Jeff Goodwin, "Symbols, Positions, Objects: Rethinking Network Analysis," paper presented at the International Conference on Social Networks, London (1995).

60. See Peter Bearman, *Relations into Rhetoric: Local Elite Social Structure in Norfolk, England, 1540–1640* (New Brunswick: Rutgers University Press, 1993); Roger V. Gould, "Multiple Networks and Mobilization in the Paris Commune, 1871," pp. 716–29 in *American Sociological Review*, volume 56, number 6 (December 1991); Doug McAdam, "Recruitment to High-Risk Activism;" and David A. Snow, Louis A. Zurcher, Jr., and Sheldon Ekland-Olson, "Social Networks and Social Movements: A Microstructural Approach to Differential Recruitment," pp. 787–801 in *American Sociological Review*, volume 45, number 5 (1980).

61. Recent works on civil society include Robert D. Putnam, *Making Democracy Work: Civic Traditions in Modern Italy* (Princeton: Princeton University Press, 1993); and Jean L. Cohen and Andrew Arato, *Civil Society and Political Theory* (Cambridge, MA: MIT Press, 1992). The Marxist and class-analytic literature on revolutions and collective action is of course vast. Among the more influential recent studies are Jeffery M. Paige, *Agrarian Revolution: Social Movements and Export Agriculture in the Underdeveloped World* (New York: Free Press, 1975); Wolf, *Peasant Wars of the Twentieth Century*; and Barrington Moore, Jr., *Social Origins of Dictatorship and Democracy: Lord and Peasant in the Making of the Modern World* (Boston: Beacon Press, 1966).

62. See Tarrow, *Power in Movement*; Doug McAdam, *Political Process and the Development of Black Insurgency, 1930–1970* (Chicago: University of Chicago Press, 1982); Tilly, *From Mobilization to Revolution*; and John D. McCarthy and Meyer N. Zald, "Resource Mobilization and Social Movements: A Partial Theory," pp. 1212–41 in *American Journal of Sociology*, volume 82 (1977).

63. See Mancur Olson, *The Logic of Collective Action* (Cambridge, MA: Harvard University Press, 1965); and Samuel L. Popkin, *The Rational Peasant: The Political*

Economy of Rural Society in Vietnam (Berkeley and Los Angeles: University of California Press, 1979).

64. See the discussion in Wickham-Crowley, *Guerrillas and Revolution*, chapter five.

65. See the case studies in Jack A. Goldstone, Ted Robert Gurr, and Farrokh Moshiri, editors, *Revolutions of the Late Twentieth Century* (Boulder: Westview Press, 1991); Friedrich Katz, *The Secret War in Mexico: Europe, the United States, and the Mexican Revolution* (Chicago: University of Chicago Press, 1981); and Wolf, *Peasant Wars of the Twentieth Century*.

66. David A. Snow and Robert D. Benford, "Master Frames and Cycles of Protest," pp. 133–55 in Aldon D. Morris and Carol McClurg Mueller, editors, *Frontiers in Social Movement Theory* (New Haven: Yale University Press, 1992); and David A. Snow, E. Burke Rochford, Jr., Steven K. Worden, and Robert D. Benford, "Frame Alignment Processes, Micromobilization, and Movement Participation," pp. 464–81 in *American Sociological Review*, volume 51 (August 1986). For different approaches to integrating ideologies and cultures into explanations of revolutions, see also Forrest D. Colburn, *The Vogue of Revolution in Poor Countries* (Princeton: Princeton University Press, 1994); Eric Selbin, *Modern Latin American Revolutions* (Boulder: Westview Press, 1993); Goldstone, *Revolution and Rebellion in the Early Modern World*, chapter four; William H. Sewell, Jr., "Ideologies and Social Revolutions: Reflections on the French Case," pp. 57–85 in *Journal of Modern History*, volume 57, number 1 (1985); and John Foran's Chapter 8 on culture and revolution in this volume.

67. Erving Goffman, *Frame Analysis: An Essay on the Organization of Experience* (New York: Harper & Row, 1974).

68. Dix, "Why Revolutions Succeed and Fail;" Wickham-Crowley, *Guerrillas and Revolution*; and Booth and Walker, *Understanding Central America*.

69. Pérez-Stable, *The Cuban Revolution*, 8.

70. Ibid., 184–5, note 16.

71. Ibid., 7. Although it reappears throughout her text, and she might have treated it as an analytically independent factor, Pérez-Stable does not actually list radical nationalism as an independent cause of the revolution.

72. Ibid. Pérez-Stable also includes two other factors in her list of the causes of the revolution, namely, "sugar-centered development" and "uneven development." These particular factors, however, seem only indirectly related to the revolution. They powerfully influenced both class and state formation in Cuba, to be sure, but since they characterized the island since the nineteenth century (at least), they do not tell us all that much about why a social revolution occurred there in 1959. "Uneven development," furthermore, is a characteristic of virtually every country in the so-called Third World, including many that have never had anything remotely resembling a social revolution.

73. Ibid., 9, 56. See also 57.

74. Ibid., 69.

75. Ibid., 62, 63.

76. Ibid., 58.

77. Ibid., 57.

78. See Jules R. Benjamin, *The United States and the Origins of the Cuban Revolution: An Empire of Liberty in an Age of National Liberation* (Princeton: Princeton University Press, 1990), chapter six.

79. Pérez-Stable, *The Cuban Revolution*, 56. See also Ramón L. Bonachea and Marta San Martín, *The Cuban Insurrection, 1952–1959* (New Brunswick: Transaction, 1974), 63–4, 147–52. The Cienfuegos revolt was led by "naval officers [who] felt

frustrated at Batista's appointments of men who had not graduated from the Mariel Naval Academy to the highest ranks in the service:" ibid., 147.
80. Bonachea and San Martín, *The Cuban Insurrection*, 231, 262.
81. Luis A. Pérez, Jr., *Cuba: Between Reform and Revolution* (New York: Oxford University Press, 1988), 309.
82. Pérez-Stable, *The Cuban Revolution*, 57.
83. Ibid., chapter one.
84. Ibid., 58–9.
85. Ibid., 53.
86. Ibid., 3–5.
87. Tarrow's *Power in Movement* certainly approaches such a synthesis, although I believe that it says too little about the social-psychological dynamics of collective action. For a rather different sketch of what such a theory might look like – one that tries to reincorporate social psychology – see Emirbayer and Goodwin, "Symbols, Positions, Objects."

2

STRUCTURAL THEORIES OF REVOLUTION

Timothy P. Wickham-Crowley

STRUCTURAL THEORIZING AND THE ALTERNATIVES

What is a structural theory?

The metaphor of "structure" is certainly of ancient vintage in sociology, and arguably the concept of social structure – along with that of culture – is absolutely central to the discipline's understanding of itself and its subject-matter. The recurring feature of all structural analyses worthy of the name, I would submit, is that their analytical focus is not on the characteristic traits of the units under consideration. Instead, structural analysis, almost by definition, focuses upon the *relationships between the units*. Therefore any structural analysis of social phenomena is likely to focus upon relationships among social groups – variously defined – as the crucial element in our theorizing about such phenomena.

So much for structural analysis. What about that special word, "theory?" Much of what passes for theory nowadays is in fact better understood as "metatheory," as more and more of the space in journals dedicated to theory is devoted to words about other scholars" words, and to battles in the ether over the correct forms of discourse and language, linked to a veritable obsession with us, as makers of theory, instead of the social world we are studying (q.v. contemporary anthropology). Social science as organized skepticism thus becomes, instead, omphaloskepsis (navel-gazing). Much of such "theory" is relentlessly subjectivistic, relativistic, and "perspectivist" (an appropriately ugly neologism), dismissing the possibility of accurate theorizing about the world. An appropriate response for the serious analyst of *society*, rather than our navels, is simply to deploy the sociology of knowledge. With merciful and non-mimetic brevity, we can thus observe that the academic community – at least in the social sciences and humanities – is the one community where neophilic discourse, language, and theorizing are central to professional prestige, income, and career advancement. In such a milieu, the current obsession with metatheory and endless postmodernist philosophizing can get individuals tenure, promotion, and fame, but gets the study of society nowhere.[1]

As one might surmise, my view of theory is, by such standards of theoretical neophilia, antiquarian. While not hewing to his particular brand of theory, I nonetheless hold with the late George Homans that the office of theory is to explain, and that a theory of a phenomenon is an *explanation* of that phenomenon.[2] If that is so, then a structural theory of a phenomenon is one where the *explicantes* that we employ are structural concepts and variables. Thus structural theories of revolutionary phenomena should draw solely, or at least mainly, on structural features of the social order.

Structure versus process in revolution?

Social structures of recurring, human, intergroup activity are themselves composed of ongoing, everyday processes of social life; therefore one cannot counterpose a simple-minded "process" model of revolution as an antithesis to structural theories of revolution. Among the processes that have actively engaged scholars who, none the less, have produced largely structural theories of revolution would be the following (obviously nonexhaustive) list: (1) *unifying or solidarity-making processes* which lead to enhanced abilities of people to act collectively; (2) *conflicts*, with special attention to conflicts (a) between classes, (b) between states, especially wars, and (c) between states and classes, especially over issues such as taxation/spending and access to political office; (3) processes of *exploitation* of labor in some of those conflicts, itself related to the distribution of property, especially landed property; (4) *commercialization* of economic activity, meaning the intrusion of market relationships into economies hitherto limited from such exposure; and (5) *colonization*, meaning the expansion of a state's control to encompass a oreign population which is submitted to a form of political domination unlike that experienced in the home country. We should note that every one of the above processes suggests structural relationships among social units, rather than focusing on the characteristics of the units themselves.

Such processes produce and/or are descriptive of certain structural characteristics of the social order. Descending from the most macro to the more micro levels, we should at least specify: (1) *world-systemic structures* of international trade, finance, and investment; (2) patterns of *interstate* competition, conflict, domination, alliance, and cooperation; (3) *state–class* relations within individual nations, especially over issues such as taxation, governance, coercion, and access to state power; (4) patterns of *class, ethnic, religious, and perhaps gender* conflicts (or alliances); and (5) the relations of *formal organizations*, including social movement organizations, to the society, as mediated by social networks.

Despite my merging of structure and process above, such a merger can never be declared final, for there are large elements of historical contingency in actual human behavior. Elsewhere I have suggested that extant theories of revolution may emphasize structural patterns at the expense of contingent events and actions, or vice versa,[3] and here I wish to explore and deepen that suggestion. Those theorists of revolution who focus on the social – as opposed to the cultural – in understanding revolutions in fact are distributed along a continuum, ranging from a greater emphasis on long-standing structural relations in human behavior, on the one hand, to a greater emphasis on shorter-term changes or contingencies in behavior, on the other, which we might well term "social action" or "social agency" (the two terms have the same Latin etymology).[4] While I shall "map out" these patterns in greater detail below, we can briefly note here that the influential theories of Theda Skocpol and Jeffery Paige, despite deep substantive disagreements, both are concentrated at the structural end of that continuum. On the other hand, the narrative accounts of revolutionary events, so common among historians of revolution, especially those who focus on what Fernand Braudel termed event-centered (and short-term) history – *histoire événementielle* – are concentrated at the opposite end of that spectrum. Exponents of the "natural history" view of revolution, like George Pettee and Crane Brinton, are closer to the action-pole, and my own work closer to the structural pole of the continuum. Theorists such as Charles Tilly and Jack Goldstone can be situated, for reasons we shall explore later, in the middle of that "social" spectrum.

Structural versus cultural views of revolution: Skocpol and her critics

We may ask ourselves how a cultural approach to revolution would differ from the social-structural guidelines outlined above. While the range of definitions is enormous, classic social-scientific views of culture generally have perceived it as a system of shared beliefs that guide human behavior. In this definitional context, "beliefs" are understood very broadly as both cognitive knowledge and moral and aesthetic guidelines, obviously including as subsets specific institutional foci like political ideologies, normative kinship rules, and religious beliefs about the realm of the sacred and supernatural, but also including other institutional belief-spheres concerning economies, expressive (aesthetic) culture, law, and so forth. Since these beliefs do not float in a social vacuum, but are shared by members of social groups – by definition, even while allowing for intragroup variations – cultural theories of social phenomena would seem *ipso facto* to focus upon the cultural characteristics of groups and subgroups themselves (not on intergroup relations as such) and the manner in which such traits can explain similarities and differences in whichever social phenomenon intrigues us. Let us turn, then, to revolutions.

A growing chorus of dissenters, whose critiques usually focus on Theda Skocpol's watershed work, *States and Social Revolutions* (1979),[5] is now forcefully arguing against structural theories of revolution and insisting upon the irreducibility of cultural elements in any defensible interpretation of revolutionary phenomena. Many such theorists, especially William Sewell, Jr. and

Lynn Hunt, zero in on the internal cultural peculiarities of the French Revolution, and they criticize Skocpol and others who fail to do likewise.[6] Sewell has been the more resolute and single-minded in his critique, his attention to ideology, and his explicit call for a return to narratives. Hunt's key monograph combines (uneasily) a focus on cultural symbols and rhetoric with a substantial structural (and statistical) analysis of the social and spatial distribution of empirical indicators of revolutionism; yet her introduction and conclusions leave us in no doubt that the former phenomena are central, the latter secondary. Latin American-focused scholars have also joined voices with the "French Cultural School" (as we might well call them), notably Eric Selbin and Forrest Colburn.[7] Yet more impressively, scholars heretofore closely associated with structural theorizing, such as Jack Goldstone and Jeff Goodwin, have also added their voices to calls for a cultural analysis of revolution. Because of such shifts in foci, these two theorists must be mapped twice onto Figure 2.1 (p. 45) (see "Goldstone [Post-]" and "Goodwin II").[8]

With such impressive, multivocal harmony among the opposition, how do structural theories of revolution stand up in the light of criticism? Theda Skocpol has already responded to both Sewell and Hunt, and has yielded some interpretative ground, while still holding to the core of her structural-processual view of the French Revolution, in particular. Against Sewell's view (which is also Hunt's) that the new ideology of French revolutionaries was the crux of the revolution, Skocpol makes the potent objection that such a self-consciously created ideology among, say, the Jacobins, is not the same thing as a traditional cultural idiom held widely by very broad groups within the French population.[9] Many cultural idioms existed in France at this time, Skocpol points out, often in open conflict with one another, and the analysis of the content of one novel ideology – Jacobinism and its variants – is insufficient to explain the *intergroup* processes and patterns of revolution in France. Moreover, I think Skocpol misses the chance here to hammer home a point previously made by Eric Wolf, James Scott, and herself, to wit: the independent peasant village uprisings that destroyed seigneurial privilege and struck out at unequal land tenure and which, in themselves, could justify the term "revolution" for the French events of 1789, were emphatically not founded upon a new, Enlightenment-generated, self-conscious Jacobinism, and indeed were much like past peasant uprisings in looking to protect the subsistence basis of peasant agriculture.[10] Similar strictures apply to the analysis of peasant uprisings underlying the Russian, Mexican, Bolivian, Vietnamese and other revolutions, as Wolf and Skocpol, in particular, have shown.

Even more telling against a cultural view are the core processes leading to the collapse of states in France (and Russia and China): increasing fiscal distress linked to great military pressures from more powerful neighbors, which were simply overwhelming in the Russian case during World War I. For China and Russia, the notion that revolutionaries consciously guided by communist ideologies brought down the old regimes is laughable: the Bolsheviks were underground and Lenin in Swiss exile when February food riots and garrison desertions brought down the old regime in 1917;[11] Mao Zedong was but a child and the Chinese Communist Party not yet in existence when the Manchu dynasty collapsed in 1910–12. Skocpol argues compellingly that these two types of events – state breakdowns and peasant insurrections – are not explicable in terms of the conscious intentions of a limited group of ideologized revolutionaries. Hence she self-describes her viewpoint as "*Nonintentionalist at the macroscopic level.*"[12] Further, since those two sets of events are *the* fundamental causes of revolution, the peculiar French, Russian, and Chinese cultures (and subcultures) of the participants in the drama seem superfluous to explain the revolutionary outcomes as such.

Indeed, in her responses both to Sewell and to Lynn Hunt's critique,[13] the argument is joined on two very interesting terrains. First, Sewell and Hunt seem to argue, essentially, for the fundamental peculiarity – dare we say, uniqueness – of French events, by focusing on ideology, rhetoric, public political discourse, and new cultural creations in general (such as the novel, if short-lived, French calendar). Skocpol, in response, always insists or implies that we must consider the structural constraints and opportunities with which the highly ideological revolutionaries had to contend. Hence, whereas Hunt would account for successful mass military mobilization for war in terms of a new French political-revolutionary culture, Skocpol argues for a continuity of such military practices beyond the revolution into Napoleonic France, and sees their success in terms of the pressures of foreign invasion (constraint) and also the enhanced social mobility (opportunity) for soldiers in the new citizen army (quite apart from its sheer military advantages against various foreign adversaries). Note that both of these features are structural traits: the first involves interstate conflicts, the second concerns unprecedented career chances within a formerly "closed" formal organization.[14] A comparativist might also point out the regularity of new revolutionary regimes engaging in mass military mobilization (by use of the draft) outside of the French cultural context, notably in Russia, Cuba, Iran, and Nicaragua. Since foreign military invasion and/or pressure and post-revolutionary mass military mobilization have often accompanied one another, why seek a peculiar French cultural explanation for such a regular pattern? We should note that such collisions between revolutionaries" ideological agendas and the internal and external structural constraints they face appear not only in the stances of opposing scholars, but are also the central theme of Forrest Colburn's comparative study of revolutions since World War II, *The Vogue of Revolution in Poor Countries* (1994).

The second terrain of debate has very specific chronological boundaries: almost all the discussion has focused upon events occurring after the collapse of the old regime, and especially on the actions of the new revolutionary leaders themselves. This empirical observation leads us to an "aha!" experience: the "cultural" critics and the main "structural" theorist have in part been talking past one another. The overwhelming focus of cultural approaches to revolution has been on what the revolutionaries do to society once in power, whereas the structural approaches to revolution have largely focused on how the revolutionaries managed to come to that point in the first place.

The best evidence for this assertion comes from the topics grappled with by cultural and structural theorists in their respective works. For example, Selbin's "cultural" study, *Modern Latin American Revolutions* (1993), concerns the sources and fates of postrevolutionary policies. The new rulers may (or may not) pursue and achieve the two ideological, tension-ridden goals of consolidation (support from the populace) and/or institutionalization (state-building). Yet Selbin does not try to explain why these revolutions occurred in the first place in Bolivia, Cuba, Nicaragua, and Grenada. Forrest Colburn's *The Vogue of Revolution*, looking at the previous fifty years, also is mainly interested in why a score of new revolutionary ships-of-state so often ran aground on the problem-shoals of dependency, state-building, popular foot-dragging, wars, and carrying out their revolutionary policies (with all their contradictions). By contrast, works by Theda Skocpol, Jack Goldstone, Jeff Goodwin, Eric Wolf, and myself focus mainly on the causes of revolution, rather than on the texture of postrevolutionary policies. Goldstone's work, *Revolution and Rebellion in the Early Modern World* (1991), also provides an exception that proves the rule: in a work whose overwhelming theoretical thrust relies on the facts of cyclical demographic pressures, fiscal crisis, mass mobilization, and structures of competition and mobility among elites, his systematic analysis of culture begins only in a chapter where he discusses the reconstruction of society after the revolutionary collapse of the state.[15]

This bifurcation of attention between the two groups of theorists suggests an analogy to what Robert Merton has termed "strategic research materials" in science. Such foci are chosen precisely because they promise both fruitful and fundamental discovery.[16] In our context, we should rather term them "strategic theoretical materials," because certain topics provide better grist for the mills of cultural theory, and other topics the material for the mills operated by structural theorists. The cultural theorists have chosen to focus on postrevolutionary events precisely because the powers of ideology to remake the social order seem greatest when disorder reigns and both state and society are *already* in flux or chaos.[17] At this point in the approach of cultural theory, we should note, the central role of contingent human agency also comes to the fore, since the actions of revolutionaries, guided by these totalizing ideologies, seem to be so impressive in making revolutionary events happen. Even structural theorists have rarely sought structural accounts of postrevolutionary processes and developments, with two notable exceptions, Theda Skocpol and Susan Eckstein.[18]

On the other side of the coin, any attempt at a culture-cum-agency approach to those revolutionary phenomena regularly addressed by structural theorists – such as state collapses, peasant insurrections, and revolutionary outcomes themselves – immediately crashes into the issue of comparison. By definition we can identify multiple cases across space and time of each of those social phenomena; thus any resort to nation-specific "culture" or an appeal to "narrative" to explain a single such instance virtually surrenders to the "uniqueness" argument tendered regularly by country-specialist historians. (In contrast, cultural-structural approaches might circumvent such limitations; see my discussion of James Scott's and Timothy McDaniel's work on pp. 49–52.) To cave in thus is to exit from all social-science theorizing; indeed, it is an exit from the possibility of ever doing comparison itself, which is what we do whenever we use a conceptual term to apply to more than one situation.[19]

Mapping the terrain of revolutionary theory

The Skocpol/Sewell debate parallels my previous comments and further suggests how we might map out the terrain of rival explanations of revolutions. Ann Swidler's cultural continuum from highly structured common sense and traditions to more novel and crystallizing ideologies, for example, parallels the social continuum I proposed ranging from social structures to contingent actions and events. If we unite Swidler's approach with Skocpol's dichotomous terminology, we may draw conceptual contrasts between structured cultural idioms versus actively created ideologies (again, in the narrower sense of the latter term). Rather than two parallel continua, the intersection of these two continua then suggests a set of four algebra-style quadrants, with either beliefs ("cultural") or behavior ("social") ranging from the highly patterned and structured (cultural idioms and social structures) to the more contingent, choice-, agency-, and event-centered (ideologies and social action). In Figure 2.1 I have mapped onto that grid the various theorists of revolution discussed in this chapter, and my justifications for the cartographic locations make up the substance of my text, both *supra* and *infra*. As one moves up, one encounters theories of revolution that increasingly rely on "structural" variables, while agency-, event-, and choice-centered theories lie in the lower portions. Theories emphasizing the visible, behavioral conditions explaining revolutionary phenomena lie to the right side of the grid; theories emphasizing ideational and belief-centered explanations lie to the left side.[20] A theorist who has signalled a shift in explanatory focus over time in her/his writings may get two separate entries (e.g., Goodwin); that is also true if a theorist has a different take on explaining, for example, prerevolutionary breakdowns and seizures of power as opposed to postrevolutionary policy-making (e.g., Goldstone).

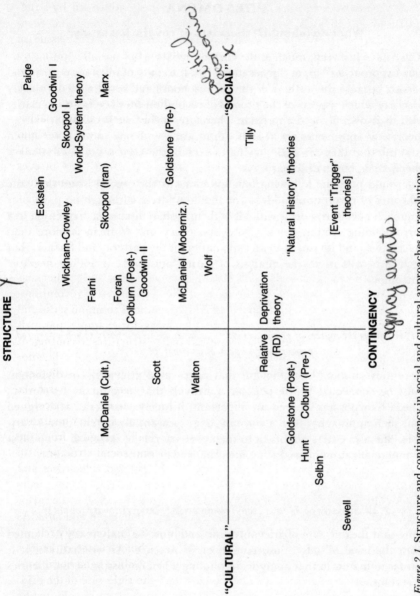

STRUCTURE Y

"SOCIAL" X
politics

Paige
Goodwin I
Skocpol I
World-System theory
Marx

Eckstein
Wickham-Crowley

Goldstone (Pre-)

Skocpol (Iran)

Tilly

Farhi
Foran
Colburn (Post-)
Goodwin II

McDaniel (Moderniz.)

Wolf

"Natural History" theories

[Event "Trigger" theories]

Deprivation theory

CONTINGENCY
agency events

Relative (RD)

McDaniel (Cult.)

Scott

Walton

Goldstone (Post-)
Hunt
Colburn (Pre-)

Selbin

Sewell

"CULTURAL"

Figure 2.1 Structure and contingency in social and cultural approaches to revolution

TIMOTHY P. WICKHAM-CROWLEY

STRUCTURAL THEORIES OF REVOLUTIONARY PHENOMENA

What do (should?) theorists of revolution study?

As we have just seen, much of the current debate – but not all – among various "approaches" to, or "generations" in, the study of revolution exists and persists because the authors of the various books and articles do not specify precisely which aspects of the process of revolution they are trying to clarify with their own favored approach. Therefore, before we decide that various theoretical approaches are at odds – or at war – with one another, we should establish that they are really trying to explain the same set of revolutionary phenomena, but in different ways.

I would pose the following four questions as the crucial issues that true "theories of revolution" address, or should address, although no particular approach necessarily deals with all of them. I shall discuss each question in a corresponding section below. Note that every one of them is more than descriptive, and invites us to an explanation of the pattern, and further, that each also calls us to the analysis of varied outcomes, including negative outcomes.

1. What are the sources of grievances in the population (as compared to non-aggrieved population groups in other times, places)?

Here most authors have thought that aggravated grievances or discontent must be connected to the popular upheavals that accompany revolution; Theda Skocpol has entered an important, if lonely, demurral, and argued that such approaches turn a constant (e.g., peasant discontent) into a variable. She also enters doubts as to the necessary role of imperialist-capitalist commercialization in producing such changed grievances.[21]

2. What makes population (sub-)groups actively insurrectionary (or not)?

Note that the question of grievances can and must be analytically decoupled from the issue of active insurrection or its absence. As we shall see, it is harder to maintain that analytic decoupling when discussing actual theories of revolution.

3. Which societies experience successful social revolutions, and which do not?

Here I embrace a slight variant of Theda Skocpol's widely used definition, arguing that social revolutions should be defined as "rapid, basic transformations of a society's state and class structures; and they are accompanied and in part carried through by [mass]-based revolts from below."[22] While this question has certainly been the central issue in the study of revolutions, the second half of the sentence has been routinely ignored: scholars rarely have included negative cases of revolution to support arguments that their particular array of operative causes routinely produced revolution, while the absence thereof led to nonrevolution.[23]

4. What explains the similarities and differences in state policies and social changes following the revolutionary seizure of power?

This particular issue has received the least attention of the four, and I know of only one attempt at a deep structural interpretation of the crucial questions, that by Theda Skocpol.[24]

These are certainly not the only possible foci of interest for the study of revolution, and here we can easily concede much to certain cultural analysts. The four issues above are largely defined in terms that lend themselves well to structural approaches, notably the binary (yes/no) codings of insurrection and of revolutionary outcomes. These issues are, of course, fundamental to understanding revolutions, yet they are relatively "content-empty" when, for example, we look back upon the heady events in France so carefully described – and analyzed – by Sewell, Hunt, Tilly, and others. We might well say similar things about the rich historiography of all revolutions. Works such as those of Lynn Hunt on France, Barrington Moore's briefer analysis of Russia, and Charles Tilly's dissection of the counterrevolutionary Vendée in France provide especially visceral satisfaction because they manage to combine textually rich narrative and attention to detail with more or less analytically precise explanations of change.[25] If one were to stretch for a metaphor here, one might say that structural theories are especially adept at telling us how the "vessels" of revolution take shape and substance, but are relatively poor in providing us with a taste of the heady revolutionary "brews" that fill them. None the less, since the four issues raised above certainly are substantively important, I need apologize no further for detailing the ways that structural approaches have enlightened us about them, or failed to do so.

Structural theory and population grievances

Mass grievances

Structural theories of grievances should be contrasted with earlier approaches which focus on the short-term precipitants thereof, or those theories which translate macrosocial processes directly into a mass psychology of discontent, without structural mediation by any type of intergroup context. Both such approaches resemble what the late E. P. Thompson pungently termed the "spasmodic" approach to collective unrest, for example, his caricatured "eighteenth-century English collier who claps his hand upon his stomach, and responds to elementary economic stimuli," especially via the food/grain riots to which Thompson forcefully drew our attention.[26] (Thompson's critique, we should note, could just as forcefully be directed against unmediated structural theories as well.) Theories which focus on short-term precipitants of revolution are relatively few, although the "natural history" approaches to the subject regularly include such "triggers" in their list of events.[27] As careful studies and thinking about collective violence can show, however, such precipitants capture our attention only when followed by volcanic social responses (such as the 1960s' ghetto riots following certain arrests or after the first Rodney King verdict in the United States). The dozens, if not hundreds of incidents which are not succeeded by such outbreaks get no attention, as for example, those cities and locations where the same trigger produces no such responses. Yet such approaches do not hold center stage in current debates, so we need not dwell on them.

The relative-deprivation (RD) approach to revolution, by contrast, did long hold exactly such a preeminent role. The core of RD theory involved the claim that a growing gap between the actual ("social") rewards/capabilities/conditions of people's lives and their ("cultural") desires/expectations/moral claims would lead to a build-up of discontent, resulting in a mass explosion of the aggrieved. In one widely cited version, that of the (inverted) J-curve, the explosion comes because expectations of continuous betterment, conditioned by a long-term rising trend, diverge from a sharp fall-off of actual conditions/rewards (e.g., long economic boom followed by a bust).[28] Since its heyday, however, vigorous critiques by competing theorists and, I would argue, the lack of specificity in how to measure RD on the y-axis of its signature graphs, have led to a sharp decline in the theory's influence on thinking about revolution. The most devastating flaw was the in-built assumption that intensified grievances would transmute readily into insurrection. As Leon Trotsky most aptly put it, "the mere existence of privations is not enough to cause an insurrection; if it were, the masses would always be in revolt."[29] Thus organizational capacity, as Tilly noted most clearly,[30] and all types of structural-institutional constraints on, and opportunities for, actual insurrectionary activity were glossed over or simply ignored. Much later theorizing about revolution has been filling in all the previously empty, mediating social spaces ignored by RD theory with the organized activities of unions, guilds, peasant movements, revolutionary undergrounds and guerrilla organizations, elites and estate-groups, and, of course, states themselves, including their military organizations.

In general, scholars began to seek other ways to think systematically about mass grievances, their source(s), and the manner(s) of their expression. In my own work on peasants and their (non-)support for guerrilla movements in Latin American from 1956 to 1990, I advanced the idea of "rebellious cultures," which I inductively inferred from the long-term historical rebelliousness against governments and landed elites in certain regions of a country, but not in others; for example, I found a greatly disproportional concentration of Cuban rebellions in the far east of the island (Oriente Province), going back to the early 1800s, with few such signs elsewhere in the island. I argued that such patterns were not reducible to either class-conflictual or class-transformational sources, and could independently contribute to our understanding of variations in peasant support for revolutionaries.[31] To assert that there are cultural roots for such rebelliousness is surely to claim that such "orneriness" can in part be decoupled from particular social-geographical situations or structural locations.[32] My analysis strongly suggests that cultural practices can, indeed, supplement structural analysis of grievances. Yet it also suggests that cultural analysis can still be transsocietal in nature, in finding parallels, not contrasts, in peasant cultural practices such as relative "quiescence" or relative "resistance" in the face of elite impositions.

The "moral economy" theoretical "school" also draws our attention to certain cultural elements in the production of mass grievances, both urban and rural. Yet its distinctive approach to the subsistence pressures on particular social groups and classes, in particular regions, under particular economic/political pressures (such as the Great Depression), grounds that perspective in both space and time in ways unlike RD theory. In effect, moral economy theory conjoins structural to cultural approaches, apparently creating an analytically inseparable fusion. The normative foundations of the moral economy – subsistence first and local needs first – are clearly cultural standards, often of great antiquity, which provide both fuel and texture to the indignation that occurs when such norms are violated. Yet in both of the watershed works on the moral economy, the urban and rural rioters/ insurrectionaries are responding to the expanding forces of the market economy, which threaten the subsistence-protections provided by more traditional economic mechanisms.[33] Thus commercialization becomes a master-process through which two different economic principles and systems come into collision, and *that* process should be understood as structural. Scholars from an enormous variety of perspectives have now embraced some form of this argument (which is usually decoupled from moral economy theory *per se*), usually uniting two propositions: (1) aggravated mass grievances derive from the commercialization of hitherto "protected" economies, and (2) such commercialization usually stems from intrusions by international capitalist markets.

In John Walton's variant of moral economy theory – as I would consider his *Reluctant Rebels* – the two driving processes of world-market commercialization and (neo-)colonization elicited three similar rebellions; but Walton also insists on rooting such mass resistance irreducibly in a "cultural nation-alism" generated among the aggrieved lower classes of the Philippines, Kenya, and Colombia. Thus Walton's cultural-nationalist response is here wedded to the violation of the moral-economic subsistence-first ethos.[34] Yet Walton's case for cultural elements here, which I would endorse, and the claims of Scott's moral-economy approach both draw transsocietal parallels in the forms of cultural response to grievances. (In this respect they resemble my idea of "rebellious cultures," also found in different societal contexts.) To discern such fundamental similarities – in depression-era peasant griev-ances and revolts in Burma, Vietnam, and (briefly) Indonesia and the Philippines,[35] or in "reluctant rebellions" in the even more diverse cases of Colombia, Kenya, and the Philippines – is surely to suggest structured paral-lels. In any event, those transsocietal parallels are a far cry from the distinc-tively new, Enlightenment-derived, rhetorics, discourses, and ideologies to which the French cultural theorists have directed us.

Another way of viewing the impetus behind collective action undertaken by the aggrieved lower classes in situations of commercialization or (neo-) colonization is to understand them as "antisystemic movements" within the world system. A deeper way to tie such patterns of international commercial-ization to revolutions is to relate revolutionary activity and/or success to worldwide business cycles (the Kondratieff curves) or to shifts in world-leadership patterns.[36] Unlike Scott's or Walton's approaches, however, world-system theorists have resolutely minimized the role of cultural elements in their theories – they are almost always treated as epiphenomenal – instead focusing on the structures and processes of global economic relations.

Marginal elite grievances

In contrast to such varied explanations of mass grievances among the lower classes, more purely cultural and contingent approaches to the production of grievances have tended to center instead on the consciously adversarial, sometimes utopian, ideologies of marginal elites, including of course the revolutionaries themselves. Hence both Sewell and Hunt focus on the rhetorics, symbols, discourses, and "poetics" actively and consciously pro-duced by the revolutionary leaders and others before and during the period of revolutionary effervescence. They both therefore zero in on the politics of revolutionary events, and the choices that revolutionaries make therein.[37] Yet that apt term "effervescence" comes from Durkheim, the positivist-supreme among sociologists, and it hints at the possibility of a deeper sociological understanding, even of the headily creative milieux wherein revolu-tionaries come to define their contrarian stance against the *ancien régime* and their visions of a *nouveau régime*.[38]

50

In *The Vogue of Revolution*, Forrest Colburn aligns himself with the French cultural school by acknowledging a primary intellectual debt to Hunt, Darnton, Furet, and Schama. He then proceeds to argue for a revitalization of the politics of revolution, as do they. Yet his argument about socialist ideologies ironically undermines that revitalizing goal (without in the least detracting from the book's many deep virtues), for Colburn himself gathers a wealth of information documenting the systematic appearance of socialist and communist ideologies among university-educated intellectuals from the Third World, especially under the direct or indirect influence of European university educators.[39]

That conclusion closely parallels certain findings in my *Guerrillas and Revolution in Latin America* (1992), which themselves owed substantial intellectual debts to both Alvin Gouldner and Karl Mannheim.[40] Mannheim, Gouldner, and myself all pay attention to a set of sociological facts: we have witnessed the structured production of an adversarial and socialist culture among university-trained intelligentsia in both Europe and the Third World. To put it in the blunt words of Carlos Rangel, "in a Latin American university, it is just about as daring and heretical to be 'revolutionary' as it is for a student in an Irish seminary to be a fervent Catholic."[41] Furthermore, such "production" has led to the great increase of a new "white-collar left" which at best has a deeply uneasy relationship with the traditional left rooted in the economic grievances of the working class.[42] Thus any academic narrative implying that the revolutionism of the (also academic) intelligentsia is pure agency, largely a self-actuation or a self-creation, seems to suffer from self-delusion.

These adversarial, intellectual revolutionaries do indeed work best in the realms of discourse, symbols, and rhetoric, all typical of what one British wag termed "the chattering classes." In this respect they are like university faculties everywhere – surely the havens of Gouldner's "culture of critical discourse" – but it is wrong to see such discourses as themselves free-floating, socially unconditioned creations. And it is further wrong-headed to see discourses and rhetorics as a resolutely non-material philosopher's stone for all social analysis.[43] Gouldner noted earlier the quite parallel failure of Marx and Engels in *The Communist Manifesto* to follow through on any sociological analysis of that segment of the bourgeoisie which suddenly sees reality plain, cuts itself off from the ruling class, and joins with the revolutionary project of the proletariat. As Gouldner put it, the analysis there is likewise strictly ideational, "a silence concealed by a gloss" wherein "Marxism has here abruptly reached the limits of its self-understanding."[44]

Between the structured (re-)production of revolutionary intelligentsias documented by Gouldner, Colburn, and myself, on the one hand, and the image of ideological self-creation advanced by the French cultural school, on the other, lie gray areas in between. Hence John Foran's contribution in this volume lies closer to the latter school with respect to his partial theoretical focus on "political cultures of resistance," which are described more than traced back to systematically produced origins. Likewise Farideh Farhi insists on the importance to revolution of "ideology" (albeit she oddly defines it not as a system of ideas, but as a "social process," which will promote only more terminological confusion in a discipline already befuddled). She also perceives such ideologies and ideological mobilization as crucial to producing revolutionary outcomes in both Iran and Nicaragua, but only in the broader context of two peripheral capitalist societies and the (atypical?) class structures and political systems produced therein. Yet she roots such creative ideologies in specific, internal, historical situations more clearly than does Foran. Finally Tim McDaniel's analysis of "cultures of rebellion" provides a series of (clearly structural) parallels in the positions of marginal-elite intellectuals in prerevolutionary Iran and Russia such as to "push" them toward revolutionary stances. More strikingly, by abstracting from the national contents and contexts of Shi'ism and Bolshevism, he can identify similar ideological themes involving elitism, dualism, superior knowledge, a transhistorical mission, universality, the importance of consciousness, and martyrdom. His analysis of cultures is thus far more structural than we find in the French cultural school, but his accompanying analysis of modernization processes that also underlie the Russian and Iranian Revolutions is rather more process-oriented, thus placing his overall argument in two different locations in Figure 2.1.[45]

Structural theory and mass insurrections

Latter-day Marxist analyses of revolutions are generally noteworthy only for their outright absence or "canned Marxist" tendentiousness.[46] The most important and clear-headed exception rooted in the Marxian tradition is surely Jeffery Paige's *Agrarian Revolution* (1975). That work first precisely defines rural class structures on the basis of cultivators" income sources (wages or land) in combination with noncultivators" income sources (capital or land) to generate a fourfold table of different types of rural class structure; a fifth is then generated by subdividing the wage laborers facing land-based elites into two subgroups, sharecroppers and migratory estate laborers. He then predicts five different forms of collective action to flow regularly from those five types (and, of course, not from the other types), and demonstrates just such patterns in a world statistical analysis. He then adds country studies of Peru, Angola, and Vietnam which show four of the types in historical-contextual "action," yet still buttressed by systematic statistical measures. Particularly for our concerns, Paige predicts and demonstrates that share-cropping will be related to revolutionary socialist collective action and migratory labor to revolutionary nationalist collective action.[47] The assumptions linking (class-)structural positions to different class interests and hence different forms of collective action are certainly those of "rational (i.e., material) choice;" but the variation-inducing source is the structure, not the psychology.[48]

Capacities and opportunities

While Theda Skocpol has been one of the vigorous critics of Paige's work, in our present context her work is similarly situated, in so far as she seeks to explain peasant insurrections – whether in revolutionary situations or not – in structural terms. First of all, she takes peasant resentment as a given, and resists theoretical attempts to explain uprisings in terms of increased grievances. That approach, she argues, "tries to turn a constant feature of the peasant condition into an explanatory variable." In effect, she proposes a theory of peasant insurrections that combines the capacity to rebel with the opportunity to rebel.[49]

The capacity to rebel among the lower classes derives from a combination of their internal structural solidarity and their external structural autonomy from elite control. Skocpol also extends this logic to her analysis of the Iranian Revolution, where the urban rebellion against the Shah was rooted in the structural autonomy and solidarity of city bazaar life, strengthened by the shared religious beliefs and rituals of a newly re-energized Shi'ism.[50] Without such features the lower classes will have little capacity to rebel. In rural China, for one such case, cross-class clan-strength and regional marketing-patterns reduced both the solidarity and autonomy of peasant villagers; the absence of such features "delayed" peasant insurrection for several decades, until the mobilization of parts of rural China by the Red Army provided a "structural umbrella" under which such resistance could emerge and express itself.[51] Skocpol's approach certainly echoes that of her former teacher, Barrington Moore, who concluded that peasant insurrections were most frequent wherever a "damaged but intact" peasantry was given room to maneuver (notably so in the rebellion-littered histories of modern Russia and China).[52] In my own essay, "What Makes Peasants Insurrectionary?" I have tried to combine Moore's and Skocpol's ideas of damage and solidarity-cum-autonomy to illuminate historical situations where peasant rebellions were common, and those where they were not. This approach can incorporate Paige's revolutionary sharecroppers and migratory estate laborers, whose high levels of solidarity derive, like factory workers, from being paid in wages. In that essay I also argue that external mobilization of resistance does indeed function as a structural substitute where solidarity and/or autonomy are weakened, or as an accelerator where they are present.[53]

In a related approach to the issue of capacity, a number of authors have focused upon the manner in which *organizational networks* have been critical elements in bringing people into revolutionary activism, or not.[54] Other authors have used organizational memberships and embeddedness as alternative ways of predicting in which direction actors of the lower class and middle class will move, given revolutionary situations and revolutionary opportunities.[55]

In Skocpol's approach the opportunity to rebel arises when the repressive apparatus that "holds" the peasantry in place is removed, when the lid comes off the political pressure-cooker. Such an "opportunity" now presenting itself, the aggrieved lower classes with the proper capacities are then able to act.[56] Hence, in Skocpol's theory, the weakening of repression, above all of state repression, takes the place of the "increased grievances" of RD and moral-economy theories in helping us to understand the timing and actual appearance of uprisings. In her analysis of Russian events of 1905, for example, the weakening of the state came when the Tsar's military was deeply involved in losing the Russo-Japanese war in East Asia. The Tsar's concessions, made under the gun to rebels both urban and rural, were rescinded when the state's power reinflated upon the military's return.

States and rebels

There can also be a spatial counterpart to the temporal weakening of state power, that is, regions of a nation where the state is always weak, especially in frontier, peripheral, or inaccessible sections of a nation's territory. While later scholarship has not necessarily supported Eric Wolf's claim that the "middle peasant" − as such − is the key to twentieth-century peasant wars, his companion claim that the peasantry's "tactical mobility" is a key to their rebellions has proven most fruitful.[57] Skocpol's idea of a peasantry with autonomy clearly echoes this idea, as does my own attempt to link squatters (in frontier zones) regularly to revolutionary guerrilla movements.[58] The best extension of this idea has come in the writings of Jeff Goodwin. Goodwin borrows Michael Mann's concept of the "infrastructural power" of the state, argues that such power varies systematically by national region and is certainly weaker in such inaccessible areas, and uses such weaknesses to explain why insurrection is likely to take shape and flourish in such regions, but not others. Furthermore, where the state is unable to control and administer such a region effectively, but is none the less able to terrorize populations therein, such regions are likely to harbor "persistent insurgencies," guerrilla movements that grow quite strong in numbers and support and survive for long periods, yet without being able to seize state power.[59]

If the varied infrastructural reach of the state might explain the likelihood of regionally based rebellions, then perhaps the very structure of the state itself might also promote rebellion. Skocpol, following Moore, argues that "agrarian bureaucracies" are especially likely to promote widespread rebellions, in part because peasantries are subjected simultaneously to material demands by both the state and landed elites; opportunities to rebel are likely to multiply where the landed elite has a foothold in state office and can paralyze state capacity, especially for repressive action.[60] In a related view, Goodwin and Skocpol have argued that the "growth of revolutionary coalitions" is especially likely to occur in societies ruled by "exclusionary, as well as organizationally weak . . . authoritarian regimes."[61]

As opposed to such highly structural views of the conditions promoting actual insurrection, we might suggest that Charles Tilly's approach to the growth of revolutionary contention is a much more process-oriented one, and hence located closer to the contingency pole of our continuum. I specify "contention" here, because Tilly has pointedly argued that "we cannot predict revolutionary outcomes, only predict revolutionary situations," and thus we should direct our scholarly attention, instead, to the regular appearance of systematic challenges to incumbent rulers (that is, to "revolutionary contention").[62] That, he argues, will mean our constant attention to the mostly political processes through which all forms of political conflict – of which revolutionary contention is a special case – regularly emerge. In exiling "revolutionary outcomes" to the domain of unsolvable scholarly puzzles, Tilly of course increases his distance from all those scholars who think that a revolutionary outcome – defined (differently from him) as involving great political and social changes – is something which demands a separate and special type of scholarly attention.[63]

In his latest book-length work on the topic, *European Revolutions, 1492–1992* (1993), Tilly has advocated this agenda again with characteristic force and clarity. Let us get to the quintessence of this book and a great deal of his previous work. Tilly has argued that, given states and state-making he has so pithily described and conceptualized as "organized crime," the processes through which states secure obedience and commitments from their national populations *must* be understood as deeply contingent ones.[64] For Tilly there is never any deep structure to what many scholars easily term "legitimacy" and "legitimation," nor could we imagine him casually using some yet-deeper term like "hegemony" to describe state power and influence over a populace.[65] In his view, instead, commitments to such orders (and order-givers) should be understood as an ongoing process of "structuration" that never really ceases.[66] Given this view of states and peoples, we can now understand why "revolutionary contenders" for European power should have appeared so regularly over the past 500 years. His portrait also includes many periods of "revolutionary situations," when substantial population groups committed themselves to the challenging group(s) and the rulers were unwilling or unable to suppress such contenders. Nearly 20 percent of that half-millennium could be so characterized in Russia, France, and the Low Countries; almost 25 percent in the British Isles (including the Irish "troubles" that English rulers have regularly faced); and almost one-third of the time in Iberia, the Balkans, and Hungary.[67]

Structural theory and successful social revolutions

As we move to Jack Goldstone's *Revolution and Rebellion in the Early Modern World*, we also move to a work whose focal interest is the breakdown of states, and thus very close to the core issue in all theories of revolution. As Goldstone carefully and clearly argues, in a manner not unlike Tilly, not all state breakdowns necessarily carry with them all of the indicators necessary to identify a particular outcome as fully "revolutionary." In fact, Goldstone does scholars the great service of specifying eight conditions which may (or may not) be met by any society at a given point in time. If all eight are present few scholars would doubt that a social revolution had occurred; fewer than eight would lead to deeper debates about our use of such a common term, but at least we would be in the same universe of discourse, and not wasting our energies on essentialist debates over "true" revolutions versus pretenders. Hence Goldstone discusses a number of cases which fail to qualify on all eight criteria, but are still worthy of our attention here.[68]

Goldstone's demographic-structural theory of state breakdowns is like Tilly's in so far as he gives deep attention to long-term processes, in this case those of (cyclic) population growth, as the "prime movers" underlying state breakdown. Such growth in turn partly (only) accounts for the intensification (1) of state fiscal crisis and (2) of elite-competition, especially for state office. He then combines these issues with measures of (3) the potential within the population for mass mobilization. Each of these three measures involves an interesting mix of structural issues (involving patterns of inter-group relations) with historically unfolding processes by which "pressure" on the state increases. As if this were not impressive enough by itself, Goldstone then develops, for each European case, a three-part numerical measure of political pressure called *psi* (the Greek letter epsilon), which combines quantitative measures of fiscal distress, mobility/competition, and mass mobilization potential. He then shows that *psi* in fact peaks at the time of historical state breakdowns or massive social eruptions and – this is quite important for careful theorizing about negative cases and alternative explanations – is lower at other times and declines in the aftermath of state breakdown, that is, as states are being rebuilt. Goldstone's approach thus "solves" an inherent problem of structural theorizing to which few critics have been attentive: how can pure structural theories account for the precise timing of social revolution? To such a question Goldstone's model, unlike most, has a ready response.[69]

Marx's theory of revolution, like Goldstone's non-Marxian one, draws attention to long-term "pressure," but within a continuing substructure of discontent. Marx's approach to predicting revolutionary outcomes rests uneasily on the cusp between the "increased grievance" viewpoints visible in RD and moral-economy theory and a more purely structural one. In particular, the emphasis in the classic texts on the transformation of intensified exploitation and poverty – the famed "immiseration" thesis – into, first, class consciousness, and then revolutionary upheavals does not itself give center stage to the organizational embodiments of revolution. Thus James Davies's original view that RD theory draws heavily on Marxian ideas (as well as Tocqueville's) is not without substance.[70] Yet Marx's view is still best understood as largely structural because of the pivotal role of bourgeois–proletarian class conflict as the "structural engine" behind revolution. As all serious theorists of revolution now know and concede, however, this model of revolution has fared badly in predicting real revolutions and transitions to socialism – however fleeting – and the vast majority of theorists of revolution recognize rather the crucial roles of certain urban artisan groups and, especially, various peasantries in the mass uprisings that qualify as revolutionary in import.

Theda Skocpol is now well known (supposedly) as the hyper-structural theorist of revolutionary outcomes, the one engaged in theoretical "statolatry," as Mexican historian Alan Knight so strikingly (but misleadingly) put it.[71] Her basic argument has occasionally been misleadingly summarized, so it should be done properly here, following her tabular aids.[72] Given the world-historical conditions of the uneven development of the capitalist world-economy and (the partially resulting) contention among nation-states, certain agrarian bureaucracies fell victim to social revolution. Those agrarian bureaucracies are the second given of her analysis, and consist politically of "absolutist" monarchical systems ruled in partly bureaucratic, tax-collecting fashion, and economically of often-backward agrarian economies, with peasantries in constant class tensions with landlords. Revolutions occurred where the collapse or paralysis of the state was followed by widespread peasant insurrections; those are her two "causes" of revolution, but those "events" have structural sources. States collapsed due to intense international pressure, generally in the form of war(s), in conjunction with a state in fiscal paralysis because a landlord class lodged in bureaucratic office staved off potentially state-saving fiscal/tax reforms. In Russia, so intense were the military pressures of World War I that they produced a state collapse in the absence of the "paralyzing" elite. Note how closely Skocpol's argument fits her "nonintentionalist" claims: surely neither foreign powers nor domestic upper classes desired revolutionary outcomes in France, Russia, and China, yet their actions in part brought on such outcomes, willy-nilly. As we have seen, peasant insurrections came after the collapse of the state, and were in part made possible by it. Those insurrections were not based on the novel, "intentional" ideologies of the self-styled revolutionaries, yet they, too, had structural causes: the combination of peasant solidarity and autonomy, already discussed. In the absence of both sets of fundamental causes, agrarian bureaucracies did not fall victim to social revolution from below, and Skocpol details such contrasts in her (often-ignored) analyses of Japan, Prussia, Germany (1848), England, and Russia (1905).

Jeff Goodwin has also crafted brilliant, structural, state-centered theories which account for both strong revolutionary movements (discussed above) and for the emergence, or not, of revolutionary outcomes (see his Chapter 1 in this volume). His explanations have consistently pointed to the key role of (1) regime-structures themselves and (2) the nature of state–elite alliances and conflicts (thus Goodwin I in Figure 2.1). In his most comprehensive work to date, he studies four cases from Southeast Asia after World War II (Vietnam, Malaya, Indonesia, and the Philippines), and four cases from Central America since roughly 1970 (Nicaragua, Guatemala, El Salvador, and Honduras). Widespread anti-colonial or left-wing revolutionary movements appeared in most such nations, but a social-revolutionary outcome emerged only in the first case in each group. While carefully attending both to historical events and processes and to structural types, he uses his well-matched comparisons and contrasts to make a persuasive case that neither movement-size or type, nor the mere presence or absence of a militarily strong "foreign" element was sufficient to produce revolution. Instead, revolutionary movements only came to power in two situations: when colonial powers chose to rule their colonies directly (Vietnam) rather than through the indirect cooptation of native elites (the other Asian cases); and when Latin American revolutionaries faced a neopatrimonial (or "Sultanistic") form of personal, narrowly based authoritarian regime (Nicaragua), rather than a democratic regime or a more impersonal and bureaucratic form of authoritarian regime (the other Central American cases). Goodwin and Skocpol further strengthen the case for structural obstacles/opportunities in revolution by extending the comparisons and contrasts to other countries and cases.[73] Finally, despite his concurrent appeals for a return to the analysis of "culture" in our studies of revolution – thus Goodwin II in Figure 2.1 – his analysis of the revolutionary collapse of Eastern European regimes is an innovative but still structural theory that cleverly extends his previous analyses. His argument is particularly compelling in pointing to the unusual structure and consequences of Ceauşescu's "neopatrimonial socialism," which led to a violent social revolution in Romania, in contrast to mostly peaceful transitions elsewhere in the region.[74]

My own work parallels Goodwin's (and Skocpol's) argument about the peculiar vulnerability of neopatrimonial regimes to revolution, which I have termed, less accurately but more evocatively, "mafiacracies." In *Guerrillas and Revolution in Latin America*, however, the work is less purely social (versus cultural) and structural (versus contingent) than either Goodwin or Skocpol's work, although still well within that "tradition," if that term is not premature. The work is less purely social-cum-structural because of the active role I attribute to revolutionary mobilizers in generating the revolutionary movements that appeared in so many nations; such Latin American mobilizations were not structurally produced by state breakdowns dovetailing with lower-class solidarity/autonomy (but there are definite resemblances here to

Skocpol's analysis of Chinese Communist activity in the 1930s and 1940s). Yet the movements still cannot be understood as purely contingent because the impetus to form the movements came at a peculiar "historical moment" for Latin American, university-educated, political activists, in the impact of the Cuban Revolution on their "cultural repertoires."[75] More importantly, the movements are not even largely contingent because their ability to expand and grow strong – to become real challengers to the state, in Tilly's terms – depended on the largely structural characteristics of the peasantries they sought to mobilize; to wit: while ideology proposes, the peasantry's condition disposes. The argument is also in part cultural because one such condition is the presence or absence of "rebellious cultures" among specific groups of peasants. In the end, revolutionary movements came to power in Latin America only where strongly supported guerrilla movements faced and defeated "mafiacracies" in Batista's Cuba and Somoza's Nicaragua, regimes from which the United States had withdrawn military support. The Boolean-algebraic analysis – also called QCA, or qualitative comparative analysis – of conditions producing revolution (or not) also shows that, if each condition is taken by itself, neither regime-type, guerrilla attempts, strong peasant support for guerrillas, the military strength of guerrilla forces, nor the level of foreign military support can predict such outcomes.[76]

Finally, John Foran has essayed an ambitious attempt in this volume to explain social revolutions, anti-colonial revolutions, reversed revolutions, attempted revolutions (e.g,. El Salvador), political revolutions (e.g., China 1911), and the absence of revolution. His arguments are strengthened by the study of negative cases, implied by the inclusion of that final category. His theory is mostly structural because, like Goodwin and myself, he attends to personalist-authoritarian regime types and also to the structural type he calls "dependent development." Yet his analysis is pulled further in the direction of both culture and contingency in Figure 2.1 because he looks at "political cultures of resistance," and also at emergent processes (if still partially structured ones) such as economic downturns and world-systemic openings.[77]

Structural theory and postrevolutionary changes

As I have argued, the French cultural school has focused its attentions on events following the collapse of the state and I suggested that this is a strategic theoretical decision on their part. Any scholar not already hypnotized by the theoretical imperialism of purely sociological explanations would also be drawn into the sheer dramas of revolutionary choices, actions, and events that seem to be deeply implicated in turning the world upside down. Who could not be drawn to Lenin's ride in a sealed car to the Finland Station and his relentless hectoring of both the Kerensky government and his own comrades until the October Revolution? Who is not deeply impressed, whatever their politics, by Mao's "Long March" across China and the later reconstitution of his revolutionary movement on a rural base? Thus the call of William Sewell to a return to narrative in the study of revolution, or Lynn Hunt's loving attention to the poetics of revolutionary imagery and language, have great power for they are what drew so many of us to the study of revolution in the first place.

Clearly, the structural theorists have a rather more difficult task in accounting for the direction and texture of postrevolutionary political policies and social changes. Yet help can be found immediately in a most unlikely quarter, that of those very early works in the genre now known as the "natural history" approach to revolution, such as historian Crane Brinton's *The Anatomy of Revolution*, first published in 1938.[78] Brinton's work has been critically discussed by a number of scholars,[79] yet those critical writings miss some elements of it that are crucial not only to the construction of explanatory theories but also to a critique of "culturalist" calls for a return to a series of national narratives of the revolutionary process.

Oddly enough, while social scientists criticized this approach as "too historical,"[80] the great strength of Brinton's work (and that of George Pettee and Lyford Edwards) was to begin with the historical materials of several revolutions and then to discern a parallel sequencing of processes. For example, Brinton argues that, after the fall of the old regime (1) the moderates (among the opposition) tend to seize power in the short term, but find themselves opposed by the far left, creating (2) a situation of dual power, with competing claims to rule, followed (3) by an extremist *coup d'état* that leads to (4) centralized authoritarian rule ("reigns of terror and virtue"), and finally, a society in exhaustion that moves toward (5) "Thermidor," or a relaxation of revolutionary effervescence, but under dictatorial (if calmer) rule.[81] If we then accept that Brinton has indeed detected largely parallel patterns, then he has begun to undermine deeply the "general case" made by Sewell and others against general explanations.

Two cases in point may be instructive. Lynn Hunt provides an illuminating discussion of the French revolutionary obsession with "conspiracy" and a consequent search for those counterrevolutionary, conspiratorial "interests" seeking to undo the accomplishments of the revolution. She then links this to a campaign of public vigilance, embodied later in the terror unleashed by Robespierre. Now such elements are just as obvious in the history of Stalinist and Maoist attempts to root out their enemies from the new society; indeed, such comments are no longer revelatory and hardly require documentation. Yet we can also observe a roughly similar pattern in the earlier English Revolution: which also exhibited the internal "wars" between the extremists and the moderates; which also saw the seizure of power by the former from the latter; which also saw terror (some of it directed by Cromwell against the Irish) and attempts to eradicate those even more extreme segments of the left and others who failed to fit the new forms of propriety (such as the Diggers and the Quakers); and which also saw power concentrated in, and at times used terroristically by, a newly and deeply centralized authority (Cromwell and the Army Council).

William Sewell provides a second such example, arguing for the great importance of ideology in creating the uniquely French aspects of the French Revolution. He points to varied ideologies in the old regime and among the revolutionary groups themselves – as if these were uniquely French? – yet we consistently see this pattern in Brinton's half-century old treatise as well. In a section on the "ideological restructuring of social life" he also dwells lovingly on the elaboration of the metric system and on the novel French calendar.[82] Yet Brinton in 1938 discussed carefully "the revolutionary mania for renaming," and he and others have for over a century now – e.g., Tocqueville – noted that these and other ideologically induced changes were part and parcel of the centralization of power that has followed inexorably after every revolution until the 1989 events in Eastern Europe.[83] To read Sewell alongside Brinton is thus to experience yet another "aha!" experience: Brinton observes many, many of the same phenomena, yet where Sewell "sees" only ideological creativity, novel action, and uniqueness, Brinton documents dozens of parallels to events both before and after the events in France. And Brinton achieves this simply by abstracting from the particulars of each nation's language, context, and specific contents, while still noting them. Such scholarly efforts sound suspiciously like a definition of analysis, as opposed to mere description or narrative.

Thus Brinton provides a wedge of "empirical generalizations" to open the hermetically sealed door behind which scholars of the unique-cum-cultural-cum-ideological have tried to seal themselves off from the virus of general theory. Eric Selbin, despite his endorsement of culture-and-agency theories, in *Modern Latin American Revolutions* actually does something rather similar. He abstracts from the specific contents of postrevolutionary policies in Bolivia, Cuba, Nicaragua, and Grenada, and suggests that the array of policies these regimes pursued might usefully be grasped under the two rubrics of consolidation (developing regime-support within the populace) and institutionalization (building up the new state organization[s]). He tries to avoid the trap of either/or thinking by straightforwardly assessing the success of each regime on both such issues, and relating those successes to the different strengths of consolidators and institutionalizers within the new government. Despite those abstractions, Selbin sticks closely to the events in each nation, and argues vigorously that we take policy-makers and policy-choices seriously.

In *The Vogue of Revolution in Poor Countries*, Forrest Colburn is arguably closer yet to both Brinton and the structural theorists. In insisting that the socialist ideologies of new revolutionary leaders cannot avoid dealing with basic issues like the structures of both the domestic and international economies, wars and invasions, building new states (like Selbin) and administering national affairs, Colburn creates a post-war world of revolutionary political irony. In that world the widespread (and supposedly inexorable) socialist/communist ideological project for solving such problems consistently collides with those structural (and rather immovable) objects, and consistently fails to achieve its greater goals. While Colburn directs us to study more closely the politics of revolution, he shows us, more thoroughly than any scholar has to date, that structural obstacles to the creation of socialism cannot be wished away by strongly held ideologies (let alone by acts of "renaming").

Surprisingly then, Colburn's brief for and claimed alliance with the French cultural school appears in a work that, instead, limns the limits of ideology in revolution. Ironically, that juxtaposes his work with that of Theda Skocpol. In words presaging the form of Colburn's argument, Skocpol seeks to understand the divergent outcomes of revolution in Russia and China and quickly decides that "leadership choices are not enough to explain the divergent courses of the Russian and Chinese revolutions," instead seeking the causes thereof in "structural legacies from the old regimes."[84] Those "outcomes" are not simply communist regimes, but the crucial differences between a Soviet state focusing on heavy industrialization-cum-urbanization, one based upon a surplus-producing peasantry, on the one hand, and a Chinese regime pursuing (after 1958) more agriculture-focused, light-industrial, egalitarian policies with a clear preference for the rural populace. She explains these differences via several structural differences the new revolutionary rulers confronted: (1) the greater level of urban, industrial, and railroad development of Russia; (2) the greater central government control over economic life, and the more solidary villages in prerevolutionary Russia, versus collapsing central authority and the trans-village social structures typical of prerevolutionary China; and (3) the fact that the Russian Bolsheviks came to power via mobilization of the urban working class, with few roots in the peasantry, as contrasted with the growth of the Chinese Red Army on a base of rural supporters following the Long March. Those varying structural and processual (re: mobilization) preconditions provided to the new rulers both constraints and opportunities, with which they contended, and to which they adapted. Ironically, far more than Colburn and even Selbin, Skocpol is attentive to the variations in the policies of new rulers; she simply insists that those policies be seen in other than ideological terms. Given our greater hindsight about the Great Leap Forward and the Cultural Revolution, and the later *mea culpa*-laden reversals of those policies after about 1978, perhaps we can now question Skocpol's desire to drive such a large wedge between those two historical trajectories, and stress rather their similarities, as most conservative critics have done from the start. None the less, none can dispute that substantial differences did indeed emerge for some time, and Skocpol makes a strong argument that ideological choices were not the decisive driving forces that explain those differences. A similar approach, both in its method and its excellence, appears in a recent attempt by John Foran and Jeff Goodwin to understand the aftermath of revolutions in Iran and Nicaragua.[85]

Finally, Susan Eckstein has for some time contributed largely structural analyses of the impact of revolution on the lives of Latin Americans. Her works combine minute and indefatigable attention to detail, especially the search for comparable detail, in order to understand the consequences of revolutions for the societies in which they occur.[86] In one ambitious model of an explanatory essay, she seeks to compare the postrevolutionary fortunes of Mexico, Bolivia, Cuba, and Peru to a closely matched quartet of non-revolutionary cases (respectively), Brazil, Ecuador, the Dominican Republic, and Colombia. She then examines data to determine whether various structural-historical conditions contribute to better or worse performance with respect to land distribution, income distribution, health-care, and nutrition. Those features include revolution or not; (type of dependent) position within the world economy; the class base of insurrection; revolution from above (Peru only) or below; a revolution resulting in a socialist (Cuba only) or capitalist economy; private or state ownership of property after the revolution; and the historical epoch of, and passage of time since, the revolution. The analysis and drawing of inferences is so carefully carried out that it is difficult to dispute her conclusions (unless one were to challenge certain short-term statistical changes that might affect those inferences). Her conclusions are extensive and complex and by no means always support the hypotheses tendered before the data were analyzed. Apart from such details, this essay and the corpus of her work on revolutions convey the message that all revolutions face real structural constraints upon their abilities to (re-) make the good society, yet nonetheless effect certain social changes that are quite difficult to ratchet back to the *status quo ante*.[87]

CONCLUSIONS

Since I have been a relentless advocate and conclusion-drawer throughout this chapter, I need spend little more time on the crucial issues. Suffice it to say that, like Mark Twain, reports of the death of "structural theorizing" about revolution in the face of the challenges of pure process or culture-and-agency theories are greatly exaggerated. Again one of the great methodological virtues of careful structural theorizing lies in dealing with negative cases, as in the exemplary work of Eckstein just discussed, but also in the works of Barrington Moore, Skocpol, Goldstone, Goodwin, Foran, and myself. Those theories and theorists that seek refuge from such general theorizing in the particularities of one nation's revolutionary course of events are engaged in a fruitless quest for scholarly security. Whenever we select certain social data and events and use concepts while talking about them, we are engaged in the business of theory. It is only – or should be – much more patently obvious that we are theorizing when we then provide a

63

sequential-narrative of such events that contains or implies causal orderings. Thus we all theorize, even when we write resounding denunciations of the perils of theory. As John Maynard Keynes put it, those scholars who imagine themselves emancipated from philosophy (read: structural theory) are apt to be the slaves of some defunct philosopher.[88]

It is also true that nation-specific "cultural" views of revolution will almost surely never surmount their fundamental problem, that $n = 1$. Thus a French cultural theorist certainly could tell us something about the "Frenchness" of the French Revolution, just as, say, an English cultural theorist might convey the "Englishness" of the English Revolution of the 1640s.[89] But the peculiar "cultural" traits of the people or of the revolutionaries are very unlikely ever to tell us why a revolution occurred here but not there, now but not then. For there is simply too much variation within the taxonomic universe of "culture-types" to provide clear answers to crucial questions about the systematic recurrence, or not, in different cultural contexts of mass grievances, lower-class insurrections, and social-revolutionary transfers of power. For such issues structural-processual theories will continue to be, far and away, the best available guides.

We can certainly, however, concede the abilities of culture- and agency-theories to make greater sense of the roles of conscious mobilization, new ideologies, and even the convergent and divergent policies pursued by post-revolutionary regimes. Yet, having made just those concessions, theorists such as Jack Goldstone can still delve deeply into the historical-structural situations in which such ideologies gain the power to remake society, and are constrained by changing social and political conditions as the post-revolutionary process unfolds.[90] Thus Goldstone, like Forrest Colburn – both scholars committed to the value of cultural views of postrevolutionary policies and social changes – ends up showing a range of structural constraints on those very policies. How much more serious seem the constraints on ideologically driven choice when we consider the multiple parallels drawn by Brinton, the Russia/China divergences dissected by Skocpol, and the economic and social achievements – and their limits – in Eckstein's Latin America. Structural theories are here to stay, and their analytical points, far from being blunted by the critics, will probably extend ever more deeply into the postrevolutionary milieu.

ACKNOWLEDGEMENTS

I would like to thank Jack Goldstone, Jeff Goodwin, Richard Lachmann, Charles Tilly, and especially John Foran for thoughtful and critical comments on an earlier (and longer) version of this chapter. (Non-standard "disclaimer" follows.) My attempts to respond to their critiques are, of course, the only sources of vice in this chapter, all virtues being my own.

NOTES

1. Given one of its signatures – barbarous prose – postmodernism receives an exceptionally clear tour-guide in Pauline Marie Rosenau, *Post-Modernism and the Social Sciences* (Princeton: Princeton University Press, 1992). On the limits of perspectivism, the definitive statement is still Robert K. Merton, "Insiders and Outsiders: A Chapter in the Sociology of Knowledge," pp. 9–47 in *American Journal of Sociology*, volume 78, number 1 (July 1972); on the leftism of intellectuals and their structurally conditioned obsession with discourse, the classic statement is Alvin W. Gouldner, *The Future of Intellectuals and The Rise of the New Class* (New York: Continuum, 1978), 53–73. For works that critically focus on the social embeddedness of contemporary (postmodern) theorists themselves, see David Lehman, *Signs of the Times: Deconstruction and the Fall of Paul de Man* (New York: Poseidon, 1991), chapter three; Ernest Gellner, *Postmodernism, Reason, and Religion* (London: Routledge, 1992), especially 29–49.
2. George C. Homans, "Bringing Men Back In," pp. 809–18 in *American Sociological Review*, volume 29, number 6 (December 1964).
3. Timothy P. Wickham-Crowley, *Exploring Revolution: Essays on Latin American Insurgency and Revolutionary Theory* (Armonk: M. E. Sharpe, 1991), 176–80, especially table 6.1.
4. The clearest referent for this distinction is surely the theoretical tugs between the poles of "order" and "action" emphasized in Jeffrey C. Alexander's *Theoretical Logic in Sociology*, four volumes (Berkeley: University of California Press, 1983), and *Twenty Lectures: Sociological Theory Since World War II* (New York: Columbia University Press, 1987). I differ from Alexander in that I do not treat these varied approaches as if they were only "presuppositions;" instead, I accept that the authors in question put those assumptions to the test in search of explanations of revolutionary phenomena, thus in principle subjecting them to the possibility of falsification.
5. Theda Skocpol, *States and Social Revolutions: A Comparative Analysis of France, Russia, and China* (Cambridge: Cambridge University Press, 1979).
6. For his debate with Skocpol on this question, see William H. Sewell, Jr., "Ideologies and Social Revolutions: Reflections on the French Case," pp. 57–85 in *Journal of Modern History*, volume 57, number 1 (March 1985). See also Lynn Hunt, *Politics, Culture, and Class in the French Revolution* (Berkeley: University of California Press, 1984); her chapters four through six vary in content, but all are structural and the giveaway is the section title, "The Sociology of Politics." Other writers consistently mentioned in this French context are Robert Darnton, Simon Schama, and François Furet.
7. Eric R. Selbin, *Modern Latin American Revolutions* (Boulder: Westview Press, 1993); Forrest D. Colburn, *The Vogue of Revolution in Poor Countries* (Princeton: Princeton University Press, 1994).
8. Jack Goldstone, *Revolution and Rebellion in the Early Modern World* (Berkeley: University of California Press, 1991), chapter five, for "Goldstone (Post-)". Jeff Goodwin's thesis advisor at Harvard was Theda Skocpol, and his dissertation combines a state-centered analysis with a clearly structural theory of revolutionary failure and success; cf. his "States and Revolutions in the Third World: A Comparative Analysis" (Ph.D. dissertation, Harvard University, 1988), followed by his "Colonialism and Revolution in Southeast Asia: A Comparative Analysis," pp. 59–78 in Terry Boswell, editor, *Revolution in the World System* (Westport: Greenwood Press, 1989), and (with Theda Skocpol) "Explaining Revolutions in the Contemporary Third World: A Comparative Analysis," pp. 489–509 in

Politics and Society, volume 17, number 4 (December 1989). All such works justify the mapping of "Goodwin I" in Figure 2.1. Yet his most recent writing contains a clear call for the insertion of cultural analysis into studies of revolution, in his "The New Sociology of Revolutions," pp. 731–66 in *Theory and Society*, volume 23, number 6 (December 1994), thus suggesting a separate mapping, "Goodwin II."

9. Theda Skocpol, "Cultural Idioms and Political Ideologies in the Revolutionary Reconstruction of State Power: A Rejoinder to Sewell," pp. 86–96 in *Journal of Modern History*, volume 57, number 1 (March 1985), 88–92. Sewell's usage of "ideology" reflects the influence of Clifford Geertz's views on culture/ideology. Marxist philosopher Louis Althusser's definition of ideology is also virtually identical to a standard sociological definition of culture. In both cases such usage creates only endless confusion among certain theorists who mix these two narrower and broader meanings of ideology as if they were interchangeable. For Althusser's definition of ideology (read: culture), see Alex Callinicos, *Althusser's Marxism* (London: Pluto Press, 1976), 60–6; see also Clifford Geertz, "Ideology as a Cultural System," pp. 193–233 in his *The Interpretation of Cultures* (New York: Basic Books, 1973).

10. For key writings in this tradition, see Eric R. Wolf, *Peasant Wars of the Twentieth Century* (New York: Harper & Row, 1969), chapter 7, especially 293–6; James Scott, "Hegemony and the Peasantry," pp. 267–96 in *Politics and Society*, volume 7, number 3 (1977), and *The Moral Economy of the Peasant* (New Haven: Yale University Press, 1976) – the strongest groundings for an understanding of the economic aspects of peasant culture. On French rural events, see Skocpol, *States and Social Revolutions*, especially 114, 118–28; Barrington Moore, *Social Origins of Dictatorship and Democracy* (Boston: Beacon Press, 1966), 70–101 (especially on tensions between the aims of the urban sans-culottes and the peasants); and Victor V. Magagna, *Communities of Grain: Rural Rebellion in Comparative Perspective* (Ithaca: Cornell University Press, 1991), chapter five and *passim*.

11. Barrington Moore, Jr., *Injustice: The Social Bases of Obedience and Revolt* (White Plains: M. E. Sharpe, 1978), chapter ten.

12. Skocpol, "Cultural Idioms," 86–7; my emphasis.

13. Theda Skocpol, "Reconsidering the French Revolution in World-Historical Perspective," pp. 53–70 in *Social Research*, volume 56, number 1 (Spring 1989); on the topic of pre- and postrevolutionary mobilization for war, see also her "Social Revolutions and Mass Military Mobilization," pp. 147–68 in *World Politics*, volume 40, number 2 (January 1988).

14. Here I "read" a structural analysis "into" Skocpol's own prose in a fashion, however, that I feel is consistent with her views here and elsewhere.

15. Goldstone, *Revolution and Rebellion*, chapter five; see the similar view I (later) encountered in Theda Skocpol, *Social Revolutions in the Modern World* (Cambridge: Cambridge University Press, 1994), 336.

16. Robert K. Merton, "Three Fragments from a Sociologist's Notebooks: Establishing the Phenomenon, Specified Ignorance, and Strategic Research Materials," pp. 1–28 in *Annual Review of Sociology*, volume 13 (1987).

17. A crucial work which crystallized my (rather more amorphous) views here is Ann Swidler, "Culture in Action: Symbols and Strategies," pp. 273–86 in *American Sociological Review*, volume 51, number 2 (April 1986), where she elaborates and applies quite practical views of culture as a "tool-kit." Swidler carefully distinguishes culture as it appears in the most settled of lives, from "common sense" (most so) to "tradition" (less so), and sets those two forms apart from the "ideologies" that may be created and (later) take hold in unsettled lives. Unlike theorists

such as Sewell, however, Swidler leaves open the key issue: will such consciously created "ideologies" take hold and eventually become more "settled" forms of culture, or not (280–1)? To collapse all such variants into "ideology," à la Althusser, is therefore quite unhelpful to the careful analyst. Swidler's usages neatly parallel Skocpol's distinction, noted above, between "cultural idioms" and "ideologies."

18. Skocpol, *States and Social Revolutions*, part two, especially the ringing rejection of a crucially independent role for political leaderships and ideology (164–71); and also her "Old Regime Legacies and Communist Revolutions in Russia and China," pp. 284–315 in *Social Forces*, volume 55, number 2 (December 1976). See also Susan Eckstein, "The Impact of Revolution on Social Welfare in Latin America," pp. 43–94 in *Theory and Society*, volume 11 (1982), and "The Impact of the Cuban Revolution: A Comparative Perspective," pp. 503–34 in *Comparative Studies in Society and History*, volume 28 (July 1986), among other works.

19. For a parallel view, see Goldstone, *Revolution and Rebellion*, 50–60; see also the rebuttal to Sewell's older and forthcoming critiques by Skocpol, *Social Revolutions in the Modern World*, 326–34.

20. One could easily have reversed the grid's layout; as a largely structural theorist, however, I prefer to reside in the upper right-hand quadrant, where the algebra was always more straightforward.

21. Skocpol, *States and Social Revolutions*, 114–15, and her "What Makes Peasants Revolutionary?" pp. 351–75 in *Comparative Politics*, volume 14 (April 1982), especially 370–1.

22. Skocpol, *States and Social Revolutions*, 4; the bracketed "mass" replaces Skocpol's original term, "class," to allow for the possibility of ethnic-based revolutions or ones involving populist upheavals.

23. The main studies that carefully attend to negative as well as positive cases are Skocpol, *States and Social Revolutions*; Goodwin, "States and Revolutions in the Third World," "Colonialism and Revolution in Southeast Asia," and, with Skocpol, "Explaining Revolutions;" Goldstone, *Revolution and Rebellion*, where his negatives more strikingly include both nation-cases and specifically nonrevolutionary time-periods for nations that at other times experienced state breakdowns; and my own work, whose best exemplar is *Guerrillas and Revolution in Latin America: A Comparative Study of Insurgents and Regimes Since 1956* (Princeton: Princeton University Press, 1992), especially chapters eight, eleven, and twelve. Ongoing work by John Foran also respects this crucial issue; see Chapter 9 in this volume.

24. *States and Social Revolutions*, part two, and "Old Regime Legacies." Notably, the first half of Skocpol's book – the causal analysis of social revolutions – has received the vast bulk of the scholarly attention, while her structural analysis of varied/similar postrevolutionary paths has generated little comment of any sort. See my discussion below and also a brief roundup of such studies in Goldstone, *Revolution and Rebellion*, 22–3.

25. Hunt, *Politics, Culture, and Class*; Moore, *Injustice*, reading chapter ten in the context of the book as a whole; Charles Tilly, *The Vendée* (Cambridge, MA: Harvard University Press, 1964). Further, despite his critique of Skocpol's comparative theorizing, Sewell actually compliments part of Skocpol's *States and Social Revolutions* for its narrative; see Skocpol, *Social Revolutions in the Modern World*, 329–33. Charles Ragin has graciously suggested that my *Guerrillas and Revolution* also unites the twin virtues of careful explanation and rich narrative; see his review in *Contemporary Sociology*, volume 22, number 2 (March 1993), pp. 190–1.

26. E. P. Thompson, "The Moral Economy of the English Crowd in the Eighteenth Century," pp. 76–136 in *Past and Present*, number 50 (February 1971), 78.

27. See, for example, Crane Brinton, *The Anatomy of Revolution*, revised and expanded edition (New York: Vintage, 1965), chapter three; see also the discussion of "precipitants" versus "preconditions" of revolution in Colburn, *The Vogue of Revolution*, chapter three. The classic treatment of collective action that places "precipitating events" properly in a severely limited causal role is Neil J. Smelser, *Theory of Collective Behavior* (New York: Free Press, 1962).

28. The key foundational works in this "school" are James C. Davies, "Toward a Theory of Revolution," pp. 5–19 in *American Sociological Review*, volume 27, number 1 (February 1962); and Ted Robert Gurr, *Why Men Rebel* (Princeton: Princeton University Press, 1970).

29. From Trotsky's *History of the Russian Revolution*, here quoted from Michael S. Kimmel, *Revolution: A Sociological Interpretation* (Philadelphia: Temple University Press, 1990), 91. I must note that Gurr's later writings on this subject have moved substantially away from RD theory in its 1970 variant.

30. Charles Tilly, *From Mobilization to Revolution* (Reading, MA: Addison-Wesley, 1978); see also Skocpol, *States and Social Revolutions*, 8–10,14–16.

31. Wickham-Crowley, *Guerrillas and Revolution*, 130–7, 246–50, 304–11; the term "cultures of rebellion" is also used by Tim McDaniel to discuss the emergence of revolutionism among the Russian and Iranian intelligentsias, and its (partial) transfer to the masses, prior to the revolutions in those two nations; cf. his *Autocracy, Modernization, and Revolution in Russia and Iran* (Princeton: Princeton University Press, 1991), chapter seven.

32. On this point, Ann Swidler is again a clear guide; see her "Culture in Action," 277–8, and my *Guerrillas and Revolution*, 130–1.

33. For urban processes, see Thompson, "Moral Economy of the English Crowd;" for rural processes, see Scott, "Hegemony and the Peasantry," and *The Moral Economy of the Peasant*. Karl Polanyi's foundational work, *The Great Transformation* (Boston: Beacon Press, 1944), underlies many of the tenets of this approach.

34. John Walton, *Reluctant Rebels: Comparative Studies of Revolution and Underdevelopment* (New York: Columbia University Press, 1984), chapter five, especially 154–6, where his focus is "Explaining Revolutionary Situations."

35. Scott, *The Moral Economy of the Peasant*, especially chapter five.

36. For one such analysis, see David Kowalewski, "Periphery Revolutions in World-System Perspective," pp. 76–99 in *Comparative Political Studies*, volume 24, number 1 (April 1991).

37. Sewell, "Ideologies and Social Revolutions;" Hunt, *Politics, Culture, and Class*, introduction and part one, "The Poetics of Power."

38. Emile Durkheim, *Selected Writings*, edited and with an Introduction by Anthony Giddens (Cambridge: Cambridge University Press, 1972), 228–32. In fact, Durkheim applies the term to certain French events of 1789 in this very passage.

39. Colburn, *The Vogue of Revolution*, x, 9–17, 20–35, 89–96. Against those who might try to explain the revolutionary outcomes via such ideological "causes," he also states flatly (36) that "the prevalence of an intellectual culture intoxicated with revolution, Marxism-Leninism, and socialism does not in itself explain either the sizable number of revolutions among the poorer countries in the aftermath of World War II or, more importantly, the configuration of countries that did and did not experience revolutions."

40. Wickham-Crowley, *Guerrillas and Revolution*, 23–5, 30–7, 213–15, 327–39; Karl Mannheim, *Ideology and Utopia* (New York: Harcourt, Brace & World, 1936), 153–64; Gouldner, *The Future of Intellectuals*, 53–73.

41. Carlos Rangel Guevara, *The Latin Americans: Their Love–Hate Relationship with the United States* (New York: Harcourt Brace Jovanovich, 1977), 214. As Mannheim noted half a century ago, intellectuals tend to define themselves against prevailing social currents; cf. Karl Mannheim, "The Problem of Generations," in his *Essays in the Sociology of Knowledge*, edited by Paul Kecskemeti (London: Routledge & Kegan Paul, 1952), 318.

42. For one analysis which nicely documents both the traditional leftism of intellectuals and the widespread emergence of the white-collar "new left," see Seymour Martin Lipset, *Political Man: The Social Bases of Politics*, second edition (Baltimore: Johns Hopkins, 1981), 332–71, 503–21.

43. Compare my analysis to Randall Collins, "Maturation of the State-Centered Theory of Revolution and Ideology," pp. 117–28 in *Sociological Theory*, volume 11, number 1 (March 1993), 122–3 where he comments on Jack Goldstone's post-revolutionary focus on cultural determinants of change. For useful comments suggesting the deep limitations of discourse–centered social theory, see Gellner, *Postmodernism, Reason, and Religion*; and Charles Tilly's review essay, "Domination, Resistance, Compliance . . . Discourse," pp. 593–602 in *Sociological Forum*, volume 6, number 3 (September 1991).

44. Karl Marx and Friedrich Engels, *The Marx–Engels Reader*, second edition, edited by Robert C. Tucker (New York: W. W. Norton, 1978), 481; Gouldner, *The Future of Intellectuals*, 58.

45. John Foran, "The Comparative-historical Sociology of Third World Revolutions," Chapter 9 in this volume; Farideh Farhi, *States and Urban-Based Revolutions* (Urbana and Chicago: University of Illinois Press, 1990), especially chapter four; McDaniel, *Autocracy, Modernization, and Revolution*, 185–202.

46. That unfortunately too-apt term was coined by C. Wright Mills, in *The Marxists* (New York: Dell, 1962).

47. Jeffery M. Paige, *Agrarian Revolution: Social Movements and Export Agriculture in the Underdeveloped World* (New York: Free Press, 1975), *passim*. Especially invulnerable to any as-yet published critiques are his worldwide, statistical correlations between structural types and collective-action frequencies. For those who do not think Paige has, in fact, supported his theoretical predictions well, see Margaret Somers and Walter Goldfrank, "The Limits of Agronomic Determinism: A Critique of Paige's *Agrarian Revolution*," pp. 443–58 in *Comparative Studies in Society and History*, volume 21 (July 1979), and Skocpol, "What Makes Peasants Revolutionary?" 354–9. For the first serious statistical challenge to his findings, one echoing Skocpol's call for attention to political contexts, see Leslie Anderson and Mitchell A. Seligson's analysis of a Costa Rican data set in "Reformism and Radicalism among Peasants: An Empirical Test of Paige's Agrarian Revolution," pp. 944–72 in *American Journal of Political Science*, volume 38, number 4 (November 1994). For Paige's attempt to extend the logic of nationalist revolution to Guatemala, while criticizing his theoretical rivals, see his "Social Theory and Peasant Revolution in Vietnam and Guatemala," pp. 699–737 in *Theory and Society*, volume 12, number 6 (November 1983). For attempts at a synthesis between the views of Paige, his critics on the issue of peasant radicalism, and other theories of revolution in general, see my *Guerrillas and Revolution*, chapters six, seven, and ten, as well as my *Exploring Revolution*, chapters six and seven.

48. Paige traces through the logic of structure/interest/action with great care in chapter one.

49. Skocpol, *States and Social Revolutions*, 114–15.

50. Skocpol, "Rentier State and Shi'a Islam in the Iranian Revolution," pp. 265–83 in *Theory and Society*, volume 11, number 2 (May 1982); reprinted in her *Social*

Revolutions in the Modern World. For a more detailed treatment and extension of the these ideas concerning solidarity and autonomy, see my *Exploring Revolution*, chapter six.

51. Skocpol, *States and Social Revolutions*, 147–54, 252–62.
52. Moore, *Social Origins of Dictatorship and Democracy*, 460 and all of chapter nine.
53. Wickham-Crowley, *Exploring Revolution*, chapter six.
54. The earlier work of Tilly provides substantial materials of this type, including his *From Mobilization to Revolution*, and Skocpol's logic is similar in much of *States and Social Revolutions*. Hunt uses just such a network-approach in *Politics, Culture, and Class*, chapter six, as do I in *Exploring Revolution*, chapter four, and *Guerrillas and Revolution*, 138–53, 250–61.
55. The most cited work showing the advantages of organizational analysis over class analysis is Mark Traugott, *Armies of the Poor: Determinants of Working-Class Participation in the Parisian Insurrection of June 1848* (Princeton: Princeton University Press, 1985); I make a vaguely similar, if considerably less developed, argument about military personnel in *Exploring Revolution*, pp. 158–61, while I analyze peasants, their networks, and their consequent responses to guerrilla movements in chapter four of that work.
56. See Skocpol, *States and Social Revolutions*, chapter three, and "What Makes Peasants Revolutionary?" for her strongest statements; the latter essay sets forth the idea, developed later, that systematic mobilization by outsiders, e.g. guerrillas, can provide a "functional substitute" for an absence of solidarity and autonomy.
57. Wolf, *Peasant Wars of the Twentieth Century*, "Conclusion."
58. Wickham-Crowley, *Guerrillas and Revolution*, chapters six and ten, and *Exploring Revolution*, chapters six and seven.
59. Jeff Goodwin, "The New Sociology of Revolutions," in commenting on my work, and his "Why Insurgencies Persist, or the Perversity of Indiscriminate State Violence" (unpublished ms.). I provide the "infrastructural power" linkage of the first piece to the "state terror" argument of the second essay; while Goodwin himself does not link the two arguments in this fashion, it seems a reasonable inference to combine the two ideas.
60. Skocpol, *States and Social Revolutions*, especially the summary tables on 155–57.
61. Goodwin and Skocpol, "Explaining Revolutions in the Contemporary Third World," 495; see also 495–7.
62. This version appears in a journal with a most apt name: see Charles Tilly, "The Bourgeois Gentilshommes of Revolutionary Theory," pp. 153–8 in *Contention*, volume 2, number 2 (Winter 1993), 157; also "In Search of Revolution," pp. 799–803 in *Theory and Society*, volume 23, number 6 (December 1994). In a private communication, Tilly argues slightly differently, for the "partial independence" of situations and outcomes, and hence our scholarly need for partly different explanations of each.
63. "Revolutionary outcome" has become for him a variable defined in strictly political terms, when power is transferred to a new (i.e., non-incumbent) political group. The "outcome" thus is not defined in terms of certain deep social, economic, or cultural changes following the power-shift. Tilly recognizes such special cases, but as variable types within the universe of "revolutionary outcomes," which may require a separate form of explanation. For many scholars, myself included, this implies a collapsing together of barracks revolts, *coups d'état*, competing claims to the throne (e.g., the War of the Roses), ethnic separatist movements, and social revolutions (in Skocpol's narrow sense) into a single

catch-all category, with all the theoretical problems such a stew creates; see my *Exploring Revolution*, 163–7.

64. Charles Tilly, "War Making and State Making as Organized Crime," pp. 169–91 in Peter B. Evans, Dietrich Rueschemeyer, and Theda Skocpol, editors, *Bringing the State Back In* (Cambridge: Cambridge University Press, 1985).

65. In his review essay, "Domination, Resistance, Compliance," Tilly, in the end, comes clearly down on the side of each actor, individual or collective, as a *zoon politikon*, "pursuing personal agendas by maneuvering among obstacles . . . the exercise of power consists of placing obstacles and of offering rewards" (601). In adopting this position, Tilly clearly distances himself greatly from any scholar who believes in the powers of ideology and hegemony to instill false consciousness, but even from James Scott's argument that subordinates can at times collectively and strategically appropriate dominant ("cultural") discourses, even as they maintain their own – separate, feisty, even rebellious – discourses and views of the world; cf. James C. Scott, *Domination and the Arts of Resistance: Hidden Transcripts* (New Haven: Yale University Press, 1990).

66. "Structuration', an ugly but useful term, comes from the work of Anthony Giddens.

67. Charles Tilly, *European Revolutions, 1492–1992* (Oxford: Basil Blackwell, 1993), 43–51, 104–41, 233–48.

68. Goldstone, *Revolution and Rebellion*, 10–12.

69. Ibid., chapter two, especially 141–8 where *psi* is first discussed and his explanation defended against rivals; also 156–69, 281–318, 384–415. His measures of *psi* are more qualitatively developed for his three Asian cases.

70. Davies, "Toward a Theory of Revolution," 5–8.

71. Alan Knight, *The Mexican Revolution*, volume one: *Porfirians, Liberals, and Peasants* (Lincoln: University of Nebraska Press, 1986), 314–15, 559 note 386. Knight's own explication of that pointed term suggests that it does not apply very well to Skocpol: she most certainly thinks of peasant actions as "genuine popular movements" (just ones not sharing the novel ideas of the revolutionary ideologists), and just as certainly never buys into any assumptions concerning peasants" "false consciousness," in so far as she recognizes their longstanding material grievances finally given room to vent themselves.

72. Skocpol, *States and Social Revolutions*, 155–7.

73. Goodwin, "States and Revolutions in the Third World," which is revised and submitted for book publication, and "Colonialism and Revolution in Southeast Asia;" Goodwin and Skocpol, "Explaining Revolutions." For earlier views about the vulnerability of "neo-patrimonial" regimes, see Jack Goldstone, "The Comparative and Historical Study of Revolutions," pp. 187–207 in *Annual Review of Sociology*, volume 8 (1982); and Robert H. Dix, "Why Revolutions Succeed and Fail," pp. 423–46 in *Polity*, volume 16, number 3 (Spring 1984). For a more recent and expansive treatment, see Jack Goldstone, "Revolutions in Modern Dictatorships," pp. 70–77 in his edited work, *Revolutions: Theoretical, Comparative, and Historical Studies*, second edition (San Diego: Harcourt Brace Jovanovich, 1993).

74. Jeff Goodwin, "Old Regimes and Revolutions in the Second and Third Worlds: A Comparative Perspective," pp. 575–604 in *Social Science History*, volume 18, number 4 (Winter 1994).

75. *Guerrillas and Revolution*, 31–3; the concept of "cultural repertoires" was elaborated by Charles Tilly, *From Mobilization to Revolution*, 151–8, 224–5.

76. Wickham-Crowley, *Guerrillas and Revolution in Latin America*, *passim*, especially chapter twelve. For useful critical responses to this argument, see John Foran's

review essay, "Revolutionizing Theory/Theorizing Revolutions," pp. 65–88 in *Contention*, volume 2, number 2 (Winter 1993), 78–87; Jeff Goodwin's review, pp. 922–4 in *American Journal of Sociology*, volume 98, number 4 (January 1993), and also his "Toward a New Sociology of Revolutions." Theda Skocpol, *Social Revolutions in the Modern World*, 308–11, generally praises the book, but notes, like Goodwin, "too much socioeconomic determinism" in my analysis of peasant responses to guerrilla attempts at mobilization.

77. See Chapter 9 in this volume, "The Comparative-historical Sociology of Third World Social Revolutions."

78. Brinton was, by the way, a historian specializing in French revolutionary history, and author of a long-in-print work on the Jacobins.

79. See, for example, Goldstone, "The Comparative and Historical Study," and Skocpol, *States and Social Revolutions*, 37–8.

80. Skocpol, *States and Social Revolutions*, 37.

81. Brinton, *The Anatomy of Revolution*, chapters five through eight.

82. Sewell, "Ideologies and Social Revolutions," *passim*, especially 77–8.

83. Brinton, *The Anatomy of Revolution*, chapter seven (quote on 178).

84. Skocpol, "Old Regime Legacies," 288.

85. John Foran and Jeff Goodwin, "Revolutionary Outcomes in Iran and Nicaragua: Coalition Fragmentation, War, and the Limits of Social Transformation," pp. 209–47 in *Theory and Society*, volume 22, number 2 (April 1993).

86. For one such work, largely devoted to comparative descriptive statistics which still render the service of clearing the air of much of the cant and posturing about Cuban conditions, see Eckstein, "The Impact of the Cuban Revolution."

87. Eckstein, "The Impact of Revolution on Social Welfare in Latin America." For examples from some of her other articles, constraints and real achievements are also the two thematic issues, respectively, in her "Capitalist Constraints on Cuban Economic Development," pp. 253–74 in *Comparative Politics*, volume 12, number 3 (April 1980), and "Comment on 'Revolution and the Rebirth of Inequality,' by Kelley and Klein," pp. 724–7 in *American Journal of Sociology*, volume 84, number 3 (November 1978).

88. David Hackett Fischer, *Historians" Fallacies: Toward a Logic of Historical Thought* (New York: Harper & Row, 1970), xii for the Keynes quote and, on the unavoidability of generalizing, 103.

89. I borrow those terms in quotations from writings by Gertrude Himmelfarb.

90. Goldstone, *Revolution and Rebellion*, chapter five.

3

AGENTS OF REVOLUTION

Elite conflicts and mass mobilization from the Medici to Yeltsin

Richard Lachmann

Revolutions are defined most often by their combination of extraordinary means and ends, drastic social and political transformations that occur during and in the wake of vast mobilizations of mass forces. Scholars compare such historic episodes to understand why masses take action when they do and to explain how popular forces combine with the actions and reactions of elites to produce the structural and ideological results of revolutions. The sharpness of revolutionary definitions and comparisons becomes blurred when we widen our gaze beyond the great modern revolutions. Popular forces mobilized in great numbers and often with much violence yet had little effect on social relations in various instances, especially in the centuries before 1789. Recently, we have seen the overthrow of seemingly permanent and brutal regimes in Eastern Europe by vast, though poorly organized and nonviolent, street demonstrations. In those cases, weak means appear to have produced ends of profound change.

This chapter makes a plea for setting aside definitions of revolution and instead broadening the scope of our analysis to encompass a range of instances of attempted and achieved political change, cases in which mass mobilization was absent as well as present, and cases in which structural change was narrow as well as broad. I shall argue that the structure of elite relations provides the best basis for a typology of comparisons because the degree of conflict among elites determines the efficacy of mass action. This chapter seeks to understand how revolutions matter by locating the great revolutions within a historically broader yet theoretically more precise study of the interaction of elite conflicts and mass mobilization.

Participants and scholarly observers find it difficult to gauge the short-term political and long-term structural effects of revolutionary mass action because notions of revolution conflate two parallel and only occasionally interacting processes: ongoing elite conflict and episodic mass mobilizations. Mass mobilization occurs most often during periods of unusually intense elite conflict. Mass action has structural consequences only to the extent that

73

non-elites are able to affect, in otherwise unpredictable ways, the outcomes of elite conflicts.[1] The long-term structural effects of revolutionary mass action can be determined by comparing the pre- and postrevolutionary organizational bases of elite power and the forms of political domination and economic exploitation by elites of non-elites enabled by those organizations.[2]

Figure 3.1 summarizes my model of the relationship between elite conflict and revolutionary mass action, and the effects of both upon social structure. Societies usually are ruled either by a single unified elite or most commonly by a set of multiple elites. Under those conditions elite conflict is restricted within "normal" bounds and may gradually shift resources and power from one elite to another but does not threaten the continued existence of any elite nor provoke significant mobilization by non-elites. Stable systems of political domination and economic exploitation by elites of non-elites persist during times of normal elite conflict.

An elite's autonomous identity (its "eliteness") is threatened by rival elites if they are able singly or in concert to eliminate its organizational base and subordinate that elite and its institutional powers within the organizational structures of its rivals. Alternately, non-elites can sever their relations of exploitation with an elite or elites, thereby eliminating the affected elite's capacity to sustain its organizational base and to pursue its interests. In reality, such non-elite challenges to an elite are effective only when carried out in concert with an elite attack on a rival. Non-elites can develop programs and ideologies independent of elite allies. However, non-elites, like elites, are not usually stupid or self-defeating; they take action when they perceive a realistic chance of attaining their goals. Non-elites mobilize when heightened elite conflict creates the opportunities and alliances which can justify the risks of collective action.

If mass mobilization occurs (its uncertain potential is denoted in Figure 3.1 by a dotted line), it can have a revolutionary effect upon the outcome of elite conflict. The new structure of elites created by a mass revolution will be different from one formed through elite conflict alone. Similarly, the transformed systems of political domination and economic exploitation (i.e., of

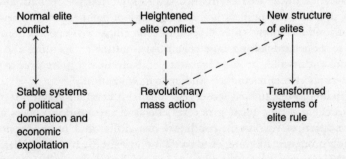

Figure 3.1 A model of elite conflict and revolution

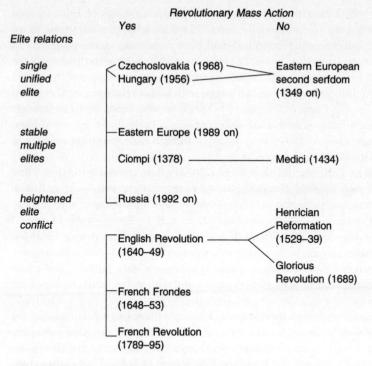

Figure 3.2 Typology of comparisons

the organizations through which elites rule and live off of non-elites) will differ depending on whether they are the products of just elite conflict or of a revolution combining elite conflict and mass mobilization.

I test the above propositions in the rest of this chapter. I do so through a series of paired comparisons. Figure 3.2 presents the cases that I shall address. I look at relatively rare instances in which societies were ruled by a single unified elite (the social structure which most closely approximates the Marxist image of ruling-class hegemony), at more common situations of stable multiple elites, and at moments of heightened elite conflict, which I predict are the settings most conducive to mass revolutionary action. I compare moments in which revolutionary mass action was present with cases in which it was absent for each of the three main states of elite relations.

I begin with a comparison of eastern European societies, separated by six centuries but linked by conditions of rule by a single unified elite (albeit a somewhat different elite in the fourteenth as opposed to the twentieth century). In the fourteenth century a single elite reimposed serfdom on a largely quiescent peasantry. In Hungary in 1956 and in Czechoslovakia in 1968, single elites crushed mass opposition to their rule. I then compare those defeated revolutions with the revolutions in Eastern Europe of 1989–90 and the 1991 break-up of the Soviet Union. Mass mobilization occurred in all those cases; however, the trajectories of elite structural change differed in Eastern Europe from that in the Soviet Union. All those societies began the 1980s ruled by a single unified elite. In much of Eastern Europe the single elite divided into multiple elites, although with stable relations, by the end of the 1980s. In that context the end of Soviet hegemony over Eastern Europe and mass mobilization had a far different effect than in the Soviet Union, where a single elite shattered into multiple though highly conflicted elites as a result of Gorbachev's perestroika.

The third and fourth comparisons parallel the first one in their logic. They are all designed to hold the structure of elite relations relatively constant while varying the presence or absence of revolutionary mass action. The third set of cases are instances of changes in rule in Renaissance Florence: the Ciompi rebellion of 1378 and the Medici seizure of power in 1434. A stable system of rule by multiple elites existed at both times, allowing for a clear measure of the effects of mass action upon elite conflict and upon social structure, and of how elite divisions determine the limits of non-elite mobilization.

In the fourth section of this chapter, I compare the English Revolution of 1640–49, in which non-elites played a crucial role, with two other instances of elite conflict when revolutionary mass action was absent, the Henrician Reformation of 1540 and the Glorious Revolution of 1688. That comparison will allow us to analyze the ways in which mass action can affect and alter the course of intense conflict among multiple elites and to explain why heightened elite conflict is not always accompanied by mass mobilizations.

Finally, I compare the French Revolution of 1789–95 with the French Frondes of 1648–53 and with the English Revolution. Revolutionary mass mobilization occurred in all three cases, yet the effects of mass action were dramatically different in each instance. This comparison highlights the importance of specific elite structures, which provide the contexts within which mass action has causal force.

I deliberately avoid defining revolutions in terms of changes in the "state." I do so because the state often is used anachronistically as the object or measure of revolution. In fact, unitary nation-states are relatively recent creations. Until the eighteenth century each European elite's organizational apparatus made state-like claims and exercised an element of sovereignty over some unit of territory (and usually divided sovereignty over overlapping territories). From the perspective of an emerging European system of states, monarchs and their organizational apparatuses were the nuclei of states-in-formation. Prior to 1789, however, revolutions were consequential to the extent to which they rearranged sovereign relations among elites and their organizational apparatuses rather than because (or whether) they decapitated and replaced the "head of state." This study takes as a topic of inquiry, and not a part of the definition, the relationship between revolutionary out-comes and changes in state leadership or political organization.[3]

SINGLE UNIFIED ELITES

Single elites enjoy unusual freedom of action in dominating and exploiting non-elites in those rare instances when they are unimpeded by rival elites. A signal example of social change instigated by single unified elites was the reimposition of serfdom in eastern Europe following the Black Death of 1349. Faced with the loss of peasant labor and the potential of a bidding war for tenants by landlords which would have had the effect of reducing rents and landlord incomes, the lords of eastern Europe were able to impose draco-nian restrictions upon peasant mobility which enabled each manor lord to increase labor obligations upon peasants.

Landlords throughout Europe needed state-like mechanisms to block peasant mobility if they were not to suffer declines in revenues following the Black Death. Monarchs and clergies in eastern Europe were not separate elites by my definition since they lacked truly autonomous organizations of appropriation and were subordinated to collectivities of landlords. As a result, manor lords were unimpeded in their efforts to mobilize the legal and military mechanisms of their proto-states to re-enserf their tenants, resulting in a decisive shift in income from peasants to lords especially in relation to the dramatic rise in English and French tenants" incomes in the century following the Black Death.[4]

Does mass revolutionary action matter in the face of a single unified elite? Brenner attributes the success of eastern European landlords in imposing restrictions upon peasants to the low level of peasant communal solidarity.[5] Ironically, in Brenner's view, peasants were not unified because of the high level of legal and customary rights they had been granted by landlords who had been eager to recruit migrants from the more crowded west in previous centuries. Brenner's interpretation has been challenged by historians of eastern Europe who find strong peasant solidarity in some parts of eastern Europe and attribute the second serfdom to demographic and market forces.[6]

Whether Brenner or his critics are correct about peasant solidarity is beside the point. Peasant communities, whether united or atomized, were re-enserfed throughout eastern Europe while French and English peasants, regardless of their level of solidarity, were not. The different outcomes were determined by the organization of elites, not of peasants. In England and France multiple elites prevented manor lords from controlling peasant labor to guard their own tax and tithe interests.[7] In contrast to the monarchs and clerics of Eastern Europe, autonomous royal and clerical elites in England and France preserved peasant freedoms in order to guard their independent access to tax and tithe revenues.[8] Peasant unity and mobilization varied within and between western and eastern Europe, while elites were multiple and in conflict in the west and unified in the east. Peasant protest was ineffective against single unified elites in the east; against divided elites in the west even weak peasant mobilization won major concessions.

REVOLUTIONS UNDER CHANGING ELITE STRUCTURES

While opposition to single unified elites was localized and infrequent in post-plague eastern Europe, revolutionary mass action has been more common in eastern Europe since World War II. When directed against single unified elites, as in Hungary in 1956 or in Czechoslovakia during 1968, non-elite mobilizations were ineffectual. However, when masses have challenged multiple elites, as they did throughout Eastern Europe in 1989–90 and the Soviet Union in 1990–91, the mobilizations transformed social relations. The difference does not lie in the level or organization of mass mobilization. The Hungarian uprising of 1956 was arguably better organized than any of the Eastern European mobilizations of 1989–90, and in the willingness of its participants to face death exhibited an intensity of commitment far greater than those of three decades later.

The crucial transformation in Eastern Europe in the 1980s was in elite structure. Prior to that decade, Eastern Europe was ruled by a single unified elite which encompassed the "national" communist parties whose cadres staffed the state administrations, industrial firms, and other institutions which extracted resources and dominated non-elites. Those single elites were integrated with the single ruling elite of the Soviet Union which provided the military muscle and formulated the legitimizing ideology for the national elites of Eastern Europe. Those elites demonstrated their internal unity and their indivisibility from their Soviet sponsors at moments of mass rebellion. Even when individual members of the ruling elites defected to the rebels" side, they did not carry with them an organizational sector capable of sustaining a new elite. The essential transnational unity between Soviet and Eastern European elites was revealed by the seamless way in which the Soviets found new individuals to replace rebellious members of local elites following military intervention in Hungary in 1956 and Czechoslovakia in 1968. Those personnel changes, even at the top, did not disrupt ongoing systems of political domination and economic exploitation, demonstrating the utter lack of effect which revolutionary mass action has upon social structures dominated by single unified elites.

Two key changes in the structure of Eastern European elites occurred in the 1980s. First, the Soviet Union under Gorbachev abandoned its military defense of Eastern European communist elites, leaving the elites of each nation in control of autonomous organizations of extraction and domination. Second, partly in response to their abandonment by the Soviet Union and partly in reaction to economic crises, the unified elite of each country divided. Those members of the elite most directly in control of organizations of production sought to convert their political positions into private capital capable of surviving the transformation or demise of communism.

When non-elites faced divided elites in 1989–90 their challenges had far different outcomes than in previous decades. The old governments and constitutions were swept away (constituting a revolution in Tilly's 1993 definition) and new structures of extraction and domination were established. Figure 3.2 presents the multiple elites of Eastern Europe in 1989 and after as stable, while characterizing the Soviet Union as a site of heightened elite conflict. The stability of most of Eastern Europe is reflected in the division of powers between state and economic elites, the secure boundaries of property rights among new owners of former state assets as well as foreign investors, and the integration of old state institutions (with mechanisms for determining the legal and political standing of members of the former communist parties) into the current state structure. In contrast, Russian elites remain in conflict over control of property, both among individuals and between state and non-state organizations. Administrators and agencies of the old Soviet and new Russian regimes are still fighting over powers and resources.[9]

Clearly the Eastern European and Russian mass mobilizations of 1989 and after have been far more effective than the peasant rebellions following the Black Death or the rebellions of the 1950s and 1960s. They sparked the replacement of party-based elites by hybrid or multiple elites (albeit with a greater degree of continuity of personnel in some countries than in others). Whether or not the masses are pleased with the results, their mobilizations strengthened to varying extents in each country the claims of elites based in firms (those already privatized and managers of state enterprises looking to profit from their privatization) at the expense of state elites, who now enjoy a much diminished degree of political domination over non-elites than did their predecessors in communist governments.

It is difficult to determine how much these social structural transformations are due to mass mobilizations as opposed to the splitting off and withdrawal of the Soviet elite from its former allies in Eastern Europe. We can best evaluate the role of revolution in structural change by holding elite structure constant. That is not possible in comparing Eastern Europe and Russia in the decades since 1945, since elite change preceded the mass upheavals of 1989 and after. The next two comparisons, of the Ciompi and Medici takeovers of Florentine government and of the English Revolution of 1640–49 with the Henrician Reformation and the Glorious Revolution, allow us to do so.

STABLE MULTIPLE ELITES

Politics in Florence was characterized by elite factionalism from the eleventh century until the Medici family achieved hegemony over Florence in the fifteenth century. Indeed, urban-based aristocrats achieved *de facto* independence for Florence in the eleventh century by taking advantage of similar competition among the great powers of Europe, allying with one or another putative conqueror of Italy in return for recognition of the rights of the Florentine commune.[10] The long-standing nature of the stalemate among the great powers in northern Italy had the dual effect of preserving urban autonomy and of ensuring that factional conflicts would not be decided, except during brief interludes of foreign occupation, by the intervention of a single dominant power from above.[11] Lack of closure from above, unique in western Europe in that era, led urban nobles to rely upon non-aristocratic allies in communal politics.

Factions in the newly autonomous city-state were indistinguishable in their class characters and in their organizational bases (i.e., in their elite characters). The urban aristocrats who led each faction in the twelfth century received much of their income as rentiers of rural estates and landlords in the city. Their power was derived from their collective control of the communal government of Florence and the hinterlands controlled by the city. Each noble faction recruited allies from the same pool of bankers, international merchants, and cloth manufacturers. The nobles won support from below by granting economic rights and organizational privileges to non-aristocrats and their guilds. The top stratum of the major guilds, known as patricians, constituted a new elite by the early 1200s. Their income was derived from business rather than land.[12] They shared power with the aristocrats at the start of the thirteenth century and had almost totally displaced them by the end of that century.[13] Patricians were able to displace aristocrats because of their greater wealth and because the abrupt decline in great power intervention in central Italy in the late thirteenth century meant that guildsmen no longer had to defer their demand for power to what had been "the most urgent issue faced by the Italian cities . . . the preservation of their independence against imperial authority, a task best entrusted to the aristocracies."[14]

The two main sources of patrician factionalism in fourteenth-century Florence were external to the city-state's polity. First, when Florence was involved in war, minority factions of the elite were given an opening to ally with foreign powers in return for aid against the ruling patrician oligarchy.[15] Second, the main avenues to wealth – banking and commerce – were largely unregulated by the commune nor could they be accessed through state office.[16] Thus, in the course of the fourteenth and early fifteenth centuries there was a growing disjuncture between political power, which remained in the hands of a self-perpetuating patrician oligarchy, and economic wealth, which was increasingly held by non-patrician bankers and merchants known as "new men."

War precipitated the two greatest challenges to patrician rule: the Ciompi of 1378 and the Medici takeover of Florentine government in 1434. The former challenge began in the early 1370s when patrician factionalism (which centered on control of ecclesiastical offices and other papal patronage) allowed an anti-oligarchic faction of patricians and new men to gain control of Florentine government. These insurgents banned most oligarchs from office and precipitated a war with the oligarchs'' papal ally. The insurgents financed the war with taxes that fell most heavily on the oligarchs and through seizures of clerical properties. The old oligarchs allied with many of the remaining aristocrats to launch a *coup* in 1378.

The *coup* was defeated by a popular uprising of guild members and of proletarianized workers. The oligarchy was broken. For a brief time, proletarianized cloth workers belonging to a new guild, the *Ciompi* (hence the name of this revolt), held high communal office.

The Ciompi is viewed by Marxist historians as perhaps the first proletarian revolution in European history. It was "remarkably modern . . . there were strikes, secret meetings, the beginning of working men's associations. Food riots were rare."[17] However, within a few months the Ciompi were eliminated from government, and within a few years the oligarchy was reconstituted and ruled without serious challenge from rival factions, guildsmen, or the once again unorganized and unrecognized masses. The proletarian revolt had the effect of fostering elite unity. The guildsmen's capacity to exploit their workers had been undermined by communal recognition of those workers as a guild and by the guild's presence in government. Guildsmen subordinated themselves to the oligarchy in order to ensure government support for the guildsmen's efforts to suppress the Ciompi. Marxists and non-Marxist historians agree that the Ciompi frightened the patricians, acting as a permanent brake upon excessive factionalism and ensuring a closing of elite ranks against any of their number who sought advancement through an alliance with the lower guilds, or even with non-patrician members of the upper guilds.[18]

The Medici takeover of the Florentine government in 1434, and their success in permanently breaking oligarchic rule and creating a ruling coalition beholden to the Medici family, occurred in the absence of mass mobilization. Indeed, an unwillingness to reach down to the guilds or to the former Ciompi for support guided both the oligarchs and the Medici in their death struggle in the 1430s.

The new men's resentment of the oligarchs'' exclusionary practices intensified during Florence's wars against Milan (1423–28) and Lucca (1429–33), which the oligarchic government attempted to finance on the backs of the new men. When the Medici, the patrician champions and business partners of the new men, won temporary control of the commune government the dominant patrician faction sought to use armed force to drive the Medici and their allies from government and out of the city.[19] The new men rallied to the Medici's defense, driving the oligarchy's leaders into exile.

Why did the patrician oligarchy retain, and within a few years greatly enhance, its control of Florentine government in 1378, while losing power in 1434? Part of the answer is that the new men gained wealth, both absolutely and relative to the patricians, in the half century between 1378 and 1434.[20] That wealth made the new men inviting business partners for the Medici, creating links of obligation between the Medici and their developing coalition of political allies. The lack of non-elite political mobilization was the most crucial factor in the emergence and success of the Medici-led opposition to the oligarchs. The very quiescence of politically marginalized patricians and new men, brought on by the fear of empowering lower guildsmen and proletarians, allowed the oligarchs to narrow the ruling circle with seeming impunity. As more and more patricians and wealthy new men were excluded from power, they had reason to support Medici political ambitions. The oligarchs" attempts to make other wealthy Florentines, but not themselves, pay for wars which furthered the oligarchs" special interests, added a material interest to the excluded men's political and social resentments. The Medici's ability to mobilize allies without also arousing guildsmen and proletarians allowed patricians and new men to take to the streets against the oligarchs" coup without danger of setting off a popular rebellion which could threaten their own means of domination and appropriation.

Revolutionary mass action does affect the course of elite conflict and elite structure, but not necessarily in an obvious or direct way. In Florence, the structure of elite factions was relatively stable from the years before the Ciompi revolt until the consolidation of Medici rule. Prolonged elite factionalism in the 1370s allowed and encouraged popular organization and mobilization. Further, elite factionalism and elite efforts to reach down for allies were inhibited by the threat which mass action posed to all elites and their organizational bases of power, a threat made real during the Ciompi's brief months of power-sharing. Mass action and elites" extended memories of the dangers they faced during the Ciompi fostered stable relations among the multiple Florentine elites while an oligarchy consolidated control of government. With the acquiescence of the other elites, the oligarchy reduced guilds to guardians of economic privilege and enforced political passivity among the *popolo di dio*. Justified confidence in the political emasculation of non-elites allowed the Medici-led elite party to engage and defeat the oligarchs without threatening their elite positions. Under conditions of stable elite relations, revolutionary mass action is inversely related to the intensity and structural efficacy of elite conflict.

HEIGHTENED ELITE CONFLICT

Sometimes an elite seeks to harness revolutionary mass action or even attempts to incite non-elites to rebellion to further its aims. Unlike the Ciompi revolt, which was an unintended and undesired product of elite factional conflict, the English Revolution of 1640–49 and the French Revolution of 1789–95 were strengthened in their violence and in their radical consequences by prolonged cooperation between elites and non-elites. Elites ally with revolutionaries only when their continued existence as elites is mortally threatened by rival elites. The Florentine elites of the 1370s were not in danger of being eliminated by rivals; they were threatened only with a relative loss of power and income to rival elites.[21] Under such serious though not desperate conditions mass mobilization in the Ciompi was taken as a threat to all elites. No Florentine elite viewed the Ciompi as a last hope for salvation from final defeat by rival elites.

Prolonged elite conflict in England in the sixteenth and seventeenth centuries and in France during the seventeenth and eighteenth centuries threatened several elites in each country with extinction. Those elites did attempt to harness non-elite mobilizations in their struggles with other elites. In this section, I compare the consequences for the structure of elite and class relations of successful elite-mass alliances in the English Revolution with the absence of such cooperation during the Henrician Reformation and the Glorious Revolution. In the following section of this chapter, I compare the effects of two mass mobilizations, during the Frondes of 1648–53 and the French Revolution, upon somewhat different elite structures. The first comparison of English cases addresses questions of causes by distinguishing the sorts of social structures in which elite conflicts enhanced the possibility of revolutionary mass action from structures in which elite conflict proceeded without the losing elites gaining an opportunity to mobilize non-elites. The next section looks at the two French cases. That comparison addresses questions of effects by asking what are the salient aspects of social structure which determine the effects of revolutionary mass action upon the course of elite conflict and the resulting transformation of elite and class relations.

England was characterized by a tripartite elite structure at the outset of the sixteenth century. A long-standing division of power among the crown, clergy, and lay landlords was grounded in each elite's own institutional capacity to regulate the organization of production on manors and to extract resources from peasants. Peasants' rights were guarded and their opportunities were shaped by the particular relations of regulation and exploitation between tenants and their landholdings on the one hand and the three elites on the other.[22] As I already noted, the eagerness of each elite to guard its particular interests against rival elites prevented English manor lords from matching the strategy of eastern European lords in re-enserfing their tenants and effectively preventing peasant mobility following the Black Death.

Elite conflict sharpened in England following Henry VIII's conflict with Rome over his remarriage and the succession to the crown. In essence, the landlord majority in Parliament approved Henry VIII's replacement of the pope by the king as head of the English Church, the diversion of clerical payments from the pope to the crown, and most significantly the dissolution of the monasteries and the appropriation by the crown of their properties which included most of the manors and tithe rights which had been held by the English Church. This crown–lay landlord alliance virtually eliminated the clergy as an independent elite.

The clergy proved unable either to counter the attack from the two enemy elites on its own or to mobilize significant non-elite support. The Pilgrimage of Grace in 1536, a peasant protest against the Dissolution of the Monasteries, was isolated and posed no serious threat to the plans of the crown and lay landlords to disempower the clergy and absorb clerical properties. Peasant support for the clergy was purely ideological and confined to the most backward and religiously conservative rural residents. Peasants were unaware of any material consequences that might stem from the loss of the clergy as one of its three elite regulators and exploiters. Thus, the Henrician Reformation was an instance of elite conflict which resulted in the almost total elimination of one elite without significant mass mobilization.

The clergy's political authority and institutional capacity to regulate production and appropriate resources initially were divided by the crown and lay landlords. The Reformation was a disaster for the crown in the long term and also decisively altered agrarian relations of production. In brief, the English crown lacked the organizational means to administer the manors and offices it had seized from the clergy. Unable to realize much income from the former monastic properties, Henry VIII and his successors sold most of the windfall to lay landlords and urban merchants to pay the costs of periodic wars. While selling estates and tithe rights, the crown also surrendered most of the former clergy's and crown's judicial powers over peasant land tenure to the gentry. Lay landlords (the gentry) had become the sole regulators of agrarian production and virtually the sole appropriators of resources from the peasantry by the start of the seventeenth century.

The Stuart monarchs of the seventeenth century were able to realize income from land (still the overwhelming majority of the British economy) only to the extent to which the gentry in their dual capacities as landowners and as local officials were willing to transfer a share of the income to the crown. The gentry used their new position as the sole regulators and exploiters of the peasantry to transform relations of production. The majority of peasants were dispossessed from their manor tenancies in the century following the Reformation and reduced to landless wage laborers. The gentry were motivated to confront peasants by a short-term benefit: extinguishing traditional peasant rights and tenancies, the gentry eliminated the legal bases from crown and clergy to reassert tax and tithe rights on manors. Of course, the gentry gained an unintended and unanticipated long-term benefit from the transformation of agrarian relations of production: as owners of land, instead of one of three elites with income rights to feudal manors which no one in fact "owned," the gentry received almost all the benefit from the enormous improvements in agricultural yields in the seventeenth and eighteenth centuries.[23]

The transformation of agrarian class relations in England and the immiseration of a plurality of peasants proceeded, as did the Henrician Reformation, without significant mass mobilization. Tenant dispossession was localized and often stretched over years and decades, making it difficult for peasants to resist and certainly impossible for tenants on one manor to make common cause with tenants elsewhere who were already dispossessed (and therefore no longer part of a stable peasant community) or with tenants who had yet to suffer at the hands of their landlords. Further, while crown and clergy had interests in guarding tenant rights (to preserve their claims to tax and tithe revenues) they no longer had the organizational means to intervene at the local level and could not serve as mobilizers or allies of disaffected tenants. Finally, peasants were not unified in the sixteenth and subsequent centuries as they had been in resisting labor obligations after the Black Death. While most tenants were harmed by the demise of feudal tenure following the Reformation, a minority of peasants (all freeholders and some copyholders) themselves gained private property rights in their tenancies as a result of the ascertainment of tenancies and enclosure.

The Henrician Reformation, along with the dispersal of former clerical lands, tithe rights, and judicial powers to lay landlords and the gentry's rolling transformation of agrarian class relations combined to permanently alter the balance of powers between the two remaining elites. The crown's elite position was precarious. Lacking independent organizational means to extract resources from producers, it could collect revenues only so long as it was able to command gentry loyalty through ideological appeals to the crown's legitimate role as head of the nation, of the national church and of state, and/or by manipulating gentry and merchant factions to win political battles of the moment. Charles I was singularly inept at reconciling high and low politics.[24] However, even a more skillful monarch would not have been able to force or entice the gentry to pay for military, church, or state-building projects which would have reestablished the crown's organizational capacities while inevitably challenging the gentry's monopoly of direct access to and control over agrarian production.

Tudor and Stuart monarchs, through their consistent strategy of building a "horizontal" national level absolutism (eliminating an autonomous clerical elite and disarming magnates and fragmenting their county political machines, all at the cost of undermining the crown's ability, alone or through allies, to regulate the behavior of locally based gentry),[25] left Charles I with the dismal choice of pursuing only those policies which the gentry were willing to support and pay for, or of trying to play factional conflicts even unto civil war. Charles not only sparked Civil War in 1642 in an effort to get out of abiding by his 1641 concessions to Parliament, but also took advantage of Parliament's conflict with its obstreperous Scottish allies in 1647 and struck a deal with his Catholic Irish supporters, setting off the "second Civil War" of 1648 which culminated in his execution and that of some of his leading aristocratic allies in 1649.

The crown also played rival groups of merchants against one another in order to raise revenues; that strategy factionalized London city politics.[26] Merchant politics was important for two reasons. First, as long as Charles I kept out of war, he could support himself and forestall calling Parliament into session by offering trade monopolies to one or another group of merchants in return for tariff revenues. Second, and far more important, the merchants were centered in London, the capital. Hence Charles I's consistent lack of recognition for the interests of the interloper-colonial merchants led that faction to become stalwarts of radical Parliamentarians. The interloper-colonial merchants mobilized popular forces in the capital to guard Parliamentary leaders from royal arrest and to support those merchants in their takeover of London city government. Thus, merchant factionalism, which the crown encouraged for its own short-term advantage in national elite conflict, resulted in the weakest merchant faction's decision to mobilize popular revolutionary forces which, once unleashed, pressured Parliament away from compromise and toward more radical positions on constitutional and religious issues than it would have taken had it been responsive only to its gentry and merchant bases of support.[27]

The Revolution of 1640–49 was anomalous in English history for its radicalism and for the significant involvement of popular forces. Elite factionalism was a necessary precondition for Civil War; however, only in London and in the army did elite factionalism reach a degree of divisiveness sufficient to lead some elites to elicit and encourage mass revolutionary action. (No gentry faction ever sought to mobilize the rural peoples under their control, nor were rural uprisings a significant factor in the Civil War. Rural rebellion steadily declined through the sixteenth and seventeenth centuries.)[28]

Once London was quieted and the New Model Army was disbanded, almost all of the radical achievements of the revolution were overturned. While religious pluralism and tolerance became a permanent feature of the English polity, the radical sects of the revolution lost adherents, were suppressed, or became quietist even under the Commonwealth.[29] While the interloper-colonial merchants won a permanent share of power in London city government and the British state pursued foreign policies favorable to those proto-capitalist international investors, popular forces in London lost any role in city or national politics after 1649.[30] The monarchy was reinstated in 1660.[31]

From the perspective of the Glorious Revolution of 1689 and the "settlement" between King William and Parliament of 1690, the radicalism of the English Revolution had virtually no lasting effect on the structure of elite and class relations in England. The limitations upon royal power which Charles I agreed to under duress in 1641 were virtually the same as the constraints accepted by Charles II upon his assumption of the throne at the end of the Commonwealth in 1660 and those enshrined in the 1690 settlement. Those limitations upon royal power, which recognized the gentry's sole authority over agrarian class relations, religion, and government in the counties and gave the landed elite a role in national and foreign policy through a revivified Parliament, were nothing more nor less than royal recognition of the results of sixteenth- and early-seventeenth-century elite conflicts which had been set in motion by Henry VIII's grab for national level absolutism.

Popular forces in the Revolution of 1640–49 had mainly temporary effects. They allowed the most militant and confrontational Members of Parliament to issue demands which Charles I would never accept, preventing the sort of compromise which a majority of gentry probably would have accepted in 1642. The militants repeatedly relied upon mass forces in London and drew upon the financial resources of the interloper-colonial merchants to sustain their rebellion. The ultimate product of the alliance between Parliament and London radicals was an independent armed force capable of defeating the crown and those gentry who allied with Charles I to prevent the victory of political and religious radicalism. That armed force, the New Model Army, became the constituency which forced Charles I's execution and sustained the Commonwealth. Thus, London mass mobilization prevented a successful *coup* by Charles I against Parliament in 1642, sustained the Civil War, and backed the New Model Army, which became the real center of political power in England for the crucial last years of the Civil War and early years of the Commonwealth.[32]

Non-elite participation in the political conflicts of the 1640s did have two long-term effects. First, it united the gentry and most London merchants in the conviction that factional differences must be limited to prevent future outbreaks of popular radicalism.[33] Second, by advancing and prolonging the Civil War, popular revolution indirectly disrupted both royal and Presbyterian plans for religious uniformity. During the years of elite conflict and Civil War, ministers recruited followers across parish lines, so disrupting and confusing hierarchical control of both elite and mass religion that all future rulers of England were forced to tolerate religious pluralism.[34]

Mass revolutionary mobilization was confined to the rare times, places, and issues over which elite divisions were so extreme that elites were willing to fight (individually and institutionally) to the death. Temporally, that was the 1640–49 period. Earlier and later, kings backed down (or in the case of James II fled) rather than provoke civil war. The clergy was so quickly isolated and overcome during the Henrician Reformation that its efforts to incite popular rebellion in its behalf were readily suppressed. Geographically, elites called up mass support mainly in London because that is where Parliament and the king were based. Outside the capital, armies rather than unarmed peasants were the currency of political power. Thus, the New Model Army was the main non-elite force brought into politics by the anti-royalist faction of the gentry elite. Non-elites were recruited into elite coalitions primarily by religious issues, for those were the ideological terms upon which elite alliances were built in the country following the demise of kin-based networks and magnate politico-military machines. Urban and army radicalism, both animated by powerful religious convictions, sustained elite divisions through the Civil War. However, once Charles I was executed and the monarchy temporarily eliminated, the gentry were able to reunify behind a program for the permanent suppression of non-elite political mobilization and for a reassertion of the constitutional settlement of 1641 in 1660 and again in 1690.

Elite conflict fostered mass revolutionary action which deepened elite conflict, resulting in Civil War and a temporary Commonwealth. Elite reunification demobilized and depoliticized non-elites, which facilitated a rapid consensus to replace an obstreperous king (James II) with another monarch and a new royal dynasty willing to reign within the confines of gentry hegemony in the counties and gentry power in Parliament. As long as elite unity lasted (which it did until a new industrial capitalist elite was created in the nineteenth century), popular mobilization was minimized.

EFFECTS OF REVOLUTION UPON ELITE CONFLICT AND SOCIAL STRUCTURES

The previous section identified variations in the presence or absence of revolutionary mass action over time, place, and issues to show how elite divisions determined the limits of non-elite mobilization. This section compares the English Revolution with two moments in French history when elites that were threatened by other elites encouraged mass mobilizations in hopes of gaining an advantage in elite conflict. However, popular uprisings had very different effects in France during the Frondes of 1648–53 as compared to the Revolution of 1789–95, and both those instances differed profoundly from the English Revolution. This section explains those differences in terms of the structures of elite and class relations against which the revolutionary mass actions occurred. Essentially, some elites were disadvantaged especially by revolution. It was those elites (who often were the instigators of peasant and urban uprisings during the Frondes and the Revolution) whose standings and plans were disrupted by mass action rather than other elites (who often were the intended targets of popular uprisings).

French monarchs never achieved national level hegemony in the manner of their English counterparts who, as we have seen, eliminated the clergy as an autonomous elite and disarmed the magnates. French kings contended with magnates who fielded their own armies and with autonomous provincial estates throughout the *ancien régime*. Unable to eliminate national level rivals, French kings pursued a second-best strategy of "vertical absolutism," selling offices to raise revenues and to create corps of venal *noblesse de robe* who could compete with magnates and the older *noblesse d'épée* for political hegemony and for access to revenues within the provinces. Sales of offices and the later development of intendants (royal officials who were not native to the provinces they administered and hence were not tied to provincial elites) expanded the ranks of "state officeholders" and resulted in drastic increases in taxes and duties. However, most of those "state revenues" never came under the control of the crown or of national officials; they were retained by the venal officeholders in their provinces.[35]

The crown and its venal and administrative appointees were locked in a contentious but symbiotic relationship by the middle of the seventeenth century. The crown was dependent upon the sale of offices, sales of rights to towns, and loans upon future revenues to sustain the royal court and to finance periodic wars abroad. The greater the crown's fiscal needs, the broader the grants of rights that were needed to make to provincial officials, aristocracies, and towns. Provincial elites continually resented the payments which the crown demanded of them and resisted crown supervision through the intendants and all other efforts by the crown to transfer provincial authority to royal officials.

Venality affected class as well as elite relations. While the crown failed to organize venal officials into a reliable and continuing revenue source, venality did serve to undermine the direct seigneurial relation between landlords and peasants. Nobles increasingly depended upon the rulings of royal officials in their efforts to increase rents from peasants.

The Frondes were a series of provincial rebellions instigated by elites to counter royal revenue demands and expanding royal claims of authority over venal officials. They were accompanied by peasant rebellions, some encouraged by the aristocratic Frondeurs to cut off tax revenues to the crown. The Frondeurs, official and seigneurial alike, were not making autarkic claims to the surplus of their domaines. Instead, they were "asserting a common front in defense of provincial 'privileges' which were subject to differing interpretations and which were defined only in reference to the king."[36]

Once Frondeurs had rejected crown regulation of crown-granted privileges, provincial elites were left to sort out their overlapping jurisdictions among themselves. As a result, the weaker elements in the Frondeur coalitions faired less well in competition with provincial rivals than they had when subordinated to the crown and intendants. Officials and nobles whose positions had only recently been established by the crown and who were not clients or allies of the leading Frondeurs were the men most likely to have never joined the Frondes, or to have abandoned the rebels" common front first.[37]

The Frondeurs were handicapped by peasant rebellions as well as by internal elite conflicts. Contrary to their expectations, it was the Frondeurs and not the crown who were most harmed by peasant rebellions. Venality had disrupted the networks of surplus extraction and political organization centered around magnate-governors in the provinces. Each element of the old provincial structures had been integrated within a crown-centered venal system. Venal and corporate bodies could attempt to improve the terms of their relations with the crown. However, they were unable to sustain or reconcile their state-like claims against those of similarly situated aristocrats, clerics, and officials. Frondeurs" political disunity and ultimate dependency on the crown were demonstrated by their inability to extract the resources needed to keep their armies in battle. Peasant rent and tax strikes affected the Frondeurs most severely. In the end Condé (the putative leader of the Frondeurs) was forced to sue for peace because his party was bankrupt.[38] In contrast, the crown continued to raise funds from financiers who had invested in tax farms and offices at the national court.[39]

The configuration of elite and class relations, and hence the consequences of urban and peasant rebellions, were quite different in 1789. French aristocrats and bourgeois had become even more closely incorporated within the French state during the century and a half from the Frondes to the French Revolution. Liquid capital increasingly was invested in state debt, while aristocrats derived a growing share of their income from state offices rather than from rents on land. The long-term rise in total state revenues as the French economy expanded in the eighteenth century allowed both financiers and officeholders to profit from their state positions. However, the drastic increase in royal debt, caused by France's intervention against Britain in the American Revolutionary War, created an insoluble state fiscal crisis. Efforts by Controller-Generals Turgot and Necker to finance state debts by taxing the aristocracy and clergy caused implacable opposition by provincial elites, culminating in the "revolt of the aristocracy" of 1787–89.[40]

Provincial nobles incited popular riots against royal officials in 1788, forcing the crown to agree to call an Estates General in 1789 for the first time in more than a century.[41] However, the popular forces unleashed by the aristocracy proved to be its undoing. When the Estates General were chosen, the largely conservative representatives of the clergy and aristocracy were foiled in their efforts to use the convention to regain power at the expense of the crown and great financiers. The Third Estate seized the initiative, meeting as a National Assembly and passing legislation guaranteeing state debt, and abolishing aristocratic and corporate privileges and most feudal obligations, while preserving private ownership of estates and tenancies. Those measures reflected the interests of the big financial capitalists and lawyers who held most of the state debts and of provincial bourgeois who were excluded from the most lucrative offices of the *ancien régime* and who profited from land-holdings but not from the old aristocrats" feudal privileges.[42]

Most leading aristocrats and clerics rejected the new legislation and supported royal efforts to call troops to Paris to dismiss the National Assembly. Those royal efforts were blocked by the popular forces which had first been unleashed by provincial aristocrats. The Great Fear of summer 1789 fatally undermined aristocratic control of the countryside, while revolts in provincial towns ended both aristocratic and royal authority in the provinces. Most critically, the Paris bourgeoisie mobilized "sans-culottes" who took to the streets at key moments to counter the troops under royal control, forcing the crown to allow the National Assembly to remain in session.[43]

The strategic unfoldings, though not the structural consequences, of the French Revolution were similar to those of the English Civil War. In both instances, the presence of mass forces in the capital, mobilized by a particular elite, led "rump" national legislatures to enact and implement legislation more radical than would have passed in the absence of mass action.[44] Popular forces in both France during the 1790s and England in the 1640s were more effective at disabling the monarchs and their elite allies than at advancing their own interests. By contrast, the popular Frondes harmed the elite Frondeurs more than the crown, while also accomplishing little for the non-elite rebels.

Elites during both revolutions made momentary concessions to win popular support. In England, Parliamentarians gave commercial concessions and control over London city government to interloper merchants and their less wealthy shopkeeper and commercial allies. In France, the National Assembly ratified popular control over Parisian government, supported popular coalitions in provincial cities, imposed price controls on food for the masses, and pretended to help peasants escape from rent obligations on land. In both countries, the ultimate elite victors of the revolutions moved to demobilize their non-elite allies once they were confident they had defeated the royalist forces. In France, the National Guard and army were firmly under elite control and so were easily used to suppress mass risings in 1794–95 and to implement the White Terror of 1795. In England, the independent New Model Army continued to set state policy on its own even after the execution of Charles I, being demobilized only with difficulty and at great expense in 1648. Again, the Frondes stand in strategic contrast to the two revolutions. Because elite Frondeurs were endangered more than the crown by the popular Frondes, aristocrats" armed forces joined the royal army in suppressing the popular Frondes.

The structural consequences of the French Revolution were dramatically different from both the Frondes and the English Revolution. The English gentry's ownership of private property in land, and its control over county government to protect those property rights, was absolute and settled before 1640. The English Revolution was a successful gentry response to the crown and allied clergy's efforts to construct rival mechanisms of political domination and economic extraction in the provinces. While the gentry divided during the Civil War over an array of issues and in pursuit of personal advantages, at no point did either side in the Civil War threaten the organizational bases for economic exploitation and political domination by the landed elite. Parliamentarians, royalists, and neutrals retained their common organizational capacities and therefore, once Charles I was executed, regained a common interest in demobilizing and subordinating popular forces.

No single French elite of the seventeenth and eighteenth centuries matched the English gentry in its control over a distinct organization of political domination and economic extraction. However, by 1789 several small elites were able to achieve organizational capacities which were more threatened by the king and his nobles and clerical allies than were aided by continuing subordination to the crown. Financiers, manufacturers, and some landowners came to share an interest in the defeat of the first two estates and the capacity to preserve their organizational integrity without royal support. The royalist elites in France, unlike Charles I's allies during the English Civil War, were so dependent upon the crown for recognition of their official bases of power and income that they could not survive the temporary victory of the popular revolution in any form. The "bourgeois" victors of the French Revolution created new state-based mechanisms of patronage and extraction for themselves.[45]

The new elites concretized their own organizational capacities through the revolutionary state in the early 1790s. The possibilities of a counter-revolution by the old elites of the *ancien régime* were ended by the Republic's war victories in late 1793. The new elites then moved to demobilize popular forces in Paris and the provinces with the executions of Danton and the Indulgents, the drafting of sans-culottes to the war front (removing them from Parisian politics), the subordination of popular organizations within the Jacobin Club, and the Terror in 1793–94. Those actions against popular forces proved fatal for the Jacobins of the National Assembly and the Committee on Public Safety (personified by Robespierre) who could not call upon street forces to save them when they were marked for execution in the Thermidorian reaction of July 1794 and in the subsequent White Terror.[46]

The 1794 reaction, like the 1648 denouement of the English Civil War, killed individual members of elites who belonged to losing factions without disrupting the political and economic hegemony of whole elites: hegemonies determined in England by elite conflict before the Revolution, in France by elite conflict during the Revolution. The consolidation of a new elite and class structure in England before the Revolution served to minimize the long-term effects of popular participation in that revolution and the Civil War. The heightened and unresolved nature of elite conflict in France from 1787 to 1793 made mass revolutionary action critical to the outcome of elite and class conflict and thereby made the long-term consequences of the French Revolution far more significant than were those of the English Revolution and Civil War (not to mention the insignificant structural effects of the failed Frondes).

CONCLUSIONS

We are now in a position to draw some conclusions from the various sets of comparisons presented above. Any generalizations must be prefaced with a plea to recognize the importance of the specific structural context within which a revolution occurs and upon which revolutionary mass action has an effect. Our comparison of the Frondes and the 1789 French Revolution illustrates how similar mass mobilizations had different consequences because they affected elites that were locked into structures of elite and class relations which had changed from the seventeenth to the eighteenth centuries.

Detailed historical study is necessary before any revolution can be inserted into a typology. Any typology is useful only in so far as it recognizes the range as well as the limits of variation of revolutions within each category. If this chapter's typology has value it is as much to alert us to the need to discover the structural causes for the differences among the Frondes and the English and French Revolutions as it is to contrast the latter two cases with such "failed" revolutions as the peasant uprisings against the second serfdom or the challenges to Communist hegemony in 1956 Hungary or with the non-violent revolutions of Eastern Europe in 1989.

The comparisons in this chapter do suggest four general conclusions, despite the important differences within and across categories. First, elite conflict encourages non-elite mobilization and decisively shapes the structural effects of revolutionary mass action. Non-elites, like elites, are not suicidal and try to read social structures and conflicts to determine when and where mobilization can be effective. Like elites, non-elites may misread social structure, seeing broad openings in unusual local conditions. All actors, elite and non-elite, often fail to see how the interweaving of elite and class conflicts in complex social structures can yield unintended and unwanted (or occasionally unanticipated though wonderful) consequences.

Non-elites are best able to sustain their struggle and achieve their aims when they are able to find an elite in a strong structural position with which they can ally. When an elite was weak (as were the clergy following the Henrician Reformation), then the rebellions by their non-elite allies were intense but isolated and therefore easily defeated (as was the Pilgrimage of

Grace in England in 1536) or were poorly organized and therefore ineffective even if broad-based (as in the cases of Hungary in 1956 or Czechoslovakia in 1968).

Elites were effective allies and helped to sustain mass action as long as the elite allied with popular forces remained unified and was able to command resources over an extended period of time. The English and French Revolutions were instances where an elite both was threatened with extinction and had the resources to mobilize non-elite forces and so sustain revolutionary conflict over years. The Ciompi and the Frondes were instances where elites felt themselves under threat, yet in mobilizing popular forces undermined their capacities to remain unified and to mobilize resources for a revolutionary challenge; thus the Ciompi and the Frondeurs became disunified and were suppressed by reconstituted multi-elite alliances.

Second, foreign military ventures influence the occurrence and outcomes of revolutions, though more narrowly and specifically than in Skocpol's and Tilly's models.[47] Elites can disagree over whether their nation should fight a war, because elites differ in the benefits they may derive from a war and in the share of military costs they will have to shoulder. The monarch or "state elite" was not always the militarist. Kings Charles I and Louis XIV were less eager to mount wars against their foreign enemies than were the most radical members of the Parliament and National Assembly.

Each elite in Renaissance Florence pursued its own foreign policy, forming alliances and promising their city-state's participation in wars, often on the opposite side from that suggested by a rival elite. Florentine and English elites developed foreign policies to protect their trade and religious interests. Louis XIV and the National Assembly each saw war as a way to mobilize domestic and foreign forces against their opponents. Many dissidents in Eastern Europe from the 1950s to the 1990s were committed, at least ideologically, to the opposite side in the Cold War from their opponents in the regime.

Wars can strengthen or weaken various elites in addition to the monarch or "state elite." Florentine expenses for wars, which were placed by the ruling elite upon rival elites outside the state, precipitated the oligarchic *coup* in 1378 and brought the new men into alliance with the Medici in the 1430s. Charles I was forced to recall Parliament, which served to organize opposition to his reign, to pay for war in Ireland. The war in Afghanistan and the costs of the Cold War mobilized opposition to the Soviet regime.

Conversely, provincial war weakened the Frondeurs and gave relative advantage to the crown. The National Assembly successfully used foreign wars which it instigated to mobilize financial and human resources against domestic enemies and to build the revolutionary state. Foreign war was vital in consolidating the French revolutionary regime and for securing long-term power for the elites served by the new state. The effects of war depend upon the specific structure of elite relations and upon the nature of each elite's

organization of fiscal appropriation. Broad generalizations about wars"
effects upon the origins and especially upon the outcomes of revolutions are
belied by the variety of causal sequences which developed in the few cases
compared in this chapter.

Third, the overthrow or transformation of the state is not necessarily the
primary object or result of revolutions. All three English conflicts examined
above were about the local control of organizations of domination and
extraction. The two revolutions, though not the Reformation, did result in
changes of rulers, but had virtually no effect on the structure of national
government which had been determined by previous elite conflicts. The
English elite transformation with the greatest immediate and long-term
effects on the national constitution was the Henrician Reformation which
overthrew the parallel national administration of the church, an entity
not contained in the definitions of the state offered by any sociologist of
revolution.

The Florentine Ciompi and Medici takeover and the French Frondes and
the 1789 Revolution (in the ambitions of both aristocrats and bourgeois)
were concerned with gaining improved positions within the existing state for
the revolutionaries. The 1789 Revolution overthrew the old state inadver-
tently, only because of the particular compounding of elite and popular
actions. Among all the cases examined in this chapter, only the Eastern
European and Soviet revolutions of the twentieth century were initiated
with the goal of overthrowing and replacing states.

The long-term consequences of revolutions are even more distant from the
ideal notion of state transformation than are the initial plans and events of
each revolutionary moment. Each revolution mattered in the long term to
the extent to which elites and non-elites succeeded in disabling and/or
absorbing the state-like mechanisms of domination and expropriation controlled by defeated elites. The Ciompi briefly, and the Medici takeover
permanently, transferred mechanisms of taxation, borrowing, and military
mobilization from one elite to another. These were cases of Pareto-like circu-
lations of elites without affecting the overall form in which non-elites were
ruled and exploited by the combined organizational capacities of elites.

Only the first of the three English conflicts, the Henrician Reformation,
seriously and permanently affected the structure of elite rule. The two later
English revolutions merely ratified the changes in elite and class relations set
in train by the Reformation. The French Revolution, and perhaps the recent
Russian and Eastern European revolutions, are unusual in that they initiated
transformations of elite and class relations in the course of overthrowing
state regimes.

The point of this review is not to sort revolutions into two piles and
see which one is bigger. Many of the major twentieth-century revolutions
not discussed here are close to Tilly's ideal type. Indeed, modern revolutions became increasingly state-centered as all elite organizations were

incorporated within or regulated by national states. I want to emphasize that revolutions matter structurally only when they extinguish, amalgamate, or destroy elite capacities which may reside within states but which historically have been found more often within state-like and other elite organizations not included in most definitions of revolutionary targets. The current weakening of national states may once again direct revolutionaries toward non-state targets.

The comparative study of revolutions will stagnate (and it will continue to misinterpret the structural import of recent historical studies of specific revolutions) as long as the Marxist strawman of revolution as class war is challenged only by state-centered theorists who counter by viewing 500-plus years of European history as a struggle between state and civil society and revolutions as victories or setbacks for one side and the other. Ruling classes and "state elites" must be examined more finely, in terms of multiple elites and their organizations (which may be states or state-like). Then we can answer comparative questions such as: How do elites depend upon states or state-like mechanisms to extract resources and to dominate non-elites, and what interest do elites have in the preservation, modification, or overthrow of states or state-like forms? Answers to these questions provide the essential groundwork for analyzing the ultimate effects of revolutions.

Finally, the focus on elite and class structures allows one to account for the unanticipated effects of revolution. Marx himself does that in his *Eighteenth Brumaire of Louis Napoleon*, with its careful tracing of alliances and conflicts among multiple class fractions which he identifies at various points through their elite-like control of organizations as well as their specific relations of production. The interweaving of elite and non-elite conflicts is what makes a revolutionary era different from previous elite conflict. It also explains why revolutionary eras are so confusing to those who live through them as well as to scholars trying to reconstruct historical events and their meanings.

Revolutionaries and their opponents use ideologies to understand choices and make alliances. The discontinuities of elite and class conflicts account for the lack of correspondence between the ideological claims for and the actual structural effects of revolutions. We can explain how non-elites matter to the ultimate victory of one or more elites, identify what victorious elites and non-elites have gained once a revolution is "won," and specify the long-term effects of revolutions for their participants and for societies as a whole only by distinguishing between the dynamics of elite and class conflict, and then highlighting their interactions. This chapter is intended to suggest ways that such an analysis can be carried out for individual revolutions and comparatively.

ACKNOWLEDGEMENTS

I want to thank John Foran, Julia Adams, Jeff Goodwin, and Eric Selbin for their helpful comments.

NOTES

1. Mass action also can have ideological consequences which are not measurable from before and after pictures of social structure. Failed as well as successful mass mobilizations can introduce new methods of collective action which may facilitate later more consequential elite and mass mobilizations.

2. I define an elite as a group of rulers with the capacity to appropriate resources from non-elites who inhabit a distinct organizational apparatus. A society is ruled by a single elite if, and only if, (1) all resources are taken from non-elites through a unified organization; (2) no putative elite is able to construct a rival organization of appropriation; and (3) individual members of groups within the elite cannot disrupt the existing organization of rule by withdrawing their support for the remaining members of an elite. When all three conditions hold, a single elite is indistinguishable from a ruling class. More often multiple elites exist in a society, meaning that several elites have developed the organizational capacities to extract resources from non-elites in such a way that other elites must tolerate them to preserve their own access to non-elite resources. Elites have two vital interests: to preserve their organizational autonomy and power against rival elites and to reproduce their exploitative relationship with non-elites (i.e., the producing class).

   For a more detailed working out of this model see Richard Lachmann, "Class Formation Without Class Struggle: An Elite Conflict Theory of the Transition to Capitalism," pp. 398–414 in *American Sociological Review*, volume 55 (June, 1990).

3. Charles Tilly, *European Revolutions, 1492–1992* (Oxford: Blackwell, 1993), 14–16 and *passim* takes the opposite approach, defining revolution in terms of the transfer of power, by which he means a change in the leadership of nation-states.

4. Wilhelm Abel, *Agricultural Fluctuations in Europe from the Thirteenth to the Twentieth Centuries* (New York: St. Martin's Press, 1980), 35–95.

5. Robert Brenner, "Agrarian Class Structure and Economic Development in Pre-Industrial Europe," pp. 30–75 in *Past and Present*, number 70 (1976).

6. Heide Wunder, "Peasant Organization and Class Conflict in East and West Germany," pp. 47–55 in *Past and Present*, number 78 (1978); and Arnost Klima, "Agrarian Class Structure and Economic Development in Pre-Industrial Bohemia," pp. 49–67 in *Past and Present*, number 85 (1979) both speak directly to the Brenner thesis.

7. See Richard Lachmann, "Feudal Elite Conflict and the Origins of English Capitalism," *Politics and Society*, volume 14, number 3 (1985), pp. 349–78 for a fuller discussion of the English case in relation to the Brenner debate.

8. The evidence for England is summarized in Richard Lachmann, *From Manor to Market: Structural Change in England, 1536–1640* (Madison: University of Wisconsin Press, 1987), 52–65. For France see J. Russell Major, *Representative Government in Early Modern France* (New Haven: Yale University Press, 1980), 1–204; Ferdinand Lot and Robert Fawtier, editors, *Histoire des Institutions Françaises au Moyen Age* (Paris: Presses Universitaires de France, 1957), volume one; Hugues Neveux, "Déclin et réprise: la fluctuation biseculaire," pp. 123–38 in *Histoire de la France rurale*, volume two: *L'Age classique des paysans 1340–1789*, edited by Emmanuel Le Roy Ladurie (Paris: Seuil, 1975); Pierre Goubert, *L'Ancien Régime* (Paris: A. Colin, 1969), volume one, 74–5; and Guy Bois, *The Crisis of Feudalism: Economy and Society in Eastern Normandy ca. 1300–1550* (Cambridge: Cambridge University Press 1984 [1976]).

9. Michael Burawoy and Pavel Krotov, "The Soviet Transition From Socialism to Capitalism: Worker Control and Economic Bargaining in the Wood Industry," pp. 16–38 in *American Sociological Review*, volume 57 (February, 1992), describe the demise of the single party elite's control over production within firms and of exchange across firms in favor of *ad-hoc* linkages between firm managers or owners. Their finding, that elite anarchy strengthens worker control over production even more than did the revolution of 1917, is consistent with the model I develop here.

10. J. K. Hyde, *Society and Politics in Medieval Italy: The Evolution of Civil Life, 1000–1350* (London: Macmillan, 1973); and Brian Pullan, *A History of Early Renaissance Italy: From the Mid-Thirteenth to the Mid-Fifteenth Century* (New York: St. Martin's Press, 1972).

11. I address the role of war and foreign domination more generally and comparatively in the conclusion to this chapter.

12. Patricians bought rural estates mainly in the sixteenth century and after: R. Burr Litchfield, *Emergence of a Bureaucracy: The Florentine Patricians, 1530–1790* (Princeton: Princeton University Press, 1986), 215–32. During the earlier period under discussion here, aristocrats and patricians were close to being separate classes, although over time patricians became aristocratized. That process is beyond the scope of this chapter. I present a broader and more detailed discussion of Florence, from which the evidence in this section is derived, in Richard Lachmann, *Capitalists in Spite of Themselves* (Oxford: Oxford University Press, 1997).

13. John Najemy, *Corporatism and Consensus in Florentine Electoral Politics, 1280–1400* (Chapel Hill: University of North Carolina Press, 1982) provides the best summary and analysis of Florentine politics from 1280 to 1400, the heyday of patrician power.

14. Najemy, *Corporatism and Consensus*, 4; see also George Holmes, *Florence, Rome and the Origins of the Renaissance* (Oxford: Clarendon Press, 1986), 3–43.

15. Gene Brucker, *The Civic World of Early Renaissance Florence* (Princeton: Princeton University Press, 1977), 39–44; and Brucker, *Florentine Politics and Society, 1343–1378* (Princeton: Princeton University Press, 1962).

16. Richard Goldthwaite, *The Building of Renaissance Florence* (Baltimore: Johns Hopkins University Press, 1980), 29–66.

17. Samuel K. Cohn, *The Laboring Classes in Renaissance Florence* (New York: Academic, 1980), 205.

18. Both the Marxist Cohn and Brucker, who is critical of earlier Marxist analysis of the Ciompi as a proletarian breakthrough, agree on this point.

19. My main sources on the Ciompi are Najemy, *Corporatism and Consensus*, 166–262; Brucker, *Florentine Politics*, 183–396; and Cohn, *Laboring Classes*. For the Medici takeover and the events leading up to it see John Padgett and Christopher Ansell, "Robust Action and the Rise of the Medici," pp. 1259–319 in *American Journal of Sociology*, volume 98, number 6 (May, 1993); Anthony Mohlo, *Florentine Public Finances in the Early Renaissance, 1400–1433* (Cambridge, MA: Harvard University Press, 1971); Dale Kent, *The Rise of the Medici: Faction in Florence, 1426–1434* (Oxford: Oxford University Press, 1978); and J. R. Hale, *Florence and the Medici* (New York: Thames & Hudson, 1977).

20. Goldthwaite, *The Building of Renaissance Florence*, 29–66.

21. Of course, the relative loss of power and income for an elite as a whole often means the bankruptcy or total political exile for individual members of that elite. Those members may find reason to ally with non-elites. However, unless a plurality of an elite is so endangered, there is not enough of a base for an effective elite alliance with non-elites. Thus, those few members of elites who allied with

Ciompi, or were involved with other emergent mass movements, appear to us not as revolutionaries but as failed instigators of *coups* or mutinies since they lacked the necessary elite allies if not the mass support to plausibly attempt to effect structural change.

22. I present an extended analysis of elite structure and class relations in fourteenth-through seventeenth-century England in *From Manor to Market*, which provides the basis and offers the empirical support for the more schematic discussion here.

23. From 1450 to 1850 rents received by landlords and then landowners rose 600 per-cent in real terms, while food prices rose (so consumers lost), wages fell (so land-less laborers lost), and the value of capital investment stagnated (meaning that commercial farmers did not share with landowners in the gains from the improve-ments which commercial farmers financed and implemented): Robert C. Allen, *Enclosure and the Yeoman* (Oxford: Clarendon, 1992).

24. John Morrill, *The Nature of the English Revolution* (London: Longman, 1993).

25. I discuss English horizontal absolutism in contrast to the "vertical" absolutism of French monarchs in "Elite Conflict and State Formation in 16th- and 17th-Century England and France," pp. 141–62 in *American Sociological Review*, volume 54 (April 1989).

26. Robert Brenner, *Merchants and Revolution: Commercial Change, Political Conflict, and London's Overseas Traders, 1550–1653* (Cambridge: Cambridge University Press, 1993).

27. Brenner, *Merchants and Revolution*, identifies in exhaustive detail the times when the interloper-colonial merchants and their popular allies in London affected Parliamentary policy and the course of the Civil War. The merchants and their popular allies had an influence far beyond their numbers because of their location in London, the capital. See Mark Traugott, "Capital Cities and Revolution," pp. 147–68 in *Social Science History*, volume 19 (Spring, 1995) for a discussion of the temporally limited importance of revolutionary forces in urban capitals in Europe.

28. Andrew Charlesworth, *An Atlas of Rural Protest in Britain, 1548–1900* (Philadelphia: University of Pennsylvania Press, 1983), 10–39; Morrill, *Nature of the English Revolution*, 1–29.

29. Christopher Hill, *The World Turned Upside Down* (Harmondsworth: Penguin, 1972), *passim*.

30. Brenner, *Merchants and Revolution*, 528–637.

31. John Morrill, *The Nature of the English Revolution*, 359–453, offers a discussion of the 1640–49 and Glorious Revolutions in the context of long-term continuities in British politics and constitutional order.

32. Brenner, *Merchants and Revolution*, 633–7 and *passim*.

33. Hill, *The World Turned Upside Down*, *passim*; and David Underdown, *Revel, Riot, and Rebellion: Popular Politics and Culture in England 1603–1660* (Oxford: Clarendon Press, 1985).

34. Brenner, *Merchants and Revolution*, 460–93, 565–9; and Morrill, *The Nature of the English Revolution*, 17–19 and *passim*.

35. David Parker, *The Making of French Absolutism* (London: Arnold, 1983), 64 and *passim*. See also Jonathan Dewald, *The Formation of a Provincial Nobility: The Magistrates of the Parlement of Rouen, 1499–1610* (Princeton: Princeton University Press, 1980), 69–112; David Parker, *La Rochelle and the French Monarchy: Conflict and Order in Seventeenth-Century France* (London: Royal Historical Society, 1980), 56–95; Richard Tait, "The King's Lieutenants in Guyenne, 1580–1610: A Study in the Relations Between Crown and the Great Nobility," Ph.D. dissertation, Oxford University (1977), 1–20; and Sharon Kettering, *Judicial Politics And*

Urban Revolt in Seventeenth-Century France: The Parlement of Aix, 1629–1659 (Princeton: Princeton University Press, 1978), 13–50, for descriptions of the relations between crown, intendants, venal officials, and provincial aristocrats in the decades leading up to the Frondes.

36. William Beik, *Absolutism and Society in Seventeenth Century France: State Powers and Provincial Aristocracy in Languedoc* (Cambridge: Cambridge University Press, 1985), 219.

37. Kettering, *Judicial Politics And Urban Revolt*, and "The Cause of the Judicial Frondes," pp. 275–306 in *Canadian Journal of History*, volume 17 (1982); A. Lloyd Moote, *The Revolt of the Judges: The Parlement of Paris and the Fronde, 1643–1652* (Princeton: Princeton University Press, 1971); Richard Bonney, *Political Change in France Under Richelieu and Mazarin, 1624–1661* (Oxford: Oxford University Press, 1978), and *The King's Debts: Finance and Politics in France, 1589–1661* (Oxford: Oxford University Press, 1981).

38. Parker, *The Making of French Absolutism*, 95–117.

39. Bonney, *The King's Debts*, 238–41.

40. On the consolidation of state finances see Daniel Dessert, *Argent, pouvoir et société au Grand Siècle* (Paris: Fayard, 1984); and George Tennyson Matthews, *The Royal General Farms in Eighteenth-Century France* (New York: Columbia University Press, 1958). George Tennyson Matthews and J. F. Bosher, *French Finances 1770–1795: From Business to Bureaucracy* (Cambridge: Cambridge University Press, 1970) discuss the rise in state revenues, income from offices, and the fiscal crisis of the 1770s and after.

41. Albert Soboul, *The French Revolution, 1787–1799* (London: New Left Books 1974 [1962]), 105–6.

42. There is a long and ongoing debate over the class character of the "Third Estate" in the National Assembly and throughout France. While bourgeois could buy offices which gave them aristocratic status, and both aristocratic and bourgeois landlords pursued similar strategies of leasing unencumbered lands to commercial farmers while trying to extract greater feudal dues from peasants in a "seigneurial reaction" there were clear divisions between elites, even if members of those elites were ambiguously feudal and capitalist at the same time. Financiers, who derived revenues from their sole access to the great amounts of capital needed by the crown and their control over the administration of state debt and tax collection, were a different elite, inhabiting a different organizational apparatus than did the provincial officeholding elites. The aristocratic reaction of 1787–89 was an attack by the latter elite on the former; the legislation of the Third Estate in the National Assembly was a response which favored the former elite at the expense of the latter. The National Assembly's legislation on feudal dues and landownership favored those who primarily held land as property over those who retained ancient dues rights by virtue of their old aristocratic titles – again the former elite over the latter. Soboul is clear on those fundamental distinctions of interest, although he anachronistically expresses them in class rather than elite terms. The most useful recent discussions of these issues are contained in George Comninel, *Rethinking the French Revolution: Marxism and the Revisionist Challenge* (London: Verso, 1987), 179–207, and Immanuel Wallerstein, *The Modern World-System III: The Second Era of Great Expansion of the Capitalist World-Economy, 1730–1840s* (New York: Academic, 1989), 57–112, who provides a penetrating review of debates on this issue.

43. Georges Lefebvre, *The Great Fear of 1789* (New York: Vintage, 1973 [1932]); Soboul, *The French Revolution*, 119–58.

44. Traugott, "Capital Cities and Revolution"; Brenner, *Merchants and Revolution*, 393–459 and *passim*; Soboul, *The French Revolution*.
45. This is the key insight offered by Comninel, *Rethinking the French Revolution*, 203–5.
46. The events and political alliances of those years are analyzed in Soboul, *The French Revolution*, 255–449.
47. In *States and Social Revolutions: A Comparative Analysis of France, Russia, and China* (Cambridge: Cambridge University Press, 1979), Theda Skocpol sees foreign wars as generally destablizing of old regimes. For Tilly, in *European Revolutions as well as Coercion, Capital, and European States, AD 990–1990* (Oxford: Basil Blackwell, 1990) and *From Mobilization to Revolution* (Reading, MS: Addison-Wesley, 1978), wars have the long-term effect of strengthening states against civil society, while leading to the demise of nations and regimes unable to keep up in the continually escalating scale of human, financial, and technological resources needed to compete in European (and later worldwide) military confrontations.

4

POPULATION GROWTH AND REVOLUTIONARY CRISES

Jack A. Goldstone

Much of the talk about population and world crises these days is apocalyptic. Such talk misses two vital issues – precisely *how* population growth is going to impact developing areas and *what* can be done about it. To determine whether population growth will produce a more unstable and dangerous world in coming decades, we need to identify the precise institutional pathways through which population growth creates political crises and discuss ways to intervene in those pathways to avert the worst effects. There certainly will be crises, but there are also sensible policy responses, and our ultimate future is not written in stone.

The obvious fears since the mid-1970s – that we shall run out of food, of water, of energy, of land, etc. – have been proven false, at least on a global scale. Julian Simon and his followers are correct that over the long haul, the human race has survived repeated crises to become richer and more numerous than ever.[1] However, *over the short run and for specific regions*, all of these shortages have occurred and will occur, with severe consequences. To ignore this fact and say that "population growth is not a problem" is like saying that since the human race has triumphed over numerous diseases, we need no longer concern ourselves with medical research or clinical treatment of diseases. In fact, we devote enormous resources to medical research and treatment not merely to save the human race (although large parts of it would surely perish without it), but to mitigate human suffering and improve the quality of our lives. It is for these same reasons, rather than only to avert apocalypse, that the effects of population growth demand our attention.

Given that many of the crises we now see stemming from population growth and accompanying environmental degradation are short term and local in their effects, economists and political scientists sometimes tell us that the real problem is not population growth; the problem lies in the political and social institutions that fail to distribute the available resources. Fair enough; in theory one could view a situation in which population growth is overwhelming the immediately available supply of housing as one in which better policy should have previously allocated more resources for building houses. But in practice, if a locality faces a housing shortage, certain questions must be answered – can the supply of housing be quickly increased? Is anticipated population growth going to overwhelm existing supplies for new construction? Most important for politics, will there be inflation, riots against housing authorities, fights over existing housing, migration to new areas?

Although economists have little to say about the distribution of goods and resources, seeing that as a political issue, it is precisely on distributional issues that population growth has its largest impacts. Every human society has its cleavages. They may be based on economic status, race and ethnicity, regions, religion, education, or some combination of these; but societies also develop social, political, and economic institutions designed to manage the conflicts that such cleavages can produce. Systems of patronage, justice, and governance may be fair or unfair, they may mitigate or sustain inequalities, but if they are working at all, they discourage violence by producing stable expectations regarding different groups" shares of land, power, and income. As long as those expectations are met, societies tend to remain politically stable. It is when large numbers of people, both elites and popular groups, find their expectations are *not* met that demands arise for dramatic change. It is an unfortunate consequence of population growth that its distributional effects tend to undermine expectations in distressing ways.

In particular, population growth, whether in the context of economic stagnation or rapid development, often distributes resources away from those who labor – such as peasants and traditional workers – to those who employ labor, raising the resentment and fears of the working poor. Moreover, if different elite groups have different degrees of influence over the growing population, and differential access to the fruits of their labors, intra-elite competition and conflicts may increase. And finally, population growth often distributes resources away from the government, as demands for development and social services increase faster than government revenues, weakening the legitimacy of government and its ability to manage conflicts just at the time that social conflicts are growing more intense.

For example, let us say for simplicity's sake that a developing society has two sectors: a labor-intensive sector of local crafts, migrant or hacienda labor, and agricultural production for local consumption, and a human and financial capital-intensive sector of professions, government, industrial production, and processing and wholesaling of agriculture for export. In developing countries, it is usually a minority of the population that is ensconced in the capital-intensive sector, and a majority that remain in the labor-intensive sector. If the flow of individuals into both sectors matches the growth of job and income-creating opportunities in these sectors, then conflict is unlikely. But in practice, that rarely happens. Generally, the fastest rate of population growth occurs in the labor-intensive sector, where the job and income opportunities are most limited by resource constraints: especially

103

the amount of land available for peasant farming, but also the incomes of local families who provide the market for traditional foods and crafts. As a result, underemployment and income stresses build in the labor-intensive sector, creating pressures for migration and redistribution of income.[2]

Moreover, the growth of such pressures is highly non-linear. To continue with our example, let us suppose that one-fifth of the population has jobs in the capital-intensive sector; three-fifths of the population has jobs or a livelihood in the labor-intensive sector, and one-fifth of the population is unemployed or underemployed. What happens if the population grows by 20 percent? If the labor-intensive sector has reached a point of saturation – whether through population growth or deterioration of land and other resources – that sector can no longer provide expected jobs and incomes. What then happens to that additional population? Assuming that the capital-intensive sector is growing rapidly, it might expand by 50 percent. But since that sector is small, such growth will absorb only *half* the new population, leaving the other half un- or underemployed. This will increase the number of un- and underemployed by *fully 50 percent*. Moreover, further population growth leads to ever faster spiralling pressures. If population grows not by 20 percent, but by 50 percent, then even a doubling of the opportunities in the capital-intensive sector still leaves a 150 percent increase in the un- and underemployed! The result of such arithmetic is clear and frightening: even with rapid growth in the capital-intensive sector, the combination of population growth and limited land and other labor-intensive employment resources can lead to wretched distributional problems. Even moderate population growth, if it occurs where resources and opportunities are limited, can lead to underemployment growing much faster than the overall population increases. Given that in many developing countries, populations are projected to double in the twenty-five–thirty-five years following 1996 while available land for peasant farming will likely stagnate or decline, the question looms: How will governments provide for and manage the coming tens of millions seeking a livelihood?

As this question suggests, the immediate effects of population growth are *political*. Well before societies experience widespread absolute deprivation, the institutions that deal with the distribution of goods and power and the resolution of social conflicts may be overwhelmed and collapse in the face of persistent population pressure and limited resources. And as we have seen in Somalia, Rwanda, and a host of other troubled countries, it is precisely when political institutions collapse that we see the most terrible outcomes – mass starvation, mass migrations, civil wars.

My point in this chapter is that population problems cannot be viewed apart from their institutional context. Unfortunately, far too little attention has been given to the impact of population shifts on *political institutions*. Yet where such effects are large, institutions, far from being part of the solution to demographic crises, become a major part of the problem. It is possible to trace in some detail the way that population pressures can undermine political institutions. That knowledge can help us intervene in ways to improve and sustain institutions, averting the worst effects of demographic pressures while policies are put in place that will, in the long run, offer hope of alleviating those pressures.

POPULATION GROWTH AND POLITICAL CRISES IN HISTORY

The relationship between population growth and institutional failures leading to revolts, civil wars, and revolutions is nothing new. European history shows its effects as clearly as the crises in modern developing countries. Europe and Asia experienced two major "waves" of violent political crises since the Renaissance. Between 1580 and 1650 the first such wave rolled across Eurasia, including the English Revolution, the Religious Civil Wars and Fronde in France, rebellions in Catalonia, Portugal, Italy, Sicily, Bohemia, the Ukraine, and the Ottoman Empire, and the collapse of the Ming Empire in China. There followed a century of relative domestic peace, followed by the second wave from 1770 to 1870, this time including the French Revolution, the European Revolutions of 1848, the Pugachev revolt in Russia, and the Taiping rebellion in China. It should come as no great surprise that demographic historians can now document a doubling or tripling of populations in Europe and Asia from 1500 to 1650, followed by a century-long pause, and then a renewed burst of population growth – in Russia and China as well as in western Europe – from 1730 to 1870.[3]

After 1870, population growth in the developed world began to slow. However, growth in the developing world just began to take off. Unsurprisingly, we are now in the midst of another worldwide wave of revolts and revolutions beginning right after World War II and continuing to the present day.

As a simple example of the correlation between population pressure and political crises, one can make a list of the twenty-five countries in the world in the low- and middle-income range with the highest population growth rates of the 1980s (see Figure 4.1).

These twenty-five countries represent those nations with population growth at or above 3 percent per year in the decade 1980 to 1991. And although not all of them have been riven by strife and conflict, a remarkable number of the major sites of recent civil wars, revolutions, and violent demonstrations are on this list: Ethiopia, Rwanda, Kenya, Nigeria, Nicaragua, Yemen Republic, Tadzhikistan (which was one of the most violent of the post-Soviet Union new republics), Namibia, Iran, and Algeria (which is hovering on the edge of a possible revolution). Other countries on this list – Ghana, Madagascar, Pakistan, and Côte d'Ivoire (Ivory Coast) – are also

Tanzania	*Yemen Republic*
Ethiopia	Honduras
Madagascar	Côte d'Ivoire
Malawi	Senegal
Rwanda	Jordan
Niger	Congo
Kenya	*Tadzhikistan*
Nigeria	Syria
Benin	*Namibia*
Ghana	*Algeria*
Togo	*Iran*
Pakistan	Paraguay
Nicaragua	

Figure 4.1 Countries with population growth rates of
3 percent per year and above, 1980–91

candidates for a considerable amount of internal violence and struggle in the
next few years.

This coincidence between high rates of population growth and violence is
more than just a statistical coincidence. Yet neither is it an iron law. Rather,
the answer lies in institutions. Not all institutions are overwhelmed by population pressures. Nor are population pressures the only causes of political
crises. State corruption, government incompetence, and economic or military setbacks, if sufficiently severe, can all give rise to political crises even in
the absence of sustained population growth. However, rapid and sustained
population growth is widespread in the developing world, and history shows
that such population growth frequently imposed tremendous strains on political and social institutions, leading to their extensive breakdown. Understanding the future of political stability and crises in the developing world
therefore seems to require that we grasp the institutional mechanisms by
which sustained population growth has produced political crises.

POPULATION PRESSURES AND INSTITUTIONAL
FAILURES

Figure 4.2 shows the key relationships linking population pressures and political crises. The left-most box lists fundamental factors which, in combination, create difficulties for political regimes: population growth and limited
or uneven development. The combination of these factors undermines states
through three main routes: bringing a decline in state capacity, producing
elite displacement and conflicts, and generating increases in mass mobilization potential.

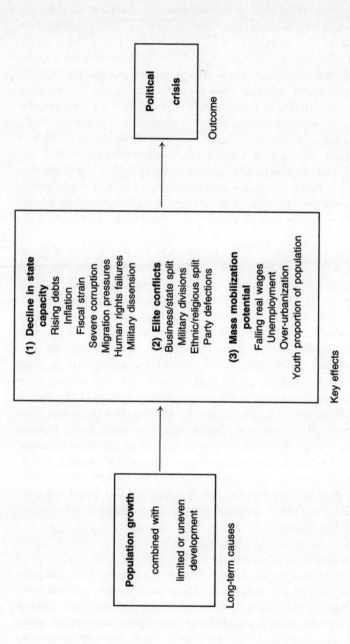

Figure 4.2 Population and political crisis

Decline in state capacity

States need resources. Whether a dictatorship or a democracy, no state can last long if it cannot pay its bureaucrats and its military, if it fails to provide opportunities for its elite supporters, if it cannot assure even minimal standards of work, justice, and security for its middle-class and working populations. One of the most striking effects of population growth and resource shortages is the decline of the capacity of the state to carry out the necessary functions of a state, relative to the demands imposed by a growing population. As population rises, the costs of administering justice, providing roads, schools, health-care, and education sharply escalate. Subsidies to farmers or city-dwellers, if part of the state budget, can rise precipitously with population increases. And frequently, a larger bureaucracy and/or larger military is needed both to absorb a growing number of aspirants to those positions and to carry out the growing tasks of governing. But will a government automatically get the resources it needs to carry out these tasks? All too often the answer is no.

If economic development is slow or uneven, while population grows rapidly, it is likely that for many people per capita income will decline, while for a lucky few wealth will accumulate. This is simply due to the laws of supply and demand. If some resource – land, timber, water, industrial capacity – becomes scarce relative to the number of people who rely on it, then the few people who control that resource will find their wealth sharply rises, while those who depend on that resource will have to pay more and their real incomes will fall. In countries where some key resources are growing scarce as population is rising, elites that control such resources will be enriched and ordinary workers, peasants, and even members of the middle class will find themselves in tighter straits. Where then can the government get the income it needs to cope with sharply rising demands? Either it raises taxes on the majority of the people who are already being hurt by economic trends – which raises resentment and feelings of injustice or is simply ineffective because they cannot pay much more – or the government tries to take a much larger portion of the new wealth of the elites who are benefiting from scarcity – again a route that is politically dangerous or impossible because of the influence of those enriched elites.

Since both of these approaches often fail, the government simply becomes weaker, increasingly unable to maintain justice, order, and welfare or to keep elites in line. What are the early warning signs of this condition? The government may take on a rising load of debt or print money, creating inflation. The government may show fiscal strain through a measurable decline in income and defaults on obligations. Severe corruption may replace regular pay as the main sustenance of state servants. Migration – either internal from the jobless seeking work or external as economic refugees leave for greener pastures – may burden cities or neighboring countries, creating more problems of disorder. Human rights failures may indicate the break-down of law and order. And an underpaid military, chafing at the rising impotence and failures of the state, may stand aside and not support the troubled regime or even talk of taking matters into its own hands through a coup.

In short, the combination of rising population and limited or uneven development in developing countries may lead to a recognizable "syndrome" of state capacity decline. This may include rising debt, inflation, fiscal strain, severe corruption, mass migrations, human rights failures, and military dissension, in varying combinations. Even strong states – such as that of mainland China – are not immune from such pressures. China's agricultural sector, despite its astounding progress since 1980, is in the process of being overwhelmed by a combination of rapid population increase (an expected 200 million to 250 million by the year 2011) and a decline in the amount and fertility of arable land due to erosion, water shortages, overuse of artificial fertilizers, and the expansion of roads and housing onto prime agricultural land.[4] With agriculture up against a ceiling of productivity growth, the only place for the population to turn is to the cities. The result has been a headlong rush of migrants – perhaps 100 million – to the cities, resulting in a building boom and rapid inflation. As economic wealth has mushroomed in the cities in the new private and foreign-investment sectors, agriculture and state-owned enterprises have, by comparison, grown slowly. As a result, the income of the central government – dependent on the latter two sectors – has declined from 34 percent of GNP in 1970 to 19 percent in 1990. Faced with this decline, the government has sped up the printing of money, let credit balloon, and taken on a vast increase in state debts. Due to these measures, as Richard Hornik wrote in an article in *Foreign Affairs*, "China's fiscal and monetary policies remain a shambles," with a state deficit approaching 25 percent of government revenues.[5]

Not surprisingly, as the private sector offers rapid and concentrated wealth and the resources of the state have declined, corruption has become a way of life. Internal migration has overwhelmed the old system of residence registration and party control and the panicked party leadership has turned to various repressive and human-rights violating policies to try to preserve its privileges and some kind of order. Yet the military, reeling from the public distrust and disapproval of its actions in suppressing the Tiananmen Square protests, has tried to professionalize and distance itself from party/ society conflicts. The latest government budget promises (but will it deliver?) a 25 percent increase in the military budget, an increase that suggests the degree to which the Communist Party now depends on the army, rather than the other way around. Yet all the signals from the military suggest that it is positioning itself to take advantage of nationalist sentiment to justify its existence, becoming the guardian of China as a whole, rather than taking the now unpopular line of supporting the Party in its attempts to control

Chinese society. Many provincial governments are now openly defying decrees from Beijing, and the rising impotence of the central government reminds many of the waning days of the Chinese Empire, with Deng Xiaoping playing the role of the Dowager Empress.

If a country with a government as powerful as that of Communist China can undergo massive state capacity decline, it is hardly surprising that weaker states, facing even faster population growth and resource degradation, are wallowing in debts, corruption, human rights failures, mass migrations, and dangerously independent militaries. From Somalia to Rwanda to Haiti, the burdens on states have shattered regimes, leading to civil wars, *coups*, and humanitarian problems that have humbled the ability of the developed world to provide solutions. Unless population growth and environmental degradation of resources are slowed or mitigated, the future offers more of the same in much of the developing world.

Elite displacement and conflicts

The decline of state capacity would not be fatal in a society that had the capacity for renewal. A society basically wealthy in resources and with loyal elites united in their support for the government could effect reforms to help put the government on a sound fiscal basis. But state capacity decline can trigger devastating civil wars and humanitarian disasters in countries that are *not* so united. Where deep fissures divide society's elite groups and the conflicts between those elites and their supporters is exacerbated by population pressures and resource scarcities that enrich certain groups and hurt others, the ability of a strong government to keep order, provide an outlet for elite ambitions, and offer a framework for compromise and distribution of society's wealth is absolutely vital. Where government weakens, elites will go into business for themselves, resolve their conflicts by force, and, all too often, turn on the government or tear their societies apart.

Where ethnic or regional divisions exist, population growth and resource shortages can intensify them. These factors can also create splits between the state and the business community, within the military, and within ruling parties. These phenomena can be grouped under the concept of "elite displacement." When a population grows, the number of people who aspire to elite positions – positions of leadership, wealth, and influence – is also going to grow. In a healthy society that is rich in resources and is building its institutions and its economy, there is usually room to accommodate a growing elite. But what happens if a country does not have a growing economy, but has invested in universities that are trying to develop an elite for the future, and that future does not come? This is what we see in many developing countries. We see far too many individuals who have been endowed with a higher education, who have been endowed with ambition and aspirations to count for something in their society, while there are simply not enough positions in the government, in the military, or enough wealth in the ordinary channels of society to satisfy all of these people. The result is a heightened competition between elites to see who is going to control what wealth there is, and what government there is.

It is such struggles that have convulsed countries like Rwanda and Burundi, where sustained population growth and environmental degradation have undermined traditional Hutu–Tutsi economic roles and created a sharp struggle for the remaining spoils. Rwanda and Burundi were characterized for most of their history by a mix of cattle-raising and farming: Tutsi dominated cattle-raising (and leadership of the societies), while the far more numerous Hutu were predominantly farmers. The exchange of cattle for grain helped maintain reciprocal relations among Tutsi and Hutu. But over the course of this century, as population growth led to farming encroachment on rangeland, cattle-raising diminished, and the Tutsi lost their distinctive livelihood, turning to farming and becoming in many ways (except for an identity system imposed by the Belgian colonial regime) indistinguishable from the Hutu. The efforts of Tutsis to maintain their distinctive position shifted to an effort to control the army and post-colonial government, an effort that was abruptly contravened by the Belgian insistence on a majority-based, Hutu-dominant regime. Tutsis and Hutus have been at war, on and off, ever since. In recent years, with population growing rapidly and per-capita output falling, competition between Tutsi and Hutu elites has intensified with each group seeing political domination as essential to its survival. The result has been a failure of compromise regimes, and either a military-imposed Tutsi dominance (in Burundi) or genocidal warfare (in Rwanda).[6]

Even rapid economic growth will not prevent such conflicts, if the state and elites come into conflict over the loyalty of a rapidly growing population. For example, in Iran the government's efforts to keep control of a rapidly growing society and to increase the state's resources led to conflicts with the business and merchant communities over control of economic growth, and with religious elites over the leadership of rapidly expanding urban populations. If the government loses the confidence of elites, and elites are divided and competing for resources, only turmoil can result. If the government weakens and elites feel that whoever first takes over the vacuum of power will win all the spoils, a situation of apparent peace or harmony, or multi-ethnic or multi-racial government, can rapidly degenerate into an all out war between different groups led by leaders seeking to take their place at the head of the pack.

Mass mobilization potential

In addition to bringing state capacity decline and exacerbating conflicts among elites, population growth and resource degradation have yet a third set of destabilizing effects, raising the willingness of people to be recruited to fight in situations of violence.

The two major dimensions determining mass mobilization potential are contentment and control. A population that is relatively content is unlikely to take major risks and follow leaders into revolt. Similarly, even discontented popular groups are unlikely to take the risks of violent action if they are well controlled by the government, either closely monitored or dependent on the state for basic needs.

The keys to keeping a population content are physical security and security of incomes. We have already seen that state decline and elite conflicts can undermine physical security as order breaks down and elites "go into business for themselves," or a state resorts to human rights abuses as normal law and order break down and the state fears it is losing control of society. At the same time, rapid population growth and resource degradation generally lead to falling real wages and various kinds of actual or disguised unemployment for much of the population. China offers a telling example. Despite the most rapid and sustained economic growth in the world between 1986 and 1995, 80 million Chinese have persistent worries in finding food and shelter. Two-thirds of China's manufacturing workers still work in state-owned firms, most of which are unprofitable and are laying off millions of workers and cutting wages. The combination of rapid population growth, limited and uneven development, and the degradation of rural resources has produced a situation in which most of the population shares relative poverty, while a small fraction competes for extraordinary wealth. Inflation can further intensify this skewed distribution of resources and is the greatest threat to the income security of the middle class.

Whether in the hills of Peru and the Philippines, where Sendero Luminoso (Shining Path) and the New People's Army respectively recruit, or in the cities of Iran, Egypt, and North Africa, where Islamic fundamentalists recruit terrorists and popular followings, or in the migrant laborer settlements that are growing in and around the cities of South Africa and mainland China, where independent labor unions have made or are making their mark, various combinations of physical threats, declines in jobs and incomes, and stubborn inflation are creating potential foot-soldiers for political violence.

Of course, governments have typically met popular discontent with various kinds of state repression and control. But population growth can defeat those efforts as well. Where population growth interacts with declining resources in the countryside, migration to the cities creates concentrations of population that are increasingly difficult to control. And these migrants are available to be recruited into new kinds of organizations, so that urban growth can greatly increase the number of people mobilized into new opposition movements.

Finally, there is a subtlety to the impact of population growth. When a population grows, it is usually because more children are being born and more of those children are growing up rather than succumbing to the childhood diseases that used to keep population growth very small. This means that the population is going to get rapidly younger. People do not just enter the population nicely distributed across all different age groups, they come in as youngsters. And youngsters tend to be more swaggering than adults, having less to lose and more to prove. If a very large youth cohort is coming of age in a situation where normal economic opportunities are contracting and elites are competing to offer opportunities and attract followers, the potential for mobilization into political opposition is high. If, in addition, the central government starts to collapse, there develops a setting for something like gang warfare to develop on a national scale.

Activating ideologies of opposition

Although the mass killings in Rwanda, the tribal struggles in Somalia, and the ethnic cleansing and battles for territory in Bosnia are redolent of non-ideological, large-scale gang warfare, other struggles that are considered more truly "revolutionary" – in Iran, Nicaragua, Palestine, Peru, the Philippines, Algeria, and South Africa – do appear to depend more for their existence on some form of ideological mobilization. It may be based on religious fundamentalism, nationalism, socialism, liberalism, or some combination of these, but giving meaning to civil violence and opposition to the government in terms of pursuing an alternative vision of the social order seems a crucial component of these conflicts.

No doubt such ideological mobilization gives a different character to these conflicts from conflicts based mainly on efforts by one group to gain territory or power at the expense of others. Yet even such ideologically colored crises are rooted in material conditions that often stem from the combination of population pressures and weak or uneven economic development. In fact, such material conditions seem to be a necessary foundation for the activation of these ideologies into effective cultures of opposition.

By this I mean that ideologies providing alternative visions of the social order are, in themselves, rather fluid and pervasive. Hardly any societies exist that do not harbor some ideological opponents of the existing regime; more commonly a number of opposition ideologies are in the air, competing for adherents. In the Middle East, this century has seen revolutionary ideologies drawing mainly from Islamic fundamentalism (as in the Wahabi movement in Saudi Arabia) and constitutional liberalism (as in the Constitutional Revolution in Iran) in the first decade of the 1900s; followed by anti-imperialism and nationalism during the era of World Wars I and II; followed by authoritarian state socialism (as Nasserism in Egypt and the Ba'athist regimes in Syria and Iraq); followed by a return to Islamic

113

fundamentalism (as in Iran, Algeria, and Egypt). All of these ideologies were "in the air" throughout the century; all of them provided the ideological basis for revolutionary mobilization at some time in the twentieth century.[7]

What distinguished times and places where ideologically inspired revolutionary mobilization became significant from times and places where the existing regime preserved stable rule was *not* the presence or absence of an alternative vision of the social order. What mattered was whether elites and popular groups *were motivated* to withdraw their assent from the existing order and to lead or join opposition movements. Existing ideologies could then be "activated" through the formation of elites and their followers into organized communities of opposition. And this in turn depended on whether the state had the capacity to fulfil its promises and commitments regarding economic development, distribution of goods and power, and conflict resolution; whether elites were satisfied or struggling with the state and other elites to preserve their position; and whether the population found sufficient security and justice in their lives, or felt so lacking in these areas that they were willing to take risks to change the *status quo*. Where growing populations consistently encountered restricted opportunities and limited state capacity (as throughout the Middle East, much of south Asia, Central America, and sub-Saharan Africa), revolutionary movements have also been consistently recurrent, even though their ideological bases show a bewildering variety of shifts in content over time.

The specific cultures and ideologies of the communities of opposition contribute much to the character, goals, and policies of revolutionary movements. Yet such communities cannot grow and be effective in the absence of material conditions that provide extensive motivation for elites and popular groups to shift their allegiance, as well as weaknesses in state capacity that provide the opportunity for the growth of an opposition.[8] Population growth can thus play a key role in providing the conditions in which ideologically motivated communities of opposition grow and achieve significance.[9]

To sum up, the most immediately threatening effects of population growth are *political*. Population growth and resource degradation in developing nations will cause demands for services and opportunities to escalate to levels that many states cannot meet, leading to debt, fiscal distress, inflation, and corruption in the government that ruins its legitimacy and effectiveness. Population growth and scarce resources will also lead to intensified elite conflicts as relative scarcities provide opportunities for a few to get rich while many lag behind. Moreover, population growth and limited resources in developing societies will often mean that the society cannot provide elite rewards to all those who believe they deserve them, leading to struggles for control of the government and economy. Population growth is further likely to expand the number of people willing to take the risk of following leaders into a fight, especially if these people are facing declining employment, rapid urban growth, and a shift toward an ever younger population. Lastly, this combination of material conditions often leads to the "activation" of ideologies of opposition, allowing ideologies which have long been present to become the focus of communities actively mobilizing in opposition to the existing regime.

PREVENTING AND MITIGATING POLITICAL CRISES

There is hardly a major arena of US foreign policy that will not be affected by the political consequences of population pressures. In the Middle East and North Africa, burgeoning populations are fueling Islamic radicalism. In Mexico, Central America, the Caribbean, and North Africa, the ill-fit between population growth and economic opportunities is producing huge streams of migrants seeking to enter the developed economies of North America and western Europe, creating increasing problems in absorbing immigrants, regulating immigration, and dealing with resulting resurgent racial conflicts. In sub-Saharan Africa, population growth, resource decline, and state decay are producing humanitarian crises that place an enormous burden on the will and means of the international community. Affecting all these areas, policies to deal with the sources and consequences of population growth may be the most comprehensive and vital element of international security in the post-Cold War world.

There are two levels of policy that are needed to deal with these problems. The first level is to offer help in dealing with the *fundamental long-term causes* of these problems: policies addressed to slowing down population growth, conserving resources, and aiding broad-based (rather than narrow, highly uneven) economic development. The second level is to offer help in dealing with the *key political effects* of population growth and resource depletion, namely, state capacity decline, elite displacement, and mass mobilization potential. A two-pronged approach involving both levels is vital. Policies addressed to the fundamental long-term causes will take years to have an impact; in the meantime, the short-term political effects of continuing population pressures need to be mitigated or the implementation of longer-term policies will fail. At the same time, policies to mitigate the political impact of population pressures *must* be accompanied by sufficient attention to reducing the long-term population and environmental pressures for conflicts, otherwise the results will be like putting out a forest fire but letting even more dry underbrush accumulate. The long-term result will be an even larger conflagration.

Thankfully, demographic research since the mid-1960s has demonstrated that population growth is relatively easy to address. It is now increasingly clear to the leaders of developing nations that the stability of their own governments and the prosperity of their societies depends on slowing the freight train of population increase.[10] Thailand and Indonesia have led the way in showing what is possible with non-coercive, voluntary family planning made available to the population. In many of the most rapidly growing countries of the world today, all that is needed to slow population growth is widespread availability of family planning clinics. Where such clinics have government support and choice is freely left to the people themselves, most families have shown a preference for smaller families than would be the case in the absence of convenient support for voluntary fertility control. Moreover, fears that cultural barriers to contraception will undermine fertility control have proven ungrounded. The largest Muslim country in the world, Indonesia, is one of the greatest success stories in fertility control, having reduced its annual population growth rate from 2.4 per cent to 1.4 percent between 1976 and 1996. Widespread adoption of voluntary contraception in Catholic Latin America and Europe, and even in Hindu and Confucian nations in Asia, point the way to what can be done. It is astonishing that only 1 percent of the international foreign aid budget goes to family planning and only slightly more to the medical support and primary education that amplify the effectiveness of family planning programs.[11] It is likely that an increase of $1 billion in making family planning assistance widely available can lead to saving hundreds of billions in dealing with military conflicts, migration, and humanitarian crises a decade or two later.[12]

Addressing environmental degradation and problems of limited and uneven development are more difficult and more contentious. Developing nations are entitled to use their resources to advance their wealth as the developed nations did on their paths to growth, and imperious efforts by developed nations to urge developing nations to stop using their forests, coal, and water are ill-received. However, the demonstration that resource degradation joined with population growth produces political instability may convince leaders in developing nations to put more emphasis on renewable and sustainable development paths. The realization that uneven development raises great political risks may increase the receptivity of leaders in developing nations to development strategies that stress broad-based development and are designed to maximize job creation and avoid severe maldistribution of incomes rather than simply to maximize GNP growth or short-term returns. It is heartening that major international aid and lending organizations have recently put a greater emphasis on such broad-based policies, for example, focusing on primary education and health-care rather than on post-secondary education and acute-care facilities in their development programs.

With population growth slowed, resources being used with greater care and efficiency, and the reach of development policies broadened to spread benefits widely, the fundamental causes of most political crises in the developing world will recede. Yet even with such efforts, population growth and its consequences will be with us for many decades as the demographic momentum developed since the 1940s plays itself out. Thus policies that mitigate those consequences will also demand attention.

In the past, much US development aid was linked to military assistance, precisely because development aid concerns have generally been linked to concerns about international security. Thus, two of the largest AID missions in recent history were those in Saigon and Iran; quite frankly neither was a great success in sustaining governments friendly to the USA. Today one of the largest US AID missions, also in part for reasons of international security, is in Cairo; one has to hope that the future of this mission will be brighter than that of its predecessors.

The failure of past security/aid missions is not really surprising, inasmuch as they were poorly designed to deal with the population-induced political conflicts described above. Military aid went into building the ambitions of the military and often ended up destabilizing the government. Too much development aid was targeted at building up small numbers of elites or building up export agriculture that actually took people off the land and concentrated wealth in fewer hands. Such policies were politically destabilizing. Vietnam and Iran were thus lost to revolutionary movements that proved hostile to the USA, hostility fueled in large part by US aid to the previous regimes. And Egypt is currently facing great difficulties; it too harbors an anti-Western opposition that has already assassinated a pro-US leader, Anwar Sadat. Moreover, while radical opposition leaders may be captured and overt violence periodically kept in check, that opposition is likely to continue to grow, for it is fueled by the frustrations of increased numbers of young underemployed Egyptians and the anger of religious and nationalist elites, all of whom feel displaced and badly served by Egypt's current economic and political institutions.

To improve the political return on foreign aid spending, it will be necessary to plan that aid with close attention to the precise pathways by which population and environmental pressures create political crises. That is, aid should be directed in ways that help mitigate state capacity decline, avoid heightening elite conflicts, and reduce mass mobilization potential. For example, current aid to governments often addresses state capacity simply by offering debt relief, credit, and/or military assistance. However, such aid often does little to improve political stability, as it does nothing to help the state secure a stable revenue base, while making the state more dependent on foreign assistance than on domestic popular and elite support.

Where political problems are already well advanced, where state capacity is low and popular mobilization potential is high, different policies are needed. In such cases, the most crucial aid should be addressed to supporting a coalition of moderate elites and thus avoiding the degeneration of elite conflicts into civil wars and revolutions. The USA's greatest success with such a policy was in the Philippines; by withdrawing support from the Marcos regime and supporting a coalition of moderate elites that had formed around Corazon Aquino, rather than supporting Marcos to the bitter end, an Iranian-style débâcle was avoided.

117

Probably the greatest failure in the US Haiti policy was the lack of invest-ment in building a coalition of moderate elites to support the Aristide government. Instead, relations between the Aristide government, which was tending in a populist, anti-elite direction, and Haiti's conservative church and business elites became polarized. As a result, Haiti's wealthy elites felt they would find greater security in a military government than in the Aristide regime, and hence tolerated (and in many cases supported) the mili-tary *coup*. Given Haiti's demographic and institutional conditions – a dense population on scarce and increasingly deforested and eroded land, and a government with weak capacities facing a largely impoverished and under-employed population – it is absolutely vital to any regime's stability that it enjoy reasonably strong elite, as well as popular, support. The forced rein-statement of the Aristide regime can lead only to greater conflicts and crises in Haiti unless a significant part of international reconstruction policies and aid is aimed at reducing elite conflicts and building broader elite support for the new regime.

More generally, the reduction of mass mobilization potential is a difficult task. Where decades of population growth and resource exploitation have constricted opportunities for productive employment, there is no easy and immediate fix. Yet much can be done by spending current aid allocations differently. One very simple measure is to increase the amount spent on primary education in the developing world as opposed to university educa-tion. Currently, typical foreign aid programs will spend about $500 per uni-versity student but only $1–2 per primary student per year in a country receiving educational assistance. Aside from the developmental aspects of these policies, the *political* effects create difficulties. Building up primary edu-cation leads to the recruitment of large numbers of school teachers. If even moderately well paid, that large number of school teachers can be the basis for a widespread regionally dispersed conservative middle class. University professors, by contrast, tend to produce radicals. But beyond that, the university professors will produce only students who also expect to have some influential position. And what developing countries need is not a large production of ambitious leaders. What they need is the type of regional grass roots leaders who can produce stable organizations and develop the lineaments of a civil society.

CONCLUSIONS

Of course, specific aid programs will have to be tailored to the needs of speci-fic countries. But to a large degree we have learned what works and what needs to be done. Attention to both the *long-term fundamental causes* and the *key political effects* of population and resource pressures in a two-pronged strategy can head off some of the worst humanitarian and international security crises of the next two decades as well as help eliminate the sources of these problems in the first half of the twenty-first century.

Much attention has been paid to the notion of "authoritarian" development and the economic advance of Asia's tigers. Yet underlying their political stability was not a particular type of regime, but a particular set of economic and development policies. In every case, declining population growth rates, fiscal stability, primary education, broad-based agrarian reform, and combined agricultural and manufacturing development lay behind their success. With aid policies designed to address both the fundamental sources and the consequences of population pressures, there is every hope that in coming decades we shall see many tigers emerging in the world and reap great gains from their stability and prosperity.

NOTES

1. Julian Simon, *The Ultimate Resource* (Princeton: Princeton University Press, 1981); Julian Simon and Herman Kahn, editors, *The Resourceful Earth: A Response to Global 2000* (Oxford: Basil Blackwell, 1984).
2. In some Asian countries (China, South Korea, Taiwan) land reforms provided new opportunities for expansion in agriculture; in other areas the "Green Revolution" and expansion of irrigated lands (e.g., the Punjab in India) accomplished the same end. But in many parts of Africa, Latin America, South Asia, and the Middle East, the expansion of population in the labor-intensive sector has led to land hunger, depressed wages, and/or massive migration to urban centers.
3. See my book *Revolution and Rebellion in the Early Modern World* (Berkeley: University of California Press, 1991) for a detailed look at this period in world history, and for a more formal version of the argument presented here.
4. See Vaclav Smil, *China's Environmental Crisis* (Armonk: M. E. Sharpe, 1993).
5. Chinese budget figures from *The Economist* (November 6, 1993), 32, (April 30, 1994), 78, and (May 21, 1994), 38. The quotation from is from Richard Hornik, "Bursting China's Bubble," pp. 28–42 in *Foreign Affairs*, volume 73 (1994), 29.
6. Valerie Percival and Thomas Homer-Dixon, "Environmental Scarcity and Violent Conflict: The Rwandan Case," Occasional Paper, Project on Environment, Population, and Security, The Peace and Conflict Studies Program, University of Toronto, and the American Association for the Advancement of Science (Washington, DC: AAAS, 1995).
7. Mansoor Moaddel, *Class, Politics, and Ideology in the Iranian Revolution* (New York: Columbia University Press, 1993).
8. See Robert Wuthnow, *Communities of Discourse: Ideology and Social Structure in the Reformation, the Enlightenment, and European Socialism* (Cambridge, MA: Harvard University Press, 1989) for illustrations of how ideological shifts depend on what he calls "communities of discourse" which in turn require material foundations and political openings to grow in the face of existing orthodoxies.
9. I borrow the term "communities of opposition" with some obvious modification from John Foran's concept of "cultures of resistance," developed in John Foran, *Fragile Resistance: Social Transformation in Iran from 1500 to the Revolution* (Boulder: Westview Press, 1993). However, I strongly prefer to speak of "communities of opposition," since "cultures" do not themselves resist any particular regime. Rather, they are adapted and combined with particular ideological elements

designed to mobilize communities against specific regimes; the term "cultures of resistance" thus risks reifying cultures and misplacing the concreteness that belongs to the human groups that make use of them.

10. Kaval Gulhati and Lisa M. Bates, "Developing Countries and the International Population Debate: Politics and Pragmatism," pp. 47–77 in Robert Cassen *et al.*, editors, *Population and Development: Old Debates, New Conclusions* (New Brunswick: Transaction, 1994), 56–58.

11. *The Economist* (May 7, 1994), 20.

12. These deficiencies in international family planning assistance, and the primacy of family planning as a matter of free choice and education of and by women, have recently been recognized by the United Nations Conference on Population and Development (Cairo, 1995).

Part II

RE-CENTERING CULTURE
AND AGENCY

5

REVOLUTION IN THE REAL WORLD

Bringing agency back in

Eric Selbin

In 1958, at a critical juncture in the struggle of the Cuban revolutionaries for political power, Fidel Castro made a consequential decision. In one of the most important military and psychological campaigns of the revolution, Castro paired his most charismatic lieutenants and sent Ché Guevara and Camilo Cienfuegos out to replicate the famous "incendiary" march of the Cuban War of Independence when national heroes Antonio Maceo and General Máximo Gómez lit up the sugar cane fields. This exploit was hugely successful, consciously evoking the link with Cuba's struggle for independence from Spain and capturing the popular imagination. Moreover, the ability of Guevara and Cienfuegos to rally the population to the revolutionary cause, along with their military skill, became important elements in Cuban revolutionary mythology as well as a component in the enshrinement of both Guevara and Cienfuegos as national heroes.

Symbolic politics, collective memory, and the social context of politics – all profoundly voluntaristic constructions – are central to understanding and exploring revolutionary processes. What I want to propose here is that ideas and actors, not structures and some broad sweep of history, are the primary forces in revolutionary processes. Revolutions are human creations – with all the messiness inherent in such a claim – rather than inevitable natural processes. The focus, therefore, needs to be on people, not structures; choices, not determinism; and the transformation of society, not simply transitions.

With apologies to Thomas Jefferson, it would appear that the tree of theory must be refreshed from time to time with at least the words of those committed to agency and structure.[1] While the patriots and tyrants may not be clear in this context, the saliency of Margaret Archer's claim is: "the problem of structure and agency has rightly come to be seen as the basic issue in modern social theory."[2] Certainly recent discussions and debates among scholars of revolution suggest that the issue remains alive and well.

Forrest Colburn and I have called for the return of people and their ideas to a place of prominence in understanding and exploring revolutionary

123

processes.[3] Some of the leading young figures in the field, such as John Foran, Jack Goldstone, Jeff Goodwin, and Timothy Wickham-Crowley, have cast their nets somewhat wider, calling for increased attention to the role of culture as at least a variable in the mix of factors.[4] All of us have sought to varying degrees to wrestle with the paradox of agents and structures and their role and utility in theorizing about revolutions.

Since 1979 theorizing has been dominated by Theda Skocpol's brilliant, paradigmatic statement in *States and Social Revolutions*,[5] which has led perhaps unfairly to her consignment to the whipping post as some sort of unrepentant, unapologetic structuralist.[6] None the less, her memorable invocation of Wendell Phillips's declaration that "revolutions are not made; they come" stands as the *sine qua non* structuralist position.[7] A structuralist perspective, according to Skocpol, stresses "objective relationships and conflicts among variously situated groups and nations, rather than the interests, outlooks, or ideologies of particular actors in revolution."[8] People's responses to structural conditions are construed as irrelevant and those who make the revolution are conspicuous by their absence. The failure to include the efforts and intentions of people assumes that structural conditions dictate absolutely what people can do.

The fourth-generation scholars of revolution mentioned above have moved beyond the smothering structuralism of the third generation.[9] Meaningful places for agents and the impact of culture have crept into the discussion and been treated by and large as having a legitimate place at the table, although the place traditionally reserved for children – seen and not heard unless politely asking for someone to pass the platter. Most of these scholars remain profoundly in the thrall of structuralist perspectives; the small place made for agents and culture needs to be expanded.

In Chapter 2 in this volume, Wickham-Crowley assures us that "structural-processual theories will continue to be, far and away, the best available guides" and concludes that "structural theories are here to stay, and their analytical points, far from being blunted by the critics, will probably extend ever more deeply into the postrevolutionary milieu."[10] But, as I suspect Wickham-Crowley would agree, we are not well served by "one-sided structuralism" but rather, as Susanne Jonas argues, by analyses that view "political, cultural, and subjective factors as more than simple 'reflections' of the material or economic base." "Human actors," she continues, "are not simply 'carriers of structures' but also 'generators of them'." A "dialectical and interactive approach" allows us to explore and understand actors who "are real men and women, in particular historical situations."[11]

I believe that it is possible to construct sophisticated and substantively grounded theories that recognize the power and importance of people *and* structures; the utility gained by holding these analytically distinct pales next to the violence done to reality. The cases with which I am most familiar, the modern Latin American revolutions, have been typified by profoundly multi-class alliances and high degrees of voluntarism: the conscious choices and intentional actions of people have played clearly critical roles throughout the revolutionary processes. The structuralist tendency to omit people and their choices serves us poorly in our efforts to be theoretically sophisticated and substantively grounded.

THE BRIEF FOR AGENCY AND CULTURE

The legacy of revolutionary activity in Latin America and the Caribbean is most commonly symbolized by places, dates, and, above all by heroes: Túpac Amaru, Toussaint L'Ouverture, Jóse Martí, Zapata, Mariátegui, Sandino, Farabundo Martí, Prestes, and "Ché." From the first defiance against the Spanish conquerors, subsequent generations of revolutionaries have sought to enable and ennoble their efforts by invoking these figures and the concomitant ideals that they and their struggles purportedly represent; conversely, populations have sought to identify and understand their struggles through the mythos generated around these figures. The cult of the heroic revolutionary has produced in many places a popular political culture of resistance, rebellion, and revolution.

The proposition here is that a crucial component of the revolutionary potential in any population is an understanding of the population's perception of the options that are available and seem plausible to them; these options constitute "repertoires of collective action" and/or a "'tool-kit' of symbols, stories, rituals and world-views," which provides actors with resources necessary for constructing "strategies of action" for dealing with their society.[12] In societies where revolution is considered a viable response to oppression – due to a long-standing history of rebellious activities being celebrated in folk culture or to revolutionary leaders having created, restored, or magnified such traditions in the local culture or some combination of these – revolutionary activities are more likely to be undertaken, more likely to receive broad popular support, and more likely to conclude successfully when such traditions are invoked.

The complaints of most fourth-generation scholars with regard to bringing people and culture back in are simple: Goodwin and Emirbayer contend that "it remains very far from clear how this might actually be done without lapsing into idealistic, voluntaristic, or simply ad-hoc forms of explanation."[13] Echoing this last concern, Wickham-Crowley counsels that "nation-specific 'cultural' views of each revolution . . . will almost surely never surmount their fundamental problem, that $n = 1$."[14] Goldstone, the most sympathetic of this trio, asks for "more detailed suggestions for *how* to integrate culture into the analysis of 'revolutions'."[15]

In what follows, I shall undertake to make a case that it is imperative that agents and the world they manufacture, the culture they create, be included in any serious analysis of revolution. Some of the nuances and subtleties will be missed, sacrificed to the constraints of space; I apologize in advance. Primarily what I shall seek to do here is advance an argument that we must remedy the failure to appreciate and account for both the conscious choices and intentional actions of people, who play identifiable and clearly critical roles across the revolutionary process, as well as for the often remarkable verve and creativity with which revolutionaries struggle for power and when successful attempt to create new societies.

Agency: ideas, ideals, and learning

People's thoughts and actions – even if haphazard or spontaneous[16] – are the mediating link between structural conditions and social outcomes. Structural conditions, moreover, do not unconditionally dictate what people do; instead, they place certain limits on people's actions or demarcate a certain range of possibilities. Within the revolutionary process, there is more than one path and more than one potential outcome. Structural conditions may define the possibilities for revolutionary insurrections or the options available after political power has been seized, but they do not explain how specific groups or individuals act, what options they pursue, or what possibilities they may realize. The question is where and how people enter the revolutionary process.

There are two places in which the critical role of individuals is discernible in the revolutionary process. Leaders play a unique role in the social revolution, organizing the population and, perhaps most importantly, articulating the vision – the ideas and ideals – around which they rally. The population, in turn, responds to these entreaties or not; if they do, it is they who determine how far and how fast the process unfolds and often shape the efforts of the leaders to their reality. We need fundamentally to refocus the discussion of profound change or transformation on the power and possibility of individuals to control their destiny.

Social revolutionary leaders invoke, manipulate, and build on timeless conceptions to arouse and mobilize the population. The ideals of justice, liberty, equality, democracy, opportunity, and freedom (from fear, from hunger, from disease; of assembly, of speech, of religion) remain powerful and compelling in a world where many people's daily lives reflect none of these. Aware of the dangers, some people none the less chose to struggle to transform their world. Revolutionary ideals become the talisman or the touchstone which carries the revolutionaries and the population through the arduous struggle.[17]

Idea streams – transmitted via people – are powerful and pervasive and travel across time and space. People learn, taking into account past experiences and factoring in new information. While it would be disingenuous to suggest that social revolutions somehow constitute an unbroken process, it is evident that modern revolutionaries have to some degree imitated the "classic" revolutions of France, Russia, Mexico, and China. There are also strong historical and contemporary connections among the modern revolutions. Both types of connections are discernible in the modern Latin American revolutions.

The Cuban revolutionaries drew on a wide array of sources, including their own struggle for independence, Mexico, Sandino in Nicaragua, the incomplete revolution in Bolivia, even the destruction of democracy in Spain (1936–39) and Guatemala (1954). Alberto Bayo, a loyalist Spanish Air Force officer forced into exile after the destruction of the Spanish Republic in 1939 by the fascist forces, hooked up with and trained surviving Sandinistas in Costa Rica who sailed against Papa Somoza in 1948. Bayo subsequently trained Castro's Cuban exiles in Mexico, where his "star" student was Ché Guevara. In Cuba, Bayo and Guevara helped train a new generation of Nicaraguan exiles, passing on to them lessons from Spain, Sandino, Guevara's 1954 experiences watching the destruction of democracy in Guatemala, and the ill-fated Caribbean Legion (a collection of progressive fighters in the region).[18] The connections are across time and within time, across cultural boundaries and within them.

The Nicaraguan revolutionaries were inspired and influenced by Mexico, their own past, and the Cubans. The Grenadians drew on the Eastern Caribbean's anti-colonial and socialist legacy, the Cubans, the contemporaneous Nicaraguan revolution, and the various socialist experiments in Guyana, Jamaica, and Suriname. And connections were not solely limited to the continent. Iran's leftist guerrilla movements, inspired in part by the Cuban revolution and the writings of Ché Guevara, had been battling the Shah since 1963 and played a decisive role in the 1979 victory of the Iranian Revolution.[19] Although Iran's secular leftist groups were brutally repressed by the Ayatollah Khomeini and driven underground by 1981,[20] in the spring and summer of 1979 one of the most popular items in Teheran were Ché T-shirts.[21] Across and within time, across and within cultural boundaries.

Culture: stories of resistance and rebellion

Traditionally, history has been constructed from above, composed by the victorious, orchestrated by the powerful, played for the population. There is another history, rooted in people's perception of how the world around them has and continues to unfold and their place in that process. This is a history informed by people's ideology and which reflects the context – material as well as ideological – of people's everyday lives; a history revealed and articulated by the various instruments of popular political culture.

The supposition here is that this history is accessible to us in people's narratives of their lives and the popular political culture of their society, and that these create the possibility – or lack thereof – for fundamental change. The proposition is that through in-depth interviewing and the collection of instruments of popular culture – folk tales, songs, plays, etc. – it may be possible to

127

ascertain the extent to which high-profile collective action, specifically rebellion or revolution, is possible, perhaps even probable in any given society.[22]

It seems simultaneously risky and trite to invoke culture. Risky thanks to the rather sordid legacy of "cultural explanations" which once and, on occasion, continue to besmirch the social sciences: stolid Brits, hot-blooded Latins, obedient and efficient Germans, indolent Italians, breezy "Americans," mysterious Asians, and so on. Such gross and racist generalizations did little to advance either social science or humanity. Trite because any number of scholars have directly or indirectly recognized the importance and utility of culture in the study of a wide array of issues, including those that fall within the social sciences. There are sightings aplenty among students of revolution and popular collective action.

None the less, "culture" poses a problem, not least with the word itself, a wildly imprecise term that in its promiscuity veers dangerously close to losing any utility at all. In an effort to surmount such problems, I start with a fairly traditional notion of culture and seek to expand it by invoking the power and depth of collective memory and the potency and prominence of symbols. These are drawn together by the now familiar demand that a focus on individuals is critical in our efforts to understand revolutionary processes.

How much did the Cuban revolutionaries" ability to invoke Martí and his vision figure in their success? Did the Bolivians" unwillingness to evoke a revolutionary or even rebellious tradition serve to derail the revolutionary process? There seems little question that in Nicaragua the revolutionaries" use of the figure and persona of Sandino was central to their success. Might a similar culture of resistance and rebellion have made a difference for the Grenadians? How were/are the efforts of Salvadoran, Peruvian, and, most recently, Mexican revolutionaries affected by their ability to invoke, evoke, and manipulate the legacies of Farabundo Martí, Mariátegui and Amaru, and Zapata, respectively?

Culture alone is not enough. The ability of revolutionaries, specifically revolutionary leaders, to conjure a context in which such traditions play out – are summoned, manipulated, rewritten – is often significant. Yet the population is not passive, waiting to be acted upon. While the revolutionaries may provide an impetus and may present the population with a vocabulary or intellectual framework that helps organize and channel their visions, revolutionary leaders can go no farther than the population is prepared for them to go. People have their context, independent of the desires of the revolutionaries.

The means by which we can gain access to such stories is primarily through narrative. There is, apparently,

> an old Andean tradition, specifically female, which conceives of history as a woven cloth; it consists in recognizing the warp and weft, the texture, the forms of relationships, in knowing the back from the front,

the value and significance of the detailed pattern, and so on. In other words, we are trying to read in the book of life that which has never been recorded in written form; we are attempting to capture the image brought to mind and revealed in the moment of the interview before it is lost again to silence.[23]

The scattered shards and remnants are out there for us to gather.

Finding a balance between the important and powerful information that a cultural perspective can provide us with and the powerful and compelling picture provided us by structural perspectives seems crucial. Those of us labeled as advocates of a more culturally oriented position have an obligation to match the rigorous and sophisticated methods of our more structuralist colleagues; they might do well to recognize that in their concern with independent and dependent variables they too often omit critical elements of the story. A surprising number of people under an array of circumstances have left the private space of their homes and fought in public space for public goods in pursuit of private desires. How and why they cross that threshold from the inside to the outside in an effort to transform their world remains the central puzzle for us all.

The marriage of agency and culture: the social context of politics

In Chapter 8 in this volume, Foran asks what the precise mechanisms of cultural influence on revolutionary processes are and how we might marry increased roles for agency and culture with previous insights on structure and political economy. His answers involve "the concept of 'political cultures of resistance and opposition' . . . and how these interact with the social forces that make revolutions."[24] While I share Wickham-Crowley's concern that culture may be "too multifarious" for our purposes, I concur with Foran's prescription.[25]

Students of revolution need to take seriously the notion that theories of revolution are rooted in and driven by a focus on individuals and the culture that they create and transmit. This occurs through the mechanisms of collective memory, symbolic politics, and the social context of politics they create. While any good theory must blend elements of agents and structures, the contention here is that without people articulating compelling stories with engaging and empowering plots, revolutions will not come.

Culture denotes "a system of shared meanings, attitudes, and values and the symbolic forms (performances, artifacts) in which they are expressed or embodied;" in this sense, "culture . . . is part of a total way of life but not identical with it,"[26] a place where simultaneously life is justified and explained and where the possibility of changing that life is raised. The capacity of people to create, enshrine, manipulate, and discard symbols is central to the conception of culture. Those symbols which can integrate the past, present, and future into a coherent view of the world, into one usable myth with near universal overtones, are of particular importance and power. Those in power endeavor to invoke/create symbols which will maintain their status; those arrayed against them seek to use symbols – sometimes the very same symbols – to overturn them. Thus popular culture, beliefs and practices held by a wide array of those in any given society, becomes a battleground.

The term popular culture has long been used to denote unofficial culture, "mass" culture, and usually to denigrate that which was not considered "high culture." More recently the term has become almost as omnipresent as "culture" and generally refers to

> folk beliefs, practices and objects rooted in local traditions, and mass beliefs, practices and objects generated in political and commercial centers. It includes elite cultural forms that have been popularized as well as popular forms that have been elevated to museum tradition.[27]

Here then we may find many of the symbols which help define any given society and the various places of the people within. Contention and confrontation over these symbols is intense and the ramifications and implications profound. The material and ideological conditions of people's everyday lives lead inexorably to issues of power and choice and their attendant interplay. Political culture, at least in theory, should offer us access to that world.

Political culture remains unfortunately associated with the modernization theorists of the 1960s for whom it denoted the abstract values, beliefs, and emotions that a population holds towards politics.[28] While there is nothing inherently problematic in this conceptualization, in practice attention was largely devoted to the salutary place of "civic culture" and its seemingly "natural" support for the sustenance of liberal democracy. Furthermore, this perspective was profoundly structural in character; people were accorded no role in creating their society but rather were captive to and the creatures of institutions and structures beyond their control.

Perhaps the most notable response to this has been that of the "interpretivists," for whom political culture is embedded in human beings and therefore in their practices; as a result, we can describe and seek to map the context from which this political culture emerges.[29] This conception of political culture refers to a collective memory which often resists the dominant discourse and allows itself to be spoken only in the act of narration – it charges life everyday with symbolic meaning.

Collective memory and symbolic politics

Remembering serves a multitude of functions; primarily it places the past in the service of the present; as the maxim has it, those who control the past control the present. The implication is clear: there is a societal memory which is up for grabs, a battlefield where various groups struggle to protect and extend their interpretations of a society's past.

Most resistance movements conceive of and understand their struggles as continuing some long process of struggle that many societies hold in their collective memory. Such collective memory is usually long on the grand and glorious but often features the implicit and the informal as well; this "shared memory" includes the "origins, purpose, development, and group life."[30] Similar to ideology, collective memory gives shape to people's lives, providing not only a base from which individuals can look back and explain their experiences and actions, but also a platform on which to build and guide the future. Revolutionaries, historically, have recognized the need to tap into and build on popular expressions of this collective memory.

How do societies remember? "What are 'the channels and repositories of memory'?"[31] Collective memory, Jelin suggests, "is the part of history that can be integrated into a current value system; the rest is ignored, forgotten, although at times it may be reclaimed and remembered."[32] Jelin's analysis is compelling but incomplete; reclamation and remembering do not occur "at times." People's history, captured in their memories, runs constantly in the background, always available.

As a result, the past is continually rewritten, often to fit the exigencies of the present. This is especially the case when "current reality" makes people "think harder about their role in shaping that process."[33] This process may not be entirely intentional, since the past is not conveniently organized "like a filing cabinet or library, where events or facts are recalled in toto."[34] Intentionality is evident, however, in the degree to which people use memory "to explain themselves, justify themselves, and to give legitimacy to the current order, or to contest it."[35] The result is that "the historical present is constructed by subjects in dispute about the meaning of history and the contents of tradition and values," a dispute that centers largely on individual and collective memories.[36]

And when those individual memories are shared, perhaps quietly in the evenings, perhaps more openly in songs or skits, together those individual memories form a collective memory, a shared history. This history is "a reservoir where glimpses of freedom, and the remembrance of atrocities and triumphs are all preserved."[37] Such a "reservoir" need not be "reclaimed and remembered;" it is, rather, in use or on tap, waiting to be drawn upon. These reservoirs are not the province of any one individual; rather, human repositories contribute to a collective maintenance of knowledge.[38]

The importance of symbolic politics has been ignored for too long in the study of revolution; as I note elsewhere, revolutionary thinkers have all discussed at length the complex but critical process whereby the revolutionaries must gain the support of the people, that is, to win their hearts and minds.[39] In 1995 Alison Brysk provided a wonderful and compelling reintroduction to the power and persuasiveness of symbolic politics.[40] Noting that dominant "models of collective action slight this ancient, universal source of social change," she invokes "a renewed consideration of the subjective influences of ideas, learning, and information as sources of political change."[41] Perhaps most importantly for our purposes, Brysk claims that "symbolically mobilized political actors can create new political opportunities by revealing, challenging, and changing narratives about interests and identities."[42] The concept of symbolic politics thus "expands the treatment of change offered by 'political culture' . . . suggest[ing] several channels for the transformation of beliefs into behavior."[43] In her very persuasive effort at "bringing meaning back in,"[44] Brysk brings us to popular political culture.

Where symbolic politics and collective memory meet and create the social context of politics is in the popular political culture. Popular political culture represents "the historically created idioms and symbols which shape the capacity of actors to construct revolutionary ideologies and build revolutionary movements . . . political culture *is* the product of human beings – i.e., it is a historical legacy of previous human actions."[45] This is where we seek the population's perception of the options that are available and seem plausible to them.

This is not meant to imply highly rational actors whose economistic calculations lead them to consider culture as simply one more resource to be mobilized. Rather Swidler's "tool-kit" is like Rudé's "inherent" ideology, "a sort of 'mother's milk' ideology based on direct experience, oral tradition or folk-memory and not learned by listening to sermons or reading books."[46] In those societies where resistance, rebellion, and revolution are part of the popular political culture, revolutionary activities are more likely to be undertaken.

Popular political culture may be accessed by turning to popular attitudes, a belief system less formal and less rigid than that denoted by the term "ideology." Neither wholly independent sets of ideas nor sets of justifications dependent on the exigencies of political power, popular attitudes form the loosely knit world-view that each person brings to bear on the events and processes around her. Such attitudes, composed of a myriad of factors, are best understood as the ways in which people wed the practical political ideology with which they judge events and their practical knowledge about how their lives operate day-to-day.[47] Central to these popular attitudes are people's cognizance and interpretation of their own history and the stories they tell themselves and each other about that history. Symbolic politics, collective memory, and the social context of politics provide us with the tools.

CONCLUSIONS

The historical world, that is, the world's past as we understand it, is fundamentally the world of human action. Structures have their place. Few subscribe wholeheartedly to one extreme or the other anymore in the debate over the relative weight and dialectical relationship between individual and collective will as opposed to historical circumstances in determining the outcome of a given event or process. Structuralism and agency may each, in particular circumstances, be significant; the scope for human action depends on historically specific conditions. People's actions clearly confront certain limits that structures engender; often structures demarcate a certain range of possibilities. But structures do not unconditionally dictate what people do. The interplay of circumstance and action – neither of which can exist without the other – creates human history; options are considered, choices are made, paths are pursued. Meaningful explorations and satisfactory answers lie with those theories which can take agents and structures, both with meaningful roles, into account.

Assessing the degree to which traditions of revolutionary activity and struggle broaden the array of possibilities that oppressed citizens view as accessible to them is a larger project which remains to be undertaken. The focus needs to be on what options populations consider available to them when they seek redress of their grievances and to what extent popular political culture and its instruments serve to keep alive and glorify people and processes which can serve as latent forms of empowerment, memories waiting to be animated either by popular leaders or by the population themselves. Such a project would endeavor to map out the ways in which the populations of a variety of countries have told and retold their history with specific reference to rebellion and revolution and the impact these acts have had on the possibilities for and occurrence of such phenomena in the respective countries.

Foran has argued that it was critical to better integrate "understandings of how culture . . . becomes effective in the causation, course, and outcomes of social revolutions . . . [and] the whole issue of agency . . . who makes revolutions and why."[48] The key here is accepting the mutually reinforcing arguments of Goldstone and Tilly with regard to analyzing revolution: the former has argued that "analyzing revolutions does not depend on identifying a particular fixed characteristic set of causes – there is none. Instead, analyzing revolutions depends on understanding the process of revolution and being able to track its trajectory in diverse cases;"[49] the latter has maintained that we must "break revolutions into components . . . which [are] theoretically coherent, then construct separate theories of those components."[50] People are part of that trajectory; culture is a key component.

With great respect, I would turn around Wickham-Crowley's challenge that cultural analyses are "unlikely ever to rival structural theories in explaining one particular type of variable: did a social revolution occur here or not?"[51] The contention here is that structural theories alone will never allow us to ascertain whether a social revolution occurred in any particular instance. We must, to echo George Homans's plea, bring people back in.[52] It is time to turn around Phillips's statement: revolutions do not come, they are made.

ERIC SELBIN

ACKNOWLEDGEMENTS

A much longer and rougher version of this was first presented at the 1995 meeting of the Latin American Studies Association and was influenced by the insights and arguments of Helen Cordes, Margaret Dorsey, Jennifer Mathews, Meredith McKittrick, Robert Snyder, and Jenny Suchland and benefitted from conversations with Steve Davidson, Jan Dawson, Florence Gould, Kathryn Hochstetler, James Mahoney, Gwen Kennedy Neville, Wendy Rahn, Katherine Roberts-Hite, Shannon Winnubst, and the students in my Spring 1995 class on the Politics of Latin America and the Caribbean. This brief essay was additionally shaped by the responses of Jeff Goodwin, Cynthia McClintock, and particularly Timothy Wickham-Crowley, who were on that LASA panel. I am indebted to John Foran for seeking out this contribution and encouraging me to develop this argument. None of these generous people, obviously, are responsible for any of the flaws and some of them disagree rather strongly with its contentions; I am most appreciative of their time and energy.

NOTES

1. In 1787 Jefferson wrote to William Stevens Smith: "What country before ever existed a century and a half without a rebellion?. . . The tree of liberty must be refreshed from time to time with the blood of patriots and tyrants. It is its natural manure."
2. Margaret Archer, *Culture and Agency: The Place of Culture in Social Theory* (Cambridge: Cambridge University Press, 1988), ix.
3. Forrest Colburn, *The Vogue of Revolution in Poor Countries* (Princeton: Princeton University Press, 1994); Eric Selbin, *Modern Latin American Revolutions* (Boulder: Westview Press, 1993).
4. See, e.g., John Foran, "Revolutionizing Theory/Theorizing Revolutions: State, Culture, and Society in Recent Works on Revolution," pp. 112–35 in Nikki Keddie, editor, *Debating Revolutions* (New York: New York University Press, 1995); Jack Goldstone, *Revolution and Rebellion in the Early Modern World* (Berkeley: University of California Press, 1991); Jeff Goodwin, *State and Revolution in the Cold War Era* (1997); and Timothy Wickham-Crowley, *Guerrillas and Revolution in Latin America: A Comparative Study of Insurgents and Regimes Since 1956* (Princeton: Princeton University Press, 1992). Other calls are now collected in *Debating Revolutions*.
5. Theda Skocpol, *States and Social Revolutions: A Comparative Analysis of France, Russia, and China* (Cambridge: Cambridge University Press, 1979).
6. A charge she responds to in the conclusion of *Social Revolution in the Modern World* (Cambridge: Cambridge University Press, 1994).
7. Skocpol, *States and Social Revolutions*, 17.
8. Ibid., 291.
9. The designation of a potential "fourth generation" is from John Foran, "Theories of Revolution Revisited: Toward a Fourth Generation," pp. 1–20 in *Sociological Theory*, volume 11, number 1 (March 1993). This builds on Jack Goldstone's insightful "Theories of Revolution: The Third Generation," pp. 425–53 in *World Politics*, volume 32, number 3 (April 1980).
10. Timothy Wickham-Crowley, "Structural Theories of Revolution," Chapter 2 in the present volume.

11. Susanne Jonas, *The Battle for Guatemala: Rebels, Death Squads, and US Power* (Boulder: Westview Press, 1991), 4.
12. Respectively, Charles Tilly, *From Mobilization to Revolution* (Reading, MA.: Addison-Wesley, 1978), 143; and Ann Swidler, "Culture in Action: Symbols and Strategies," pp. 273–86 in *American Sociological Review*, volume 51, number 2 (April 1986), 273.
13. Jeff Goodwin and Mustafa Emirbayer, "Symbols, Positions, Objects: Toward a New Theory of Revolutions and Collective Action," Working Paper No. 223 (New York: New School for Social Research Center for Studies of Social Change, 1995), 2.
14. Wickham-Crowley, "Structural Theories of Revolution."
15. Jack Goldstone, "Analyzing Revolutions and Rebellions: A Reply to Critics," pp. 178–99 in *Debating Revolutions*, 195.
16. I concur with Wickham-Crowley's counsel that scholars be wary of our "claims of privileged perception" in such assessments and chary about the invocation of hegemony "and its theoretical cousins 'false consciousness' and 'consciousness-raising'." Timothy Wickham-Crowley, "Discussion," Washington, DC: Latin American Studies Association, 1995, 3.
17. In practice many of these ideals may be betrayed once political victory has been achieved. Historically, the achievement of political victory has not been sufficient to guarantee that the visions of the revolutionaries or the population – which are not necessarily, may rarely be, the same – will be realized. None the less, slogans predicated on trust, opportunity, and a vision of the future abound.
18. Donald Hodges, *Intellectual Foundations of the Nicaraguan Revolution* (Austin: University of Texas Press, 1986), 167–72. See also the introduction to Bayo's classic *150 Questions for a Guerilla Fighter* (Boulder: Paladin, 1963).
19. Ervand Abrahamian, "The Guerrilla Movement in Iran, 1963-1977," in Haleh Afshar, editor, *Iran: Revolution in Turmoil* (Albany: State University of New York Press, 1985), 152.
20. Valentine Moghadam, "The Left and the Revolution in Iran: A Critical Analysis," pp. 23–40 in Hooshang Amirahmadi and Manoucher Parvin, editors, *Post-Revolutionary Iran* (Boulder: Westview Press, 1988), 24.
21. Amir Taheri, *The Spirit of Allah: Khomeini and the Iranian Revolution* (Bethesda: Adler & Adler, 1986), 254.
22. Debates over the "predictability" of revolutions can be found in *Debating Revolution* and the "Symposium on Prediction in the Social Sciences," pp. 1520–626 in *American Journal of Sociology*, volume 100, number 6 (May 1995).
23. Andean Oral History Workshop (THOA)/Silvia Rivera Cusicanqui, "Indigenous Women and Community Resistance: History and Memory," pp. 151–83 in Elizabeth Jelin, editor, *Woman and Social Change in Latin America* (London: Zed, 1990), 180.
24. John Foran, "Discourses and Social Forces," Chapter 8 in this volume.
25. Timothy Wickham-Crowley, "States and Societies in Revolution: Two Steps Forward, Perhaps One Step Back?" pp. 777–83 in *Theory and Society*, volume 23, number 6 (1994), 781. Wickham-Crowley's influential *Guerrillas and Revolution in Latin America* does support the concept of "rebellious cultures."
26. Peter Burke, *Popular Culture in Early Modern Europe* (New York: Harper & Row, 1978), 1.
27. Chandra Mukerji and Michael Schudson, "Introduction: Rethinking Popular Culture," pp. 1–61 in Chandra Mukerji and Michael Schudson, editors, *Rethinking Popular Culture: Contemporary Perspectives in Cultural Studies* (Berkeley: University of California Press, 1991), 3–4.

28. Classic statements of this position are found in Gabriel Almond and Sidney Verba, *The Civic Culture* (Princeton: Princeton University Press, 1963) and Lucian Pye and Sidney Verba, editors, *Political Culture and Political Development* (Princeton: Princeton University Press, 1965).
29. Probably best represented by Clifford Geertz's classic "Thick Description: Toward an Interpretive Theory of Culture," pp. 3–30 in *The Interpretation of Cultures* (New York: Basic Books, 1973), 14.
30. Tracy K'Meyer, "Shared Memory in Community," paper presented at the International Oral History Conference, Columbia University (October 1994).
31. Elizabeth Jelin, "The Politics of Memory: The Human Rights Movement and the Construction of Democracy in Argentina," pp. 38–58 in *Latin American Perspectives*, volume 21, number 2 (Spring 1994), 50.
32. Ibid.
33. Jeffery Gould, *To Lead As Equals: Rural Protest and Political Consciousness in Chinandega, Nicaragua, 1912–1979* (Chapel Hill: University of North Carolina Press, 1990), 10.
34. Christopher Kaplonski, "Collective Memory and Chingunjav's Rebellion," pp. 235–59 in *History and Anthropology*, volume 6, numbers 2–3 (1993), 236.
35. Ibid.
36. Jelin, "The Politics of Memory," 50.
37. D. Watson, "Can *Memory* Survive the *Storm*?" pp. 14–16 in *New Internationalist*, number 247 (September 1993), 15.
38. Rob Smith, "Simultaneity and Identity: The Imagining, Making, and Politics of a Transnational Mexicano Migrant Community Between the United States and Mexico," paper presented at the International Conference on Oral History, Columbia University (October 20, 1994).
39. Selbin, *Modern Latin American Revolutions*, 35. See 164 note 2 for a brief discussion of the origin of this phrase and its appropriateness to revolutionary situations.
40. Alison Brysk, "'Hearts and Minds:' Bringing Symbolic Politics Back In," pp. 559–85 in *Polity*, volume 27, number 4 (Summer 1995).
41. Ibid., 560.
42. Ibid., 561.
43. Ibid., 562–3.
44. Ibid., 570.
45. James Mahoney, "Social Structure and Political Culture in the Explanation of Third World Social Revolutions: Iran and Cuba Compared," unpublished paper, Department of Political Science, Berkeley (1993), 9.
46. George Rudé, *Ideology and Popular Protest* (New York: Pantheon, 1980), 28.
47. "Practical political ideology" is from Harry Vanden, "Ideology of the Nicaraguan Revolution," pp. 25–39 in *Monthly Review*, volume 34, number 2 (1982); "practical knowledge" is from Geertz, *The Interpretation of Cultures*.
48. Foran, "Revolutionizing Theory/Theorizing Revolutions," *Debating Revolutions*, 133.
49. Jack Goldstone, "Predicting Revolutions: Why We Could (and Should) Have Foreseen the Revolutions of 1989–1991 in the U.S.S.R. and Eastern Europe," pp. 39–64 in *Debating Revolutions*, 45–6.
50. Charles Tilly, "In Search of Revolution," pp. 799–803 in *Theory and Society*, volume 23, number 6 (1994), 802.
51. Wickham-Crowley, "States and Societies in Revolution," 781.
52. George Homans, "Bringing Men [*sic*] Back In," pp. 809–18 in *American Sociological Review*, volume 29, number 5 (December 1964). I thank Tim Wickham-Crowley for introducing me to this piece.

6

GENDER AND REVOLUTIONS

Valentine M. Moghadam

The scholarship on revolution is prodigious and rich, but it is deficient in incorporating gender into the analysis. The study of revolution has not yet considered systematically the prominent position assumed by gender issues in the discourse of revolutionaries and the laws of revolutionary states. In the sociology of revolution, gender, unlike class or the state or the world-system, is not seen as a constitutive category.

In contrast, feminist scholarship has been attentive to the theme of women and revolution. Feminists have produced prolific research into the role and position of women in revolutionary France, Russia, China, Vietnam, Cuba, Algeria, Nicaragua, Iran, and elsewhere.[1] This body of literature strongly suggests that gender relations constitute an important part of the culture, ideology, and politics of revolutionary societies. Some scholars of the French Revolution have examined how gender was constructed in the political discourse and discovered the legal disempowerment and exclusion of women based on the "natural fact" of sexual difference. Siân Reynolds makes the interesting point that the participation of women as mothers and food distributors has a profoundly legitimizing effect on a revolution – at least in its early stages.[2] Mary Ann Tétreault observes that all twentieth-century revolutionaries retain or recreate private space and family forms.[3] Hanna Papanek maintains that the construction of the "ideal society" entails a notion of the "ideal woman."[4] In a previous essay I have classified revolutions in terms of gender outcomes: one group of revolutions is modernizing and egalitarian, with women's emancipation an explicit goal; another group is patriarchal, tying women to the family and stressing gender differences rather than equality.[5] Certainly revolutionary states expend considerable effort legislating the social positions of women, revising family law, and defining the prerogatives of men.

In this chapter I hope to show not only that women – like men – have been active participants in revolutionary movements, but also that revolutions have a gender dimension that must be taken into account in analyses of their causes, courses, and outcomes. Gender is an integral part of the social structure, a basic element of production and reproduction, and a central

137

feature of concepts of the ideal society and of national identity. For these reasons, gender affects and is affected by revolutionary processes in profound ways, as the empirical sections in this chapter will show. I shall further try to show that since the French Revolution, and especially during the twentieth century, revolutions have evinced either patriarchal or emancipatory agendas for women. Outcomes for women seem to be determined by the explicit ideology, goals, and social program of the revolution, by the nature of pre-existing gender relations, and by the scope of women's involvement in the revolutionary movement.

EN-GENDERING REVOLUTION

What is a revolution, and in what way is it gendered? The major theories of revolution have linked revolution to the dynamics and contradictions of modernization (including population change and other demographic factors) and to struggles over configurations of state power, from the French Revolution of 1789 to the Eastern European Revolutions of 1989. Social scientists have disagreed about whether revolutions are purposive or structural in nature: are they "made" or do they "come about"? There is also disagreement as to their dominant causal features: are these political, social, economic, cultural, or a combination? John Dunn's definition includes the purposive and violent dimensions of revolution: revolutions are "a form of massive, violent, and rapid social change."[6] They are also attempts to embody a set of values in a new or at least renovated social order. Perez Zagorin includes the ideational in his definition:

> A revolution is an attempt by subordinate groups through the use of violence to bring about (1) a change of government or its policy, (2) a change of regime, or (3) a change of society, whether this attempt is justified by reference to past conditions or to an as yet unattained future ideal.[7]

Few studies focus on culture or ideology, although Lynn Hunt is a notable exception, and the Iranian Revolution sparked a number of studies that emphasize these factors principally by Iranian scholars (such as Farideh Farhi and Mansoor Moaddel).[8] There is growing agreement among scholars that revolutions should be studied in terms of the interaction of economic, political, and cultural developments within national, regional, and global contexts.[9]

What do revolutions have in common? In all revolutions, the explicit goal is thorough upheaval of the previous system and its replacement by a new system. In general, revolutionaries have some idea, if not a detailed program or blueprint, of what they mean the new society to look like. The basic premise is that it should look as different as possible, in all aspects – economic, political, and cultural – from the previous system. Gender-specific outcomes are very much influenced by this aspect of revolutions. In all revo-lutions, the system of social stratification changes, and relations of domi-nation and subordination are sometimes reversed; in many cases, the revolutionary rhetoric includes the promise that previously disadvantaged groups will see an improvement in their situation. All revolutions entail downward and upward social mobility; the political and economic elites lose their power and are replaced by other groups; there is disempowerment of some and empowerment of others. Even occupations invariably change: some lose status while others are valorized (for example, in postrevolutionary Russia, medicine lost status and remuneration while production work was upgraded in status and income); those who are fired or let go are replaced by those who are either more politically correct or more in line with the eco-nomic vision of the new elite (as in postrevolutionary Iran, where Islamic women occupied civil service positions vacated by non-Islamic employees, and in East Central Europe, where teachers of Marxism or Communism lost their jobs). In all cases, the system of social stratification remains, though its contents are rearranged. Almost always, the family is redefined, usually in the new government's body of laws. Women experience the effects of revolu-tionary upheavals differentially by class (and in some societies, by race or ethnicity). However, laws on women and the family, especially those per-taining directly to reproductive issues or legal status, may affect all women in similar ways.

A synthetic definition of revolution might be the following: revolutions are attempts to rapidly and profoundly change political and social structures; they involve mass participation; they usually, but not always, entail violence or the use of force; they include notions of the "ideal" society; and they have some cultural reference points. As revolutions entail constructions of national identity, reorganizations of production, and reformulations of (social) repro-duction, class, ethnicity, and gender all figure prominently. In their analysis of Mexico, Diane Bush and Stephen Mumme conceptualize revolution "as a process whereby traditionally subordinate groups attempt to transform the culture and structure of power relations within a society."[10] They stress the need to examine how the revolutionary situation and the revolutionary out-come are related to the social organization of gender. Similarly, I argue that prerevolutionary social conditions, including the gender system, as well as the nature of the revolutionary coalition and its principal objectives, largely determine whether a revolution's outcome for women will be patriarchal or modernizing.

Changes in gender relations are especially obvious in revolutionary outcomes, most dramatically in such twentieth-century revolutions as Russia, China, and Iran (albeit in very different ways). There is less evidence thus far to support a role for gender in causality. In the case of the Iranian Revolu-tion, however, it is plausible to hypothesize that gender intersected with class to constitute a causal factor in the revolt against the Shah and the turn to

Islamization, at least for a section of the revolutionary coalition. That is, the growing visibility of middle-class women and the "Westernization" of bourgeois women offended the men of the lower middle class who sought to recuperate traditional gender roles as part of their revolutionary goals. For all revolutions it is possible to posit that gender ideology profoundly *shapes* all manner of actions and decisions, from macro to micro, from patterns of revolutionary mobilization, state-building, and the establishment of constitutions, laws, and policies, to household dynamics and relations within families. For example, Guida West and Rhoda Blumberg have identified the gendered nature of social protest, in terms both of the types of issues that draw women into protest, and of gender differentiation within social protest and justifications for protest.[11] Maxine Molyneux's analyses of the Nicaraguan Revolution and its impact on women's mobilization and emancipatory prospects reveal the constraints imposed by the contra war as well as the role of "the pervasive *machismo* of Nicaraguan life."[12] Bush and Mumme have explored the interactive process in which gender intersected with church, state, and ideology pertaining to women's place in the family in the Mexican revolutionary situation, with contradictory effects on family, church, and state and on the relations among them.[13]

REVOLUTIONS AND WOMEN'S INTERESTS

Do revolutions have the same gender outcomes for all women? Molyneux has distinguished women's interests, practical gender interests, and strategic gender interests. "Women's interests" are specific to particular class, ethnic, or age groups within a given society. Women's interests are revealed by specifying "how the various categories of women might be affected differently and act differently on account of the particularities of their social positioning and their chosen identities." In contrast, strategic gender interests "are derived . . . deductively . . . from an analysis of women's subordination and from the formulation of an alternative, more satisfactory set of arrangements."[14] Thus, strategic gender interests often take the form of broad reforms which question the structural basis of gender inequality: suffrage, legal reform of family law, freedom of choice over childbearing, abolition of the sexual division of labor. Practical gender interests are inductive and usually formulated by women (or men) in concrete positions within the gendered division of labor. Practical gender interests do not challenge the division of labor itself or gender inequality more broadly, but focus on women's basic needs and their access to resources and welfare. Molyneux's threefold distinction of women's interests, practical gender interests, and strategic gender interests correctly emphasizes the gender dimension of revolutions, with attention to the differential impact of revolution and social transformation of women of different social classes, and with an understanding that different types of revolutions and revolutionary state policies will have different outcomes for women. In her analysis of Nicaragua, Molyneux has explored the effects of economic resources, conflict, and religious pressures on women and gender, pointing out that the Nicaraguan Revolution's legal reforms, redistributive policies, and political mobilization positively affected women's practical needs and strategic gender interests "even though fundamental structures of gender inequality were not dismantled."[15]

On the other hand, many feminists have noted that revolutionary movements subordinate women's interests and gender interests to "broader" or "basic" goals of emancipation. For this reason, there has been a veritable indictment of all revolutions and liberation movements as essentially inimical to women's interests. Maria Mies, for example, has pointed to a dramatic shift in nationalist imagery in postrevolutionary states:

> In this phase, the female image of the nation, found on the revolutionary posters mentioned above, is replaced by the images of the founding-fathers: Marx, Engels, Lenin, Stalin, Mao, Ho Chi Minh, Castro, Mugabe, to name only a few. Typically, among this gallery of socialist patriarchs, there are no women.[16]

It cannot be denied, however, that some revolutionary experiences have been profoundly liberating for women *as women*, especially in those cases where patriarchal gender roles are challenged, and where new legislation is enacted towards greater equality and autonomy for women. For example Molyneux and Norma Chinchilla are very positive in their assessments of Nicaragua.[17] According to Linda Lobao, of the five Latin American guerrilla movements she discusses, the issue of women's rights was recognized as significant for the movements" present and future success in Nicaragua and El Salvador.[18] Chinese communism brought about a genuinely revolutionary change in women's legal status and social positions, especially in the urban areas.[19] Stephanie Urdang writes, correctly, in my view:

> In Mozambique and other postrevolutionary societies, there are real gains that have been made by women. To ignore these and the kind of support – economic and political – that women get from their governments and political party is to ignore some real, tangible advances.[20]

REVOLUTIONS AND GENDERED OUTCOMES: A TYPOLOGY AND FRAMEWORK

Molyneux has argued that in reforming the position of women, revolutionary governments seek to accomplish three goals: "(1) to extend the base of the government's political support; (2) to increase the size or quality of the active labor force; and (3) to help harness the family more securely to the process of social reproduction."[21] In my reading of revolutions, the goal of harnessing the family is more evident in some revolutions than in others, while the importance of deploying female labor and drawing political support from women is also a feature of some but not all revolutions. Furthermore, the "emancipation of women" is not exclusively tied to development goals, but is also a matter of principle and ideology – a point made by Molyneux in an earlier study.[22] For these reasons, I distinguish two types of revolutions, social transformation, and national-identity construction: (1) the "woman-in-the-family" or patriarchal model of revolution, and (2) the "women's emancipation" or modernizing model. These conform to events in revolutionary France and revolutionary Russia, respectively, which also happen to be the reference points for most twentieth-century revolutions (see Figure 6.1).

Combining my terminology with that of Molyneux, I would propose that the women's emancipation model of revolution serves (at least some) strategic gender interests, especially through its explicit espousal of gender equality and the full integration of women in public life; addresses practical gender interests to the extent that resources allow it to; and is in the interests of most strata of the female population – although some groups of women may oppose it due to class and ideological differences. By contrast, the woman-in-the-family model of revolution, by virtue of its insistence on gender differences and female domesticity, is inimical to the strategic gender

Type of revolution	Bourgeois revolutions	Socialist revolutions and Third World populist revolutions
Women's emancipation a major goal or outcome	Kemalism in Turkey	France (1848) Russia (1917) China Cuba Vietnam Democratic Yemen Eritrea Afghanistan Nicaragua El Salvador
Family attachment of women a major goal or outcome	French Revolution	Mexico
	Perestroika in the Soviet Union	Algeria
		Iran
	'1989 revolutions' of Eastern Europe	

Figure 6.1 Revolutions by gender outcomes: a typology

interests of women, though it may address some practical gender needs and the specific interests of some groups of women.

Our theoretical framework thus rests on the following propositions:

1. Revolutions entail conscious attempts at economic, political, cultural, and ideological transformations. As an integral part of the social structure, gender shapes these processes and is implicated in the course and outcome of revolutions.

2. While preexisting gender relations affect revolutionary goals, discourses, and patterns of mobilization, they may themselves be affected and altered in the course of the revolution or its aftermath. Some aspects of the preexisting gender system may profoundly shape the revolutionary movement and the policies of the new revolutionary regime, while others may be fundamentally altered, often through conscious efforts, policies, and laws. The relationship between the gender system and the revolutionary process is an interactive one.

3. Revolutionary regimes almost always set about legislating new gender relations, redefining male and female prerogatives, enacting social policies pertaining to men, women, the family, and so on. These are frequently drastic measures which are intended to make the new society as different as possible from the old one. This is indicative of the centrality of gender to state-building, reorganizations of production and reproduction, and constructions of national identity.

4. Revolutions may serve practical needs only and be inimical to feminist goals, or they may advance gender emancipation, or both. Due to the social differentiation of women (class, ethnic, and ideological divisions), women's involvement in revolutionary movements and their responses to the new regimes and its policies are diverse and cannot be assumed.

In the sections that follow, I present my two types of revolutions. Elaboration of each will be supplemented by examples from twentieth-century revolutions. Whether the cases are examples of patriarchal or modernizing revolutions, they highlight the centrality of gender issues in the revolutionary process. What follows are ideal types, but they represent fairly faithfully the kinds of revolutions that have occurred and their gender dynamics.

THE WOMAN-IN-THE-FAMILY MODEL OF REVOLUTION

This type of revolution excludes or marginalizes women from definitions and constructions of independence, liberation, and liberty. It frequently constructs an ideological linkage between patriarchal values, nationalism, and the religious order. It assigns women the role of wife and mother, and associates women not only with family but also with tradition, culture, and religion. Although family issues and especially improvement of the quality of life of families among the popular classes may be among the goals of modernizing revolutions, here the family is exalted and women's role within it made paramount. The historical precursor of the patriarchal model was the French Revolution which, despite its many progressive features, had an extremely conservative outcome for women.

Popular sovereignty, civil liberty, equality before the law – these are among the rich legacy of the French Revolution and of the Enlightenment. But many of the French revolutionaries associated women with weakness, corruption, frailty, and specifically with the court and *ancien régime*. Indeed, under the *ancien régime*, certain privileged women of all three estates took part in the preliminary voting for the Estates General of 1789.[23] This may be one reason why the French republicans did not extend the new liberties to women. Thus did the playwright Olympe de Gouges utter her famous *cri de coeur*: "O my poor sex! O women who have gained nothing from the Revolution!"

With the collapse of the authority of the church and the old regime, the French revolutionaries sought a new moral basis for family life. They made divorce possible, accorded full legal status to illegitimate children, and abolished primogeniture. They also abolished slavery and gave full civil rights to Protestants and Jews. (Napoleon later reversed the most democratic provisions of the laws on family life, restoring patriarchal authority.) But there was another trend at work during the revolution. Darnton notes that at the height of the French Revolution virtue was the central ingredient of a new political culture.[24] To the revolutionaries, virtue was virile. At the same time, the cult of virtue produced a revalorization of family life. Darnton explains that the revolutionaries took their text from Rousseau, and sermonized on the sanctity of motherhood and the importance of breast-feeding: "They treated reproduction as a civic duty and excoriated bachelors as unpatriotic."[25] According to Sheila Rowbotham, banners and slogans proclaimed: "Citizenesses! Give the Fatherland Children!" and "Now is the time to make a baby." Mothers had a certain legitimacy which unmarried *citoyennes* did not. Robespierre's Reign of Virtue involved an ideal of women as passive nurturers. Women should bear children for the revolution and sacrifice them for France. He abhorred the active women in the revolutionary club, describing them as "unnatural" and "sterile as vice." Rowbotham notes that in contrast the action of women in the crowd over prices or in pushing for a part in popular sovereignty hinted at an active creation of women's roles, while Claire Lacombe attempted to appropriate revolutionary virtue for an extension of the power of the left-wing women. When the deputation of the Society of Revolutionary Republican Women came to the National Convention to protest because their society was banned they described it as "composed in large part of mothers of families."[26]

Considering the revolution's outcome for women, it is ironic or paradoxical that in its early stages, the symbol of the revolution was female. Hunt's study reveals that the radical break with tradition and with the justification of authority by reference to historical origins implied the rejection of paternalist or patriarchal models of authority. On the official seal, in the engravings and prints representing the new republic, and in the *tableaux vivants* of the festivals, feminine allegorizations of classical derivation replaced representations of the king. These female figures, whether living women or statues, always sat or stood alone, surrounded most often by abstract emblems of authority and power. The republic might have her children and even her masculine defenders, but there was never a father present.[27] In the early years of the French Revolution, the symbol of the republic was Marianne.

Eventually Marianne was replaced by the image of Hercules, which recaptured and rehabilitated a distinctly virile representation of sovereignty, a concept that had connotations of domination and supremacy in any case.[28] The introduction of Hercules served to distance the deputies from the growing mobilization of women into active politics. For both the Jacobin leaders and their sans-culottes followers, politics was a quarrel between men.[29] On the grounds that women's active participation in politics would lead to "the kinds of disruption and disorder that hysteria can produce," the Convention outlawed all women's clubs at the end of October 1793. The Jacobin Chaumette said, "The sans-culottes had a right to expect his wife to run the home while he attended public meetings: hers was the care of the family, this was the full extent of her civic duties."[30] If the revolution had been female, the republic was to be male. And what was to be the place of women in the new society of revolutionary France? According to the Jacobin deputy André Amar:

> Morality and nature itself have assigned her functions to her: to begin the education of men, to prepare the minds and hearts of children for the exercise of public virtues, to direct them early in life towards the good, to elevate their souls, to educate them in the cult of liberty – such are their functions after household cares. . . . When they have carried out these duties they will have deserved well of the fatherland.[31]

The exclusion of women from the construction of the republic, their relegation to the sphere of the family, and their education in Catholic schools (until the 1850s) made them especially vulnerable in the anti-clerical politics of the Second and Third Republics. The association of women with cultural and political conservatism led to their exclusion from the "universal suffrage" of 1848. As Michelet put it, giving women the vote would mean "giving thousands of votes to the priests."[32] This argument peaked under the Third Republic (1870–1940), and was shared by all anti-clerical parties. Not until after World War II did women in France obtain the right to vote.

Carol Pateman argues that woman was the marginalized other in the development of the liberal democratic state.[33] Bonds between men *qua* men were constituted in opposition to women; the division between the public sphere of state and civil society was conceptualized in opposition to the family, which was constructed as a natural and private institution headed by a man. Similarly, Harriet Applewhite and Darlene Levy write:

> In the most general terms, for men, the revolutionary period established the principle of democratic citizenship, constitutionally guaranteed rights, and collective empowerment through participation in new political, economic, and social institutions. For women, revolutionary outcomes were far more complex and confused. . . . The age of democratic revolution nowhere produced political democracy that included women as citizens; nowhere did women achieve political and civil rights that middle-class white male proprietors had established for themselves. . . . In the aftermath of revolution or civil unrest in the political cultures treated here, women were excluded from modern political institutions like labor organizations, political parties, militias, and legislatures.[34]

In twentieth-century revolutions that had similarly patriarchal outcomes for women – notably Mexico, Algeria, and Iran – women were relegated to the private sphere despite the crucial roles they had played in the revolutionary movements. In these three cases, men took over the reins of power, assigned to women responsibility for family, religion, and tradition, and enacted legislation to codify patriarchal gender relations, including second-class citizenship for women. Similarly, in the "1989 revolutions" of East Central Europe and in the former Soviet Union the new revolutionaries resurrected patriarchal discourses on women and the family, launched an attack on reproductive rights, and proceeded to establish what East European feminists called "democratization with a male face" and "male democracies."

The Algerian case

The French took over Algeria in June 1830. Unlike colonial policy in Morocco after 1912 and Tunisia after 1882, an attempt was made in Algeria to dismantle Islam, its economic infrastructure, and its cultural network of lodges and schools. By the turn of the century, there were upwards of a million French-speaking settlers (*petits colons*) in Algeria. European competition ruined most of the old artisan class by 1930. Small shopkeepers such as grocers and spice merchants survived, but other small shopkeepers suffered severely from the competition of the *petits colons*. Industrialization in Algeria was given a low priority by Paris during the inter-war period. Local development and employment generation were severely hampered and there was considerable unemployment and male migration. Fierce economic competition, cultural disrespect, and residential segregation characterized the Algerian situation.

In this context, many Algerians regarded Islam and Muslim family law as "sanctuaries from French cultural imperialism."[35] To many Algerian men the unveiled woman represented a capitulation to the European and his culture; she was a person who had opened herself up to the prurient stares of the foreigners, a person more vulnerable to rape. The popular reaction to the *mission civilisatrice* was a return to the land and to religion, the foundations of the old community. Islam was reinforced, the patriarchal family became increasingly important, and the protection and seclusion of women were seen by Algerians as imperative to their identity and integrity.

When the *Front de Libération Nationale* (FLN) was formed there was no provision for women to enjoy any political or military responsibilities. None the less, military exigencies soon forced the officers of the *Armée de Libération Nationale* (ALN) to use some women combatants. Upwards of 10,000 women participated in the Algerian Revolution. The overwhelming majority of those who served in the war were nurses, cooks, and laundresses.[36] But many women played an indispensable role as couriers, and because the French rarely searched them, women were often used for carrying bombs. (This recalls the function of women in the street processions of Paris in 1792.) Among the heroines of the Algerian Revolution were Djamila Boujhired (the first woman sentenced to death), Djamila Bouazza, Jacqueline Guerroudj, Zahia Khalfallah, Baya Hocine, and Djoher Akrour. Women who fought and did not survive the war of liberation included 20-year-old Hassiba Ben Bouali, killed in the casbah, and Djennet Hamidou, who was shot and killed as she tried to escape arrest. She was 17. Yamina Abed, who was wounded in battle, suffered amputation of both legs. She was 20.[37] These Algerian women, like the women of Vietnam after them, became the stuff of legends.

After independence, the September 1962 Constitution guaranteed equality between the sexes and granted women the right to vote. It also made Islam the official state religion. Ten women were elected deputies of the new National Assembly and one of them, Fatima Khemisti, drafted the only significant legislation to affect the status of women passed by the National Assembly after independence.[38] In this optimistic time, when heroines of the revolution were being hailed throughout the country, the *Union Nationale des Femmes Algériennes* (UNFA) was formed. Indeed, one consequence of the Algerian Revolution and women's role in it was the emergence of the "*Moudjahidates* model" of Algerian womanhood. The heroic Algerian woman fighter was an inspiration to the 1960s and 1970s generation of Algerians, particularly Algerian university women.[39]

But another, more patriarchal, tendency was at work during and after the Algerian Revolution. One expression of this was pressure on women fighters during the liberation struggle to get married and thus prevent spurious talk about their behavior. Moreover, despite the incredible sacrifices of Algerian women, and although the female militants "acceded to the ranks of subjects of history," Cherifa Bouatta argues that the Algerian Revolution has tended to be cast in terms of male exploits, while the heroic female feats have not received as much attention.[40]

In the 1960s, Algerian marriage rates soared. In 1967 some 10 percent of Algerian girls were married at 15 years of age; at 20 years of age, 73 percent of the women were married. The crude fertility rate was 6.5 per woman. The Boumedienne government's policy on demographic growth was predicated on the assumption that a large population is necessary for national power. It was, therefore, opposed to all forms of birth control unless the mother had already produced at least four children.[41] By the end of the Boumedienne years in 1979, 97.5 percent of Algerian women were without paid work. (Some 45 percent of Algerian men were unemployed or underemployed.) The UNFA had become the women's auxiliary of the FLN, devoid of feminist objectives.

The Algerian Revolution has frequently been identified as one of the clearest cases of postrevolutionary marginalization of women – notwithstanding their critical roles during the liberation struggle. As such, it conforms to the woman-in-the-family model of revolution.[42]

The Iranian case

The Iranian Revolution against the Shah, which unfolded between early 1977 and February 1979, was joined by countless women. Like other social groups, their reasons for opposing the Shah were varied: economic deprivation, political repression, identification with Islamism, aspirations for a socialist future. The large street demonstrations included huge contingents of women wearing the veil as a symbol of opposition to bourgeois or Westernized Pahlavi decadence. Many women who wore the veil as a protest symbol did not expect *hijab* (veiling) to become mandatory. Thus when the first calls were made in February 1979 to enforce *hijab* and when Ayatollah Khomeini was quoted as saying that he preferred to see women in modest Islamic dress, many women were alarmed. Spirited protests and sit-ins were led by middle-class leftist and liberal women, most of them members of political organizations or recently formed women's organizations. Limited support for the women's protests came from the main political groups. As a result of the women's protests, the ruling on *hijab* was rescinded – but only temporarily. With the defeat of the left and liberals in 1980 and their elimination from the political terrain in 1981, the Islamic state was able to make veiling compulsory, and to enforce it strictly. Iranian women were deeply divided over the revolution, and the Islamization of Iran had its many female adherents, drawn mainly from the lower middle class, which was also the class base of the new Islamist leadership.

The idea that women had "lost honor" during the Pahlavi era was a widespread one. Anti-Shah oppositionists decried the overly made-up "bourgeois dolls" – television announcers, singers, upper-class women in the professions – of the Pahlavi era. As in Algeria, the Islamists in Iran felt that "genuine Iranian cultural identity" had been distorted by Westernization or what they called *gharbzadegi* (a coinage literally suggesting "West-struck" or "Westoxicated"). The unveiled, publicly visible woman was both a reflection of Western attacks on indigenous culture and the medium by which it was effected. Many Iranian analysts have observed that the growing number of educated and employed women "terrified" men who came to regard the modern woman as the manifestation of Westernization and imperialist culture and a threat to their own manhood. Islamists projected the image of the noble, militant, and selfless Fatemeh – daughter of the Prophet Mohammad, earlier popularized by the radical Islamic sociologist Ali Shari'ati – as the most appropriate model for the new Iranian womanhood.[43]

Such attitudes were behind the early legislation pertaining to women. The 1979 Constitution spelled out the place of women in the ideal Islamic society which the new leadership was trying to establish in Iran: within the family, through the "precious foundation of motherhood," rearing committed Muslims. Motherhood and domesticity were described as socially valuable, and the age of consent was lowered to 15 (or 13, in some accounts). Legislation was enacted to alter gender relations and make them as different as possible from gender norms in the West. In particular, the Islamic Republic emphasized the distinctiveness of male and female roles, a preference for the privatization of female roles (although public activity by women was never barred and they retained the vote), the desirability of sex segregation in public places, and the necessity of modesty in dress and demeanor in public and in media images. The Iranian Islamists were aware, however, of modern sensibilities. The Introduction to the Constitution mentions women's "active and massive presence in all stages of this great struggle," and states that men and women are equal before the law. But this stated equality is belied by differential treatment before the law, particularly in the area of personal status or family law, based on the shari'a, or Islamic canon law.

The signal importance of the woman question to the Islamist revolutionaries and state-builders and in particular the significance of veiling has been widely discussed in the (expatriate) literature on Iranian women. Afsaneh Najmabadi, for example, has discussed an editorial that appeared in a 1984 issue of *Zan-e Rouz* (Today's Women), which described the veil as "a shield that protects [woman] against conspiracies aimed at her humanity, honor and chastity" as well as the means to protect Islam from cultural imperialism. The editorial maintains that the revolution "transformed everyone, all personalities, all relations and all values" and that "woman was transformed in this society so that a revolution could occur."[44] Other publications of the

149

Islamic Republic and speeches by its leaders indicate the importance of the family unit, and the links between veiling and family values: "*hijab* is a spiritual bulwark around the family which protects it against degeneration,"[45] and "the family is the basic unit of the society and plays a crucial role in prosperity, public morals and education of new generations, as well as social integration and social stability."[46] That it devolves upon women to maintain family and social cohesion and the integrity of the Islamic revolution through veiling and proper comportment is the distinctive Iranian contribution to the patriarchal model of revolution.

The case of East Central Europe

In 1989, the decision to reject communism, privatize the economy, and adopt Western-style electoral systems entailed concerted efforts to transform economic structures, political institutions, laws, and even values and attitudes. A new ideology took shape in explicit opposition to the previous dominant ideology (of socialism/Marxism/communism), borrowing heavily from neoclassical economics and from liberal and conservative political thought. In the context of anathemization of the socialist discourse of common ownership, workers'' management, and equality, the objectives of gender equality or the emancipation of women were dismissed as irrelevant to urgent economic concerns or as an unwelcome legacy of communism.[47]

Notwithstanding the participation of women in the democracy movements, especially in Poland, Czechoslovakia, and East Germany, the first democratic elections resulted in a dramatic decline in female parliamentary participation, from an average of 30 percent to shares as low as 3 percent.[48] Cultural images of women began to change as well. Liberalization and an almost automatic imitation of anything Western transformed the public image of the woman into a sex object. With the end of government subsidies and the proliferation of new and independent presses engaged in a fierce battle for survival, most newspapers began to adorn their articles with nudity. Democratization, unemployment, and inflation seem to have had another outcome: a burgeoning traffic in women. The sex trade is a growing industry, and includes migration of sexual workers to places such as Helsinki and Istanbul from the Baltics and Russia, and Berlin and Amsterdam from Central and Eastern Europe, for hard currency.

In the immediate post-communist transition period, women's maternal, domestic, and family roles were exalted, and there was a fierce battle over the right to abortion. The controversy over reproductive rights and abortion was indicative of the new gender realities and seemed to reflect both the growing power of the church and conscious efforts by the new leadership to distance itself as much as possible from aspects of the former regime. In a manner strikingly reminiscent of post-independence Algeria and the early Islamic Republic of Iran, the first group of post-communist leaders and elites in East Central Europe and the former Soviet Union stressed not equality and empowerment of women, but "liberation from work" and a return to the joys of domesticity. This was apparently supported by some women, and in 1989–90 there was much talk of women's *relief* at no longer having to be employed, and the importance of *choice* under the new arrangements. But as Barbara Einhorn has noted, since women's only experience was of full employment and of jobs awaiting them after extended childcare leave, "women initially had no way of knowing that exercising choice in a decision to 'stay at home with the children for a few years' might result in their becoming long-term unemployed."[49] Since then, market reforms have led to high levels of unemployment among women and an apparent trend towards appropriation by men of now-lucrative occupations such as banking and accounting which were previously female-dominated.[50] In the late 1980s, support for the end of communism was apparently overwhelming among women. Later, however, as the new market and gender realities took shape, unemployed women and those who felt insecure about their jobs, income, and ability to look after their children in the absence of socialist-era supports grew more wary. Dobrinka Kostova reports on a survey of Bulgarians that showed women to be especially critical of the new situation.[51]

What was the basis for these startling and unexpected outcomes for women? In the former Soviet Union, notwithstanding the achievements of early communism, female disadvantage remained, pervaded the spheres of production and reproduction alike, and was manifested in gender inequalities in economic life, in political power, and even in attitudes towards "feminine" and "masculine." There was a similar patriarchal legacy in Central and Eastern Europe, probably enhanced by hostility to Soviet communism, which is what the new post-communist leaderships were able to draw upon. Einhorn and others have noted that women are viewed by conservative parties and the church as the guardians of traditional morality, entrusted with the sacred duty of bearing children "for the nation" and rearing them in the spirit of national linguistic and cultural identity and ethical virtue:

> In Polish literature and culture the woman is equated with suffering Polonia, who in turn, in the figure of the Holy Virgin of Czestechowa, is named Queen of Poland. In both Poland and Czechoslovakia national identity is fiercely upheld precisely because of its historical fragility, as their respective territories have been for much of their history simply the staging posts in other people's campaigns. This sense of an ethnic and cultural heritage to be retrieved after the period of state socialism has deeply affected current views of women's role in this renewal, in many cases appearing to instrumentalize them in the name of nationalism. The need to boost numbers in the ethnic group also provides one explanation for the almost universal attack on abortion rights.[52]

151

VALENTINE M. MOGHADAM

THE WOMEN'S EMANCIPATION MODEL OF REVOLUTION

The women's emancipation model holds that the emancipation of women is an essential part of the revolution or project of social transformation. It constructs Woman as part of the productive forces and citizenry, to be mobilized for economic and political purposes; she is to be liberated from patriarchal controls expressly for that purpose. Here the discourse is more strongly that of sexual equality rather than difference. The first example historically of such a revolution is the Bolshevik Revolution in Russia which, especially with respect to its early years, remains the avant-garde revolution *par excellence*, more audacious in its approach to gender than any revolution before or since.

World War I brought more Russian women into factory production, leading the Bolsheviks to recognize them as a potential social and political force. The Bolsheviks also had supporters among laundresses, domestic servants, restaurant and textile workers, and soldiers" wives. They launched *Rabotnitsa*, a paper for women workers, and encouraged women to join factory committees and unions. Wendy Zeva Goldman writes that although the party was theoretically opposed to separate organizations for women, "in practice, the success of *Rabotnitsa*'s staff resulted in the organization of the Petrograd Conference of Working Women in November 1917 and the formation of the *Zhenotdel*, or women's department, within the party in 1919."[53]

Under Alexandra Kollantai, People's Commissar for Social Welfare, labor legislation was passed which gave women an eight-hour day, social insurance, pregnancy leave for two months before and after childbirth, time at work to breast-feed, and prohibition of child labor and night work for women. The early months of the revolution also saw legislation to bring in equality between husband and wife, civil registration of marriage, easy divorce, abolition of illegitimacy, and the ending of the wife's obligation to take her husband's name and share his domicile. Under Kollantai's directorship in particular, the women's section of the Party, the *Zhenotdel*, saw itself as a force to represent women's interests in the party and to transform society. In Central Asia, it organized mass unveilings of Muslim women and ran literacy classes. (As we shall see, this was attempted fifty years later in South Yemen and Afghanistan.) All this followed from the view that the emancipation of women was an essential part of the socialist revolution, and that this was to be accomplished through "the participation of women in general productive labor," as socialists put it, and through the socialization of domestic duties. Lenin's views on the subject of women, revolution, and equality were sometimes expressed in rather forceful terms:

> woman continues to be a domestic slave, because petty housework
> crushes, strangles, stultifies and degrades her, chains her to the kitchen

152

and to the nursery, and wastes her labor on barbarously unproductive, petty, nerve-racking, stultifying and crushing drudgery.[54]

Enlightenment, culture, civilization, liberty – in all capitalist, bourgeois republics of the world all these fine words are combined with extremely infamous, disgustingly filthy and brutally coarse laws in which woman is treated as an inferior being, laws dealing with marriage rights and divorce, with the inferior status of a child born out of wedlock as compared with that of a "legitimate" child, laws granting privileges to men, laws that are humiliating and insulting to women.[55]

The Bolsheviks also stressed the need for the political participation of women, or as Lenin put it:

We want women workers to achieve equality with men workers not only in law, but in life as well. For this, it is essential that women workers take an ever increasing part in the administration of public enterprises and in the administration of the state.[56]

The Bolsheviks took the initiative in calling the First Communist Women's Conference and prepared the position paper for the occasion, *Theses of the Communist Women's Movement*. Apart from its commitment to the political equality of women and the guarantee of their social rights, the *Theses* included an attack on housewifery and "the domestic hearth." The document reflected the Engelsian view that female emancipation would be a two-fold process, incorporating both the entry of women into the national labor force, and the socialization of domestic labor.[57] The document also reflected the views of the outstanding Communist women who contributed to its formulation, among them Alexandra Kollantai, Inessa Armand, and Clara Zetkin.

Like the French revolutionaries before them, the Bolsheviks strongly supported "free union," and therefore legalized divorce. But in other matters they parted company with the French revolutionaries. Debates on sexuality reflected the Bolsheviks" commitment to gender equality and their critique of the family. The liberation of peasant women could come about only through a massive change in the mode of production, as well as a revolutionary transformation of social values and practices. The implementation in the 1920s of the land code and the family code, with their emphasis on individual rights and freedoms – including women's rights to land and for maintenance – was an extremely audacious act that challenged centuries of patriarchal control. It also undermined the collective principle of the household, the very basis of peasant production, and was thus strongly resisted. In Soviet Central Asia in the 1920s, where there was virtually no industrial working class, Bolshevik strategists directed their campaigns at women because they were considered the most oppressed social category.[58]

Goldman writes that material scarcity weakened the Bolshevik vision of liberation, although jurists and party officials maintained their commitment to the "withering-away" of the family, and the Women's Congress in 1927 showed the potential of an active socialist women's organization. This potential was cut short in the 1930s with the consolidation of the power of Stalin and his associates, who ushered in a more culturally conservative era. This led to the decision to disband the Zhenotdel, to end open discussions of women's liberation, and to resurrect the family. The earlier critique of the family was replaced by a strong emphasis on the "socialist family" as the proper model of gender relations. Family responsibilities were extolled for men as well as for women.

The Bolshevik Revolution and communist legislation inspired socialists and feminists throughout the world, and for many decades. It was truly an exemplar of the "women's emancipation" model of revolution. Other revolutions in which "The Woman Question" assumed a prominent position in revolutionary discourse and in the policies of the new states include the socialist and populist revolutions of China, Vietnam, Democratic Yemen, and Nicaragua (see Figure 6.1). At least one "bourgeois revolution" also conforms to the women's emancipation model: Kemalism in Turkey in the 1920s and 1930s.

The case of Turkey

If "the Woman Question was the Achilles Heel of the [European] Enlightenment,"[59] it was central to the Turkish Enlightenment and the Kemalist Revolution. To the Turkish reformers, the women of Turkey were both participants in the nationalist and political struggles and symbols of the new Turkey. Kemal Atatürk viewed women's equality to men as part of Turkey's commitment to Westernization, secularization, and democracy.

Toward the end of the nineteenth century, opposition to the sultanate was manifested in the Young Turk movement, officially called the Committee of Union and Progress. One of the principal tenets of the Young Turks was the need for modernization; they were also unabashedly for Westernization. Closely linked to the need for modernization through Westernization was the emancipation of women. Kumari Jayawardena reminds us that the process of Europeanization not only was ideological, but also meant the forging of economic links with the capitalist countries of Europe. Around this time, the writer and sociologist Ziya Gökalp, often referred to as the theoretician of Turkish nationalism and strongly influenced by the Comtean and Durkheimian tradition in French sociology, advocated equality in marriage, divorce, and inheritance rights for women.[60] In 1871 the American College for Girls was started, although it was for two decades restricted to Christians. The first Muslim girl to complete her studies there was Halide Edip, a future women's leader.[61]

World War I hastened the break-up of the Ottoman Empire and the emergence of a new group from among the Young Turks which advocated the building of a modern Turkish national state that was "republican, secular and non-imperialist." Mustafa Kemal, an army captain, set up a revolutionary government in Ankara in 1920 and oversaw a peace treaty with the British and the establishment of the Turkish Republic in 1923, with himself as president as well as leader of the Republican People's Party. The Kemalist reforms were far-reaching in both intent and effect. Atatürk – Father of the Turks – as he came to be known, furthered the process of Europeanization through economic development, separation of religion from state affairs, an attack on tradition, Latinization of the alphabet, promotion of European dress, adoption of the Western calendar, and the replacement of Islamic family law by a secular civil code. The influence of the French Enlightenment and anti-clericalism is clear in these reforms. Ziya Gökalp urged the Turks to "Belong to the Turkish nation, the Muslim religion and European civilization."[62] But by 1926 the shari'a (Islamic legal code) was abolished and the civil and penal codes thoroughly secularized.

Where the Turkish reformers diverged from their French predecessors was on the woman question. Indeed, Turkish women obtained the legal right to vote in 1934, many years before French women did. Legislation mandating compulsory education, enacted in 1924, provided for equal access of girls to schooling. Unlike the French, for whom the emancipation of women was not on the agenda, a central element of the conceptualization of Turkish nationalism, progress, and civilization was "Turkish feminism" – the exact words of Gökalp.[63] Not only Atatürk and Gökalp, but Kemalist feminists such as the nationalist fighter and writer Halide Edip and Atatürk's adopted daughter Afet Inan, author of *The Emancipation of the Turkish Woman*, played major roles in creating images of the new Turkish woman. Various Turkish writers stressed the harmful individual and national effects of the subordination of women. Stories and essays depicting individual women who suffered from subjugation, children who suffered because of their mother's ignorance, and households that suffered because women could not manage money properly highlighted the need for education for women. Writings depicting women who descended into abject poverty when their husbands or fathers died underscored employment for women as the solution.[64] Other stories sought to show that society and progress suffered when women were kept illiterate and subordinated to men. According to Deniz Kandiyoti, in many writings the new Turkish woman was depicted as a self-sacrificing "comrade-woman" who shared in the struggles of her male peers, and as an asexual sister-in-arms whose public activities never cast any doubt on her virtue and chastity. Turkish national identity was "deemed to have a practically built-in sexual egalitarianist component."[65] In this sense the image of the emancipated Turkish woman was in line with the "true" identity of the collectivity – the new Turkish nation.

Why was the question of women's rights so strategic to the self-definition of the Turkish reformers? It would appear that women's emancipation was necessary for purposes of economic development and social progress, which were high on the agenda of the Kemalists. Women's emancipation was also a way to distance the new Turkey from the old and a response to European prejudices. As Atäturk was quoted as saying in 1923: "Our enemies are claiming that Turkey cannot be considered as a civilized nation because this country consists of two separate parts: men and women."[66]

Another reason was that Mustafa Kemal had been highly impressed by the courage and militancy of Turkish women during the Balkan wars and World War I. As Jayawardena notes, Turkish women had taken up new avenues of public employment as nurses on the war fronts and had worked in ammunition, food, and textile factories as well as in banks, hospitals, and the administrative services. The occupation of various parts of Turkey by European troops in 1919 aroused protests in which women joined and women in Anatolia were part of Mustapha Kemal's army in its war against the invaders. In his speeches in later years Kemal constantly referred to the role played by Anatolian women in the nationalist struggle. In a speech at Izmir in 1923 he said, "A civilization where one sex is supreme can be condemned, there and then, as crippled. A people which has decided to go forward and progress must realize this as quickly as possible. The failures in our past are due to the fact that we remained passive to the fate of women."[67]

In the 1935 elections, eighteen women were elected (4.5 percent of the Assembly), the highest number of women deputies in Europe at that time.[68] Clearly the Turkish case exemplifies the women's emancipation model of twentieth-century revolutions.

The case of South Yemen

Following 5 years of guerrilla fighting against 128 years of British colonial rule, the People's Democratic Republic of Yemen (PDRY) was born in the southern part of Yemen, with its capital city in Aden. In June 1969 the revolutionary government took a more radical turn, which aimed at "the destruction of the old state apparatus," the creation of a unified, state-administered legal system, and rapid social structural transformation.[69] Tribal segmentation and the local autonomy of ruling sheikhs, sultans, and emirs had resulted in a country devoid of a unified national economy, a political structure, or a legal system. Such a social order was seen by the revolutionaries as an obstacle to economic development and social reform. At the same time, it was clear that development and change required the active participation of women, as Maxine Molyneux has shown in her writings on the PDRY. Kin control over women and the practice of seclusion had consequently to be transformed. In this context the Constitution of 1970 outlined the government's policies toward women, and a new Family Law was proposed in 1971 and passed in 1974.

Quite unlike the Algerian FLN, the NFL (National Front for Liberation) of Yemen described itself as "the vanguard of the Yemen working class," and its official doctrine was inspired by the writings of Marx, Engels, and Lenin. Article 7 of the Constitution, which described the political basis of the revolution as an "alliance between the working class, the peasants, intelligentsia, and petty-bourgeoisie," went on to add that "soldiers, women, and students are regarded as part of this alliance by virtue of their membership in the productive forces of the people."[70] The Constitution recognized women both as "mothers" and "producers," and consequently as forming part of the "working people." In giving all citizens the right to work and in regarding work as "an obligation in the case of all able-bodied citizens," the Constitution called upon women not yet involved in "productive work" to enter the paid and agricultural labor force.[71]

Molyneux's analysis of the legal reforms in the PDRY reveals that according to the preamble of the Family Law, the "traditional" or "feudal" family is "incompatible with the principles and programme of the National Democratic Revolution . . . because its old relationships prevent it from playing a positive role in the building up of society." The law began by denouncing "the vicious state of affairs which prevails in the family," and proclaimed that "marriage is a contract between a man and a woman who are equal in rights and duties, and is based on mutual understanding and respect." It established the principle of free-choice marriage; raised the minimum legal of age of marriage to 16 for girls and 18 for boys; abolished polygamy except in exceptional circumstances such as barrenness or incurable disease; reduced the dower (*mahr*); stipulated that both spouses must bear the cost of supporting the family's economy; ended unilateral divorce; and increased divorced women's rights to custody of their children.[72]

As in Soviet Russia before and in Afghanistan later, family reform was regarded not only as mandated by socialist concepts of emancipation and equality but also as necessary for the integration of women into the development process. Unlike the Bolsheviks, the PDRY revolutionaries had to contend with Islamic religious forces that enjoyed strong institutional bases, economic power, and traditional authority. After 1969 they took control of religious education in schools and transferred its responsibility to lay teachers. School textbooks were replete with references to working women, frequently shown as engaged in agricultural as well as domestic work.[73] As Maxine Molyneux has noted, women were interpellated in new ways – as workers, national subjects, political subjects – in order to help construct the new order. The rearticulation of gender was an integral part of the restructuring of state and society. Gender redefinition was both a reflection of the new regime's political agenda *and* the means by which the new state could establish its authority and carry out its revolution.[74]

The case of Afghanistan

In April 1978, the People's Democratic Party of Afghanistan (PDPA) seized power in what came to be called the Saur (April) Revolution, and established the Democratic Republic of Afghanistan. Soon afterwards, the PDPA introduced rapid reforms to change the political and social structure of Afghan society, including patterns of land tenure and gender relations. The government of President Noor Mohammad Taraki targeted the structures and relations of "tribal-feudalism" and enacted legislation to raise women's status through changes in family law, including practices and customs related to marriage, and policies to encourage female education and employment. As in other modernizing and socialist experiments, the woman question constituted an essential part of the political project. The Afghan state was motivated by a modernizing outlook and socialist ideology which linked Afghan backwardness to feudalism, widespread female illiteracy, and the exchange of girls. The leadership resolved that women's rights to education, employment, mobility, and choice of spouse would be a major objective of the "national democratic revolution." The model of revolution and of women's emancipation was Soviet Russia, and the Saur Revolution was considered to belong to the family of revolutions which also included Vietnam, Cuba, Algeria, the PDRY, and Ethiopia.

Landlordship and early marriage for girls transacted monetarily were the first targets of the Marxist revolutionaries, who were inspired by earlier efforts in Soviet Central Asia and in South Yemen. A series of decrees was enacted to wrest power from traditional leaders and Afghan society; these included land redistribution, the cancellation of peasants'' debts and mortgages (Decree no. 6), and changes in marriage laws (Decree no. 7). The latter was especially bold, as its dual purpose was to reduce material indebtedness throughout the country and enhance the status of women. In a speech on November 4, 1978 President Taraki declared: "Through the issuance of Decrees no. 6 and 7, the hard-working peasants were freed from bonds of oppressors and money-lenders, ending the sale of girls for good as hereafter nobody would be entitled to sell any girl or woman in this country."[75] This was clearly an audacious program for social change, one aimed at the rapid transformation of a patriarchal society and decentralized power structure based on tribal and landlord authority. Revolutionary change, state-building, and women's rights went hand-in-hand. The emphasis on women's rights on the part of the PDPA reflected: their socialist/Marxist ideology, their modernizing and egalitarian outlook, their social base and origins (urban middle class, professionals, educated in the USA, USSR, India, and Western and Eastern Europe), and the number and position of women within the PDPA.

Although the PDPA sought merely to carry out the reforms that earlier Afghan modernizers had attempted, efforts to change marriage laws, expand literacy, and educate rural girls met with strong opposition by rural vested interests. Decrees nos. 6 and 7 deeply angered the rural tribesmen and the traditional power structure. In the summer of 1978 refugees began pouring into Pakistan, giving as their major reason the forceful implementation of the literacy program among their women. The new marriage regulations and compulsory education for girls raised the threat of women refusing to obey and submit to family authority. The attempt to impose a minimum age for marriage, prohibit forced marriage, limit divorce payments, and send girls to school "inevitably aroused the opposition of Afghan men, whose male chauvinism is as massive as the mountains of the Hindu Kush," in the words of one account.[76] An Islamist opposition began organizing and conducted several armed actions against the government in the Spring of 1979. By December 1979 the situation had deteriorated to such an extent that the Soviet Army intervened.

In 1980 the PDPA slowed down its reform program and announced its intention to eliminate illiteracy in cities in seven years and in the countryside in ten. Unlike Soviet Russia, Democratic Yemen, or Iran, the Afghan state was not a strong one, able to impose its will through an extensive administrative and military apparatus. As a result, it was far less successful than other revolutionary regimes in carrying out its program on land redistribution and women's rights. Nor did twelve years of civil war and a hostile international climate provide propitious conditions for progressive social change. It should also be noted that the women's emancipation discourse was well received by urban Afghan women but not by the wives and daughters of tribal and Islamist men in the rural areas. Even so, some village women embraced the Saur revolution (and organized self-defense brigades against the Mujahideen) while in Kabul, many middle-class and professional women and men left after 1978 due to their antipathy to the PDPA's Marxism. In 1987 the name Democratic Republic of Afghanistan was changed to the Republic of Afghanistan, and the liberation of women took a back seat to national reconciliation. In 1990 the PDPA changed its name to the National Party, Hizb-e Watan. Simultaneously, constitutional changes were made, dropping clauses which articulated the equality of men and women and reinstating Muslim family law. The revolutionary experiment collapsed altogether in April 1992, when the tribal-Islamist Mujahideen took over.[77]

The Nicaraguan case

As with the Afghan and South Yemeni revolutionaries, the Nicaraguan revolutionaries were confronted by problems of underdevelopment and poverty, exacerbated by counterrevolution and external intervention. This had implications for women's reproductive rights and the position of the family. But Nicaragua is also an example of feminist attempts to influence the process of revolutionary transition.

Many urban feminists, like many poor and rural Nicaraguan women, supported the Sandinista Revolution, viewing it as offering Nicaraguan women their best chance to obtain full equality. The revolution occurred in the period after the upsurge of the "new feminism" of the late 1960s, at a time when Latin American women were mobilizing around feminist demands in such countries as Mexico, Peru, and Brazil. In 1977, the Association of Women Confronting the National Problem (AMPRONAC) was formed, and combined a commitment to overthrow the Somoza regime with that of struggling for women's equality. Unlike many of its counterparts elsewhere, the Sandinista Front (FSLN) did not denounce feminism as a "counter-revolutionary diversion."[78] When they came to power, sections of the Sandinista leadership recognized the legitimacy of and need for women's liberation in Nicaragua, as well as support for the objectives of the feminist wing, renamed AMNLAE. As in many other countries, however, the Sandinistas and the AMNLAE had to contend with deeply entrenched sexist attitudes and hostility to the idea of women's emancipation. Consequently, the Sandinistas began to build popular support for AMNLAE's campaigns, including an ideological attack on *machismo* similar to Cuba's. The government's own emphasis was on legal reform and the political participation of women.

In a social context of high rates of male desertion, migrancy, and serial polygamy which had contributed to the emergence of impoverished households maintained by women alone, new laws were enacted to strengthen the position of women within the family, to clarify the responsibilities of each family member, and to promote family cohesion. Improvements were made in the working conditions of women workers, and rural women workers were given the legal right to receive and control their income themselves. Women's political participation was also encouraged and a substantial number of highly visible women came to occupy high-level party and government positions as heads of provincial governments, party officers, head of the police, and minister of health.[79]

Norma Chinchilla reports that AMNLAE took a radical turn in the early 1980s and assumed a more feminist stance.[80] It made proposals to the Council of State (the precursor of the National Assembly) on gender issues and used the print and electronic media to stimulate public debate. AMNLAE encouraged the official newspaper to feature women doing nontraditional jobs, agitated for the inclusion of women in the draft, and made extensive efforts to promote international solidarity with the Nicaraguan Revolution through participation in international conferences and contacts with women from other countries. But AMNLAE did not succeed in having women included in the draft and in legalizing abortion. The draft issue was lost mainly because of extensive parental objection to the mandatory conscription of young sons in the wake of the deaths incurred in the insurrection. Abortion was illegal and criminal, the result both of government sensitivities to the Catholic lobby and the high rate of Nicaraguan mortality due to the

US-backed contra war. Birth control was legal and available through public health clinics and private pharmacies, but difficult to obtain. Eventually, the growing numbers of female deaths due to botched abortions brought the abortion controversy out into the open.

The reproductive rights controversy in Nicaragua signalled some of the emerging new divisions within the movement and in the society. Molyneux has written that while no one was against some form of women's emancipation, understandings of what constituted this emancipation varied considerably, from a limited, traditional protection of women and their mobilization behind certain national campaigns (employment, defense of the revolution, mass education, and health), to policies informed by feminism which see an alteration of gender relations and the full implementation of reproductive rights as the goals towards which the revolution should be moving.[81] On a more optimistic note, Beth Stevens wrote in 1988 that "the mere existence of this dynamic debate in Nicaragua today is one of the strengths of the Nicaraguan revolution."[82]

CONCLUSIONS: REVOLUTIONS, STATE-BUILDING, AND GENDER

Revolutions are a special case of social change and collective action that entail attempts to rapidly transform political and economic structures, social relations, and societal institutions to conform to an ideal or an ideology. The twentieth century has been called the century of revolutions and two sets of scholarship have examined revolutionary change. In one set, standard social-science studies have emphasized the international context as well as class, status, and power within a given society, but have ignored gender as an analytic category in revolutionary transformation.[83] In the other set, feminist studies have revealed the significance of gender dynamics and their links to political, economic, and ideological processes, including constructions of national identity, in times of social transformation. In this chapter I have tried to show that women and gender issues figure prominently in political discourses, state ideologies, legal policies, and the construction of a national identity. Although revolutionary transformations are shaped by preexisting gender systems, changes in societal values and ideologies and in economic strategies brought about by revolutions also affect gender relations.

At times of regime consolidation, state-building, and identity formation, questions of the construction of gender, the family, and male–female relations come to the fore. Cultural representations of women, changes to family law, and legislation on reproductive rights and women's rights reflect the importance of gender in politics and ideology and signal the political agenda of revolutionaries and regimes. Whether political discourses support women's emancipation and equality or whether they glorify tradition, morality, the family, and difference, the point remains that political ideologies and practices are gendered and that social transformation and state-building entail changes in gender relations as well as new class configurations and property relations.

In my reading of twentieth-century revolutionary transformations, two models of womanhood have emerged. One model, which I have called the woman's emancipation model, draws its inspiration from the Enlightenment, the socialist tradition, and the Bolshevik Revolution. This model is more consistent with feminist demands for equality and empowerment of women. The patriarchal model, which I have called the woman-in-the-family model, seems to occur where revolutionaries draw from their own cultural repertoire, frequently in reaction to external modes of control, as in the three cases discussed in this chapter. The cases of revolutionary transformation discussed in this chapter, and others not discussed but included in Figure 6.1, confirm the strong links among social transformation, state-building, and laws about women and the family. Revolutionizing society and transforming women are two sides of the same coin.

The differentiation of revolutions by gender outcomes shows that gender is indeed an integral dimension of the revolutionary process and should be accorded conceptual value by sociologists of revolution. This is a conclusion I have come to following several years of study.[84] Future research in the sociology of revolution, or in analyses of other types of social transformations, should examine more closely the articulation of gender with class, ethnicity, state policies, and world-systemic processes. Research should also attempt to situate gender issues, in a more systematic manner than I have been able to do, in the various stages of a revolution, including the prerevolutionary conditions, proximate causes, the course of the revolution, and its short-term and long-term outcomes. A fruitful line of inquiry could also be whether or not feminist discourses and the growth of women's movements worldwide will attenuate patriarchal outcomes in future instances of social transformation.

ACKNOWLEDGEMENTS

I wish to thank John Foran and Linda Lobao for their very helpful comments on the first draft of this chapter. This chapter draws on my previously published writings, especially Chapter 3 in my book, *Modernizing Women: Gender and Social Change in the Middle East* (Boulder: Lynne Rienner, 1993), and "Gender and Revolutionary Transformation: Iran 1979 and East Central Europe 1989," pp. 328–58 in *Gender & Society*, volume 9, number 3 (June 1995).

NOTES

1. Early writings include Sheila Rowbotham, *Women, Resistance, and Revolution* (London: Allen Lane, 1972), and Miranda Davies, editor, *Third World/Second Sex* (London: Zed, 1983).

2. Siân Reynolds, "Introduction," in Siân Reynolds, editor, *Women, State and Revolution: Essays on Power and Gender in Europe since 1789* (Amherst: University of Massachusetts Press, 1987).

3. Mary Ann Tétreault, editor, *Women and Revolution in Africa, Asia, and the New World* (Columbia: University of South Carolina Press, 1994).

4. Hanna Papanek, "The Ideal Woman and the Ideal Society: Control and Autonomy in the Construction of Identity," pp. 42–75 in Valentine M. Moghadam, editor, *Identity Politics and Women: Cultural Reassertions and Feminisms in International Perspective* (Boulder: Westview Press, 1994).

5. Moghadam, *Modernizing Women: Gender and Social Change in the Middle East* (Boulder: Lynne Rienner, 1993), chapter three. It should be noted that I use the term "patriarchal" in the strict sense of a form of social organization or an ideology which confines women to the role of wife and mother under male guardianship.

6. John Dunn, *Modern Revolutions* (New York: Cambridge University Press, 1972), 12.

7. Perez Zagorin, *Rebels and Rulers*, volume one (Cambridge: Cambridge University Press, 1982), 17.

8. Lynn Hunt, *Politics, Culture and Class in the French Revolution* (Berkeley: University of California Press, 1984), and *The Family Romance of the French Revolution* (New York and London: Routledge, 1992); Farideh Farhi, *States and Urban-Based Revolutions: Iran and Nicaragua* (Urbana: University of Illinois Press, 1990); Mansoor Moaddel, *Class, Politics, and Ideology in the Iranian Revolution* (New York: Columbia University Press, 1993).

9. Valentine M. Moghadam, "Populist Revolution and the Islamic State in Iran," pp. 147–163 in Terry Boswell, editor, *Revolutions in the World-System* (Westport: Greenwood Press, 1989); Michael S. Kimmel, *Revolution: A Sociological Interpretation* (Cambridge: Polity Press, 1990); John Foran, "A Theory of Third World Social Revolutions: Iran, Nicaragua, and El Salvador Compared," pp. 3–27 in *Critical Sociology*, volume 19, number 2 (1992).

10. Diane Mitsch Bush and Stephen P. Mumme, "Gender and the Mexican Revolution: The Intersection of Gender, State, and Church," pp. 343–65 in Tétreault, editor, *Women and Revolutions in Africa, Asia, and the New World*.

11. Guida West and Rhoda Lois Blumberg, "Introduction: Reconstructing Social Protest from a Feminist Perspective," pp. 3–35 in Guida West and Rhoda Lois Blumberg, editors, *Women and Social Protest* (New York and Oxford: Oxford University Press, 1990).

12. Maxine Molyneux, "Women's Role in the Nicaraguan Revolutionary Process: The Early Years," pp. 127–47 in Sonia Kruks, Rayna Rapp, and Marilyn B. Young, editors, *Promissory Notes: Women in the Transition to Socialism* (New York: Monthly Review Press, 1989), 128. See also Maxine Molyneux, "Mobilization without Emancipation? Women's Interests, State, and Revolution," pp. 280–302 in Richard Fagen, Carmen Diana Deere, and José Luis Corragio, editors, *Transition and Development: Problems of Third World Socialism* (New York: Monthly Review Press, 1986).

13. Bush and Mumme, "Gender and the Mexican Revolution."

14. Molyneux, "Mobilization without Emancipation?," 283–4.

15. Ibid., 297.
16. Maria Mies, *Patriarchy and Accumulation on a World Scale* (London: Zed, 1986), 199. See also Margaret Randall, *Gathering Rage: The Failure of Twentieth-Century Revolutions to Develop a Feminist Agenda* (New York: Monthly Review Press, 1993).
17. Molyneux, "Mobilization without Emancipation?;" Norma Chinchilla, "Revolutionary Popular Feminism in Nicaragua: Articulating Class, Gender, and National Sovereignty," *Gender & Society*, volume 4, number 3 (1990): 370–97, and "Feminism, Revolution and Democratic Transitions in Nicaragua," unpublished paper, Program in Women's Studies, California State University at Long Beach, 1993).
18. Linda Lobao, "Women in Revolutionary Movements: Changing Patterns of Latin American Guerilla Struggles," pp. 180–204 in West and Blumberg, *Women and Social Protest.*
19. See Kyung Ae Park, "Women and Revolution in China: The Sources of Constraint on Women's Emancipation," pp. 137–60 in Tétreault, *Women and Revolutions in Africa, Asia, and the New World.* The author notes, as others have done, that the introduction of market reforms in China may be undoing the progress achieved earlier and helping to resurrect patriarchal concepts, including son preference.
20. Stephanie Urdang, *And Still They Dance: Women, War and the Struggle for Change in Mozambique* (New York: Monthly Review Press, 1989), 28.
21. Molyneux, "Mobilization without Emancipation?," 295.
22. Maxine Molyneux, "Socialist Societies: Progress towards Women's Emancipation?" *Monthly Review*, volume 34, number 3 (1982), 56–100.
23. Siân Reynolds, "Marianne's Citizens? Women, the Republic, and Universal Suffrage in France," pp. 101–22 in Reynolds, *Women, State and Revolution*, 110.
24. Robert Darnton, "What Was Revolutionary about the French Revolution?" *New York Review of Books* (19 January 1989).
25. Ibid., 4.
26. Information and quotes from conversations with Sheila Rowbotham, Helsinki, July 1990. Rowbotham has also said that women's roles in the French Revolution, and in particular left-wing women such as Claire Lacombe and the sansculottes women in the club and society, were the precursors of the socialist women of 1830–48.
27. Hunt, *Politics, Culture and Class*, 31.
28. Ibid., 104.
29. Ibid., 109.
30. Quoted in Siân Reynolds, "Marianne's Citizens?," 113. The similarities to the discourses of the Iranian Revolution are quite striking.
31. Cited in Linda Kelly, *Women of the French Revolution* (London: Hamish Hamilton, 1987), 127.
32. Cited in Reynolds, "Marianne's Citizens?," 105.
33. Carol Pateman, *The Sexual Contract* (Cambridge: Polity Press, 1988).
34. Harriet Applewhite and Darline G. Levy, "Introduction," pp. 1–19 in Harriet Applewhite and Darline G. Levy, editors, *Women and Politics in the Age of the Democratic Revolution* (Ann Arbor: University of Michigan Press, 1990), 17–19.
35. Peter Knauss, *The Persistence of Patriarchy: Class, Gender and Ideology in Twentieth Century Algeria* (Boulder: Westview Press, 1987), 49.
36. Ibid., 75.
37. Doria Cherifati-Merabtine, "Algeria at a Crossroads: National Liberation, Islamization, and Women," pp. 40–62 in Valentine M. Moghadam, editor,

Gender and National Identity: Women and Politics in Muslim Societies (London: Zed, 1994).

38. Knauss, *The Persistence of Patriarchy*, 98.
39. Cherifa Bouatta and Doria Cherifati-Merabtine, "The Social Representation of Women in Algeria's Islamist Movement," pp. 183–201 in Moghadam, *Identity Politics and Women.*
40. Cherifa Bouatta, "Feminine Militancy: Algerian Moudjahidates During and After the War," pp. 18–39 in Moghadam, *Gender and National Identity.*
41. Knauss, *The Persistence of Patriarchy*, 111.
42. On the positive side, state-sponsored education has created a generation of Algerian women who could become a restive force for progressive social change in Algeria. These are the women who loudly and visibly challenged the Chedli Government's conservative Family Code in 1982, who continued to protest it after it was passed in 1984, and who today are courageously confronting the violent Islamist fundamentalist movement in Algeria.
43. See Nayereh Tohidi, "Modernity, Islamization, and Women in Iran," pp. 110–47 in Moghadam, *Gender and National Identity*; Afsaneh Najmabadi, "Power, Morality and the New Muslim Womanhood," pp. 366–89 in Myron Weiner and Ali Banuazizi, editors, *The Politics of Social Transformation in Afghanistan, Iran, and Pakistan* (Syracuse: Syracuse University Press, 1994); Val Moghadam, "Islamic Populism, Class, and Gender in Postrevolutionary Iran," pp. 189–222 in John Foran, editor, *A Century of Revolution: Social Movements in Iran* (Minneapolis: University of Minnesota Press, 1994).
44. Najmabadi, "Power, Morality and the New Muslim Womanhood," 370–1.
45. *Hijab: Immunity, Not Limitation* (Tehran: Center for Mosques" Affairs, Women's Section, prepared for the Fourth World Conference on Women, Beijing, September 1995).
46. Speech of Shahla Habibi, Presidential Advisor on Women's Affairs, presented at the Fourth World Conference on Women, Beijing (September 11, 1995).
47. Valentine M. Moghadam, "Gender and Restructuring: Perestroika, the 1989 Revolutions, and Women," UNU/WIDER Working Paper No. 87 (Helsinki: UNU/WIDER, 1990).
48. Ibid., 35.
49. Barbara Einhorn, "Democratization and Women's Movements in Central and Eastern Europe: Concepts of Women's Rights," pp. 48–74 in Valentine M. Moghadam, editor, *Democratic Reform and the Position of Women in Transitional Economies* (Oxford: Clarendon Press, 1993), 58.
50. Findings from the 1994–95 UNU/WIDER research project, coordinated by the present author, on economic reforms, women's employment, and social policies in industrializing and transition economies, especially commissioned papers by Renata Siemienska on Poland and Dobrinka Kostova on Bulgaria.
51. Dobrinka Kostova, in a paper prepared for UNU/WIDER, 1994.
52. Einhorn, "Democratization and Women's Movements," 63.
53. Wendy Zeva Goldman, "Women, the Family, and the New Revolutionary Order in the Soviet Union," pp. 59–81 in Kruks, Rapp, and Young, *Promissory Notes*, 61.
54. *The Woman Question: Selections from the Writings of Karl Marx, Frederick Engels, V. I. Lenin, Clara Zetkin, Joseph Stalin* (New York: International Publishers, 1977), 56.
55. Ibid., 59.
56. Ibid., 61.
57. Elizabeth Waters, "In the Shadow of the Comintern: The Communist Women's Movement, 1920–1943," pp. 29–56 in Kruks, Rapp, and Young, *Promissory*

Notes. As Engels himself put it in the preface to the *Origin of the Family, Private Property, and the State*, "The supremacy of the man in marriage is the simple consequence of his economic supremacy, and with the abolition of the latter will disappear of itself."

58. On Bolshevik strategies in Central Asia see Gregory Massell, *The Surrogate Proletariat* (Princeton: Princeton University Press, 1974).
59. Eric Hobsbawm, personal communication, Helsinki, August 9, 1990.
60. Nermin Abadan-Unat, "Social Change and Turkish Women," in Abadan-Unat, editor, *Women in Turkish Society* (Leiden: E. J. Brill, 1981), 9.
61. Kumari Jayawardena, *Feminism and Nationalism in the Third World* (New York: Monthly Review Press, 1986), 29.
62. Çaglar Keyder, "The Political Economy of Turkish Democracy," pp. 3–44 in *New Left Review* number 115 (May–June 1979), 9; Jayawardena, *Feminism and Nationalism in the Third World*, 34; Deniz Kandiyoti, "Women and the Turkish State: Political Actors or Symbolic Pawns?," pp. 126–49 in Nira Yuval-Davis and Floya Anthias, editors, *Women-Nation-State* (London: Macmillan 1989), 141.
63. Cited in Kandiyoti, "Women and the Turkish State," 141.
64. See Emel Dogramaci, *The Status of Women in Turkey* (Ankara: Meteksan Co., 1984), especially chapter three on "The Status of Women as Reflected in the Works of Namik Kemal, Huseyin Rahmi Gürpinar, Halide Edip Adirar and Ziya Gökalp."
65. Kandiyoti, "Women and the Turkish State," 142.
66. Suna Kili, "Modernity and Tradition: Dilemma Concerning Women's Rights in Turkey," paper presented to the annual meeting of the International Society of Political Psychology, Helsinki, Finland (July 1991), 7.
67. Quoted in Jayawardena, *Feminism and Nationalism in the Third World*, 36.
68. Jayawardena, *Feminism and Nationalism*, 38.
69. Maxine Molyneux, "Legal Reform and Socialist Revolution in South Yemen: Women and the Family," pp. 193–214 in Kruks, Rapp, and Young, *Promissory Notes*, 195.
70. Ibid., 203.
71. Ibid.
72. Ibid., 205–6.
73. Nagat El-Sanabary, "The Middle East and North Africa," pp. 140–65 in Elizabeth M. King and M. Anne Hill, editors, *Women's Education in Developing Countries: Barriers, Benefits, and Policies* (Baltimore: Johns Hopkins University Press, 1993), 162.
74. North and South Yemen were unified in 1990, largely to the disadvantage of the South. To this day, Arab feminists will explain a Yemeni woman's Westernized appearance or bold ideas by saying: "She comes from Aden."
75. Quoted in Nancy Tapper, "Causes and Consequences of the Abolition of Bride-Price in Afghanistan," pp. 291–305 in Nazif Shahrani and Robert Canfield, editors, *Rebellions and Revolutions in Afghanistan* (Berkeley: University of California Press, 1984), 292.
76. Thomas Hammond, *Red Flag Over Afghanistan* (Boulder: Westview Press, 1984), 71.
77. For an elaboration of this discussion, see Moghadam, *Modernizing Women*, chapter seven.
78. Molyneux, "Mobilization without Emancipation?," 287.
79. Beth Stevens, "Women in Nicaragua," pp. 1–18 in *Monthly Review*, volume 40, number 4 (September 1988).
80. Chinchilla, "Revolutionary Popular Feminism in Nicaragua."

81. Maxine Molyneux, "The Politics of Abortion in Nicaragua: Revolutionary Pragmatism – or Feminism in the Realm of Necessity?," pp. 114–32 in *Feminist Review*, number 29 (1988).
82. Stevens, "Women in Nicaragua," 18.
83. See, for example, the special issue of *Contention* on revolutions (volume 2, number 2, Winter 1993) – not a word on women or gender.
84. A paper that I wrote in 1989 and circulated in 1990 attempted to theorize gender in a structuralist vein, situating gender in the realm of culture and showing its links to politics and the economy. After this was critiqued by several friends and colleagues, I took a different approach, one that was premised on the social reality of gender and its integral role in production and reproduction. Extensive research since 1990 on a range of issues – such as fundamentalism and other forms of cultural reassertion, and structural adjustment and market reforms – convinced me that not only do such processes have gender-specific effects, but also they are profoundly shaped by gender ideologies. It seems to me that there is no gender-neutral ground, and the field of revolution is not exempt.

7

RACE AND THE PROCESS OF THE AMERICAN REVOLUTIONS

Christopher McAuley

In a footnote to *The Protestant Ethic and the Spirit of Capitalism*, Max Weber made an interesting observation on the "racial" dimension of the English Revolution, a dimension which may serve as an unexpected point of departure for our present concerns on race and revolution in the Americas. Weber noted:

> One who shared the philosophy of history of the Levellers would be in the fortunate position of being able to attribute this in turn to racial differences. They believed themselves to be defenders of the Anglo-Saxon birthright, against the descendants of William the Conqueror and the Normans. It is astonishing enough that it has not yet occurred to anyone to maintain that the plebian Roundheads were roundheaded in the anthropometric sense![1]

The rank and file of Oliver Cromwell's New Model Army were able consequently to bolster their conviction and morale in unifying race and class during the revolution in the idea of the "Norman Yoke." The New Model Army was Parliament's armed force in its dispute with Charles I over "unparliamentary taxation" and over which political body would decide British commercial policy, among other issues. Having "forgotten how to fight,"[2] Independent Members of Parliament persuaded Parliament to employ "commoners" (yeoman farmers, artisans, small merchants) as armed surrogates while royalists sought the aid of Scottish Presbyterians.

The Norman Yoke theory which surfaced forcefully during the revolution was a reinterpretation of English history (a requirement of all race and class based theories) whose vision of the past held that "Before 1066 the Anglo-Saxon inhabitants of this country lived as free and equal citizens, governing themselves through representative institutions. The Norman Conquest deprived them of this liberty, and established the tyranny of an alien king and landlords." Little did it matter, Christopher Hill continues, that "Anglo-Saxon society was already divided into classes before William the Bastard set foot in England;"[3] what the New Model Army found and employed in the English Revolution was an historical reconstruction which

168

attributed the introduction of property rights (and wrongs) to Norman intervention in a land where, according to the theory, property did not make the person. It may have been "a rudimentary class theory of politics," but the Norman Yoke was a successful analysis of "the relation between force, property, and the origin of the state."[4]

It is rarely the case, however, that race and class are so neatly solidified that to speak of one accurately speaks of the other. Normally, there are gradations and overlaps which serve to complicate and even defy (but do not deny) our tendency to think in terms of absolutes minus the "gray" areas. This was no less true of the Norman Yoke. At first the label "Norman" was reserved for those who wanted to maintain social hierarchies in landownership, religious structure, and legal matters as against the "Anglo-Saxons" who called for land redistribution (among whom the "Diggers" were the most radical), decentralized Puritan preaching, and democratic laws. Later, however, the Norman Yoke grew more inclusive, submitting even Oliver Cromwell to its blood logic when he climbed the political ranks to assume the positions of Lord General and Lord Protector, then rooted out the Levellers (those who desired an extension of the franchise) from the New Model Army, and devastated Ireland over their opposition. Red blood could change to blue without any change in lineage: a change in ideology sufficed. Still, if race rather accurately encompassed class, then the Norman Yoke was a useful device by which English commoners could understand the terms of their struggle in the English Revolution. And as we shall see in the American revolutions – by which I mean the anti-colonial ("American," Haitian, and Latin American wars of independence), Mexican, Cuban, and Nicaraguan revolutions – contending social actors also assumed racialized personas. Furthermore, we shall also assess the effects of race consciousness on revolutionary mobilizations and ultimately outcomes.

RACE IN THE AMERICAS

An "American" observer will tend to find the example of racial differences in the English Revolution puzzling on perhaps two counts: first, we tend to think of "race" in terms of skin color and phenotype due to the Amerindian, African, and European dimensions of our populations; and second, precisely because of these presences, we fail to recognize "racial" distinctions in populations we have come to think of as monolithically "white" or European. Contrary to its modern usage, "race" did not always exclusively refer to skin color: it was used to distinguish ethnicities, nationalities, and even populations from different regions of the same social formation, as in the instance of seventeenth-century England. And like the three categories already mentioned, "race" was/is simply a term of difference (biological or divinely ordained) onto which is necessarily grafted a corresponding social value or

169

lack of one. Differences notwithstanding, the Norman Yoke provides some useful parallels with events in the Americas.

Both were/are settler societies; invading armies not only conquered the indigenous populations, but also settled permanently on indigenous soil. Those directly engaged in the conquest divided the newly acquired lands among themselves and the conquered became their labor supply in a host of labor conditions ranging from slavery to wage labor. Oliver C. Cox described the racialization of the Atlantic world's division of labor thus:

> The . . . exploitation of the colored workers, it should be observed, consigns them to employments and treatment that is humanly degrading. In order to justify this treatment the exploiters must argue that the workers are innately degraded and degenerate, consequently they naturally merit their condition. It may be mentioned incidentally that the ruling-class conception of degradation will tend to be that of all persons in the society, even that of the exploited person himself, and the work done by degraded persons will tend to degrade superior persons who attempt to do it. . . . Moreover, we . . . tend to dislike people who are degraded or brutalized. A degraded person is a contemptible person who should be despised and kept at a distance – the Christian Gospels notwithstanding.[5]

These last remarks suggest that "race" or "ethnicity" is not a function of biology alone, but that one's socio-economic station is a necessary element in the making of one's race or ethnicity. In the Americas, unskilled manual labor tends to darken the worker so engaged, as "mental" labor tends to whiten. Moreover, when elites are predominantly drawn from a particular ethnic group or race, it affirms an association between race and class for the entire society. While "Race made little difference among the poorest in society,"[6] as one scholar aptly noted, when there is a high correlation between race and class or poverty and "persuasion," then race matters. The Levellers and Diggers among others, understood by Anglo-Saxonness, direct producers in the fields, while by Normanness they understood those who did not engage in direct production. Thus, a socio-racial order is maintaining itself successfully when race is stereotypically associated with class and it is actively undermining itself if those it has deemed racially inferior are able to succeed economically.

The parallels between "Norman" England and the Americas may end there, however, since in the Americas the children of European and Amerindian and European and African sexual relations were conceptualized as distinct populations which demanded corresponding labels – mestizo, ladino, mulatto, quadroon – by settler elites.[7] These biological labels were not idle but ideally active determinants of socio-economic position: color and class were made to work in unison.[8] The longevity, then of the race–class complex is due not to its uncompromising nature but rather to its bounded flexibility:

170

a portion of those conquered are assimilated into the extended family of the victors. This "tokenism" pragmatically serves to fragment the solidity of a too apparent race–class bond which would probably result in more successful revolutions than merely local rebellions, especially in the absence of a compelling ideology to transform class into caste. In some instances the assimilated are a pre-conquest ruling caste within large and well-defined state structures (the Aztec and Inca experiences with Spanish colonization, for example), while in others, the assimilated are creations (biological or by treaty) of the victor's pragmatic and conscious divide-and-rule strategies. In all cases, the intermediate or "buffer" populations, by their mere existences, "institutionalize, in a customary if not in an official way, the symbolism of race, colour and status as the idiom of social stratification and mobility."[9]

Despite its apparent explicit meaning, however, "race" is typically accompanied by two other illustrations – phenotype and culture – which demonstrate the multidimensionality of human identity. Phenotype refers not only to complexion, but also to its associates: facial structure, hair texture, etc. In the Americas, European features are normally valued most, with Amerindian and African ones finishing in a distant second and third positions. Skin tone valuations, however, have been more negotiable and at times white skin alone has not been considered the pinnacle of perfection.

Culture, more elusive, may be simply defined as a group's mechanisms of daily performance, including language, dress, leisure activities, religious practices, cooking styles, etc. Culture, like phenotype, is hierarchically "structured in dominance."[10]

> Since the cultural attributes of [a] population are inextricably associated with racial factors . . . ethno-cultural differences . . . provide the ruling classes with a powerful instrument to be used as an ideological justification of the miserable conditions, limited power and limited vertical mobility of the Indian and Black masses. Thus, in the absence of biological and cultural "purity" of the ruling class an individual [is] unfit to be a member of society: by this means, the monopoly over politico-economic power [is] legitimized.[11]

For one to have "good hair" or be labeled an "oreo" or its equivalent, therefore, is an assessment of what Michel-Rolph Trouillot has fittingly called one's "social direction" or "the path that an individual is perceived to be taking up or down the social ladder."[12]

Post-conquest European immigrants and even immigrants of color are socially molded by the racial paradigm of historical conquest into which they settle. For Cox, "The race against whom the whites are least prejudiced tends to become second in rank, while the race that they despise most will ordinarily be at the bottom. Thus more or less directly the superior race controls the pattern of all dependent prejudices."[13] For the sake of accuracy, we need to expand Cox's notion of "race" to encompass "ethnicity," which

171

the dominant group deploys and defines in the social order it guides. Eighteenth-, nineteenth- and twentieth-century German, Irish, Italian, Slavic, and other European immigrants were not immediately considered part of the ruling complex primarily because "Creole" elites (American-born Europeans of Spanish, American, and Portuguese stock) saw these new-comers as ethnically or racially inferior. In crude, but no less accurate terms, these European immigrants had yet to become "white." Still, "these European migrants . . . tended to be rapidly absorbed into the warm embrace of the ruling classes, typically through the route of commercial and matrimonial activity."[14] After all, they knew, as their children did, that their "civilisational project"[15] status placed them above people of Amerindian and African descent (even when their class position did not). On this racialized division of labor, Norman Girvan comments:

> White immigrants took the relatively highly-paid semi-skilled and skilled occupations in farming, industry and services, and benefitted along with the owners of capital, in the tremendous growth and industrialization process taking place in these areas. Therefore in these regions while it is true to say that a process of proletarianization of all races did occur, this process had a marked racial bias. It would be more true to say that the whites were proletarianized while the non-whites were lumpenproletarianized.[16]

Similarly, Chinese and East Indian laborers who had been originally imported into the Americas as indentured servants were frequently able to take advantage of their intermediate status as a means of social climbing after indentureship.

What we have just described, however, are ideal types, that is, bio-economic approximations of what has been and still is more socially variable across time and place. Still, for our purposes in this chapter, the importance of ideal types lies in their outline of power relations and the historical staying power of those relations, especially as they inform, define, and create individual and group aspirations in the American revolutions and in everyday life. For it is still the case that "In the . . . Americas generally, there remains a high correlation between income, occupational status, ownership of property and socio-economic power on the one hand, and 'physical' and 'social' race on the other hand."[17]

RACE AND THE ANTI-COLONIAL REVOLUTIONS

In the eighteenth and nineteenth centuries, the racialization of the Atlantic world's division of labor cast the majority of Amerindians and Africans as agricultural workers of various subordinate statuses. Whereas Africans in the Americas were unabashedly commercialized laborers with few unsupervised spaces of respite, surviving Amerindians still had recourse to their village communities. The collaboration, furthermore, of some mixed-race caciques with the colonial administration in Spanish America also served to stabilize the colonial dispensation and they were handsomely rewarded for their services.[18] As the Amerindian populations began to recover, however, in the mid-seventeenth century and after from the demographic destruction engendered by the conquest, the Casa Grande and the pueblo inevitably came into open conflict, especially in Mexico and Peru.

The bulk of the children that European men had with Amerindian and African women were also confined to their mothers'' stations, though some secured managerial positions and city-dwellers enjoyed a higher status ranking. In many cases, however, mestizos, mulattos, and free Blacks were prohibited from engaging in economic activities which would diminish the meaning of the race/class/culture complex. In colonial Cuba, for example,

> Whenever [free Blacks and mulattos] found an occupation that promised a fair livelihood, the whites, to reserve such forms of livelihood for themselves, put pressure on the authorities to forbid the Negroes to continue in that pursuit. Thus the Negro was forbidden to sell tobacco, except for his own use, nor could he operate an inn or bar.[19]

Similar restrictions were made on mulatto dress, access to education, and religious rites which attempted to copy European practices. Only in colonial Haiti was mulatto wealth tolerated by their plantocrat fathers, and there it was ensured by the racial division of crops: coffee for mulatto planters and the more lucrative sugar for Europeans.

What these middling populations wanted from any social movement was a rupture in the association of color and physical features with economic subordination and indignity. Racially progressive, conservative with regard to property, but too weak militarily to overthrow their colonial governments, these middling populations found themselves dependent on both crown and Creole.

Few if any mestizos or mulattos penetrated the fortress of merchant's capital in colonial America: "Spaniards . . . monopolize[d] trans-Atlantic trade and shipping . . . while Americans [Creoles] were confined to inter-colonial trade."[20] Though Creoles were among the largest landholders in colonial Spanish America, they were continuously barred from the upper echelons of political and economic power by Spanish-born merchants and bureaucrats – peninsulares. Alexander von Humboldt remarked candidly that "The lowest, least educated and uncultivated European believes himself superior to the white born in the New World."[21] What made matters worse were the increasing numbers of immigrant peninsulares who arrived at the end of the eighteenth century.[22] Understandably, Creoles could hardly stomach the sight of colonial funds subsidizing personal and imperial arrogance not to mention the harm to colonial economic development by Spain's denying them access to international markets and discouraging their industrial designs.

The tenuous adhesive of Spanish colonialism finally came unglued with Napoleon's invasion of Spain in 1808 and his replacement of the legitimate heir to the Spanish throne, Ferdinand VII, with his brother, Joseph. As the center no longer held, the contradictory anti-colonial visions unfurled. Simón Bolívar's sentiments foreshadowed the social limitations of the independence movement: "A great volcano lies at our feet. Who shall restrain the oppressed classes? Slavery will break its yoke, each shade of complexion will seek mastery."[23] Since complexion rather neatly referred to class position, Bolívar was speaking to the maintenance of the colonial socio-economic order minus its unsightly abuses. In 1815 he promised an end to slavery and other forms of unfree labor, just as he wanted to end Spanish mercantilism and its political straitjacket; however, he had not become the great "liberator" in order to make of Latin America a chain of Haitian republics. The demographic composition of his native Venezuela made Bolívar particularly anxious about the possibility of subalterns taking the independence movement beyond even mulatto intentions. This fear was quite personal for Bolívar as he was both a large slaveholder and mulatto, and it nearly compelled him to renege on his promise to the Haitian people. He had once remarked that a slave insurrection was "a thousand times worse than a Spanish invasion."[24] The emancipation promise was kept, nevertheless, with nearly all of the Latin American republics declaring slavery's termination between 1815 and 1830.

Regrettably, but characteristically, it was military pragmatism that forced Creoles to make pronouncements against unfree labor and racism in the independence struggle. Even before the independence movements, however, the military was one of the primary sites of socio-economic mobility for the mestizo, free Black, and mulatto. As the colonial militias were neither Madrid-financed nor *peninsulare*-manned, the Spanish American colonies were forced to employ their own populations for territorial defense. This reliance on proxies to defend the political order within which they were denied full citizenship raised the issue of how Creole elites would control the vision of freedom of subordinate populations. Cuba deferred its independence struggle until 1868 precisely because the plantocracy recognized that political independence would bring "free" labor. With Blacks and mulattos soon becoming the majority populations of the island, the planters were terrified by the prospect of another Haiti (even as their sugar profits swelled from European boycotts of Haiti).

Until 1814, Peru similarly became the southern bastion of counter-independence after the cataclysmic rebellion of Tupac Amaru in 1780. As in Cuba, the demographic constitution of Peru explained a great deal: Amerindians and mestizos comprised a majority with 57 and 29 percent of the population respectively, Blacks and mulattos numbered 8 percent, leaving a mere 6 percent of the population white.[25] Few Peruvians of color were willing to heed Túpac's cry for freedom, however, and the cacique, Mateo Pumacahua (who later came to understand his misdirection) and a loyal militia of color brutally crushed the movement. Order over independence became the rallying cry of a threatened white elite and it is not surprising that the independence movement had to be imported. It was, therefore, a negative independence rather than a positive one, or an independence by default: finding the application of Spain's liberal constitution of 1821 ironically too menacing to Peru's social order, independence was advocated as a defensive move or as "a case of self help."[26] The imperial armies, for their part, took advantage of the social divisions within colonial society and expediently offered African slaves and Amerindian peons emancipation and land respectively, forcing reluctant Creole elites to match the terms. The African and Amerindian presences within Latin America made both crown and Creole acknowledge that, like themselves, "Red" and "Black" understood the independence movements "in terms of their own interests and concerns."[27]

As anti-colonial revolutionaries the American elites aimed at higher political and economic places rather than the inauguration of a decisive structural break from the colonial political-economy's dictates on property and production. The revolutions' anti-racist potential was in part undermined by the devastation and debt incurred by the military effort as well as the channeling of trade toward Great Britain. Perhaps both the recognition of the structural constraints on their national economies and their own class aspirations largely explain why Latin American mestizos and mulattos opted for individual assimilation. The costs, however, were great and the strategy served only to reinforce the racialization of the national division of labor: "they made this ascent . . . only by disavowing their class [i.e., race] and becoming culturally white themselves, which meant that the most dynamic element in society worked not to dissolve the existing structure but to join and profit from it."[28]

On the other hand, we cannot deny the role that elite class interests played in the reproduction of the racialization of the Atlantic world's division of labor in the post-independence era. To the degree that the independent nation remained tied to the terms of exchange set by the European-centered world economy, it required the old labor regime. This process was graphically illustrated in the thirteen colonies: "The economic forces of the country, which had suffered most, sought to recover and rearrange themselves; and all the selfish motives that impelled a bankrupt nation to seek to gain its daily bread did not long hesitate to demand a reopening of the profitable African slave-trade."[29] Even without the post-war debts, Eli Whitney's tinkering, which produced the cotton gin in 1791, would have given the slave mode of capitalist production a new lease on life for another three-quarters of a century. The cohabitation of slavery and independence was foreshadowed in the earlier part of the eighteenth century as one of the primary causes of the independence of the thirteen colonies.

What did move the colonists was a crafty tactic by the "first full-fledged villain . . . in the American patriotic tradition,"[30] John Murray, Earl of Dunmore, who "declare[d] all indented servants, Negroes, or others . . . free, that are able and willing to bear arms, they joining His Majesty's Troops as soon as may be."[31] Despite prejudicial restrictions, Black Americans had been enlisted (admittedly as a last measure) in prior colonial wars and their military service was considered a fair exchange for freedom. Initially the same custom applied in the Revolutionary War, but many white colonists soon began to fear the potential of slave revolts that extensive Black recruitment would engender (the African population constituted 20 percent of the colonial total). Necessity combined with Dunmore's ploy, to make it clear "that if the Patriots did not make use of the blacks, the enemy would."[32] On the whole, however, Blacks were employed in the navy as sailors rather than as soldiers, and it was only in the North that Blacks served duty on land.

The Deep South, however, firmly stood its ground and refused to enlist slaves as soldiers even in the face of near defeat. Thus, the very concerns which were "mainly responsible for moving uncommitted Southern planters into the camp of rebellion" ironically made them "willing to have their country overrun by the British rather than comply with the urgent recommendation of Congress to permit the enrollment of their slaves in the American armed forces."[33] The British, however, could not take full advantage of the counterrevolutionary forces in the South which saw national independence and slave emancipation as one, since they too were constrained by similar conservative considerations from the West India Interest. Thus sections of both sides opted for social order over independence or empire.

With independence won without the need to pair it with slave emancipation, the post-colonial constitutional discourse on slavery subsided. The image of slavery, however, continued to be a powerful force in the new Republic even in areas with few slaves, as white working people declared it antithetical to both republican institutions and spirit. Not only was independence what the colonies had won from England, but also the adjectival form of the word – independent – became a proud self-description of its people. And those who were not independent, so the syllogism went, had not contributed to independence and thus were doubly slaves, "that Black oppression was the result of 'slavishness' rather than slavery."[34]

Four forces combined in the post-independence era to make this curious republican logic feasible: first, the cross-class white refusal to allow all willing slaves and free people to engage in the revolutionary cause thereby blocking a customary path to emancipation; second, the persistence of slavery and thus the continued association of Blackness and enslavement; third, the decline of white indentured servitude which enabled whiteness to be more fully associated with economic independence; and fourth, the political and military engagement which the anti-colonial struggle demanded reduced intra-white ethnic conflict and Americanized white ethnics into a more unified "white" people. Against these forces, Black Americans had become a pariah population. As in Latin America, US independence left racism intact.

But their lot was surprisingly better than others; some Amerindian nations were decimated in the course of the anti-colonial struggles for having allied themselves with the losing side. Such was the Iroquois" fate. Ironically, the independence movement which the Iroquois played no small part in cata-lyzing – from pushing the thirteen colonies to confederate following its example,[35] to providing the revolutionaries with a fitting costume idea at the Boston tea rebellion – crushed the Iroquois. The Ho-da-ne-sau-nee (League of the Iroquois) broke with its Council's tradition of unanimity at the out-break of the American Revolution when the Oneida representatives rejected siding with the British. "It was finally determined that each nation might engage in the war upon its own responsibility; so that, ultimately, the Mohawks, Onondagas, Cayugas and Senecas took up the rifle for the English."[36] Typical of European–Amerindian relations, once the latter's use-fulness to the former had run its course, so had Amerindian interests. For the Iroquois as for countless other Amerindian societies, peace with victors meant relinquishing ever larger pieces of their lands. And does not the Cayuga case speak volumes on the Amerindian experience in the wake of the revolutionary struggles? "In the brief space of twelve years after the first house of the white man was erected in Cayuga county (1789) the whole nation was uprooted and gone."[37]

Ironically, in Haiti, the one revolution which might have committed itself most to institute significant changes in both labor relations and the final destination of profits, did least in those domains. The limited vision of the Haitian revolutionary leadership was due in part to its slave origins, the source also of its strength. So formed by the "plantation" complex were Toussaint L'Ouverture and the other revolutionary leaders that the develop-ment path for which rank-and-file Haitians fought – peasant subsistence pro-duction – frightened their leadership:

> The ultimate guarantee of freedom was the prosperity of agriculture. This was Toussaint's slogan. The danger was that the blacks might slip into the practice of cultivating a small patch of land, producing just sufficient for their needs. He would not allow the estates to be broken up, but bound the interests of the labourers to their work by giving them their keep and a fourth of the produce.[38]

The "enlightened" despotism of militarized agriculture (*caporalisme agraire*) could and did quickly turn into the blind despotism of re-enslave-ment. Neither Toussaint in institutionalizing nor C. L. R. James in writing about the Haitian Revolution foresaw the staying power of the military or that it would permanently confront its now "liberated" nation with the same preparedness it planned to meet foreign re-enslavers. Where the nation "measured its liberty in Sunday markets and in the right to work in its garden plots," the developing state "was firmly attached to the plantation system."[39] The leadership of the only anti-colonial struggle that was simultaneously the overthrow of slavery failed "to face the fact that the goal of unconditional freedom was incompatible with the maintenance of the plantation system."[40] What spared the military-landed elite from the wrath of former slaves was largely its color and national prestige. This political use of pigment foreshadowed what would be termed later in the nineteenth century, the *politique de doublure*, whereby mulatto elites would deploy a Black Haitian as president in order to thinly mask the continued pillage of the peasantry.

In the aftermath of the revolution, however, race did not distinguish Haitian elites: regardless of color they were all agreed on the perceived need to reinstate the plantation economy. Where they disagreed was on the point of plantation ownership: whereas President Henri Christophe, like his predecessor Jean-Jacques Dessalines, insisted on state ownership (which the generals came to consider practically their own private lands), contender Alexandre Pétion, insisted on private ownership. Not only did this disagreement lead to the division of the Republic between Christophe's North and Pétion's West and South, but also it was now racialized: in the North, Christophe led a cadre of military planters who had been slaves before the revolution, while in the West and South, Pétion upheld the property rights of mulatto planters, a considerable number of whom had been free persons and landowners before the birth of the Republic. Color considerations, moreover, forced Pétion to make nominal concessions to the Haitian peasantry within those regions; for as a mulatto, the security of his regime depended on avoiding any visible tie to an agricultural regime that reminded former slaves of racial slavery.

By the time then that Jean-Pierre Boyer reunited the Republic in 1820, the Haitian peasantry had *de facto* implemented the land reform project which the revolution's leadership had shunned during and after independence, setting up small family farms wherever they could.[41] Former slaves strove for a more authentic vision and practice of freedom than their leadership, seeking an inversion of plantation-led economic growth with production geared toward the uplift of the "provision grounds" at the expense of the Big House. This vision of development also grew out of the slave experience, as did its opposite. None the less, former slaves did not categorically reject export agriculture in favor of subsistence production; on the contrary, they enthusiastically engaged in coffee cultivation.

The state fought back, however. If it could not control land settlement it could control (with the aid of foreign and domestic merchants) the export taxes levied on coffee thus taking revenge at the customhouse. These taxes were all the more invidious because of their invisibility to the peasant producer. "Whenever the state increased the fees and duties on coffee the exporters . . . passed the charges on to the speculators . . . who in turn imposed them on the peasants by reducing the price paid for their produce."[42] In short, while the Haitian Revolution successfully changed the form of labor, it ultimately did not change its content. In certain respects, then, American reactions to the Haitian Republic were not entirely justified.

AMERINDIANS AND IDENTITY IN THE MEXICAN REVOLUTION

British capital's assault on the Mexican economy in the post-independence era was two-pronged: first, its design was to keep Mexico a raw materials producer by the active discouragement of its industrial development, especially in textiles; and second, by the granting of loans and other credit extensions to the newly constituted Mexican state, British capital controlled the material terms of Mexican debt. To achieve the first goal, "British manufactured goods flooded the Mexican market."[43] It was not yet state mismanagement of funds which drove the Mexican state to seek loans; rather it was the cost of the war of independence in the context of colonialism.

More secure in its position as world capitalist leader, British capital saw no need to send in its troops to force either monetary or territorial concessions from the Mexican state as did Spain, France, and the burgeoning United States, though it connived with the former two to take over Mexico militarily during the tragicomic rule of Archduke Maximilian III from 1862 to 1867. American capital was fast on British heels, however, and during Porfirio Díaz's presidency (1876–1911), it had overtaken its rivals:

> By 1897, U.S. investments in Mexico totaled more than $200 million and exceeded such investment in the rest of Latin America, in Canada, in Europe, or in Asia. In the next fourteen years, this figure quintupled, and by 1911 U.S. investments were estimated to be greater than those of the Mexican bourgeoisie and double those of all other foreign investors.[44]

Little wonder that American property was frequently targeted for either expropriation or destruction during the revolution.

American and British capital built the bulk of the railways that carried Mexico's goods to market: besides oil and minerals, sugar, coffee, vanilla, chiles, chicle, chickpeas, sisal, cotton, maguey, tomatoes, and cattle. Such a vast scale of agricultural output points to extensive land concentration and this last meant the usurpation of more than 2 million acres of Indian communal lands highlighting the perennial question of what type of landownership arrangement would rule the countryside: village plots and commons or haciendas.[45] When the haciendas won the battle, displaced villagers were bitterly forced to seek employment on them.

It was ironically during Benito Juárez's tenure as president that Díaz's land monopolization policies had their precedent. Though of Zapotec stock himself and vocally against encroachment on Amerindian lands, Juárez's Ley Lerdo and the 1857 Constitution submitted communally held Amerindian lands to bourgeois property rights of individual ownership. The financial demands of the war against French imperialism, furthermore, drove Juárez to renege on the clauses partially protecting Amerindian communal lands from total alienability. Cockcroft notes that 4.5 million acres were sold for two and a half cents each between 1863 and 1867, but Warman contends, nevertheless, that "in most parts of the country many Indian communities preserved their character of relatively independent social units."[46] Where these "liberal" land policies took their toll was rather on Amerindian political institutions, languages, and culture: "Many Indian communities gradually became simple rural ones without distinctive cultural features but clearly distinguishable by their structural position in the system."[47] With this last remark we may well wonder what was, if any, the particularly Amerindian content of the Mexican Revolution or had Amerindianness come to signify merely the "poor, above all rural poor,"[48] devoid of racial/cultural awareness. Had a socio-economic condition been indiscriminately racialized out of past habit leaving the signifier ethnically empty even in the course of a revolution? Was the Mexican peasantry so racially and culturally nondescript that even a revolution could not revive its past identities especially when revolutions are normally in the habit of trying to retrieve identities lost?

In an article devoted to the role of race in the Mexican Revolution it is Alan Knight's position that "the Revolution that began in 1910 could be fought and was fought on the basis of considerable Indian participation (more so if the broad definition of 'Indian' is adopted), but in the absence of any self consciously Indian project."[49] It is furthermore Knight's contention that the *indigenismo* and then, *mestizaje* slogans which the state promulgated in post-revolution Mexico were elite constructs employed to forge both a cohesive national identity and to justify the revolutionary state's interventionist role in Mexican society. These identity slogans, Knight stresses, were not voiced by Amerindian communities themselves.

The second part of Knight's two-part argument, however, lends itself to an alternative interpretation of the initial half. It seems equally plausible to suggest that in the face of the Porfiriato's visible admiration for and alliance with the elite European and North American model of socio-economic development (as embodied in the *científicos*, the "Chicago Boys" of the time), campesinos (Amerindian-identifying or not) acutely perceived the official associations between color, class, and culture which had become state policy and which they justifiably resented. In other words, class protest metonymically invoked the color and culture that corresponded to the enemies of the protesters. This complex of associations was perhaps most true in the southern states where "antagonism between the largely Indian peasants and mestizo urban middle class"[50] was particularly pronounced. Little did it matter that in Emiliano Zapata's native state of Morelos a mere 9 percent of the population spoke Nahuatl; they referred to themselves and were perceived by outsiders as "Indians."[51] Moreover, it would have been difficult for a leader perceived as a "non-Indian" (that is, untied to local traditions) to have garnered the popular backing that a Zapata could claim. Thus, François Chevalier's suggestion that the battle between hacienda and village in Morelos "served to increase their [campesinos'] solidarity. In their efforts to avoid becoming mere peons and agricultural day-labourers, they appear to some extent to have regained their communal spirit, which they had lost through contacts with the neighbouring capital and often through neglect of their native language."[52] In other words, the engagement in the revolutionary process lent itself to the revival of Amerindian identities which no doubt informed revolutionary ideologies.

There may have been, then, a silently articulated, implicit, and/or latent Amerindian "color" content to the revolution (which at times the revolution itself forged) beyond those places where it was less timidly voiced (e.g., among the Maya in the Yucatán and the Yaqui in Sonora). In other words, there may have been an Amerindian equivalent of the "Norman Yoke" in the Mexican Revolution. This perception of events did not automatically translate into revolutionary activity (though there may have been a significant correlation between racial/cultural memory and revolutionary engagement), but it was a perspective which harbored the potential coalition among color, class, and culture independent of local caciques.

My position is taken from drawing an analogy to what some scholars consider the second American Revolution, the Civil War.[53] At the war's outset, President Abraham Lincoln had made it clear that the dispute was not over the fact of slavery, but of its boundaries. Rarely, however, do events proceed according to plans, especially when those plans are based on the prediction of how another person or group will respond to those events. Such was the case with Black American slaves, the population on which so much else pivoted yet about whom few white Americans spoke, even in a civil war. Initially even the slaves themselves were somewhat oblivious to their own importance, but as the plantations fell before the Union armies they soon realized that they were "masterless" women and men. Thus the conflagration that began in the absence of a formal Black voice took on in mid-stream the then fullest expression of Black liberation. The Civil War had become a Black American War.

Even the meagre results of US Reconstruction proved better than the Mexican returns some four years after the Decree of January 5, 1915 formally instituted land reform as government policy: "the land that changed hands was about one half of one percent."[54] Beyond the facts that the typical ejidal plot was designated on the least rich land, was not "large enough to support its occupant without need of an outside job for at least part of the year, more often than not on a neighboring hacienda," and was not offered to the peon *acasillado* (a hired hacienda worker lodging on the premises) who merited it most, hacendados had a repertoire of evasion and intimidation techniques.[55]

From this angle assimilationist *indigenismo* and *mestizaje* slogans were indeed elite socio-political strategies, as Knight contends, but also strategies to preempt the class struggle from taking on a voiced and visible ethno-cultural content. Postrevolution political elites (who until Cárdenas were northerners) may have been well aware of the threatening potential of a too transparent association between Amerindianness and rural proletarianiz-ation versus Europeanness (both Mexican and foreign) and management or ownership of capital, which they reasoned had taken place in select sites during the revolution. Without *indigenismo* and *mestizaje* projects within the racial structures of a capitalist economy, the new state risked confronting opposition movements which would successfully unite rural and urban politico-cultural aspirations, a gap which remained unbridgeable in the Mexican Revolution and which the Russian Revolution would prove the first to span, no small thanks to World War I.

Still, Knight's argument cannot be wholly dismissed and it appears to capture the ideologies of the Villista and Mexico City working-class move-ments. In fact, one could argue that there was an active anti-Amerindian bias in both these movements which weakened and eventually compromised the revolutionary struggle. It is perhaps an overstatement to claim that there was an anti-Amerindian dynamic at play in the Villista program; after all, both Villa and Zapata largely agreed on land reform projects (differing primarily on the institutions to effect them) which aided and would have continued to aid Amerindian communities. Yet, in the historical pattern of settlement in the North, there was perforce a suspicion of Amerindians. Throughout the nineteenth century, Mexicans from the southern and central parts of the country were encouraged to become military colonists in the North. This is labeled military colonization because in exchange for the license to settle, the immigrants had to quell Apache resistance to both American and Mexican appropriation of their customary lands. Thus, "land along this frontier was granted to anyone willing to take possession of it and defend it with his life."[56] Moreover, "The right to land did not derive merely from inheritance but had to be constantly reaffirmed and defended in battle."[57] These battles of will were intensified by a racial-cultural opposi-tion: the military colonists were largely mestizo or became so as they "had no villages or extended family networks to fall back on, as the peasants of central and southern Mexico had."[58]

The colonists" final success was short-lived, however, as they too would ironically fall victim to forces similar to those which they unleashed on the Apaches. It was not, however, the force of arms which threatened the integrity of northern pueblos but the "iron horse" and its repertoire of removal mechanisms: land speculation and land price inflation, monopolization, and tax increases as foreigners took tax breaks. The railroad companies also precipitated in the mid-1880s the loss of customary "access to large herds of unclaimed cattle that grazed on . . . immense public lands" as local "hacendados began exporting cattle and appropriating public lands."[59] "These developments," continues Friedrich Katz, "undermined whatever free peasantry had developed in northern Mexico in the days of the open frontier [and] . . . the tradition of cooperation among all classes of [northern] society which first emerged in the Apache wars."[60] Like Zapata, then, Villa could articulate his dissatisfaction in terms of lost rights though his referenced a different past from Zapata's:

> In all parts of the Republic we will establish military colonies composed of the veterans of the Revolution. . . . My ambition is to live my life in one of those military colonies among my companeros whom I love, who have suffered so long and deeply with me . . . and the rest of the time I would like to work on my little farm, raising cattle and corn.[61]

Villa's practices during and after the revolution, however, pointed in a different social direction than the utopian military colonies. Not only did he have few qualms with lining his own pockets through land acquisitions and commercial ventures in the supposed name of the Villista state during the revolution, but when he "retired" from the revolution on the 87,000-hectare Hacienda Canutillo, Villa proved himself to be violently against land reform. "When authorities attempted to subdivide the Hacienda El Pueblito," Ramon Eduardo Ruiz recounts, "occupied by General Albino Aranda, an old companion, Villa blocked their path with guns. Ironically, the people asking for land were his former soldiers."[62] This was a far cry from the envisioned *esprit de corps* that would bond military colonists and it was even farther removed from Zapata's "return to the origins" or "the indigenous past."[63]

An anti-Amerindian penchant in the industrial working class may also have played a significant part in keeping the Mexican Revolution from bridging the rural–industrial worker divide. We have already drawn attention to the "Indian" label that was given to rural workers in southern and central Mexico regardless of the "biological" accuracy of the term. It was rather an associative label, linking particular locations and types of labor to the Amerindian. This association was neither born nor created in the nineteenth century: it was a product of the Conquest. And if the Amerindian–campesino association was the dominant one in the countryside, it meant that another race–class association was predominant in towns and cities. In spite of the host of occupations of various statuses in the urban sphere which potentially weakened a rigid race–class overlap, city living tended to Europeanize its inhabitants. The city, like money, tended to whiten one's skin even if there had been no improvement in the economic well-being of the urban dweller (in comparison to the rural worker) or if it was biologically inaccurate. There may have been then a "psychological wage" gained in city life:[64]

> urban workers, as proud citizens of Mexico City, considered themselves more sophisticated than the seemingly primitive campesinaje. As constituents of Mexico City they enjoyed the wealth of the metropolis even if unbalanced distribution of income gave them only peripheral advantages, such as public transportation and parks, paved streets, a few schools, sewage disposals, and other public services.[65]

If we attempt to decode the Mexico City working class's description of both the Zapatistas and Villistas, it becomes apparent that in the eyes of the former the latter were for all intents and purposes a different race of people. Urban references to rural irrationality, illiteracy, religiosity, banditry, barbarism, and primitiveness revealed the perceived depth of differences separating the countryside from the city. While this perspective cannot override all other dimensions of the city–country relationship in the Mexican Revolution (like the important omission of industrial labor concerns in both the Zapatista and Villista programs until rather late in the day), it is reasonable to suggest that there was a link between the Mexican industrial working class's social assessment of the rural working class and the former's willingness or unwillingness to join forces with the latter. In the collective eye of Mexico City's working class, the less radical Constitutionalists appeared to be a more promising ally.

THE COLOR OF THE CUBAN REVOLUTION

Even an incomplete list of American interests in Cuba from the end of the "Spanish–American" War to the revolution reads like a "who's who" of corporate America. Rockefeller, Morgan, Mellon, Carnegie, Whitney, Herbert Hoover, Woodrow Wilson, Bethlehem Iron & Steel Co., General Electric, Goodyear Tire and Rubber, Sears, Woolworth's, Colgate Palmolive, Bank of America, and Chase Manhattan Bank were among the names of American investors, firms, and banks. That "the first advance guard of [US] business representatives" may also have come to Cuba "within the two weeks of the military occupation of the island as they came to Puerto Rico,"[66] meant that Cuba's second and successful bid for independence from Spain was compromised by the American intervention. In short, Spanish colonialism was replaced by its American brand in the wake of the devastation caused by the war: "By 1905, some 13,000 North Americans had acquired title to land in Cuba . . . an estimated 60 percent of all rural property."[67] Until the Depression, American capital was overwhelmingly invested in sugar production ($750 million by 1925), with railways, tobacco, and mining posting $110 million, $50 million, and $35 million respectively in the same year.[68] Only the Depression catalyzed the gradual withdrawal of American investment from Cuban sugar into the more durable profit-maker of banking.

The attractiveness of Cuba was in large part due to the tax exemptions accorded American businesses there. Not only did these tax exemptions allow American firms to repatriate nearly all of their profits (especially given that most American ownership was absentee), but they also denied Cuba a resource base for the provisioning of the basic needs of its own population. Though this was not officially a clause of the infamous Platt Amendment which *de jure* imposed American tutelage in Cuba's economic and political life, it certainly did not hinder it. Financially strapped, Cuban administrations were forced to negotiate loans with the very American banks which were major shareholders in precisely those tax-exempt Cuban industries. The principal and interest on these loans were tragically paid for by the Cuban people through the imposition of regressive tax policies. Jorge Gilbert cites one example:

> the total value of loans from Morgan House to the Cuban government . . . was, between 1913 and 1927, $111 million. Payment of interest and amortization increased the debt to $170.8 million, producing a liquid profit of $59.8 million to that House. To pay the foreign debt, taxes were imposed on beverages, tobacco cigars, and matches, taxes which were finally paid by the Cuban population. However, the main productive sectors, sugar and mining, remained practically untouched by taxation. This attitude toward fiscal policy was not due to over-sight; rather the so-called Republican Government of Cuba was not allowed to change its fiscal system without previous authorization from the Banking Houses, Speyer and Morgan, a commitment clearly specified in the contracts signed among these houses and governments.[69]

Indebtedness not only created numerous American monopolies, but also further deepened Cuba's reliance on sugar as its major revenue earner and hence debt repayer.[70] And there were considerable opportunity costs from sugar production. Stymied were Cuba's import substitution industrialization program, agricultural diversification, and most important, yeoman or middle-sized farms which could have been the basis of diversified agriculture. As in Puerto Rico, the Cuban "consumer was thus obliged to buy high-priced imported foods from the American market or, as was the case with the poverty-stricken majority, be driven back to, virtually, a starvation diet of the very simplest ground provisions."[71] Hence, coupled with the land monopolization that the sugar "central" demanded was a subsequent decline in nutritious caloric intake as less and less land and livestock were available for rural worker subsistence. Wages that were low (because it was once the work of slaves) and seasonal (due to the cane cycle which left labor idle for up to eight months of the year) in turn made medical costs and access prohibitive to the average rural worker, as were the amenities that would have lessened the causes of disease: proper plumbing, adequate housing materials, protective clothing, etc. More the cause than the consequence of poverty, working "in the cane" was even less so after the American occupation given that "the American manager['s] . . . attitude was shaped by the fact that he was an outsider likely in the future to be posted elsewhere by his distant office in the States."[72]

Rural poverty invariably drives country folk to seek out rumored fortunes in the city, and Cuba was no exception to this rule. By 1953, less than 50 percent of the Cuban population lived on the land.[73] Havana and other Cuban cities, however, could not meet employment aspirations, especially those of Afro-Cubans, 60 percent of whom were city-dwellers on the eve of the revolution. Their economic plight was particularly harsh:

> In 1959, out of a total work force of some 2,500,000 laborers, Blacks accounted for an estimated 64.1 percent. As much as 34.3 percent of the black work force was permanently and/or partially unemployed in 1959. Added to the estimated 11.5 percent of Blacks consigned to the lumpen proletariat, approximately 45.8 percent of employable Blacks were in a state of permanent and/or partial unemployment in 1959. The plight of the black worker in pre-Castro Cuba was certainly grave.[74]

Though not an insignificant number of Afro-Cubans were in the professions, representing, for example, one-fifth of Cuba's doctors in 1943 and were "in an actual majority among coopers, builders, dressmakers, launderers, shoemakers, woodcutters, and tailors,"[75] many Afro-Cubans were forced to turn to even more modest trades: shoeshining, portering, domestic work, prostitution. And here, as elsewhere, the socio-economic circumstance of the majority came to dominate the image of all.

The one sector of the Cuban economy in which Afro-Cubans were glaringly absent, however, was in the public sector. Government, the only institution that was wholly Cuban when the economy was in the hands of foreign merchants, refused to employ Afro-Cubans as it did white Cubans. The employer of last resort to which white Cubans "looked for economic security" and which "integrated into the national system the expanding ranks of the middle and working class that otherwise would face exclusion from economic livelihood,"[76] was not so for Afro-Cuba. Denied access to the machinery of government, Afro-Cubans were in turn denied the government contracted jobs which would have enlarged their job opportunities.

The renowned Caribbeanist Gordon K. Lewis aptly wrote in 1963 that "The Cuban affair . . . has done for twentieth-century Caribbean society what the Haitian revolt did for its nineteenth-century predecessor."[77] Curiously, however, he maintained that the "real strength" of the revolution was found "in the lowlier white and mestizo cultivators of rural Cuba."[78] But what of the role, if any, of Afro-Cuba in the revolutionary process? In contrast to Lewis's position, Carlos Moore maintains that "The predominantly black rural and industrial workers, the unemployed, and the white peasantry were the true social base of the regime."[79] Did an otherwise meticulous scholar miss the racial dimension of the Cuban Revolution?

What does the paucity of literature on the Black experience in the Cuban Revolution suggest? Perhaps a couple of things: first, that the depth of Cuban national identity has made the distinction between its African, Asian, and European components anachronistic and inappropriate to outside and inside observers, a remarkable feat for a Caribbean society and one which may also explain Fidel Castro's silence on the subject in *History Will Absolve Me*;[80] and/or second, that the Afro-Cuban experience in the revolutionary process does not warrant, in its own right, any special consideration. This last is, once again, quite a remarkable position given the racial composition of Cuba in general,[81] and of Oriente Province in particular, within whose boundaries lived half of the total Afro-Cuban population and where the armed struggle of the 1959 Revolution began. It is Carlos Moore's position that this last bias has prejudiced commentators from exploring the unique experience of Afro-Cubans and it is the principal motivation behind his writing of *Castro, the Blacks, and Africa*.

Moore's contention is that in the past two centuries of Cuban history, Black brawn has been conveniently used in the name of nationalist social movements whose leadership did not ask of it to be part of those movements" brains. Ultimately, this bias on the part of the leadership of Cuban social movements (the Cuban Revolution included) has resulted in the betrayal of Black aspirations and the subsequent mistrust of "white" leadership on the part of the Afro-Cuban rank and file.

As we have already seen, in all of the Americas African populations have used (when permitted) the show of military prowess as a mechanism for socioeconomic mobility. In most instances, of course, this calculation was forced upon Black populations in the Americas as few, if any, channels of social mobility were open to them. Still, Blacks have attempted to make inauspicious circumstances work to their advantage: the Black show of force was self-consciously considered proof of Black worthiness of national citizenship. Though it was a calculation which all-too-often failed against the front of unmoved racism, this shortcoming did not keep Blacks in the Americas from siding largely with progressive causes, and in Cuba this was no less the case.

In the nineteenth century's two wars for independence, Afro-Cuban fighting power and enthusiasm were no less than decisive. In the Cuban

Revolution, however, an Afro-Cuban racial reading of the opposing forces may have served to split its allegiances. Perhaps the one and only time when Afro-Cuban military might sided with an unprogressive political project was in its alliance with Fulgencio Batista; yet this alliance must be put in its proper context. Batista was able to woo Afro-Cuba on three counts. First, his 1933 coup "opened to Blacks the then racially segregated army officer corps," and in twenty years" time, "Approximately one-third of the officers in the Cuban army at the time of the revolution were probably of Afro-Cuban descent, while the noncommissioned and enlisted ranks presumably comprised a still larger percentage."[82] Second, the memory of the Cuban Communist Party's alliance with Batista in 1937 and his administration's subsequent promotion of populist policies favorable to the Cuban working class may have initially raised expectations in the Afro-Cuban community (among whom was a large membership in the Partido Socialista Popular – the new name of the Cuban Communist Party) that he would launch a similar platform after 1952, the year of his second *coup d'état*. Third,

> Batista supported and contributed to the santería and ñañigo rites, whose initiates regarded him as almost one of themselves, particularly in the city of Trinidad. Indeed, Batista paid "out of his own money" for a big reunion in the summer of 1958 for all the prominent Santeros (priests) of Guanabacoa, at which many cocks and goats were sacrificed to appease the "demons of war".[83]

Finally, as a "mulatto avanzado, a very fair-skinned mulatto who claimed to be white, but was chided by the Hispanic upper-classes on account of his 'inferior' racial background . . . he derived some of his power by courting Black Cuba."[84] This was Cuba's version of the *politique de doublure*. Still, if Batista could play the racial trump card, it meant that race mattered in pre-revolution Cuba. As long as his regime was stable Batista could and did make an effective appeal to Afro-Cuba against Fidel Castro by implying that the latter's movement was a "white" one; one, in other words, that would inevitably betray Black aspirations in light of Cuban history.

While Batista's inclusion of Afro-Cubans in the military can be interpreted as a manipulative ploy to racially split his opposition, it could very well have been his attempt to rectify a past injustice and one particularly heart-felt in Oriente Province, not only the historic home of much of Afro-Cuba but also the birth-place of many of the Afro-Cuban heroes (among whom the Maceo brothers are best known) of the Cuban Independence War. Though they sacrificed their lives out of all proportion to their percentage of the total Cuban population, as the number of Afro-Cuban widows in the post-war period confirmed,[85] color, property, and education requirements denied them jobs in all sectors of the economy, including those jobs to which their military experience should have entitled them: the army, rural guard, and police force. The Afro-Cuban response was to form the first African-based political party in the hemisphere, the Partido Independiente de Color (PIC). After five years of pressuring Havana to employ Blacks in the public sector in proportion to their number of the total population, the PIC had little to show for its efforts. Realizing that their pleas were falling on deaf ears, the PIC resorted to armed rebellion in its home province Oriente in 1912. Crushed as if it were a slave rebellion and not a revolt of freemen, hundreds of Afro-Cubans were massacred as a collective warning to the rest of Afro-Cuba.[86] It is doubtful that this event was forgotten where it took place and its memory may have added another dimension to the negotiations between the Afro-Cuban rural proletariat of Oriente Province and the crew of the Granma.

The above is in part an illustration of Moore's second point. While Afro-Cubans have historically supplied muscle power to Cuban social movements, first-generation Hispanic Cuban intellectuals have been the near-exclusive theoreticians of those movements. Moore notes more decisively: "Of all Cuban whites, first generation Hispanic Cubans would seem to be the most attached to Euro-Mediterranean traditions, and the least influenced by the home grown cultures of Cuba."[87] Not only does this bias make for a certain unwillingness to enter into "the ethno-political and psycho-cultural ramifications of the Cuban system of white supremacy," but of even greater consequence is that in speaking for Blacks, these revolutionary intellectuals deny Black people the ability "to define the content of their own oppression, or define the terms of their ethnic emancipation."[88] Placed in a larger context, Moore's sentiments are that Afro-Cuba's courting ends after the first phase of the social movement – the middle-class exhortation of subordinate groups to the revolutionary nationalist cause – and in the absence of a successful counterrevolution, they are told to await further instructions from the leaders of the movements. Thus, in spite of their service to Cuban national causes at home and abroad, Afro-Cubans have been served a political diet of "revolutionary elitism" and "'protective' benevolent paternalism," both amounting to the political silencing of Afro-Cuba in Moore's opinion.

With regard to the Cuban Revolution, however, Moore may well have overstated the initial involvement of Afro-Cubans. Hugh Thomas maintains that "It is not clear how many of the rebel army in the Sierra were black but a majority certainly were not, and [Juan] Almeida, a mulatto, was the only officer of importance who was."[89] I have been unable to find any source which either qualifies or contradicts Thomas's contention. The 1953 Moncada attack likewise included a low number of Afro-Cuban participants, a total of not more than "a dozen."[90] Thus, what a Cuban soldier once said to an Afro-Cuban at the time of the abortive Moncada siege may have contained an element of truth: "You don't know that Negroes can't be revolutionaries? Negroes are either thieves or partisans of Batista, not revolutionaries."[91] It appears then that "The black population as such never rallied to Castro before 1959. He appeared just another middle-class white radical, with nothing to say to them."[92] From this perspective, Moore's thesis may be unduly harsh and somewhat inappropriate with regard to the opening of the Cuban Revolution. Some believe, moreover, that his verdict describes developments up to and including the Cuba of 1963 (the year he went into exile) but fails to characterize Cuban racial politics since that year. Nevertheless, I believe that before Moore is dismissed as "counterrevolutionary," we should address the aspects of the Cuban Revolution which trouble him besides the simultaneity of the launching of Cuba's African foreign policy and the "discovery" of Afro-Cuba, the third part of his book.

Perhaps the gravest shortcoming of the Cuban Revolution in Moore's assessment is the scarce Black representation in the commanding heights of Cuban political power. This absence undermines the gains against racism that the revolution has made in ending the association between blackness and poverty. For in the continued absence of Blacks in political decision-making roles, the association between race and intellectual capacity has not been broken. Second, the inability or flat refusal of past and present Cuban governments to provide trustworthy figures on the racial composition of the Cuban population suggests that the race issue is far from being resolved on the island. As Gayle McGarrity and Osvaldo Cardenas note, "Although more than a million Cubans, mostly white, left the country in the post-revolutionary period, according to official statistics the proportion of whites to non-whites remains constant."[93] While the census of 1981 recorded a Black and mulatto population of less than one-third of the total Cuban population (hardly differing from the official 1953 figures despite the exodus) many Afro-Cubans believe that this figure captures instead the white minority population of the island, and not that of the Black majority. Third, Afro-Cuba's religious expression has been muted by the revolution though more Cubans practice Santería and consult Babalaos than attend Catholic mass or go to confession.[94] Thus, instead of embracing, promoting, and rendering more visible Cuba's popular religious expression which is also Afro-Cuban led, the revolution repressed it for fear of it giving rise to Black nationalism. Only since the mid-1980s has there been a reversal of state policy toward Afro-Cuban religions and it is difficult to separate this change of heart from the perceptible discontentedness of Afro-Cuba with the revolution.[95] Fourth and perhaps last is the lack of dialogue in postrevolution Cuba on the socio-historical meaning of race if only in recognition of the fact that historical associations between race, class, and culture have longer lives than revolutionary ruptures. Moreover, what the revolution must come to terms with is the fact that it too has emerged from a racialized past and is not exempt from scrutiny or criticism on that score. In short, Moore's position is not counterrevolutionary but rather a plea for a democratic revolution:

> The road to an authentic racial democracy in Cuba presupposes the emergence of new institutional and mental structures, and not just

novel socioeconomic arrangements. It presupposes, above all, the opening on the scale of the entire polity, of an honest national debate on every aspect of race, culture and ethnicity in Cuba, from slave-colonial times to the Castro-Marxist period, passing through the neo-colonial Republican era. The links between power and pigmentation throughout the centuries will have to be exposed. The interconnection between racial politics and the politics of race will have to be un-ravelled. The starting point to all this may simply be the sincere recog-nition by Cuban whites that they are racists; the products of many generations of an insidious system of white supremacy premised on an "amiable," paternalistic attachment to multiracialism . . . so long as the whites are on top.[96]

Cuba need not be singled out in this regard: what Moore says of his place of birth is applicable to all settler societies in the Americas. Still, "no other nation in the region has undergone a comparable socialist revolution that raised expectations that racism would be confronted and uprooted."[97] It should be said, moreover, that some of these issues may have been compounded by a particular brand of Marxism-Leninism in that certain interpretations of the latter subscribe to "vanguard" leadership, have difficulty addressing the legacies of racially and ethnically reinforced class oppression, are normally hostile to religions, and are beleaguered by the nagging question of whether the revolution is to be led by either democratic or vanguard consciousness when the two do not coincide.[98]

We must also consider to what degree the revolution's approach to race issues was encouraged by Washington's foreign policies toward Cuba. Washington's "low-intensity" warfare (propaganda, trade embargoes, arming of counterrevolutionaries) against Cuba may well have forced the Cuban government to take domestic positions on race issues it might not have taken in the absence of Washington's ploys. Typically, Washington's inflexible responses to revolutionary movements throughout the world have pushed these movements to become more extreme, moving what were once almost exclusively nationalist struggles toward intolerance of political expressions perceived to threaten national unity. The intention here is neither to exaggerate the role of Washington's activities in the shaping of Cuban domestic policies at the expense of national political traditions nor to offer excuses for the revolution's shortcomings, but to suggest that in contending with the United States Cuba was affected internally.

AFRO-AMERINDIANS, AUTONOMY, AND THE NICARAGUAN REVOLUTION

It warrants repeating that it is neither out of disregard for Nicaragua's social structure nor internal politics that one is forced to dwell on US intervention in the country, but rather out of an assessment of the magnitude of those interventions; interventions which took advantage of racial tensions within Nicaragua and finally drove the Sandinista government from power.

Initially American motives for intervention were limited to keeping rival contenders (Germany and Japan in particular) from constructing a transisthmian route through Nicaragua. José Santos Zelaya's ouster in 1909 came as a result of attempting to accommodate other-than-American interests in the proposed waterway, a move which would have challenged US strategic dominance over the Caribbean.[99] Following Zelaya's removal from office, Nicaraguan political developments were overseen by both the US Marines and Robert Dawson, the Department of State representative who formerly worked at then Secretary of State Philander C. Knox's law firm. Dawson engineered the Castillo–Knox Treaty "which provided for US loans of $15 million to Nicaragua in return for the right of the United States to protect its interests there and to arbitrate any dispute in which Nicaragua becomes involved."[100] Though never made *de jure*, the agreement was a *de facto* description of the forced Faustian bargain made in the heyday of North American expansionism.

Unwilling and perhaps frankly unable to comprehend what inspired Augusto Sandino, Calvin Coolidge followed what was now the old deal in Nicaragua by sending the Marines to stop anti-imperialist nationalism. Though he brought the troops back home once in office in 1933, Franklin Delano Roosevelt resorted to the new deal in foreign policy of funding conservative military men and their national armies. In the Nicaraguan case, the recipients were General Anastasio Somoza García and the National Guard, the analogues of Fulgencio Batista in Cuba. In spite of a rocky post-World War II period of internal opposition from both workers and conservatives, Somoza adroitly assumed first a populist and then a conservative stance to first ward off calls for political liberalization and redistributive social welfare measures, and then catch the attention of McCarthy's Washington. Part of the Somoza brothers'' inheritance after their father was assassinated in 1956 was US military aid which rose steadily from $200,000 yearly between 1953 and 1961 to $1.8 million annually from 1967 to 1975, while the other part included an array of landholdings and businesses.[101]

Ronald Reagan's entry into the White House ushered in a return to the anti-communist foreign policy of the Truman and Eisenhower administrations and flatly undermined the human rights basis of the Carter administration's foreign policy. Having vowed to put an end to the Sandinista government, Reagan endorsed the funding of counterrevolutionary groups both within and outside Nicaragua, including Nicaraguan Amerindian populations. The pressing question for our discussion is this: How did Nicaraguan Amerindians come to support the "counterrevolution"?

While the Sandinista Revolution of 1979 was a "multi-class coalition of aggrieved social forces,"[102] the details of which I am leaving to other sources, it was not necessarily multi-ethnic. The populations of Nicaragua's Atlantic Coast (Zelaya and eastern Río San Juan provinces) representing 12 percent of the total population,[103] in 56 percent of the country's land mass, were hardly involved in the revolutionary struggle. There were a number of factors which contributed to this costeño neutrality, besides the fact that they "had not suffered repression from Somoza's National Guard."[104]

First is the region's economic geography, the direction of which did not move toward the Pacific Coast but rather to the US Gulf Coast:

> Nicaragua, like almost all Central American nations, faced an Atlantic Coast region that had been integrated historically into a different social formation from that of the national mainstream. The entire Atlantic seaboard of Central America was penetrated by U.S. multinational corporations beginning in the late 1800's. Because of the physical isolation of these zones, the foreign companies established an unparalleled level of control. The classic examples, of course are the banana companies which established mini-nation-states on the Atlantic Coast of every single nation in Central America (except for El Salvador which only has a Pacific Coast). In Nicaragua the most important North American companies extracted minerals, lumber, and bananas strictly for export to the United States. The coastal economy had no linkage with that of the rest of the country. There was more regular transport and commerce from Bluefields to the United States than to the interior of the country. Indeed, it was easier to get to the Atlantic Coast from New Orleans than from Managua.[105]

Second is the racial/ethnic composition of the Atlantic Coast's population. Whereas Pacific Nicaragua draws on a predominantly Amerindian and Spanish genetic past, the Atlantic Coast's population includes a significant African strain. In fact, as one costeño puts it,

> If racial origin were the sole criterion used, it would appear then that the majority of the Costeños are of African ancestry, including in this calculation all of the Black Creoles, Garifunas, Miskito and Rama Indians and a sizeable percentage of the Mestizo ethnic group. Only the members of the Sumo Indian ethnic group would not be included.[106]

Clearly color and/or phenotype by themselves cannot determine one's ethnic categorization in the coastal context: culture illuminates where color leads merely to confusion. Outside conceptions of both race and culture largely explain the frequently large discrepancies in demographic figures between Managua and/or foreign estimates and those recorded by costeños themselves. Both the Sandinista government and Western researchers, for example, have the tendency to render "mestizo" those Afro-Amerindian peoples without (in their eyes) visible African features thus increasing this last population by nearly as much as 50 percent against costeño estimates.[107] Still, whatever the figures, one could not deny a racialized division of labor on the Atlantic Coast:

> The Miskitu, Sumu, and Rama were at the bottom of this local class-ethnic hierarchy, performing the least desirable, most poorly paid jobs. . . . Above the Amerindians but below the Creoles came the Mestizo population, many of whom were landless laborers, recent migrants from the Pacific provinces. Like the Miskitu, they engaged in poorly remunerated agricultural wage labor and had a high level of illiteracy and alcoholism. The Creoles dominated the skilled jobs. Because of their superior education they tended to obtain white-collar employment in disproportionate numbers. . . . Above the Creoles there was the stratum of upper-class Pacific-born Mestizos, usually of lighter complexion than the poorer Mestizos, who held administrative and political-appointee positions. Finally, until the triumph of the revolution this ethnic-class hierarchy was capped by a miniscule layer of North American and European whites who owned or ran the few companies still operating on the coast, such as the gold mines or the lumber export firms.[108]

As can be imagined from this description, as one looked toward the upper end of the socio-economic hierarchy, class was grafted onto race without fanfare, while toward the lower end class reflected culture. Again, this last dimension is due to the considerable inter-mixture of Amerindian, African, and European (predominantly British) peoples in the Miskito, Rama, and Garifuna populations. The complex class sentiments of the costeño professional class or Black Creoles, for example, can be understood only in this light: while they

> resented the political and economic domination of the elite Mestizo costeños and western Nicaraguans [and] felt that the "Spaniards" had a racist attitude towards them. . . . The Black Creoles tended to feel superior to the Miskito, Sumo, and Rama Indians, who were considered to be backward and disadvantaged as they clung to the old traditional Indian ways and mainly lived in small interior villages.[109]

Black Creole cultural identity was also shaped by its strong human ties with the English-speaking Caribbean (particularly Jamaica) which made for a pro-Anglo bent and a corresponding anti-"Spanish" bias.

A third factor was church influence. Unlike the Catholic Church on the Pacific Coast which actively joined the struggle for Somoza's ouster in the final years of the dynasty, on the Atlantic Coast the influential Moravian Church would tolerate political change only to the degree that this would not compromise the region's autonomy (as under the Somozas) and Moravian institutions there. Besides having brought schools which trained many Black Creoles among others and having "established a church-school-hospital-nursing school-sanitorium complex at Bilwaskarma in the northern Atlantic Coast region,"[110] what made the Moravian gospel all the more convincing was its messengers" willingness to "stoop to conquer", so to speak, and live among the Miskito. The Moravian Church was also instrumental in the formation of ALPROMISU (Alliance for the Progress of the Miskitos and Sumos) in 1973 whose goals included

> restoration of control over communal lands, primarily the forests; teaching of the Miskito language, which had been put into written form by the Moravian missionaries; Indian representation in the Managua government; and an arrangement whereby a portion of the money made by the government in Miskitia would be returned to the region in public works.[111]

In short, Moravian influence on the Atlantic Coast could serve to strengthen costeño resistance to the Sandinista government.

The last factor which drove some costeños to aid US imperialistic designs in Nicaragua is one to which we have already alluded: the issue of minority self-determination. Where the FSLN "tend[ed] to analyze problems from a class perspective and view ethnic distinctions as being possibly separatist in orientation," indigenous groups such as ALPROMISU (becoming in November 1979 MISURASATA – Miskitos, Sumos, Ramas, and Sandinistas together) and SICC (Southern Indigenous Creole Community) subscribed to the "view that certain government programs and policies were assimilationist in character" and consequently in direct opposition to the charters of these organizations.[112] In a region where culture and its preservation were of pronounced importance, costeños were particularly sensitive to government policies that threatened each group's cultural autonomy and ultimately survival. Costeños were already troubled by the sizeable influx of Pacific Coast mestizos into their region in the years prior to the Revolution and the Sandinista presence (7,000 troops flanked by Cuban and Eastern European technicians by 1981) seemed like yet another cultural invasion.[113] This last wave was weightier of course since it represented the state seeking now to incorporate the Atlantic Coast into the larger Nicaragua nation-state.

It can be argued, therefore, that it was less the socialism of the Sandinista government than its statism which costeños found so officious. The state not only had ultimate jurisdiction over the custody of ancestral lands but also dictated which organizations would voice costeño concerns. The Sandinista government targeted for exclusion the Black Creoles and the organization in which their membership was largest, SICC, by denying them "participation in MISURASATA as Daniel Ortega specifically requested that they not be included."[114] In January 1981, roughly a year after MISURASATA was formed, it too was labeled a counterrevolutionary organization when its leader, Steadman Fagoth, concluded that the Sandinista government was not working in the interest of the Miskito people. Fagoth and other Miskitos undoubtedly found it puzzling that "while the Sandinistas themselves were restricting private ownership on the Pacific side of Nicaragua, they could not accept the communal ownership advocated by the Miskitos. In both cases, it was something outside the control of the state."[115] With Fagoth's arrest a month later, the Atlantic Coast turned into a war zone.

An outside observer can justifiably fault the Sandinista government for not having analyzed with greater care the cultural politics of the Atlantic Coast before intervening there. An "insider" did the same.[116] A counter-argument can of course be made that the revolution was a western Nicaraguan phenomenon where the National Guard fought and did not hand over its weapons to a local priest as it did on the Atlantic Coast. Still, had a careful and unresentful inquiry been undertaken of the Atlantic Coast, one of the possible outcomes could have been the awareness that to costeños any western Nicaraguan presence in the region is considered at best an intrusion and at worst (a function of numbers and time) an invasion, regardless of western Nicaraguan intentions. From this perspective, the Sandinista presence on the Atlantic Coast as of 1980 constituted an invasion that threatened the cultural survival of the region. Had the Sandinistas subscribed to a more flexible model of nation-building or national incorporation which worked with instead of against local costeño institutions, disaster could have been avoided. Instead costeño suspicions about western Nicaraguans were confirmed and they were pushed to seek autonomy with the aid of an eager source. A region that was considered peripheral and backward in western Nicaragua proved more decisive for the country's future than anyone would ever have imagined.

CONCLUSIONS

Norman Girvan raises two critical points on social movements in the Americas which distinguish them from those elsewhere:

> The first conclusion of relevance to our theme is . . . that the terms upon which Indian and subsequently African labour were incorporated into the American colonial/capitalist economy implied a predominantly racist ideology directed against the worker; whereas for the European workers it did not. From this follows the first operational principle of relevance to the struggle against oppression in the Americas: that for the Indians and Africans the ideological aspects of this struggle must of necessity contain a strong element of racial-cultural consciousness; i.e. an assertion of race pride, dignity and worth both intrinsically and as opposed to the alleged superiority of European peoples and their cultures. . . . The second observation is that the strug-

gles on the part of white proletarians and other exploited white groups against the power of capital would entirely lack the racial dimension. This followed naturally from the fact that whites never had the experience of being a subjugated race, that an ideology of racism was never utilized to systematically denigrate their physical and cultural attributes, and that they were never restricted ascriptively to undesirable occupations considered at best miserable and at worst sub-human. Therefore, the struggles of white people against white capital would have a class content only; by definition it could not share the crucial if not predominantly racial content of the struggles of Indians and Black people. For while the large majority of white people shared a common relationship with non-whites of subordination to the capitalist mode of production, the specific content of that relationship was profoundly different for non-whites from what it was for whites.[117]

Girvan's perspective judges as necessary but not sufficient for an American Revolution "the direct interference of the masses in historic events," as Leon Trotsky offered as the most elemental feature of a revolution,[118] or even "a social catharsis that dramatically alters the prevailing economic system, and transforms the class structure as well as the patterns of wealth and income distribution," as Ramon Eduardo Ruiz has it.[119] Due to the historical settlement of the Americas and the social patterns developed in that process, for Girvan an "authentic" American Revolution must (if we dare speak normatively) weave the racial-cultural threads as well as material desires of its Black and Amerindian populations into the revolutionary tapestry. From a practical point of view, moreover, the racial-cultural expressions of both populations necessarily also embody the desires of a class revolution because of the large number of Amerindian and Black folk in the hemisphere's working class. Girvan's suggestion of what constitutes a successful American Revolution is undoubtedly a demanding one and one unfortunately that has eluded all previous American Revolutions in varying degrees.

What all the American Revolutions discussed in this chapter share is a generalized distrust of (or contempt for) either Black and Amerindian self-determination or even self-definition movements which emerge separately or as by-products of the revolutions themselves. My thesis is that this distrust is due not to the "counterrevolutionary" nature of these movements of color as their detractors label them, but to the legacy of American settler societies even where whites are few in number as in Haiti at the time of the Haitian Revolution. Rarely is the point raised, moreover, that even in the throes of a revolutionary struggle the settler nation continues to subscribe to Euro-American ideas of who constitutes the nation. In most if not all cases this has meant that the Black and Amerindian contributors to the revolutionary struggle have not been called upon to be participants in the postrevolution period of institution building or policy-making. As we have seen, in some instances these slights did not jeopardize a revolutionary movement's ability to sieze state power. This was true of the anti-colonial revolutions of what we may term the long eighteenth century and the Cuban Revolution of the twentieth. The same cannot be said for the Mexican and Nicaraguan revolutions: in the first case it prohibited the union of urban and rural revolutionary struggles; while in the second it undermined the potential forging (both nationally and ideologically) of a united Nicaragua heretofore divided by geography and ethnicity.

Where then does this mixed balance sheet leave us? Apparently here: race alone is not the ultimate arbiter of an American revolution's success or failure, yet this caveat in no way diminishes the significance of race in either the strategies of revolutionary mobilizations or their outcomes.

ACKNOWLEDGEMENTS

I would like to thank John Foran and Timothy Wickham-Crowley for their comments on an earlier draft of this chapter.

NOTES

1. Max Weber, *The Protestant Ethic and the Spirit of Capitalism* (New York: Charles Scribner's Sons, 1958), 216–17.
2. Christopher Hill, *God's Englishman: Oliver Cromwell and the English Revolution* (New York: Harper & Row, 1972), 58, 31.
3. Christopher Hill, "The Norman Yoke," pp. 50–122 in his *Puritanism and Revolution: Studies in the Interpretation of the English Revolution of the Seventeenth Century* (London: Mercury, 1962), 57.
4. Ibid., 57.
5. Oliver C. Cox, *Caste, Class, and Race* (New York: Monthly Review Press, 1970), 334, 336.
6. Alejandro de la Fuente, "Race and Inequality in Cuba, 1899-1981," *Journal of Contemporary History*, volume 30 (1995), 156.
7. Though there may have been names for and hence distinctions between the children of Norman and Saxon unions and the those of purely Saxon parentage, these labels perhaps quickly dissolved into the near-caste terms of feudal society.
8. Stuart Hall, "Pluralism, Race, and Class in Caribbean Society," pp. 150–82 in *Race and Class in Post-Colonial Society: A Study of Ethnic Group Relations in the English-Speaking Caribbean, Bolivia, Chile and Mexico* (Paris: UNESCO, 1977), 166–7.
9. Ibid., 167. See Norman Girvan, "Aspects of the Political Economy of Race in the Caribbean and in the Americas," Working Paper No. 7 (Institute of Social and Economic Research, University of the West Indies, Jamaica, 1975), 29.
10. The phrase is Stuart Hall's: see "Race, Articulation and Societies Structured in Dominance," pp. 305–45 in *Sociological Theories: Race and Colonialism* (Paris: UNESCO, 1980), 305–6.
11. Girvan, "Aspects," 28, 20.
12. Michel-Rolph Trouillot, *Haiti, State Against Nation: The Origins and Legacy of Duvalierism* (New York: Monthly Review Press, 1990), 121.

13. Cox, *Caste*, 349. See Girvan, "Aspects," 14.
14. Girvan, "Aspects," 18.
15. The term is Anouar Abdel-Malek's. See "The Civilisational Project," pp. 139–47 in *Social Dialectics*, volume one: Civilisations and Social Theory (Albany: State University of New York Press, 1981), 144.
16. Girvan, "Aspects," 16.
17. Ibid., 30.
18. Charles Gibson, *Spain in America* (New York: Harper & Row, 1966), 150.
19. Philip S. Foner, *A History of Cuba and its Relations with the United States*, volume one: *1492–1845: From the Conquest of Cuba to La Escalera* (New York: International Publishers, 1962), 51.
20. John Lynch, *The Spanish American Revolutions 1808–1826* (New York: W. W. Norton, 1973), 13.
21. *Ensayo Politico Sobre el Reino de la Nueva Espana*, sixth edition, four volumes, (Mexico, 1941), volume two, 117, cited in Lynch, *Spanish American Revolutions*, 18.
22. Lynch, *Spanish American Revolutions*, 17.
23. Bolívar to Páez, August 4, 1826 in *Cartas del Libertador*, ten volumes, Vicente Lecuna editor (Caracas, 1929–30), volume six, 32, cited in Lynch, *Spanish American Revolutions*, 23.
24. Bolívar to Briceño Mendez, May 7, 1828, *Cartas del Libertador*, ten volumes, Vicente Lecuna editor, volume seven, 257, cited in Lynch, *Spanish American Revolutions*, 224.
25. Lynch, *Spanish American Revolutions*, 157–8.
26. Ibid., 326.
27. Benjamin Quarles, "The Revolutionary War as a Black Declaration of Independence," pp. 48–64 in *Black Mosaic: Essays in Afro-American History and Historiography* (Amherst: University of Massachusetts, 1988), 56.
28. Lynch, *Spanish American Revolutions*, 225.
29. W. E. B. DuBois, T*he Suppression of the African Slave-Trade to the United States of America 1638–1870* in *Writings* (New York: Library of America, 1986), 55.
30. Benjamin Quarles, "Lord Dunmore as Liberator," pp. 35–47 in *Black Mosaic*, 35.
31. Cited in Quarles, "Lord Dunmore as Liberator," 35.
32. Philip S. Foner, *History of Black Americans*, volume one: From Africa to the Emergence of the Cotton Kingdom (Westport: Greenwood Press, 1975), 331.
33. Ibid., 334, 316.
34. David R. Roediger, *Race and the Making of the American Working Class* (London: Verso, 1991), 35.
35. See Bruce Johansen, *Forgotten Founders* (Boston: Harvard Common Press, 1982).
36. Lewis Henry Morgan, *League of the Iroquois* (New York: Citadel Press, 1962), 28.
37. Ibid., 31.
38. C. L. R. James, *The Black Jacobins: Toussaint L'Ouverture and the San Domingo Revolution* (New York: Vintage, 1963), 242.
39. Trouillot, *Haiti*, 44.
40. Ibid., 43, 73.
41. Alex Dupuy, *Haiti in the World Economy: Class, Race, and Underdevelopment Since 1700* (Boulder: Westview Press, 1989), 98.
42. Trouillot, *Haiti*, 62.
43. James Cockcroft, *Mexico: Class Formation, Capital Accumulation, and the State* (New York: Monthly Review Press, 1983), 64–5.
44. Ibid., 93.

45. Eric R. Wolf, *Peasant Wars of the Twentieth Century* (New York: Harper & Row, 1969), 16.
46. Arturo Warman, "The Historical Framework of Inter-Ethnic Relations," pp. 341–54 in *Race and Class in Post-Colonial Society: A Study of Ethnic Group Relations in the English-Speaking Caribbean, Bolivia, Chile and Mexico* (Paris: UNESCO, 1977), 351–2; Cockcroft, *Mexico*, 76.
47. Warman, "The Historical Framework," 352. François Chevalier holds a similar position: "The Ejido and Political Stability in Mexico," pp. 158–91 in Claudio Veliz, editor, *The Politics of Conformity* (London: Oxford University Press, 1967), 162.
48. Ramon Eduardo Ruiz, *Triumphs and Tragedy: A History of the Mexican People* (New York: W. W. Norton, 1992), 88.
49. Alan Knight, "Racism, Revolution, and Indigenismo: Mexico 1910–1940," pp. 70–113 in Richard Graham, editor, *The Idea of Race in Latin America, 1870–1940* (Austin: University of Texas Press, 1990), 76.
50. Friedrich Katz, *The Secret War in Mexico: Europe, the United States, and the Mexican Revolution* (Chicago: University of Chicago Press, 1981), 38.
51. John Womack, Jr., *Zapata and the Mexican Revolution* (New York: Vintage, 1968), 13, 70–1. John Mason Hart puts the figure at 20 percent: see *Revolutionary Mexico: The Coming and Process of the Mexican Revolution* (Berkeley: University of California Press, 1989), 305.
52. Chevalier, "The Ejido and Political Stability in Mexico," 162.
53. For the vast majority of former slaves the promise of freedom became the ugly terms of sharecropping and debt peonage, agricultural regimes perfected in Mexico and other Latin American countries: see W. E. B. DuBois, *Black Reconstruction in America 1860–1880* (New York: Atheneum, 1983), 55–127.
54. Ramon Eduardo Ruiz, *The Great Rebellion: Mexico 1905–1924* (New York: W. W. Norton, 1980), 311.
55. Ibid., 316, 323–31.
56. Katz, *The Secret War in Mexico*, 8.
57. Ibid., 143.
58. Ibid., 15.
59. Ibid., 38.
60. Ibid., 21, 20.
61. John Reed, *Insurgent Mexico* (New York: International Publishers, 1969), 145.
62. Ruiz, *The Great Rebellion*, 198.
63. Octavio Paz, *The Labyrinth of Solitude* (New York: Grove Press, 1985), 338,144.
64. The term is DuBois's: see *Black Reconstruction*, 700.
65. Hart, *Revolutionary Mexico*, 305.
66. Gordon K. Lewis, *Puerto Rico: Freedom and Power in the Caribbean* (New York: Monthly Review Press, 1963), 88.
67. Louis A. Pérez, Jr., *Cuba: Between Reform and Revolution* (New York: Oxford University Press, 1988), 197.
68. Jorge Gilbert, *Cuba: From Primitive Accumulation of Capital to Socialism* (Toronto: Two Thirds Editions, 1981), 123.
69. Ibid., 136.
70. Lewis, *Puerto Rico*, 73.
71. Ibid., 90.
72. Ibid., 94.
73. Hugh Thomas, "Middle Class Politics and the Cuban Revolution," pp. 249–77 in Claudio Veliz, editor, *The Politics of Conformity in Latin America* (London: Oxford University Press, 1967), 253.

74. Carlos Moore, *Castro, the Blacks, and Africa* (Los Angeles: Center for Afro-American Studies, UCLA, 1988), 50.
75. Thomas, "Middle Class Politics and the Cuban Revolution," 263. We note, however, that these are trades typically present on plantations.
76. Pérez, Jr., *Cuba*, 214, 219.
77. Lewis, *Puerto Rico*, 509.
78. Ibid., 509.
79. Moore, *Castro, the Blacks, and Cuba*, 16.
80. See Hugh Thomas, *Cuba: The Pursuit of Freedom*(New York: Harper & Row, 1971), 851.
81. The Afro-Cuban figure ranges from 25 to 50 percent of the total Cuban population: see de la Fuente, "Race and Inequality in Cuba," 135, and Moore, *Castro, the Blacks, and Africa*, 15.
82. Moore, *Castro, the Blacks, and Africa*, 32.
83. Thomas,*Cuba*, 1122.
84. Moore, *Castro, the Blacks, and Africa*, 34, 32.
85. "The proportion of widows was highest among women of color; nearly three widows for every five wives and in Havana four widows for every five wives:" Pérez, *Cuba*, 190.
86. See Aline Helg, *Our Rightful Share: The Afro-Cuban Struggle for Equality, 1886–1912* (Chapel Hill: University of North Carolina Press, 1995), 193–226.
87. Moore, *Castro, the Blacks, and Africa*, 39.
88. Ibid., 28. See also Helg, *Our Rightful Share*, 1–21.
89. Thomas, *Cuba*, 1122.
90. Thomas, "Middle Class Politics and the Cuban Revolution," 262.
91. Carlos Franqui, *Le Livre des douze* (Paris, 1965), 18, cited in Thomas, *Cuba*, 851.
92. Thomas, *Cuba*, 1122.
93. Gayle McGarrity and Osvaldo Cardenas, "Cuba," pp. 77–107 in Minority Rights Groups, editor, *No Longer Invisible: Afro-Latin Americans Today* (London: Minority Rights Publications, 1995), 98.
94. Andres Oppenheimer, *Castro's Final Hour: The Secret Story Behind the Coming Downfall of Communist Cuba* (New York: Simon & Schuster, 1992), 340.
95. Ibid., 346–7.
96. Carlos Moore, "Afro-Cubans and the Communist Revolution," pp. 199–239 in Carlos Moore, Tanya R. Sanders, and Shawna Moore, editors, *African Presence in the Americas* (Trenton: Africa World Press, 1995), 237.
97. McGarrity and Cardenas, "Cuba," 98.
98. On this last point see Alfred G. Meyer, *Leninism* (Boulder: Westview Press, 1986), 37–56.
99. John A. Booth, *The End and the Beginning: The Nicaraguan Revolution* (Boulder: Westview Press, 1985), 34.
100. Ibid., 32.
101. Ibid., 75.
102. John Foran, Linda Klouzal, and Jean-Pierre Rivera, "Who Makes Revolutions? Class, Gender, and Race in the Mexican, Cuban, and Nicaraguan Revolutions," in *Research in Social Movements, Conflicts, and Change* (1997).
103. The figures range from 180,000 to 276,000 out of a total Nicaraguan population of 2,600,000.
104. Philippe Bourgois, "Nicaragua's Ethnic Minorities in the Revolution," pp. 459–72 in Peter Rossett and John Vandermeer, editors, *Nicaragua: Unfinished Revolution* (New York: Grove Press, 1986), 461.
105. Ibid., 465.

106. Bassette Cayasso, "Afro-Nicaraguans Before and After the Sandinista Revolution," pp. 163–198 in Carlos Moore, Tanya R. Sanders and Shawna Moore, editors, *African Presence in the Americas* (Trenton: Africa World Press, 1995), 171.
107. Ibid., 169–70.
108. Bourgois, "Nicaragua's Ethnic Minorities," 468–9.
109. Cayasso, "Afro-Nicaragua Before and After the Sandinista Revolution," 179.
110. Ibid., 177, 166.
111. Shirley Christian, *Nicaragua: Revolution in the Family* (New York: Vintage, 1986), 297–8.
112. The National Network in Solidarity with the Nicaraguan People, "Atlantic Coast: Miskito Crisis and Counterrevolution," pp. 83–90 in Peter Rosset and John Vandermeer, editors, *The Nicaragua Reader: Documents of a Revolution Under Fire* (New York: Grove Press, 1983), 86.
113. Christian, *Nicaragua*, 299–301.
114. Cayasso, "Afro-Nicaraguans," 189.
115. Christian, *Nicaragua*, 302.
116. See Alejandro Martínez Cuenca, *Sandinista Economics in Practice: An Insider's Critical Reflections* (Boston: South End Press, 1992), 61.
117. Girvan, "Aspects," 10–11, 23–4.
118. Leon Trotsky, *The History of the Russian Revolution* (London: Pluto Press, 1977), 17.
119. Ruiz, *The Great Rebellion*, 4.

8

DISCOURSES AND SOCIAL FORCES

The role of culture and cultural studies in understanding revolutions

John Foran

From the seeds of culture blossom flowers of resistance and liberation.
                                                                Amilcar Cabral

Like many other specialized but historically central topics within the social sciences, the study of revolutions has not proven immune to changes in the larger currents within social theory generally. This means that since the early 1980s, and with increasing urgency in the early 1990s, the "cultural" turn within the social sciences has begun to have an impact on theorizing about revolutions. This turn constitutes a critical new moment in the actual study of revolutions, one potentially capable of affecting our thinking on a par with the previous "turn" toward structural theories in the 1970s associated with the work of Theda Skocpol, Jeffery Paige, and Charles Tilly, among others, and just before them, Eric Wolf and Barrington Moore, Jr. This development has paralleled and been affected by the rise of the sociology of culture in the United States, cultural studies in England, and poststructuralism in France and elsewhere. The purpose of this chapter is to take some stock of the many diverse currents within this most recent approach as applied to revolutions, establishing their historical lineages and identifying the major debates among them, and to set out a new research agenda for incorporating the undeniable insights of this body of work into future, better-rounded perspectives for studying revolutions.

Among the major issues involved here are the perennial questions of the causes and outcomes of revolutions; the difficulties of thinking about how culture, ideology, and discourse play a role in these; and the relationship of such factors to social structure, state, and political economy as principles of explanation. The following chapter will take up in turn the larger field of studying culture, current approaches to revolution and culture, the problem of the cultural origins of revolutions, and the role played by cultural forces in shaping their outcomes. Along the way, I shall make my own argument about the centrality of culture in the making and unmaking of revolutions, touching base empirically with a diverse set of cases across time and space, from the French Revolution, to Iran, Eastern Europe in 1989, Cuba, El Salvador, and Nicaragua. My goal is to suggest the indispensability of the idea of culture in understanding revolutions and to simultaneously place this within a larger perspective that leads away from an equally one-sided rebuttal of the structural or political economic schools in theorizing revolutions.

STUDYING CULTURE/CULTURAL STUDIES

It is impossible in such a short space to do more than point at some of the classic statements and positions informing contemporary debates in the study of culture generally. My aim here will be to indicate both the flavor of the major contending paradigms and to single out some of the more promising leads within them for the specific subfield that concerns us most here, namely the role of culture in shaping political action.

The vulnerability of classical Marxian theory on issues of subjectivity, culture, and consciousness signalled initially by Max Weber's thesis on the rise of capitalism produced the remarkable oeuvres of Lukàcs and Gramsci after the turn of the twentieth century and the Russian Revolution. The first problematized class consciousness and the second bequeathed us the concept of hegemony, thereby together laying the groundwork for the rise of such influential theoretical schools as critical theory, neo-Marxism, and Western Marxism after World War II. The English cultural critic Raymond Williams tapped these perspectives for brilliant empirical studies of popular culture, giving us the key term "structures of feeling" to characterize the outlooks and mentalities of historical actors.[1] His contemporary E. P. Thompson further concretized the significance of culture for the study of social structure and revolutionary action in his many works, most notably *The Making of the English Working Class* (1963) with its famous prefatory remarks on the irreducible subjectivity of class:

> By class I understand an historical phenomenon, unifying a number of disparate and seemingly unconnected events, both in the raw material of experience and in consciousness. . . . Class-consciousness is the way in which these experiences are handled in cultural terms: embodied in traditions, value-systems, ideas, and institutional forms. . . . Class is defined by men as they live their own history, and, in the end, this is its only definition. . . . I am convinced that we cannot understand class unless we see it as a social and cultural formation, arising from processes which can only be studied as they work themselves out over a considerable historical period.[2]

Since the 1960s Stuart Hall and many others in England loosely affiliated with the Birmingham Centre for Contemporary Cultural Studies have built on the work of Gramsci, Williams, and Thompson to found the field of cultural studies, concerned above all with the relationship between cultural forms and class, racial, and gendered political movements of resistance.[3] In the United States, James Scott has worked the same critical vein, giving us the concept of "hidden transcripts" to refer to the discourses of subaltern groups resisting domination with the tools at their disposal.[4] Yet another large current with close relations to Hall's project is the vast but uncharted field we might call Third World cultural studies, with significant contributions ranging from the work of such writers as Edward Said, Fredric Jameson, and Aijaz Ahmad, or the paradigms of subaltern studies, post-colonial studies, the postmodernism debates in Latin America, and the like.[5]

On the continent of Europe, Michel Foucault's work fashioned an alternative view of power and its effects on people. Pushing beyond the boundaries of French structuralism he pioneered the broad trend of post-structuralist social theory and a radically new way of writing history that attempted to unearth and map what he called the "genealogies" of how power intersects with discourse to produce institutions such as the modern prison, asylum, and hospital clinics or ways of thinking about sexuality, academic disciplines, and other discursive formations. Much work on culture generally since the late 1970s in the United States and elsewhere has been deeply shaped by encounters with Foucault's writings, which have proven difficult, however, to extend faithfully into the domains he left unexplored.[6]

Taking another tack entirely (and indeed sometimes in quite explicitly hostile contradistinction to post-structuralism) has been the American sociology of culture approach, which embodies an equally diverse set of empirical emphases and theoretical inflections. This field has come of age within the American academy since the 1980s, drawing on earlier work by such anthropological luminaries as Clifford Geertz. In one influential article, Ann Swidler refers to the notion of culture as a "tool-kit," a locus of symbols, beliefs, and orientations to the world that social actors may draw upon for pragmatic purposes. As we shall see, this notion has left its imprint on writings about revolutionary ideologies, yet most of the American work in the sociology of culture has remained resolutely detached from analyses of political action generally and in non-US settings in particular.[7] This sketch of the broad outlines of the social scientific literature on the impossibly large topic of "culture" must suffice for present purposes; it will be useful now to narrow the scope of this survey to the topic at hand.

REVOLUTION AND CULTURE

Alexis de Tocqueville's mid-nineteenth century views on the role of ideology in the revolutionary upheavals in France (on which more below) remained a largely minority view in writing on revolution until quite recently.[8] There was, to be sure, a generation of theorists in the 1920s and 1930s sometimes referred to as the "Natural History" school that kept de Tocqueville's insights partly alive, and a strong hegemonic paradigm in 1950s and 1960s American sociology – structural functionalism and modernization theory – that centered a certain reading of culture.[9] But perhaps because of these earlier emphases, the 1970s saw a strong turn away from culture as an explanatory strategy toward political economy, "structure," and the state, all key to Theda Skocpol's influential classic, *States and Social Revolutions* (1979).[10] Skocpol argued iconoclastically that "Revolutions are not made, they come," and that ideas were epiphenomena in the origins and outcomes of the revolutions she studied – the French, the Russian, the Chinese. Her book generated a substantial amount of further debate around issues of structure and agency, pro and contra, and the Iranian Revolution of 1979 forced her to reconsider her position somewhat to acknowledge that here was at least one revolution in which ideas – notably Islam – motivated actors and that ideological change was one of the distinguishing features of a social revolution.[11]

The debate took a step forward with a 1985 exchange between historian William Sewell and Theda Skocpol on the precise role of ideas in the making of the French Revolution. Sewell charges Skocpol with failing to recognize "the autonomous power of ideology in the revolutionary process," smuggling in ideas under the rubric of differing "world-historical contexts" in France and Russia. Invoking the works of Althusser, Foucault, Geertz, and Raymond Williams, Sewell calls for a structural, anonymous, and transpersonal analysis of ideology, arguing that such collective human products are capable of transformation.[12] Skocpol's reply offers a nice distinction between long-standing, anonymous, and socially diverse *cultural idioms* drawn upon by popular groups, and the self-consciously elaborated *ideologies* that politically articulate actors fashion out of the former for specific purposes. These conceptions then interact with the structural situations described in her earlier work, with central significance still seemingly lying in "struggles over the organization and uses of state power."[13]

These leads have been further extended in the work of political scientist Farideh Farhi on the Iranian and Nicaraguan revolutions. Drawing on Craig Calhoun, Göran Therborn, and Gramsci, she writes that "cultural practices, orientations, meaning systems, and social outlooks" play a role in the making of revolutions.[14] Ideology is *not* "a system of ideas;" rather it is a "social process" involving "knowledgeable actors" which invokes larger cultural systems rather than "consciously held political beliefs': "successful ideological mobilization always manages to fuse and condense several ideological discourses into a single major theme, usually expressed in a single slogan."[15] From feminist liberation theology she appropriates the intriguing notion of "dangerous" memories of conflict and exclusion[16] – whether of past suffering or actual or imagined instances of resistance and change (such as Shiʻi imagery in Iran or Sandino's rebellion in 1920s Nicaragua). Farhi also perceptively analyzes the legitimation claims of the old regimes and the contradictions inherent in these (the Shah's god-like creator image ironically made him responsible for Iran's problems; Somoza's branding of all opponents as communists gave the term a positive valuation).

Scholars have also begun to try to grasp the other end of the revolutionary continuum, asking how culture has affected the *outcomes* of revolutions. Jack Goldstone traces the contrasting outcomes of the "early modern" upheavals he studied to the differences between revolutionary political reconstruction in France, England, and Japan versus conservative outcomes in seventeenth-century China, the Ottoman Empire, and Spain.[17] High levels of "ideological tensions" (challenging monarchy to the core) left England and France poised for dynamic evolution after their state breakdowns, while the absence of such tension, linked to a cyclical rather than eschatological view of history, is said to account for subsequent stagnation in the Chinese and Ottoman cases. Turning to more recent revolutionary outcomes, Eric Selbin has insisted that revolutionary consolidation and institutionalization involve indispensable acts of human agency in which revolutionary leaderships make quite explicit and conscious appeals to populations for allegiance to their projects.[18] Forrest Colburn, meanwhile, has argued that socialism (or, more precisely, Marxism-Leninism) has served as a blueprint for the cultural construction of postrevolutionary regimes in such seemingly diverse settings as Cuba, Angola, Ethiopia, China, and Afghanistan; in a sense, one international political culture overriding the effect of another, local, one.[19] The writings mentioned in this section take the social scientific study of revolutions to a new theoretical plane, on which the frontiers of cultural approaches become plainly visible.

DISCOURSES AND SOCIAL FORCES: AN ALTERNATIVE APPROACH

All of this work has recentered culture in the study of revolutions, and begun to move current research agendas away from the pure structuralisms of the 1970s. Yet many questions remain for today's students of revolutionary social change, two perhaps foremost among them: What are the precise mechanisms by which culture works its independent effects on the revolutionary process? And how should the new concerns with culture and agency be balanced with the previous generation's insights on structure and the political economic?

My own sense of answers involves recourse to the concept of "political cultures of resistance and opposition," on the one hand, and to how these are interpreted and fashioned by the social forces that make revolutions, on the other.[20] By "political culture," I mean not the 1960s American political-science concept, but the plurivocal and potentially radical ways of understanding one's circumstances that various groups within a society sometimes articulate to make sense of the political and economic changes they are living through.[21] Some of the theorists already mentioned invoke much the same idea, notably Scott, Sewell, Skocpol, Tilly, Farhi, and even Swidler. The qualifier "political cultures of *resistance and opposition*," however, distinguishes this notion from the American sociology-of-culture tradition. The fact that such cultures tap everything from historical memories of past conflicts to inchoate sentiments about injustice, to long-standing religious idioms and practices, to more formally elaborated political ideologies transcends the Sewell–Skocpol debate by embracing all of what they pinpoint as relevant (although it remains to be seen how these articulate with each other). My insistence that such political cultures are plural and multiple, that they can be secular as well as religious, and that different social groups may embrace different versions, takes us beyond the work of Farhi on Iran and Nicaragua.[22]

It is therefore also critically important to link these discursive practices with actual social forces for the study of revolution. Difficult as it may be to perceive political cultures of opposition operating in revolutionary settings now lost to historical view, it is equally necessary to attempt the even more daunting task of linking what is visible with the actors who made the events, in effect mapping discourses and social forces as best we can.[23] Such social forces may be the standard ones of class, but this must be handled with particular care, as E. P. Thompson reminds us, and not in isolation from gender and race as two other central principles of social stratification and partial determinants of political identities, as much recent scholarship, including the contributions of Val Moghadam and Chris McAuley to this volume, has made manifest.[24] My previous work on this process in the Iranian Revolution has argued that social revolutions are made by broad coalitions of aggrieved social forces which may be characterized as multi-class (now also to be conceptualized as cross-racial and gendered) *populist* alliances. This chapter will attempt to extend this in two directions: to other cases empirically and with a more fine-grained discussion of the processes by which such alliances use political cultures of opposition to coalesce (or fail to do so).

Finally, in thinking about outcomes, we must continue to track the fortunes of the populist alliance, this time through a process of fragmentation into its constituent elements as both internal and external pressures are brought to bear on postrevolutionary societies. My argument shall be that culture again is central to making sense of this process, either in Selbin's sense of holding a coalition together or in the disasters that await revolutionaries once in power. The six case studies that follow are meant to further illustrate and specify something of the range of ways in which culture looms large in the revolutionary record.

THE ORIGINS PROBLEM

How then, does culture matter in the causality of revolutions? I will argue that prior to revolutions, different groups in society elaborate multiple political cultures of opposition to the regime, and that these may draw on diffuse folk beliefs and historical memories of struggle, shared "structures of feeling" fashioned out of common experiences, and eventually, perhaps, explicitly revolutionary manifestos and formally articulated ideologies. The cases of eighteenth-century France, 1970s' Iran, and Eastern Europe in 1989 will allow us to see where such political cultures come from, how they are mapped onto social actors, and how diverse orientations coalesce into a more or less unified popular alliance. I shall be necessarily brief and suggestive in this discussion, making use of some of the best recent scholarship on each case, as well as my own research, where appropriate.

France

The case of France has been brilliantly dissected in a book by Roger Chartier, for our purposes most appropriately titled *The Cultural Origins of the French Revolution* (1991).[25] Chartier takes up and complicates the thesis originating in de Tocqueville and formalized by Daniel Mornet, that the reformist and critical ideas of the Enlightenment fatefully inflected the crisis of the old regime as it moved toward the revolution.[26] Chartier argues that the creation of an essentially middle-class public sphere by writers and printers prepared the way for the French to become critical of the monarchy in the decades just before the revolution. Pamphleteers, philosophes, fiction writers, gazetteers, and their publishers constituted the key social forces driving this process, which intersected with a growing reading public of slightly lower class positions, increasingly capable of reading critically. Though he rightly problematizes this by asking who read and how they interpreted what they read, Chartier in the end accepts the broad outlines of the cultural argument, linking it with such radical developments as the secularization of the hold of religious beliefs, the desacralization of and disenchantment with the king's privileged social position, and the growth of ideas of anti-hierarchical liberty in the cities and anti-seigneurial authority in the countryside.[27] We also learn that literacy rose from 29 percent to 47 percent for men and from 14 to 27 percent for women between the late 1680s and the late 1780s; that types of books published shifted from religion to fiction and politics; and that the most radical books were published outside of France, setting off a rebellion for freedom of the press led by French publishers.[28] For all its qualifications and limitations (there is no attention to the content of the ideas that drove the revolution, and there is an emphasis on middle-class actors at the expense of those below in the social order), Chartier's analysis leaves little doubt about the conclusion that revolutions *do* have cultural origins.[29]

Iran

We can make good some of the gaps in Chartier's analysis of France with a look at the Iranian Revolution of 1977–79. This revolution put the domain of culture squarely on the agenda of a new generation of scholars (Skocpol among them), forcing an appreciation of the role played by revolutionary Islam in its making. Unfortunately, all too often this was all that was seen, making a kind of monolithic Islam the sole cause of the events. In fact, the political cultures behind the revolution spanned secular and Islamic discourses, appealing differentially to the quite varied social forces that made the revolution.[30] Khomeini's militant Islam castigated the Shah for selling the country to foreigners and neglecting the downtrodden. An important variation on this was the radical Shi'i theology of liberation elaborated by the layman Dr. 'Ali Shari'ati, who blended themes from Marxism with Shi'i emphases on suffering and the struggle against social injustices. A third strand within Islamic oppositional discourses was offered by Mehdi Bazargan (the first revolutionary prime minister), whose Freedom Movement of Iran had since the 1960s advocated a liberal-democratic solution to the country's problems within an Islamic framework. Nor should the apolitical or even pro-Shah outlook of many of the nation's clergy be overlooked in the rush to interpret the revolution as "Islamic" in its overall inspiration. Arguing further against this is the existence of important secular currents such as the democratic nationalism of the National Front, the orthodox Marxism of the Tudeh Party, and the guerrilla strategies of the Fada'ian and other Marxist and Maoist organizations. Finally, straddling the secular–religious divide and on the far left of the Islamic movement was the widely popular Mujahidin guerrilla organization, itself divided over the issue of the primacy of a Shi'i Islamic or a Marxist interpretation of society.[31] The plurality of these political cultures of resistance forecloses any simple-minded identification of Khomeini's brand of Islam as *the* ideological mover behind the revolution. There is, in addition, an important argument by Val Moghadam that Islamization set in after the revolutionaries came to power in 1979, and that accounts that read it back into the movement of 1978–79 are thus inadmissible.[32]

Beyond this, there looms the problem of mapping these diverse political cultures onto specific social actors. Here, too, the state of the literature on the Iranian case permits some preliminary observations, which may be summed up in the following way:[33]

Khomeini's militant Islam:	seminary students, some bazaaris
Shari'ati's radical Islam:	students
Bazargan's liberal Islam:	professionals
National Front democratic nationalism:	professionals
Tudeh Party orthodox Marxism:	intellectuals, some workers
Fada'ian's radical Marxism:	students, some workers
Mujahidin's Islamic socialism:	students

The problems with this mapping are readily apparent: some groups – notably professionals and students[34] – cross ideological lines, while other important actors – the working class, the urban marginals – are largely absent from it, as are women as such and Iran's important ethnic minorities (the Kurds, the Azeri-speakers of the northwest, the Turkomans, and others). What, too, is the nature of the evidence in the cases we have so seemingly confidently mapped above? And how do we know what the millions of people who marched in the streets really identified their struggle with, in political and cultural terms?[35]

This last question raises the issue of how these diverse orientations – assuming they existed and are roughly accurate – came together to topple a government. That is, if we insist that people's conceptions are multiple, even if overlapping, how is a sufficient degree of unity attained to achieve a common goal?[36] In Iran, it would seem that each of the several oppositional cultures contained two key elements in common: a demand that monarchic autocracy come to an end, and a (related) demand that Iran's relationship with the United States be redefined in less dependent ways. Khomeini was perhaps the most visible embodiment of both demands, garnering support from all sectors of the movement, or at least respect for his symbolic leadership on these issues. Equally important, he downplayed the divisive aspects of his program (Islamic state, anti-communism) very effectively from the point of view of obtaining at least the acquiescence of his organized rivals among the left and liberal forces on both sides of the secular–religious divide.

Eastern Europe

Ten years later, in 1989, Eastern Europe witnessed a sudden and vigorous movement to overthrow a system that had maintained a strong hold on society for forty years. These events are of particular interest because they shed further light on the same question of how culture catalyzes movements, presenting an instance of a rather diffuse yet extremely powerful political culture, one that did not primarily tap explicitly formulated ideologies with texts and authors, as in the French or Iranian cases. We might think about this in the following way. Socialism came to Eastern Europe *from the outside*, imposed by the Soviet Union at the end of World War II. The result was a particular form of development – a *dependent* development, to which corresponded a particular state ideology of state socialism. Eventually political repression and economic stagnation engendered political cultures of opposition, which could not appeal to socialism (an idea discredited by the system they lived in), but which took the form of the language of democratic, citizens'' rights, tinged with nationalistic resistance to Soviet domination and with a conservative undercurrent provided by religion as well.[37] Local elites proved powerless without Soviet force to back them up. Ash describes the loss of confidence of the ruling communist elite in their own rule:

> A few kids went into the streets and threw a few words. The police beat them. The kids said: You have no right to beat us! And the rulers, the high and mighty, replied in effect: Yes, we have no right to beat you. We have no right to preserve our rule by force. The end no longer justifies the means![38]

Thus the revolutions of 1989 were essentially nonviolent, except in Romania, ruled more independently of the Soviet Union by the dictator Nicolae Ceaușescu. In Czechoslovakia, for example, the events were termed "the velvet revolution." Everywhere they consisted of mass demonstrations by men and women across all classes, no longer accepting the legitimacy of the state.[39] Ash writes of their nonviolent strategy:

> Partly it was pragmatic: the other side had all the weapons. But it was also ethical. It was a statement about how things should be. They wanted to start as they intended to go on. History, said Adam Michnik, had taught them that those who start by storming bastilles will end up building their own.[40]

Their motives then were a desire for freedom, to be able to tell the truth to themselves and their children, to construct better lives. The main actors were "the people," struggling against the state, the bureaucracy, the party elite, referred to simply as "them." Their political culture thus consisted of a diffuse counter-ideology of "democracy," sovereignty, and the market, fashioned from the hard realities of everyday life in more or less diametric opposition to the official ideology of the state. Both of these insights are important: oppositional cultures are often elaborated in contradistinction to the state (this is quite clear here where the state holds the avowedly "revolutionary" discourse), but they are also always rooted in the actual experiences of diverse social sectors, that is, they have an eminently practical dimension.

These three cases – 1789 France, 1978 Iran, and 1989 Eastern Europe – could be multiplied several-fold in assessing the roles that culture may play in the origins of revolutions. Each could also be studied in much greater depth to nuance and modify our specific propositions regarding the complex interplay of culture with economy, polity, and society, and the mechanisms through which it assumes its mobilizing efficacy. Nevertheless, it is hoped that this survey makes at least the preliminary case for recentering culture in the complex, conjunctural causality of social revolutions. Let us turn to some emerging ways of thinking about their outcomes.

THE OUTCOMES PROBLEM

In taking up the question of the role that culture might play in the outcomes of revolutions, different problems arise. There is, first of all, the disjuncture between what revolutionaries say they were fighting for before seizing power, and the sorts of societies they fashion if they succeed in doing so. In *States and Social Revolutions* Skocpol used this divide as one of her arguments to discount the role of actors (and by extension their ideologies) in the making of revolutions. She reasoned that if the results were not foreseen, the activities and objectives of revolutionaries must have played little role in bringing them about. We shall examine the Cuban Revolution with this objection in mind. Another challenge – something of a mirror opposite of the first – is posed by the argument that no revolution ever failed for want of a culture of opposition; since organized revolutionaries always possess an ideology of some kind (but see the discussions of Eastern Europe on pp. 211–13) their failure to come to power must be attributed to some other cause or causes. We will examine the reasons for the lack of success of the Salvadoran Revolution in the 1980s with this debate in mind. A final problem – and one that follows from the framework adopted in this chapter – has to do with the fragmentation of the broad alliances that make revolutions; my argument is that this has as much to do with culture as with political economy and international processes. The case of Nicaragua will shed some light on this question.

Cuba

It is sometimes pointed out that since Fidel Castro embraced Marxism only after coming to power in 1959, political culture was not consequential in the shaping of the Cuban Revolution. This is not the place to analyze the distinctive blend of nationalist, egalitarian, and populist themes in the July 26 Movement's insurrectionary phase.[41] Instead, I want to engage with Skocpol's views on the inability to follow a "blueprint" as evidence for the relative unimportance of what revolutionaries actually try to do, and on how they elaborate and propagate this for society at large. This will also put us on the ground of Forrest Colburn's argument that all Third World revolutionary regimes tend to look alike in their Marxism-Leninism.

The origins of socialism in Cuba clearly owe much to the escalation of tensions between the United States and the Cuban revolutionaries between

January 1959 and mid-1961: the dispute caused by the opening of commercial relations with the Soviet Union, the nationalization of US companies, the US blockade, and finally the Bay of Pigs invasion in April 1961 prompted Castro to declare himself a socialist a month later. But Cuban socialism, as a political culture, was neither a radical turn from the earliest stated objectives of the July 26 Movement nor a faithful translation of the Soviet model into Spanish. In terms of its origins, the ideology of Castro's July 26 Movement *before* coming to power in 1959 was an already radicalized variant of nineteenth-century revolutionary hero José Martí's amalgam of anti-imperialist nationalism, humanism, and sympathy with the poor. From its formation in 1955 the July 26 Movement had declared itself for the introduction of "social justice" in Cuba; though its specific positions were often deliberately vague and consciously kept moderate in 1957–58 to attract a diverse social base, it was undoubtedly understood by many Cubans as capable of providing the land reform it openly announced in October 1958, as well as more independence from the United States, and other radical goals.[42] Castro, like Khomeini in Iran, certainly modified his message for diverse constituencies, and muted it in the interest of keeping them together, but there should be little doubt that his radical followers understood his goal as one of relatively deep social transformation well before they came to power.[43]

This is not to deny that the explicitly Marxist-Leninist cast of Cuban revolutionary rhetoric is an artifact of the post-1961 conjuncture. But this should not be dismissed as the failure to follow a revolutionary blueprint, as Skocpol would have us do, for several reasons. First, it should come as no surprise that revolutionaries, once in power, must confront new challenges, often quite severe, from inside and abroad. Here, we see the interaction of culture and social forces in a new light, one in which political culture is shaped by economy, politics, and external pressures. In responding to these forces, whether in 1792 France, 1979 Iran, or 1962 Cuba, revolutionaries work within their preexisting ideological horizons, but also go beyond and outside them, in the process elaborating new, revisioned cultures of opposition to try to keep a revolutionary coalition together. Cuba surely represents one of the most successful such cases in the history of revolutions, in so far as its broad populist coalition did not disintegrate (aided by the migration of upper and skilled middle classes in the early 1960s). Rather, it was held together even as the revolution radicalized into a project of deep social transformation. And it was held together, in no small part, by the enthusiasm of the population for the new socialist political culture.

Nor, however, does Cuba's experience fit Colburn's thesis of a purely imitative "vogue" of Marxist-Leninist Third World revolutionary ideology (letting alone the ways in which Iran bursts out of this argument). Colburn quite rightly notes that the inconclusive debate over whether Castro hid his socialism until 1961 or was a convert "obscures how ideas of socialism at the University of Havana and elsewhere in Cuba helped inspire the revolution and how, once formally adopted as the ideology of the Cuban Revolution, they played a decisive role in defining the Cuban Revolution."[44] This is far from the unwarranted conclusion that Marxism-Leninism homogenizes revolutionary ideologies into a remarkably similar-looking state and society. Here, too, the longevity of the Cuban Revolution suggests that the process of elaborating effective political cultures requires complex negotiations between such "universals" as Marxism-Leninism and much longer-standing notions of a specifically Cuban nationalism, democracy, and ideals of social, racial, and economic justice.[45] While the Cuban revolutionaries, in power, operated without a blueprint of the kind suggested by Colburn and dismissed by Skocpol, they enjoyed the benefits of the political culture they themselves had fashioned before the overthrow, now turned to the purpose of generating the wide popular enthusiasm that aided them in constructing what would become – in my view – the most impressive socialist transformation in human history. It was these inflections that gave the Cuban Revolution its particular imprint as a powerful force for socialist change within Cuba and indeed, as a model for particular rearticulation with other local traditions elsewhere (interestingly, never as successful as in Cuba).

El Salvador

One of these more recent cases is the Salvadoran Revolution of 1979–92. This case speaks to the contrary objection that no revolution has ever failed for want of a revolutionary political culture.[46] The Salvadoran revolution no doubt also reposed on a diverse set of oppositional currents, including social democracy and liberation theology, at its inception in the mid- to late 1970s. But even its roots in the struggle led by Augustín Farabundo Martí in the 1920s and early 1930s were significantly more Marxist and class-based than its counterpart under Sandino in Nicaragua, and by the 1970s the ideological center of gravity of the revolution was an uncompromising Marxist-Leninist standpoint embodied in the FMLN (Farabundo Martí National Liberation Front).[47] As the hoped-for swift uprising of 1979–80 devolved into a stalemated civil war through the decade of the 1980s, the armed wing of the revolution represented by the FMLN defined the political cultural terms of the struggle as resolutely anti-imperialist and class-based. This was not calculated to secure any broad support from the middle-class sectors, or even some of the peasantry and urban lower classes for whom they fought. Instead, the centrist Christian-Democratic Party of José Napoleón Duarte dominated the electoral opening of the mid-1980s, eventually ceding a thin hegemony to the right-wing ARENA Party which governed El Salvador thereafter, finally negotiating a peace settlement with the rebels in 1992. To this argument may be added the neglect by the FMLN of the emerging feminist revolutionary culture within its own ranks, which, as Julia Shayne has demonstrated, surfaced fully only after the 1992 settlement and is adding its part to politics there today.[48]

I am *not* arguing that only culture explains the defeat of the Salvadoran Revolution (and labeling the outcome itself presents a complex challenge, for the revolutionaries were not defeated in the field and are playing a crucial role in the new El Salvador). Other factors clearly contributed their effect as well: the very democratic opening that the regime undertook made the state less vulnerable, the massive outside aid to the government supplied by the Reagan administration helped produce the battlefield stalemate (and note that each of these factors has a cultural dimension, whether in domestic political culture or the Cold War).[49] The argument advanced here is simply that the particular configuration of revolutionary political culture in 1980s El Salvador was an important adverse factor in the outcome, just as the end of the Cold War on a certain level after 1989 and internal debates produced the willingness of the FMLN to negotiate a peace, itself another way in which political culture contributes to specific outcomes.[50]

Nicaragua

All revolutionary movements, once in power, tend to fragment. This is inevitable, given the broad alliance necessary to sustain them, the discrepancies in the goals of their constituent social groups, classes, and parties, and the great expectations unleashed by the success of the events themselves. I have traced this process elsewhere in the case of Iran, where the supporters of Khomeini in the Islamic Republican Party skillfully outmaneuvered the social forces adhering to each of the other political cultures of opposition sketched earlier in this chapter.[51] Even in Cuba, where civil society developed a remarkable cohesiveness after the seizure of power (as evidenced in the repulsion of the Bay of Pigs invasion), the years from 1959 to 1961 witnessed a power struggle that removed liberals from the government and was marked in social terms by a mass exodus of the privileged and skilled middle classes. This common process of fragmentation is as yet little studied, and its causal mechanisms remain undertheorized. It constitutes one more instance of the dialectic of discourses and social forces that underlays the theoretical framework adopted in this chapter.

The case of Sandinista Nicaragua is a challenging one to illustrate this point, for the Sandinistas in power learned from both the Cuban and Salvadoran experiences to avoid a rigid Marxist-Leninist vision of postrevolutionary society. They tried hard to create a space within the revolution for the middle classes and even the elite, especially the landowners that dominated the export economy in cotton and other products. Revolutionary pluralism politically and the mixed economy were the hallmarks of the Sandinista approach to the social transformation of Nicaragua.[52] The vicissitudes of their interaction afford us a final opportunity to assess the relationship of culture and political economy.

The Sandinista model worked rather well between 1979 and 1983: despite a severe continent-wide recession, the Nicaraguan economy grew a total of 22.5 percent, a remarkable achievement given the regional trends. By 1983, food consumption was up 40 percent, rents had been cut by 50 percent, medical care was free, and infant mortality had declined by 28 percent, as had a number of illnesses and diseases that were gotten under control by immunization and better public health services. A literacy campaign in 1980 reduced illiteracy from 50 percent to 12 percent. Land reform brought 5 million acres of land to 100,000 families, more than it had elsewhere in all of Central America combined. These accomplishments made the Sandinistas rather popular inside the country, and in the 1984 elections, they received 67 percent of the votes in what all non-US observers termed a fair and free election.

Stormclouds were already appearing on the horizon, however. The Reagan administration's fear that the model of a mixed economy and independent foreign policy would be attractive throughout Latin America and the Third World led to a cut-off of aid, loans, and in 1985, a total trade embargo on Nicaragua. More devastating still, in 1982 the United States virtually created the contras out of former members of Somoza's National Guard, who were trained, supplied, and funded by the CIA and US military. The United States also secretly mined Nicaragua's harbors. The reasoning behind US pressures was that the Sandinistas probably could not be overthrown in this way, but by imposing what is euphemistically called a "low-intensity conflict" the Nicaraguan model could be weakened and made less attractive for other countries. We see here the intersection of a particular Republican anti-communist crusade and Cold War ideology with long-standing US geostrategic visions of the places of Central America, Latin America, and the Third World within a US-dominated world-system (however much the US position is in decline, and in fact assuming greater urgency *because* it is in decline).

The war took a great toll on the economy and society of Nicaragua. Its costs have been calculated as equal to three years of GDP. The military budget ran at up to 50 percent of government spending, and 25 percent of GNP. By 1985–87, these developments had reversed the earlier successes of the economy. In 1985 alone, GDP fell by 30 percent and inflation hit 300 percent (in 1988 it is said to have reached 20,000 percent). By 1986, purchasing power was down 60 percent from the levels of 1979, although the "social wage" of free education, access to health-care and other services made up for some of this. In addition, Cuba and the Soviet Union gave Nicaragua some economic support, but this was drastically curtailed after the changes in the socialist world registered by the shock of 1989.

217

The impact of hyperinflation and the continued contra war meant a grow-ing disillusionment with the Sandinista vision of a revolutionary political culture. Deteriorating standards of living, increasing hunger in the country-side, the return of certain diseases because immunization could no longer be afforded, and a growth in illiteracy rates as children had to earn money rather than attend school, severely eroded belief in the project. This had a marked impact on the receptiveness of crucial sectors of the revolutionary alliance to the Sandinista project. Peasants, especially in the north, were on the front lines of the contra war.[53] All urban popular classes, from the mar-ginalized groups of the "informal sector" to the small industrial working class to the middle classes, felt the effects of inflation, the draft, and unem-ployment. Women's emancipation was subordinated to the immediate pro-blems and challenges of defending the revolution against the contras. Undoubtedly the economic crisis affected women by the late 1980s, and many must have supported the opposition, which was headed by an upper-class woman with traditional views, Violetta de Chamorro.[54] The church hierarchy was also a conservatizing influence after the revolution, waging a battle for hegemony with the proponents of liberation theology on issues from abortion and birth control to women working outside the family.[55] The indigenous minority on the Atlantic Coast was never integrated into the revolution.[56] The military pressure of the US-sponsored contras, the deep economic crisis, a changing world political atmosphere – all of these pro-duced considerable dissatisfaction with Sandinista policies by 1990. In Feb-ruary of that year they lost elections to Chamorro's UNO coalition of center and right-wing parties. Most observers explain the opposition's win by the weariness of the Nicaraguan people from the war, which significant numbers of voters felt that the USA would continue as long as the Sandinistas were in power, combined with the hope that US economic aid would follow a UNO victory.[57] In this case, fragmentation of the revolutionary coalition was imposed through military and economic pressures from abroad, com-pounded by errors from within, and translated through political cultures into an electoral defeat.

The lasting achievement of the Sandinistas is to have held open elections at all, something nearly unprecedented in the history of revolutions, and also following in part from the political culture they adopted. This is perhaps their best hope for the future, should the post-election leadership prove cap-able of reassessing their defeat and building upon the lasting gains of the revolutionary decade in the popular imagination.[58] In this sense, too, then, political culture will play a role in the long-term outcome of the Nicaraguan Revolution.

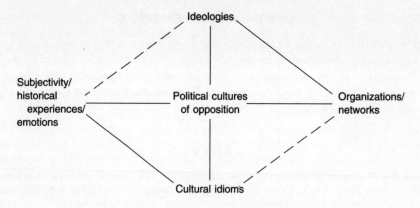

Figure 8.1 The role of culture in the making of revolutions

CONCLUSIONS

This has been a whirlwind tour through a diverse set of revolutionary movements as viewed through the prisms of culture and cultural studies. The argument has been advanced and to some degree illustrated that culture plays a complex and crucial role in the making of revolutions and in their outcomes. While it is premature to bring any closure to this discussion, and at the risk of reifying the complex realities at play, I offer the schema in Figure 8.1 by way of summary for further reflection and elaboration. This suggests that political cultures of opposition are a product of, and in turn have an impact on, a range of material and discursive elements: from the historical experiences that shape subjectivity and arouse emotions that E. P. Thompson has identified,[59] to *all* the issues uncovered by Skocpol and Sewell on the spectrum from cultural idioms to formally articulated ideologies, and through the organizations and networks of social actors who make revolutions happen (or not).[60] The dotted lines indicate the more indirect linkages between subjectivity and ideology on the one hand, and cultural idioms and social forces on the other. Everything passes through our notion of political cultures of opposition and resistance at some point in the chain, and complex two-way relations are not ruled out.

Political culture, then, spans and links culture with discourse and ideology, and puts us on the path to understanding agency as carried by social forces. It is not the same as any of these, but stands in a relationship with each of them. Much work remains to be done on the precise mechanisms at work here. Finally, culture must be rigorously linked to social structure and imaginatively synthesized with political economy and international contexts. For students of revolution and culture, *this* is the agenda for the 1990s and beyond.

ACKNOWLEDGEMENTS

I would like to thank Craig Calhoun, Lynn Hunt, and Farideh Farhi for helpful comments on this chapter, as well as the students who have read and discussed it in my graduate seminars, and the participants in the Asimov group at UCSB (Richard Appelbaum, Kate Bruhn, Fernando Lopez-Alves, and Chris McAuley).

NOTES

1. See Raymond Williams, *Culture and Society, 1780–1950* (New York: Columbia University Press, 1960), *Culture* (Cambridge: Fontana, 1981), and *Politics and Letters: Interviews with New Left Review* (London: Verso, 1979). See the discussion by Ellen Kay Trimberger, "E. P. Thompson: Understanding the Process of History," pp. 211–43 in Theda Skocpol, editor, *Vision and Method in Historical Sociology* (Cambridge: Cambridge University Press, 1984), 221–4.
2. E. P. Thompson, *The Making of the English Working Class* (New York: Vintage Books, 1966 [1963]), 9–11.
3. The works of Stuart Hall are numerous and influential. Among many others one might name (with John Clarke, Tony Jefferson, and Brian Roberts) "Subcultures, Cultures and Class: A Theoretical Overview," pp. 9–74 in *Working Papers in Cultural Studies*, numbers 7/8 (Summer 1975), (with B. Lumley and G. McLennan), "Politics and Ideology: Gramsci," pp. 45–76 in Stuart Hall, Bob Lumley, and Gregor McLennan, editors, *On Ideology* (London: Hutchinson, 1978), "Marxism and Culture," pp. 5–14 in *Radical History Review*, number 18 (1978), "Cultural Studies: Two Paradigms," in *Media, Culture and Society*, number 2 (1980), "Signification, Representation, Ideology: Althusser and the Post-Structuralist Debates," pp. 91–114 in *Critical Studies in Mass Communication*, volume 2, number 2 (1985), "The Problem of Ideology: Marxism Without Guarantees," pp. 28–44 in *Journal of Communication Inquiry*, volume 10, number 2 (1986), "Clinging to the Wreckage: A Conversation with Frederick Jameson," pp. 28–31 in *Marxism Today* (September 1990), and "Cultural Studies and Its Theoretical Legacies," pp. 277–94 in Lawrence Grossberg, Cary Nelson, and Paula A. Treichler, editors, *Cultural Studies* (London: Routledge, 1992). For a scathing critique that illustrates the uneasy reception of cultural studies in the United States and the political and ideological battle lines in the stakes drawn so far, see the review of the latter volume by Steven Jay Sherwood, Philip Smith, Jeffrey C. Alexander, "The British Are Coming . . . Again! The Hidden Agenda of "Cultural Studies'," pp. 370–5 in *Contemporary Sociology*, volume 22, number 3 (May 1993).
4. James C. Scott, *Domination and the Arts of Resistance: Hidden Transcripts* (New Haven: Yale University Press, 1990).
5. For a few key works, see Edward Said, *Culture and Imperialism* (New York: Vintage, 1993); Fredric Jameson, "Third World Literature in the Age of Multinational Capital," pp. 65–88 in *Social Text* (Fall 1986); Aijaz Ahmad, *In Theory: Classes, Nations, Literatures* (London: Verso, 1992); Ranajit Guha and Gayatri Chakravorty Spivak, editors, *Selected Subaltern Studies* (New York: Oxford University Press, 1988); John Beverley and Jose Oviedo, editors, special issue of *Boundary 2, The Postmodernism Debate in Latin America*, volume 20, number 3 (Fall 1993); and the debates over post-colonial studies represented by, for example, Anne

McClintock, "The Angel of Progress: Pitfalls of the Term Post-Colonialism," pp. 84–98 in *Social Text*, number 31/32 (Summer 1992), and Ella Shohat, "Notes on the Post-Colonial," pp. 99–113 in ibid. It is far beyond the scope of this chapter to do more than gesture toward this vast literature, citing it where appropriate. Interested readers may request a copy of my syllabus on "Third World Cultural Studies" (Department of Sociology, University of California, Fall 1994). I am indebted to the students in this class for clarifying observations on many of the issues.

6. The works of Foucault are well known. Three among the many subsequent studies that are of relevance to the topics explored in this chapter include Edward Said, *Orientalism* (New York: Vintage, 1978); Benedict Anderson, *Imagined Communities: Reflections on the Origin and Spread of Nationalism* (London: Verso, 1983) and Ana Maria Alonso, "The Effects of Truth: Re-Presentation of the Past and the Imagining of Community," pp. 32–57 in *Journal of Historical Sociology*, volume 1, number 1 (March 1988).

7. See Ann Swidler, "Culture in Action: Symbols and Strategies," pp. 273–86 in *American Sociological Review*, volume 51 (April 1986), and "Strategic Actors and Cultural Commitments: Variations in Culture's Transcendence," paper prepared for conference on "Ideology: The Turn to Practice," University of Tulsa (April 20–21, 1990) and presented also at the University of California, Santa Barbara in 1993. Among many other scholars in the US setting one may mention Wendy Griswold, *Cultures and Societies in a Changing World* (Thousand Oaks, London, New Delhi: Pine Forge Press, 1994) and Michele Lamont, *Money, Morals, and Manners: The Culture of the French and American Upper-Middle Classes* (Chicago: Chicago University Press, 1992). Clifford Geertz's classic work is *The Interpretation of Culture* (New York: Basic Books, 1973).

8. Alexis de Tocqueville, *The Old Regime and the French Revolution*, translated by Stuart Gilbert (Garden City, NY: Doubleday, 1955 [1856]).

9. On the Natural History school and 1950s–1960s approaches to revolution, see Jack A. Goldstone, "Theories of Revolution: The Third Generation," pp. 425–53 in *World Politics*, volume XXXII, number 3 (April 1980). For a neo-modernizationist view of the issues, see S. N. Eisenstadt, "Frameworks of the Great Revolutions: Culture, Social Structure, History and Human Agency," pp. 385–401 in *International Social Science Journal*, number 133 (August 1992).

10. Theda Skocpol, *States and Social Revolutions: A Comparative Analysis of France, Russia, and China* (Cambridge: Cambridge University Press, 1979).

11. Theda Skocpol, "Rentier State and Shi'a Islam in the Iranian Revolution," (including comments by Nikki Keddie, Eqbal Ahmad and Walter Goldfrank), pp. 265–303 in *Theory and Society*, volume 11, number 3 (May 1982), 265, 267.

12. William H. Sewell, Jr., "Ideologies and Social Revolutions: Reflections on the French Case," pp. 57–85 in *Journal of Modern History*, volume 57, number 1 (March 1985). Interestingly, I might add, state, class, and international structures may be similarly viewed as human constructions, in Anthony Giddens's dual sense of constraining and enabling action. This is another promising direction for a new sociology of revolution, not pursued in the present chapter (although I shall touch on it in passing on El Salvador). This paragraph, and the next two, are based closely on a passage in my essay, "Theories of Revolution Revisited: Toward a Fourth Generation?" pp. 1–20 in *Sociological Theory*, volume 11, number 1 (March 1993).

13. Theda Skocpol, "Cultural Idioms and Political Ideologies in the Revolutionary Reconstruction of State Power: A Rejoinder to Sewell," pp. 86–96 in *Journal of Modern History*, volume 57, number 1 (March 1985), 96.

14. Farideh Farhi, "State Disintegration and Urban-Based Revolutionary Crises: A Comparative Analysis of Iran and Nicaragua," pp. 231–56 in *Comparative Political Studies*, volume 21, number 2 (July 1988), 249. See also her *States and Urban-Based Revolutions: Iran and Nicaragua* (Urbana and Chicago: University of Illinois Press, 1990).

15. Farhi, *States and Urban-Based Revolutions*, 84.

16. S. H. Welch, *Communities of Resistance and Solidarity: A Feminist Theology of Liberation* (New York: Orbis, 1985). Cf. also Charles Tilly's suggestive references to "cultural repertoires" of revolution in his *From Mobilization to Revolution* (Reading, MA: Addison-Wesley, 1978), 151–9, 224–5.

17. Jack A. Goldstone, *Revolution and Rebellion in the Early Modern World* (Berkeley, Los Angeles and Oxford: University of California Press, 1991).

18. Eric Selbin, *Modern Latin American Revolutions* (Boulder: Westview Press, 1993). Selbin makes further contributions to how we might integrate culture into the causes of revolution in his Chapter 5 in this volume, especially with the notions of collective memory and symbolic politics.

19. Forrest Colburn, *The Vogue of Revolution in Poor Countries* (Princeton: Princeton University Press, 1994).

20. I have used these concepts in previous work on Iran and the origins of Third World social revolutions: John Foran, *Fragile Resistance: Social Transformation in Iran from 1500 to the Revolution* (Boulder: Westview Press, 1993) and "A Theory of Third World Social Revolutions: Iran, Nicaragua, and El Salvador Compared," pp. 3–27 in *Critical Sociology*, volume 19, number 2 (1992).

21. This concept owes much to an idea I originally encountered in the work of A. Sivanandan, "Imperialism in the Silicon Age," pp. 24–42 in *Monthly Review*, volume 32, number 3 (July–August 1980) (this was first published in *Race and Class* (Autumn 1979). Upon recently rereading this work, I noticed that I had extrapolated quite a bit from some hints in its conclusion! On the lineage of the term "political culture," see Samih K. Farsoun and Mehrdad Mashayekhi, editors, *Iran: Political Culture in the Islamic Republic* (London: Routledge, 1992). Keith Michael Baker gives us another useful definition of political culture as "constituted within a field of discourse, and of political language as elaborated in the course of political action': "On the Problem of the Ideological Origins of the French Revolution," pp. 197–219 in Dominick LaCapra and Steven L. Kaplan, editors, *Modern European Intellectual History: Reappraisals and New Perspectives* (Ithaca: Cornell University Press, 1982), 212.

22. On this point see also my debate with another student of the Iranian Revolution, Mansoor Moaddel: John Foran, "The Iranian Revolution and the Study of Discourses: A Comment on Moaddel," pp. 51–63 in *Critique: Journal of Critical Studies of Iran & the Middle East*, number 4 (Spring 1994), and Mansoor Moaddel, "The Significance of Discourse in the Iranian Revolution: A Reply to Foran," pp. 65–72 in ibid.

23. A start has been made in this direction by Mansoor Moaddel, "State Autonomy and Class Conflict in the Reformation," pp. 472–4 in *American Sociological Review*, volume 54, number 3, (June 1989), and Robert Wuthnow, "State Structures and Class Conflict in the Reformation (A Reply to Moaddel)," pp. 474–6 in ibid. The original article is Robert Wuthnow, "State Structures and Ideological Outcomes," pp. 799–821 in *American Sociological Review*, volume 50 (1985). Wuthnow's major statement is *Communities of Discourse: Ideology and Social Structure in the Reformation, the Enlightenment, and European Socialism* (Cambridge, MA: Harvard University Press, 1989). For two other recent statements on this problem, see Lyn Spillman, "Culture, Social Structures, and Discursive Fields," pp. 129–54 in

Current Perspectives in Social Theory, volume 15 (1995), and Mustafa Emirbayer and Jeff Goodwin, "Network Analysis, Culture, and the Problem of Agency," pp. 1411–54 in *American Journal of Sociology*, volume 99, number 6 (May 1994). The work of Tim Wickham-Crowley, while clearly structuralist in thrust (see his Chapter 2 in the present volume), likewise makes a place for culture in the analysis of revolution. His aphorism, "while ideology proposes, the peasantry's condition disposes," goes part of the way I feel is required in this direction: culture does not "float free" of social conditions, yet both should be treated as equally important, at least until our theoretical understanding gets closer to the bottom of the matter (which, of course, it will never reach).

24. I have attempted to bring race, class, and gender into the study of revolutions (but without the next step of considering political culture) in two essays: "Race, Class, and Gender in the Making of the Mexican Revolution," in *Revue internationale de sociologie* (1996), and John Foran, Linda Klouzal, and Jean Pierre Rivera, "Who Makes Revolutions? Class, Gender, and Race in the Mexican, Cuban, and Nicaraguan Revolutions," in *Research in Social Movements, Conflicts and Change* (1997).

25. Roger Chartier, *The Cultural Origins of the French Revolution*, translated by Lydia G. Cochrane (Durham and London: Duke University Press, 1991).

26. Daniel Mornet, *Les Origines intellectuelles de la Révolution française 1715–1787* (Paris: Armand Colin, 1933, 1967). Before him, Tocqueville had analyzed the role of the intellectuals in a chapter titled "How towards the middle of the eighteenth century men of letters took the lead in politics and the consequences of this new development": *The Old Regime*, book three, chapter one.

27. Chartier, *Cultural Origins*, 37, 44, 90, 109–10, 122–3, 143–4, 148–9.

28. Ibid., 69–73.

29. This conclusion is supported by the works of the growing list of scholars who have been revising accepted wisdom about the French Revolution in recent years, as well as the Skocpol–Sewell debate discussed already: see, *inter alia*, Edward Berenson, "The Social Interpretation of the French Revolution," pp. 55–81 in *Contention: Debates in Society, Culture, and Science*, volume 3, number 2 (Winter 1994); François Furet, *Interpreting the French Revolution* (Cambridge: Cambridge University Press, 1981); Keith Michael Baker, editor, *The French Revolution and the Creation of Modern Political Culture*, volume one: *The Political Culture of the Old Regime* (Oxford: Pergamon Press, 1987); idem, *Inventing the French Revolution: Essays on French Political Culture in the Eighteenth Century* (Cambridge: Cambridge University Press, 1990); Colin Lucas, editor, *The French Revolution and the Creation of Modern Political Culture*, volume two: *The Political Culture of the French Revolution* (Oxford: Pergamon Press, 1988); William H. Sewell, Jr., *Work and Revolution in France: The Language of Labor from the Old Regime to 1848* (Cambridge: Cambridge University Press, 1980); Simon Schama, *Citizens* (New York: Knopf, 1989); and Lynn Hunt, *The Family Romance of the French Revolution* (Berkeley: University of California Press, 1992). The important task of untangling the many issues they raise about how best to rethink culture goes beyond my knowledge of this vast literature.

30. For a more detailed discussion, see Foran, *Fragile Resistance*, and the sources cited therein.

31. On the Liberation Movement, see H. E. Chehabi, *Iranian Politics and Religious Modernism: The Liberation Movement of Iran under the Shah and Khomeini* (Ithaca: Cornell University Press, 1990); on the National Front, Sussan Siavoshi, *Liberal Nationalism in Iran: The Failure of a Movement* (Boulder: Westview Press, 1990); on the Mujahidin, Ervand Abrahamian, *The Iranian Mojehedin* (New Haven: Yale University Press, 1989); on Shari'ati, Brad Hanson, "The 'Westoxication' of

Iran: Depictions and Reactions of Behrangi, Al-e Ahmad, and Shari'ati," pp. 1–23 in *International Journal of Middle East Studies*, volume 15, number 1 (February 1983); on Khomeini, *Islam and Revolution: Writings and Declarations of the Imam Khomeini*, translated and annotated by Hamid Algar (Berkeley: Mizan, 1981), and Ervand Abrahamian, *Khomeinism: Essays on the Islamic Republic* (Berkeley: University of California Press, 1993); the Fada'ian still await their historian in English. An important discussion of the content of the writings of many of these figures is found in Hamid Dabashi, *Theology of Discontent: The Ideological Formation of the Islamic Revolution in Iran* (New York: New York University Press, 1993).

32. Val Moghadam, "Populist Revolution and the Islamic States in Iran," pp. 147–63 in Terry Boswell, editor, *Revolution in the World-System* (Westport: Greenwood Press, 1989).

33. Again see the discussion in Foran, *Fragile Resistance*.

34. On Iran's student movement, as well as cultural issues in the making of the revolution generally, important work is being done by Afshin Matin-asgari in "Revolutionary Political Culture as a 'Cause' of the 1978–79 Iranian Revolution," paper presented at the meetings of the Middle East Studies Association, Research Triangle Park, North Carolina (November 1993).

35. I take up these questions in a preliminary way in "The Dialectic of Discourses and Social Forces: Re-Mapping the Iranian Revolution of 1977–79," presented to the Islamic and Near Eastern Studies group at the University of California, Santa Barbara (Spring 1995). A good discussion of the data available for further research is found in Charles Kurzman, "Historiography of the Iranian Revolutionary Movement, 1977–79," pp. 25–38 in *Iranian Studies*, volume 28, numbers 1–2 (Winter 1995).

36. A good lead here is Gene Burns, "Ideology, Culture, and Ambiguity: The Revolutionary Process in Iran," in *Theory and Society*, volume 25, number 3 (June 1996).

37. This question of the ideal of socialism is expressed in a graffito exchange on a Bucharest wall in February 1990. Someone had written "Down with Communism." Under which was written, in another hand: "What is this phenomenon? We have never experienced it!", quoted in Alex Callinicos, *The Revenge of History: Marxism and the East European Revolutions* (University Park: Pennsylvania State University Press, 1991), 95. Humor was a potent form of underground resistance to the limits on personal freedoms.

38. Timothy Garton Ash, "Eastern Europe: The Year of Truth," pp. 17–22 in *The New York Review of Books* (February 15, 1990), 19.

39. Among the many new works on Eastern Europe, see Timothy Garton Ash, *The Magic Lantern: The Revolution of '89 Witnessed in Warsaw, Budapest, Berlin, and Prague* (New York: Random House, 1990); for a detailed account of events, and for a more analytic one, Jeff Goodwin, "Old Regimes and Revolutions in the Second and Third Worlds: A Comparative Perspective," pp. 575–604 in *Social Science History*, volume 18, number 4 (Winter 1994).

40. Ash, "Eastern Europe," 19.

41. I discuss this briefly in "The Causes of Latin American Social Revolutions: Searching for Patterns in Mexico, Cuba, and Nicaragua," pp. 209–44 in Peter Lengyel and Volker Bornschier, editors, *World Society Studies*, volume three: *Conflicts and New Departures in World Society* (New Brunswick: Transaction, 1994). Arguments about Castro's pre-1959 ideology can be found in Timothy P. Wickham-Crowley, *Guerrillas and Revolution in Latin America: A Comparative Study of Insurgencies and Regimes since 1956* (Princeton: Princeton University Press, 1992).

See also Sheldon Liss, *Fidel! Castro's Political and Social Thought* (Boulder: Westview Press, 1994), for a comprehensive look at the matter.

42. On Castro's views and the July 26 Movement's positions, see Terence Cannon, *Revolutionary Cuba* (New York: Thomas Y. Crowell, 1981), 54–57, 97; United States National Archives, 737.00/8-458, Foreign Service Despatch 5, Park Wollam, Santiago de Cuba, to State Department (August 4, 1958), 11; "Ideario Económico del Veinte y Seis de Julio," found in USNA, 837.00/3-959, Foreign Service Despatch 982, Gilmore, Havana, to State Department (March 9, 1959); and Wickham-Crowley, *Guerrillas and Revolution*, 176–8.

43. Interestingly the *reception* of Castro's message in the United States echoes the Cuban side of the story, both in its diversity and diffuseness, but also in the transparency of its reading by radicals. See the extraordinary revisionist account of these matters by Van Gosse, *Where the Boys Are: Cuba, Cold War America and the Making of a New Left* (London: Verso, 1993).

44. Colburn, *The Vogue of Revolution*, 28.

45. To be fair, Colburn notes that "From an administrative perspective, Marxism-Leninism is more a *mentalité* than a coherent and all-encompassing plan of government": ibid., 59. The thrust of his argument, however, seems to be that this ideal has had a monolithic, determinant, and negative impact on all post-revolutionary Third World societies. We agree, then, on the impact of ideology and political culture; we disagree on the meanings that inform them and the mechanisms that make them work. For further discussion of the importance of Cuban political culture in maintaining the revolutionary project into the 1990s, see my essay, "The Future of Revolutions in a Globalizing World," Working Paper No. 26, Advanced Study Center 1995–96, International Institute, University of Michigan (March 1996).

46. This objection has been put to me personally by Wally Goldfrank. It is also implied to some degree by Jack Goldstone in an early overview of theories of revolution, wherein he debunks the commonsense view that radical ideas can by themselves cause revolutions, since such radical ideologies as democracy (and by extension, socialism) existed for generations before revolutions based on them were made: Jack A. Goldstone, "The Comparative and Historical Study of Revolutions," pp. 187–207 in *Annual Review of Sociology*, volume 8 (1982), 188. It is further implied by all models of revolution that leave culture out as a causal variable, including Skocpol's and Wickham-Crowley's. The latter provides intriguing discussions of historical memories of struggle, but doesn't elevate culture to direct causal significance in his formal analysis in *Guerrillas and Revolution*.

47. For discussion of both periods in Salvadoran history, see Sheldon B. Liss, *Radical Thought in Central America* (Boulder: Westview Press, 1991); Tommie Sue Montgomery, *Revolution in El Salvador: From Civil Strife to Civil Peace*, second edition (Boulder: Westview Press, 1994); James Dunkerley, *Power in the Isthmus: A Political History of Modern Central America* (London: Verso, 1988); and Robert Armstrong and Janet Shenk, *El Salvador: The Face of Revolution* (Boston: South End Press, 1982).

48. Julia Denise Shayne, "Salvadorean Women Revolutionaries and the Birth of Their Women's Movement," MA thesis, Department of Women's Studies, San Francisco State University (April 1995).

49. I develop these arguments in "A Theory of Third World Social Revolutions."

50. In "The Future of Revolutions," I show similar cultural sources of failure in the cases of the militant Islamist movements in Egypt and Algeria, the Sendero Luminso in Peru, and Iraq in 1991.

51. John Foran and Jeff Goodwin, "Revolutionary Outcomes in Iran and Nicaragua. Coalition Fragmentation, War, and the Limits of Social Transformation," pp. 209–247 in *Theory and Society*, volume 22, number 2 (April 1993).
52. The following analysis is based on many sources, in addition to the one just cited. Overviews of the 1980s can be found in Carlos M. Vilas, *The Sandinista Revolution: National Liberation and Social Transformation in Central America*, translated by Judy Butler (New York: Monthly Review Press, 1986); and Laura J. Enríquez, *Social Transformation in Latin America: Tensions Between Agroexport Production and Agrarian Reform in Contemporary Nicaragua* (Chapel Hill: University of North Carolina Press, 1991).
53. On peasants, see Jeffrey Gould, "Notes on Peasant Consciousness and Revolutionary Politics in Nicaragua, 1955–1990," pp. 65–87 in *Radical History Review*, number 48 (1990).
54. The myriad contradictions of Sandinista policy for women's lives are chronicled by Margaret Randall, *Gathering Rage: The Failure of Twentieth Century Revolutions to Develop a Feminist Agenda* (New York: Monthly Review Press, 1993). See also Maxine Molyneux, "Mobilization Without Emancipation? Women's Interests, the State, and Revolution in Nicaragua," pp. 227–54 in *Feminist Studies*, volume 11, number 2 (1985).
55. On the church, see John M. Kirk, *Politics and the Catholic Church in Nicaragua* (Gainesville: University Press of Florida, 1992); and Michael Dodson and Laura Nuzzi O'Shaugnessy, *Nicaragua's Other Revolution: Religious Faith and Political Struggle* (Chapel Hill: University of North Carolina Press, 1990).
56. Among many other works, see Charles R. Hale, *Resistance and Contradiction: Miskitu Indians and the Nicaraguan State, 1894–1987* (Stanford: Stanford University Press, 1994); and Carlos M. Vilas, *State, Class, and Ethnicity in Nicaragua: Capitalist Modernization and Revolutionary Change on the Atlantic Coast*, translated by Susan Norwood (Boulder and London: Lynne Rienner, 1989).
57. On the 1990 elections, see Vanessa Castro and Gary Prevost, editors, *The 1990 Elections in Nicaragua and Their Aftermath* (Lanham, MD: Rowman & Littlefield, 1992), especially the essay by Bill Barnes; as well as Michael E. Conroy, "The Political Economy of the 1990 Nicaraguan Elections," in *International Journal of Political Economy*, volume 20, number 3 (Fall 1990).
58. Splits and disagreements among the factions composing the FSLN in the course of 1993 and 1994 do not bode well for this prospect. After this chapter was written, the FSLN in fact lost the elections of 1996. On the lasting shifts in the popular imaginary of revolution, however, see Jean Pierre Rivera, "Agency and Political Consciousness in the Nicaraguan Revolution," MA thesis, Department of Sociology, University of California, Santa Barbara (1993).
59. Thompson, *The Making of the English Working Class*; see also Mustafa Emirbayer and Jeff Goodwin, "Symbols, Positions, Objects: Toward a New Theory of Revolution and Collective Action," Working Paper No. 223, New School for Social Research (1995).
60. The emphasis on organizations is an important part of resource mobilization theory (e.g. Tilly's *From Mobilization to Revolution*); it is also addressed by Emirbayer and Goodwin in "Network Analysis, Culture, and the Problem of Agency."

9

THE COMPARATIVE-HISTORICAL SOCIOLOGY OF THIRD WORLD SOCIAL REVOLUTIONS

Why a few succeed, why most fail

John Foran

The twentieth century, as much as any before it, has been an age of revolutions. The locus of these revolutions, until the startling events in Eastern Europe in 1989, has been firmly rooted in the Third World, on the continents of Latin America, Asia, and Africa. The record of these revolutions is highly mixed: almost all have started as popular movements which generated wide hope and optimism both internally and internationally, yet have ended at some later point in time, in economic crisis, political repression, or social failure. This chapter is one not of ends, however, but of origins. It seeks to extend previous work on the causes of successful social revolutions to a consideration of why so few revolutions have earned the label "social" revolutions, while so many have fallen short of the sorts of deep economic, political, and social change that could justify this claim.[1]

This chapter will survey the causes of a variety of Third World revolutions, from cases of successful outcomes (measured in terms of taking and holding state power long enough to engage in a project of social transformation), such as in Mexico 1910–20, China 1911–49,[2] Cuba 1953–59, Iran 1977–79, and Nicaragua 1977–79; to their close relations among anti-colonial social revolutions, as in Algeria 1954–62, Vietnam 1945–75, and Angola, Mozambique, and Zimbabwe in the 1970s; to cases that have resulted in short-lived success, such as Guatemala under Arevalo and Arbenz from 1944 to 1954, Allende's Chile between 1970 and 1973, Jamaica under Michael Manley in the 1970s, and Grenada 1979–83; to attempted revolution in El Salvador, Guatemala, and Peru from the late 1970s to the early 1990s; to political revolutions in 1911 China, Bolivia in the 1950s, and Haiti and the Philippines in the 1980s; to the absence of revolutionary attempts in societies undergoing otherwise rapid transformation, such as post-World War II South Korea, Taiwan, Mexico (before 1994!), Turkey, Egypt, Brazil, Argentina, Zaire, and elsewhere. The aim is to discern distinctive analytic patterns for these diverse outcomes, using Boolean analysis, as

227

codified by Charles Ragin and illustrated for the comparative study of revolution by Timothy Wickham-Crowley.[3] This method is based on the careful construction of a truth table that allows the researcher to sort out significant patterns of combinations of causes leading to both success and failure. The relevant factors to be tested derive from a theoretical model of the origins of Third World social revolutions that I have been elaborating for the cases of Mexico, Cuba, Iran, and Nicaragua, to which we may now turn.

THEORIES OF THIRD WORLD SOCIAL REVOLUTIONS

The study of social revolutions, and Third World revolutions, has taken a great leap forward since the 1979 publication of Theda Skocpol's *States and Social Revolutions*, a structuralist *tour de force* that showed how international pressures could combine with state and class arrangements to produce political crises. Walter Goldfrank, John Walton, Jeff Goodwin and Theda Skocpol, Farideh Farhi, Timothy Wickham-Crowley, and Jack Goldstone and his collaborators, among others, have produced important studies of sets of particular Third World cases.[4] These perspectives have all advocated multi-causal approaches to revolutions. The question today has become: What particular mix of causes is most useful as an explanation across (which) cases? All of the above theorists have stressed structural approaches to revolution, often at the expense of agency and culture (Farhi has done the most with culture in this group). Many – Goodwin, Skocpol, and Wickham-Crowley – have placed great emphasis on the particular kind of state that is most vulnerable to revolution, often at the cost of paying less attention to social structure and the economy. And gradually, a consensus has emerged that both external and internal factors are at work, but in what way and to what degree is not yet settled.

My own work draws on many of the specific insights of this latest generation of scholars, but with its own particular synthesis that insists on balancing attention to such perennial (and all too often reified) dichotomies as structure and agency, political economy and culture, state and social structure, internal and external factors. Elsewhere I have argued that five interrelated causal factors must combine in a given conjuncture to produce a successful social revolution: (1) dependent development; (2) a repressive, exclusionary, personalist state; (3) the elaboration of effective and powerful political cultures of resistance; and a revolutionary crisis consisting of (4) an economic downturn; and (5) a world-systemic opening (a let-up of external controls).[5] Let us briefly examine each of these factors in turn.

Dependent development, taken from the work of Latin American scholars Fernando Henrique Cardoso and Enzo Faletto, is a process that may be characterized as one of "growth within limits": it refers to certain Third World economies, at certain moments in their history, that undergo both development – as measured by increases in GNP, foreign trade, industrial or agricultural output – combined with the negative consequences of the attendant social transformation in the form of inflation, debt, growing inequality, or overburdened housing and educational infrastructures, among others.[6] This complex process defines a changing social structure that creates social and economic grievances among diverse sectors of the population, ranging from the urban working, middle, and underclasses, to rural peasants, farmers, and workers, crossing gender and ethnic lines as well.

The repressive, exclusionary, personalist state which so often (but not always) accompanies dependent development reposes on the combination of repression of lower-class forces and exclusion of both the growing middle classes and the economic elite from political participation. Such states possess an elective affinity for dependent development because they are good at guaranteeing order, at least for a time, but they also tend to exacerbate conflictual relations between state and civil society.[7] Dictators, particularly of the dynastic variety (either by monarchic succession or imposition of new generations) or of long-lived duration (whether through patently fraudulent elections or other means), epitomize this personalist type of rule. They fuel the grievances generated by dependent development, often alienating the upper classes from the state, and provide a solid target for social movements from below. Because of this, under certain circumstances, they facilitate the formation of a broad, multi-class alliance against the state, because middle and even upper classes may join with lower classes, feeling less threat of being overturned along with the state. Conversely, *collective* military rule, or rule by the military as an institution, especially when given a veneer of legitimation through regular elections, however fraudulent, tends to elicit more elite support and provide a less vulnerable target for cross-class social movements.

this is the case of Guatemala

For this to occur, an opposition must coalesce. To capture the ideological dimension of this intervention of human agents onto the historical stage, I have developed the notion of "political cultures of opposition and resistance" in my previous work and in Chapter 8 of this volume.[8] To move from the structural determinants of the grievances produced by dependent development and the repressive, exclusionary, personalist state, broad segments of many groups and classes must be able to articulate the experiences they are living through into effective and flexible analyses capable of mobilizing their own forces and building coalitions with others. Such political cultures of opposition may draw upon diverse sources: formal ideologies, folk traditions, and popular idioms, ranging from ideas and feelings of nationalism (against control by outsiders), socialism (equality and social justice), democracy (demands for participation and an end to dictatorship), religion (resistance to evil and suffering), and the like. Different groups, classes, and actors will embrace complex combinations of these, sometimes weaving them into critiques of the regime with great mobilizational potential. How

229

well these multiple political cultures are capable of bringing together diverse sectors into a broad and unified opposition, I shall argue, may spell the difference between success and failure. In any case, this factor insists on the irreducible role played by human agency and meaning in the making (or not) of revolutions.

The final element in the model is the emergence of a revolutionary crisis that both weakens the state and emboldens the opposition. This has two determinants, one partly internal and the other external. Students of revolution from Alexis de Tocqueville to James Davies have insisted that economic downturns on the eve of revolutions sharpen existing grievances past the breaking point.[9] Recent scholars have disputed this point, both for their general models and in particular cases.[10] I shall argue that it is present in virtually all successful cases. When this factor is combined with a "world-systemic opening" for change, a powerful conjuncture arises for revolutionary movements to succeed (this leaves open the question of the precise *timing* of such crises, which may precede or follow revolutionary mobilization, but do seem to precede the taking of power). Such an opening refers to the letting up of external controls by the dominant outside power; it may be the result of distraction in the core economies by world war or depression, rivalries between one or more core powers, mixed messages sent to Third World dictators, or divided foreign policy when faced with an insurrection.[11]

The combination of all five of these factors makes for a favorable climate in which social revolutions may thrive. My previous work has found these factors in the cases of the Mexican, Cuban, Nicaraguan, and Iranian Revolutions. The present research attempts to extend the model to the anti-colonial cases and instances of shorter-lived social revolutions (looking for broad similarities), and to contrast these with the several types of failure (failed attempts, political revolutions, and no attempt), looking for significant patterns among these types.

RESULTS

Table 9.1 presents an overview of the data on the thirty-plus cases I have mentioned, evaluating each in terms of the presence or absence of each of the causal factors in the model for the origins of successful Third World social revolutions. It should be pointed out that this is a preliminary analysis of many of these cases, and is subject to further modification based on deeper study of individual cases.

We shall discuss each of the major types in turn, moving through the set of contrasting cases until we arrive at instances where no revolution was attempted (despite the presence of one or more of the factors facilitating revolution).

Type One: successful Third World social revolutions

I have done fairly extensive analysis of the cases of Mexico, Cuba, Iran, and Nicaragua elsewhere.[12] Each of these social revolutions presents all of the factors suggested by the model, as Table 9.2 suggests.

In Mexico, the period of rule by dictator Porfirio Díaz from 1876 to 1910 marked a surge of development led by US investments in railways, commercial agriculture, and oil that severely disrupted both rural and urban society. Díaz himself kept a firm grip on power through fraudulent elections, co-optation of elite competitors, and repression of lower-class groups when necessary. Nascent political cultures of opposition developed after the turn of the twentieth century, based on amalgams of nationalistic resistance to foreign encroachment, democratic demands for political inclusion, economic and social justice in the countryside (agrarismo), and the like. After a business recession in 1907–8, aggrieved groups came together into a broad alliance behind the presidential candidacy of Francisco Madero, while the USA stood idly by as Díaz fell in the Spring of 1911. This was just the opening blow in a long-drawn-out struggle that went on for nine more years in a devastating and complicated civil war, but it marked the first victory of the revolution.[13]

Cuba also fits the pattern for success in all major respects, with one interesting variation. It was among the most developed Latin American nations by the 1950s at the same time as it was a society marked by enormous disparities of wealth and power.[14] After seizing power by force in 1952, Fulgencio Batista ruled the island with an iron fist, the classic "mafiacracy" for Wickham-Crowley. Fidel Castro's July 26 Movement took up a broadly popular guerrilla struggle after 1957, mobilizing diverse social sectors with a syncretic ideology of national sovereignty, popular participation, and social justice, appropriately toned down for foreign and elite consumption. The USA, so tightly tied to Cuban governments since winning the Cuban–Spanish-American War in 1898, fell out with its erstwhile client, Batista, when he used American-supplied weapons to subdue a naval mutiny at Cienfuegos in September 1957, in contravention of agreements stipulating that the weapons were only for defending the hemisphere against communism. The most interesting twist (and the one variation on the model) in the Cuban case is that the economy fluctuated up and down in the 1950s, actually improving in 1956–57 until the rebels *made their own* economic downturn by disrupting the sugar harvest in the latter part of 1958. With this factor – the result of human agency – in place, Batista's regime fell to the revolutionaries by New Year's day, 1959.[15]

Nicaragua and Iran experienced revolutions in the same year, 1978–79, thereby highlighting the world-systemic opening provided to both by the impact of Jimmy Carter's human rights-oriented foreign policy on dictatorship and opposition alike. Iran under the Shah was a textbook case of

231

Table 9.1 Causes of Third World revolutions: a Boolean truth table (0 = trait absent; 1 = trait present)

| Cases | Favourable conditions | | | | | Outcome |
	(A) Dependent development	(B) Repressive, exclusionary, personalist state	(C) Political cultures of opposition	(D) Economic downturn	(E) World-systemic opening	
	Type One: successful social revolutions					
1. Mexico, 1910–20	1	1	1	1	1	1-SR
2. Cuba, 1953–59	1	1	1	1	1	1-SR
3. Iran, 1977–79	1	1	1	1	1	1-SR
4. Nicaragua, 1977–79	1	1	1	1	1	1-SR
5. China, 1949	1	1	1	1	1	1-SR/1-AC
	Type Two: anti-colonial (social) revolutions					
6. Algeria, 1954–62	1	1	1	1	1	1-AC/0-SR
7. Vietnam, 1945–75	1	1	1	1	1	1-AC/1-SR
8. Angola, 1970s	1	1	1	1	1	1-AC/1-SR
9. Mozambique, 1970s	1	1	1	1	1	1-AC/1-SR
10. Zimbabwe, 1970s	1	1	1	1	1	1-AC/1-SR
	Type Three: reversed social revolutions					
11. Guatemala, 1944–54	1/1	1/0	1/1–	1/1	1/0	1/0-SR
12. Chile, 1970–73	1/1	0/0	1/1–	1/1	1/0	1/0-SR
13. Grenada, 1979–83	1/1	1/0	1/1–	1/1	1/0	1/0-SR
14. Jamaica, 1972–80	1/1	0/0	1/1–	1/1	1/0	1/0-SR

Type Four: attempted social revolutions

15. El Salvador, 1979–92	1	1–	1–	0	0-SR
16. Guatemala, 1960s	1–	1–	1–	0	0-SR
17. Peru, 1980s–90s	1–	0	1–	0	0-SR
18. Philippines, 1980s	1–	0	1–	0	0-SR

Type Five: political revolutions

19. China, 1911	1–	1–	1–	1–	1-PR/0-SR
20. Bolivia, 1952–	1–	1–	1–	1–	1-PR/0-SR
21. Philippines, 1986	1–	1	1	1–	1-PR/0-SR
22. Haiti, 1989	1–	1	1	1–	1-PR/0-SR

Type Six: no attempt at revolution

23. South Korea, 1970s–	1+	1–	0	0	0-SR
24. Taiwan, 1970s–	1+	1–	0	0	0-SR
25. Brazil, 1970s–	1–	1–	1–	0	0-SR
26. Argentina, 1970s		0	0	0	0-SR
27. Argentina, 1983–	1–	0	1	0	0-SR
28. Mexico, 1980s	1	1–	1/0	0	0-SR
29. Turkey, 1970s–	1	1/0	0	0	0-SR
30. Egypt, 1970s–	1–	1–	1–	0	0-SR
31. Zaire, 1970s–	0	0	1	1/0	0-SR

Table 9.2 Origins of successful Third World social revolutions

	Social structure	State	Political cultures	Conjunctural factors	Outcome
Mexico	Dependent development based on railroads, oil, commercial agriculture	Díaz's "Bread and Stick" dictatorship	Nationalism, *agrarismo*, liberalism	US inaction 1910–12 and WWI/Deep recession 1907–8	Broad-based coalition – Complex civil war
Cuba	US-led dependent development of sugar, tourism	Batista's dictatorship	Castro's blend of nationalism, democracy, social justice	US non-support 1958/ Rebel-made decline	Broad-based coalition – Guerrilla success
Nicaragua	Commercial agricultural boom, 1960–70s	Somoza's repression	Sandinista nationalism and social justice/ Liberation theology	Carter human rights policy/Post-earthquake crisis, 1972–78	Broad-based coalition – Guerrilla success
Iran	State-led dependent development based on oil	Repressive Shah	Nationalism, Islamic and secular radicalism	Carter human rights policy/End of oil boom, 1976–78	Broad-based coalition – Unarmed success
China	Beginnings of commercial agriculture and industrialization	Chiang Kai-shek/ KMT dictatorship	Widespread Communist Party legitimacy	Japanese invasion and Western neglect/ Post-WWII-hyperinflation	Broad-based coalition – Guerrilla success

dependent development: as oil incomes swelled, so did inflation, substandard housing, rural landlessness, and migration. Nicaragua's much smaller economy also experienced a decided boom based on commercial agriculture in the 1960s and 1970s. Likewise the Pahlavi and Somoza dynasties were prototypically repressive, exclusionary, and personalist. Political cultures in each case articulated broad and effective combinations of nationalism,[16] social justice, and religion to bring together multi-class alliances that swelled to include upper- and middle-class groups after each economy turned down on the eve of the revolution: Nicaragua's due to government corruption in the medium-run aftermath of the 1972 earthquake, Iran's with the end of the oil boom around 1976. When the crisis came, US foreign policy proved indecisive, and no compromise could be found to preserve US interests.[17]

China's revolution, as mentioned above, is a hybrid case, in so far as it most definitely resulted in a social revolution (by 1949), but also was occupied by the Japanese during World War II and is thus in some respects the first anti-colonial revolution of the century. It is also instructive to compare conditions in 1911 (case 19 in Table 9.1), when the Manchu dynasty was overthrown by a political revolution, with 1949, when the communists came to power in a successful social revolution (case 5 in the table). Turn-of-the-century China was perhaps a dubious case of dependent development, but by the 1930s and 1940s the still largely agrarian country had begun a process of industrialization that better qualifies for the term. Both the monarchy and Chiang Kai-shek's KMT (Kuomintang: Chinese Nationalist Party) which eventually replaced it in the 1920s can be characterized as repressive, exclusionary, and personalist. Political cultures of opposition were just starting to develop by 1911 (and were largely confined to middle-class urban circles), and communist thought did not exist; by 1949, Mao's army and party had won the battle for ideological hegemony with Chiang's KMT, especially in the countryside, having also wrested from them the mantle of nationalist defenders of the country during the world war. The first signs of economic and demographic exhaustion were already visible before 1911, but the post-1945 KMT economy exhibits signs of deeper collapse, beset with a crippling inflation (prices rose thirty-nine times in Shanghai between September 1945 and February 1947, another 58.6 times by July 1948, and a further 400 times by February 1949).[18] Finally, the world-system put pressure on the Manchus by the turn of the century; Japanese occupation continued this in the 1940s, with the communists benefiting most, and the United States was unwilling and unable to intervene in the subsequent civil war.

In significant ways, then, the Chinese situation by 1949 fits the model already proposed for the cases of Mexico, Cuba, Iran, and Nicaragua. In Boolean terms, it is the *presence* of all five factors – dependent development, the exclusionary state, widely embraced political cultures of resistance, an economic downturn, and a world-systemic opening – that accounts for the success of these five Third World social revolutions. This may be represented by the equation:

$$Success = ABCDE,$$

where the capital letters represent the presence of each factor, and this single pattern is found in all the successful cases.

Type Two: anti-colonial (social) revolutions

The anti-colonial revolutions which swept the Third World after World War II bear striking resemblances to the successful social revolutions just analyzed. The fact that China in the 1940s falls into both categories is a first indication of this. The only significant difference between the two types is a relatively minor one: the target in the anti-colonial case was not a local dictator but a foreign, colonial power occupying the country (there is also the fact that the outcomes have not in all cases resulted in such deep social change as to qualify as social revolutions, but that is of secondary importance for the present study of their origins). In other respects, *with appropriate modifications that take into account the external locus of political control*, we may hypothesize that the same factors are operative as in non-colonial instances. Thus, for example, a form of dependent development obtained when foreign powers tried to transform colonial economies in certain directions for their own purposes: certainly some urbanization, infrastructural development, and growth in trade and GNP may be expected to occur in such a case (although foreign powers may not be as interested in industrialization as an indigenous government would be because they tended to be in the Third World to get access to raw materials such as minerals and foodstuffs). This last qualification explains why these colonial cases do not appear, at first glance, to warrant the term dependent *development*; I believe, in fact, that colonialism produced a distinct variant of dependent development, as suggested here. The colonial state is also, in some sense, a variant of the repressive, exclusionary state, although it is not personalist, but collective and bureaucratic in rule. On the other hand, because the government is composed of foreigners, the population may be as able (or even *more* likely) to focus its collective grievances on it as they would on an indigenous dictator. This distinction, too, should not be lost: a collective dictatorship of outsiders is not the same thing as collective dictatorship by an indigenous elite, and, I am arguing, closer to a personalist regime in emotional terms. Political cultures of opposition to colonial rule were also likely to arise: ideas of nationalism and independent rule or self-determination were obvious candidates for this role, but so were socialism and religion, as well as various local myths, legends, and heroic stories of previous struggles against the occupiers. Conjunctural factors likewise turn out to be important. Externally, one can find Goldfrank's "permissive world context" at work in various ways: most

236

generally, after World War II the global sentiment that the era of colonialism was ending, and that Africa and Asia should be independent. Those countries that resisted this process fell subject to anti-colonial revolts and international disapproval. Likewise, internal economic downturns either occurred or, as in Cuba, the guerrilla struggles themselves helped create these, thus convincing the colonial power that it was no longer profitable to remain in the country. Let us briefly survey the five most definite cases of anti-colonial Third World revolutions (four of the five resulted in social revolutions, as contrasted with the many other struggles for decolonization that were not revolutionary in either goals, strategies, or degree of mass participation).

After China (already discussed as case 5), these cases include Algeria 1954–62, Vietnam 1945–75, and Zimbabwe, Angola, and Mozambique, all in the 1970s. Their origins are summarized in Table 9.3.

The French came to Algeria in 1830 and took control at the expense of the indigenous tribal elite by force of arms, first in Algiers, the capital, and then in the surrounding countryside. By the middle of the twentieth century there were two separate societies in Algeria – an urban, French-educated and French-speaking wealthy society, and a rural and urban, Arabic-speaking, impoverished Muslim Algerian society. These two societies in a sense represented the two sides of dependent development, with the benefits of development for the French settlers, and the negative features of dependency for the Algerian population. The state was dominated completely by the French, and while not personalist it was certainly exclusionary and repressive of the Algerians. Meanwhile, political cultures of opposition were crystallizing around ideas of national independence from French control, and Islamic identity, as well as radical ideas about socialist egalitarianism, again with an Islamic veneer. The FLN (Front de Libération Nationale) urban guerrilla organization formed to carry out bombings against the French state and settlers after 1954. It included 10,000 women, some as fighters, some as couriers, most in support roles as nurses, cooks, and launderers.[19] By 1957 they had been effectively wiped out by a ferocious counter-insurgency response led by the French army, but they had shown the population that it was possible to resist the colonial state, and the struggle spread to the countryside, where it was harder for the French to repress it.

In the Algerian case, as in the Cuban, the conjunctural factors came together after the revolution had started. The disruption of everyday life by the FLN in the cities and the growing unrest in the countryside together constituted a kind of economic downturn that made the French question the continued viability of holding onto their colony. A world-systemic opening also contributed to this sentiment: the defeat of the French in Vietnam in 1954, international criticism of French methods in Algeria, and the protest of French intellectuals at home, such as Jean-Paul Sartre, all undermined French determination (although the French settlers in Algeria remained

Table 9.3 Origins of anti-colonial (social) revolutions

	Social structure	State	Political cultures	Conjunctural factors	Outcome
Algeria	Dependent development under France	French colonial rule	Nationalism, Islam, socialism	French defect in Vietnam/Rebel-made downturn	Broad-based coalition – Guerrilla success
Vietnam	Dependent development under France and USA	Colonial under France, client under USA	Nationalism, socialism	Anti-war movement in USA/Economic downturn	Broad-based coalition – Guerrilla success
Zimbabwe	Dependent development under Britain	Ian Smith's repressive, apartheid state	Nationalism, socialism, past resistance	International sanctions/ Rebel-made downturn	Broad-based coalition – Guerrilla success
Mozambique/ Angola	Dependent development under Portugal	Salazar dictatorship in Portugal	Nationalism, socialism	Portuguese Revolution/ Rebel-made downturn	Broad-based coalition – Guerrilla success

attached to the country until the end). Under this constellation of circumstances, by 1961–62, a popular insurrection resurfaced in the cities and countryside, and the French government simply gave up and withdrew. The FLN had come to power.[20]

In Vietnam, we have a revolution carried out in another French colony over a period of thirty years, involving at least three distinct moments: the liberation of the north in 1945 in the wake of World War II, the expulsion of the French from Vietnam in 1954 following their defeat at Dien Bien Phu, and a revolution in the south between 1959 and 1975 in which the north allied with southern revolutionaries to overthrow a regime massively backed by the United States. Dependent development is again a useful way to characterize the colonial situation of Vietnam under both the French, who turned the country into a rice and rubber exporter, and then under the USA, whose massive aid to South Vietnam kept the economy afloat during the 1960s. An elite of merchants, bureaucrats, and landlords tied to the world powers benefited from this arrangement, while the average peasant or poor town-dweller lived a very difficult life. The governments of the south were always perceived by the population as under the control of the French and later the Americans, and not truly representative of the will of the people. The political cultures that animated the revolutionaries in the north and south, as in Algeria, revolved around long-standing notions of driving out the foreign invaders (in this case, going back to ancient times and the struggle against Chinese encroachment), combined with a populist call for indigenous government and an emerging socialist ideology as the north joined the Soviet bloc in the 1950s. Political cultures of opposition were thus a mixture of traditional values of independence and egalitarianism overlaid by modern ideologies of nationalism and socialism.

The revolutionary crisis intensified after US military intervention escalated in the mid-1960s. The country was systematically devastated by the war (epitomized in the famous quote by an American officer: "It became necessary to destroy the town to save it.")[21] Meanwhile the rebels, using guerrilla tactics, fought the US army to a standstill, though at great cost: while some 50,000 Americans were killed, over a million and a half Vietnamese died in the struggle for independence. The world-systemic opening crystallized with the growth of a peace movement in the United States in the 1960s, the election of Richard Nixon in 1968 with promises to end the American military role, and the attenuation of the US commitment to support the South Vietnamese government at all costs after 1972. As government popularity plunged, the end came relatively rapidly, with the fall of Saigon in April 1975 and the reunification of Vietnam as a single country under socialism.[22]

Three other anti-colonial revolutions captured the world's attention in the 1970s, all in Africa. The state of Zimbabwe was created out of colonial Rhodesia, while Angola and Mozambique gained independence from

Portugal. Dependent development in Rhodesia produced a wealthy white farmer elite and a poor rural African majority. The colonial state under Britain and then under Ian Smith's independent Rhodesia was clearly repressive, and narrowly based on white rule. The Black population drew on a long tradition of political cultures of resistance going back to the driving out of the Portuguese in the 1690s and the attempted uprising of 1896. The guerrillas in Robert Mugabe's Zimbabwe African National Union (ZANU) and Joshua Nkomo's Zimbabwe African People's Organization (ZAPU) united the population around the ideals of independence, majority rule, and socialism. Eventually, by the 1970s, a guerrilla war was being waged, in which 30,000 Africans died. By the late 1970s Smith was coming under increasing pressure from the effects of the war, which created an economic downturn and drained the government's budget, as well as international public opinion. The international sanctions and guerrilla war caused economic hardship for the Smith government in the 1970s, providing the internal and external factors conducive to the negotiated settlement that brought independence in 1979 and 1980 (the same year as the successes of revolutionaries in Iran and Nicaragua).[23]

Though located on opposite sides of southern Africa (separated, interestingly enough, by what would become Zimbabwe), the revolutions in the two states of Mozambique in the east and Angola in the west are linked by a common colonial power, Portugal, and a world-systemic opening that occurred in the same period for both (I recognize that these countries have distinct historical trajectories to which I do not do justice here). Portugal made of each an exporter of primary products (oil, coffee, and diamonds from Angola; sugar, nuts, and cotton from Mozambique), yet a limited amount of industrialization and infrastructural growth also occurred in each by the 1960s and after. The dictatorships of Antonio Salazar and his successor, Marcello Caetano, sponsored the creation of colonial governments as repressive, authoritarian, and (by extension) personalist as their own in Portugal. The liberation movements that arose in each country – the Popular Movement for the Liberation of Angola (MPLA) and the Front for the Liberation of Mozambique (FRELIMO) – tapped deeply felt nationalist longings and channelled these in socialist directions. Already well organized in the 1960s, they fought long-term guerrilla wars that contributed to the favorable conjuncture of the mid-1970s by undermining the national economies and first demoralizing and later radicalizing the young Portuguese army officers who toppled the Portuguese regime in April 1974. Within the year, both countries had worked out arrangements for their independence. The MPLA and FRELIMO rebels, then, had gone a step further than the Cubans and Algerians in helping to bring about not only an economic downturn but to force a favorable international context for their revolts.[24]

This set of five anti-colonial revolutions, then, largely parallels the causal pattern of the five successful Third World social revolutions, with due con-

sideration given to the specific effects of colonial states and political economies: while development is more dependent than dynamic in these cases, still
it transforms societies enough to generate revolutionary grievances. And
while the colonialist state is not usually personalist, it still represents a concentrated target in the form of an outside force ruling above civil society.
Colonialism also shaped political cultures of opposition in the direction of
intense nationalisms, in each case overlaid with specific socialist, religious,
and indigenous currents of resistance. Conjunctural factors are similar too,
with less emphasis perhaps on sudden economic downturns, and more on
world-systemic openings (both, to some degree, subject to influence by the
rebels themselves). In Boolean terms, all five cases conform to the pattern of
the social revolutions:

$$Success = ABCDE,$$

that is, the presence of all five factors led to successful anti-colonial revolutions. Four of the five anti-colonial cases, finally, resulted in social revolutions of varying depth (Algeria being a borderline fifth case, in the sense that
different views exist on the degree to which subsequent social transformation
would qualify it).

Type Three: reversed social revolutions

A third set of cases consists of countries which experienced a relatively brief
period of revolutionary rule that was *reversed*. Here, one thinks of Chile's
experience of democratic socialism under Salvador Allende (1970–73) as the
prototypic case, and the somewhat less radical experiments with social transformation in Guatemala between 1944 and 1954 and Jamaica under
Michael Manley in the 1970s. To these may be added the 1979–83 revolution in Grenada.[25] As events radicalized in each case, internal contradictions
and external pressures reversed the revolution, often violently. These cases
present various challenges for our analysis. One is the need to reason somewhat counterfactually: How radical *were* these experiments? My sense is that
had each of them not been reversed, they could have resulted in structural
transformation as deep as in most of the successful cases discussed above.
A second problem for analysis is posed by the fact that in Chile and Jamaica
revolutionaries came to power democratically. While violence is definitely
not a feature of the definition of social revolution used in this chapter, this
means that the governments that were replaced by revolutionaries were not
of the exclusionary type posited by the model itself. Finally, there is a dual
periodization to attend to in these cases: the circumstances under which
revolutionaries came to power, and those under which they fell from
power (the latter being, strictly speaking, outside the scope of this study).
Table 9.4A presents the cases at the moment of revolution; let us see how the
theory fares.

Table 9.4A Reversed social revolutions: coming to power

	Social structure	State	Political cultures	Conjunctural factors	Outcome
Guatemala 1944	Dependent development under United Fruit Co.	Ubico dictatorship	Nascent democratic, nationalist radical currents	USA alienated by Ubico's fascism/ Recession and strikes	Urban-based coalition – Peaceful demonstration ousts Ubico
Chile 1970	Mining/industrial dependent development	Democratic	Vibrant democratic socialist challenge	USA underestimates threat/Recession in 1969–70	Allende elected with narrow plurality
Jamaica 1972	Adversely impacted and diversified by dependent development	Democratic	Social(ist) democratic challenge/ Rastafarianism	Fair elections/ Recession, unemployment	Clear-cut electoral victory for Manley
Grenada 1979	Dependent development under Britain	Gairy's repressive "autocratic democracy"	New Jewel populism/ democratic aspirations	Britain and USA passive/Economic problems	Sudden uprising brings New Jewel Movement to power

Guatemala between 1944 and 1954 lived through a period of increasingly radical social change.[26] If we focus on the circumstances under which a progressive, elected government led by Juan José Arévalo took power from the dictator Jorge Ubico in the course of 1944, we find a process of dependent development led since the turn of the century by foreign corporations such as the United Fruit Company. These companies commercialized and concentrated Guatemalan agriculture to produce coffee and bananas at the expense of the small and medium producers, mestizo and indigenous. The Depression brought renewed state repression and dictatorship to control labor; World War II brought further recession as coffee prices fell. Ubico's fascist sympathies alienated US policy-makers, and internal opposition arose based on emerging sentiments in favor of democratic rule, national economic autonomy, and to a lesser degree, indigenous demands. In June 1944 urban demonstrations and a general strike compounded existing economic conditions to force Ubico's resignation. In the fall, against a backdrop of indigenous mobilizations, elections brought the reformer Juan José Arévalo to power. While the oppositional political cultures in 1944 may not seem particularly strong, I would argue that the radicalization that they underwent by 1950 is part and parcel of what makes the later rule of Arbenz qualify as a potential social revolution.

Chile in 1970 departs from the general pattern in one significant respect: a long (if not unbroken) history of democratic institutions permitted the emergence of a vibrant socialist challenge within the rules of the democratic game.[27] Chile was unarguably one of Latin America's most developed societies by 1970, highly urbanized and industrialized, with an economy based on copper and multinational investment. In political cultural terms, it was also highly sophisticated: the labor movement, socialist and communist parties, and newer, further left groups, vied with Christian Democrats of all stripes for public support. I would argue that this constellation of a liberal political system and a well-articulated oppositional party coalition constitutes in some sense the "functional equivalent" of a repressive state and effective underground political cultures of resistance (that is, a truly democratic polity undergoing the changes wrought by dependent development is open to revolutionary electoral strategies). In 1970, the conjuncture was likewise favorable for Allende's accession to power: the centrist-reformist Christian Democratic government of Eduardo Frei had presided over an economic recession, while the United States underestimated the threat Allende posed in the three-way presidential race and did not interfere decisively in the election. Allende's victory with a slim plurality of the vote then launched his Popular Unity coalition on the "Chilean path to socialism."

Jamaica in the 1970s followed a combination of the paths of Guatemala and Chile before it.[28] Dependent development with American and British multinational corporation input focused on the bauxite and agro-export sectors, clearly transforming the economy and social structure in the period after World War II. As in Chile, a formally democratic system facilitated the eventual rise of a left-leaning electoral option in the form of Michael Manley's People's National Party (PNP). Another political culture that contributed to electoral victory in 1972 was Rastafarianism, a utopian political-religious-cultural movement that helped mobilize the Black population.[29] The internal conjuncture of 1972 was one of recession and unemployment, while an international climate that permitted reasonably free and fair elections contributed to Manley's victory and the inauguration of a leftward trajectory that would culminate in the declaration of democratic socialism in the fall of 1974.

The rise of the New Jewel Movement under Maurice Bishop on another English-speaking Caribbean island in Grenada in 1979 completes this set of cases.[30] Economically, the country fits the colonial, plantation model, with the rhythm of development set under British rule. A small elite benefited from the export of crops like nutmeg, mace, cocoa, and bananas, while a bare minimum of infrastructure and almost no industry was put in place. Eric Gairy ruled as an idiosyncratic autocrat under the Westminster system from 1951 to 1979, relying on the notorious "Mongoose Gang" to repress dissidents. Meanwhile the New Jewel Movement organized a tentative opposition based on a pragmatically radical populist alternative, influenced by the Black Power movement in nearby Trinidad, a growing sense of Grenadian national identity, and a budding labor movement. The economy, always precarious, suffered a serious recession in 1974; by 1978 export earnings were restored, but unemployment, inflation, and balance of payments problems remained acute. The conjuncture came suddenly in 1979: the New Jewel, believing that Gairy was about to arrest its leadership, moved first, leading a brief uprising that toppled Gairy before the United States or Britain could react. The fact that it took only forty-six men (of whom only eighteen were armed) to overcome the armed forces, should not obscure the popular aspect of the uprising: when a call for support went out over the radio, enormous, enthusiastic crowds answered it.[31]

These four cases, then, broadly fit the outlines of the model advanced in this chapter, if due allowance is made for the existence of democratic, rather than dictatorial, state systems in Chile and Jamaica. The effects of dependent development, vitality of political cultures (highlighted by Chile, especially), and the same conjunctural factors of internal economic downturn and favorable external situation lie in the background of the events that brought revolutionaries or radical reformers to power.

If we turn briefly to the circumstances of the falls from power of these regimes, in most cases within three or four years, some brief points may be made (for further details, consult Table 9.4B). Thinking about falls from power of *revolutionary* governments may be expected to require its own theory, differing from the fall of *anciens régimes*. This is not the place fully to work out such a theory.[32] Still, we may identify some preliminary common-

244

Table 9.4B Reversed social revolutions: falling from power

	Social structure	State	Political cultures	Conjunctural factors	Outcome
Guatemala 1954	Continued dependency amidst gains	Democratic under Arbenz	Maturing progressives facing right-wing opposition	US/UFCO plotting/ Economic hardships	CIA-supported *coup* restores dictatorship
Chile 1973	Continued dependency amidst gains	Democratic under Allende	Intense left/right polarization	US blockade and intervention/ Hyperinflation, crisis	CIA-supported *coup* establishes dictatorship
Jamaica 1980	Continued dependency amidst gains	Democratic under Manley	Increasing left/right polarization	US economic and political maneuvers/ Economic hardships	Conservative Seaga government elected
Grenada 1983	Continued dependency amidst gains	Revolutionary, popular under Bishop	Splits in New Jewel Movement	US intervention/ Economic hardships	Fall of New Jewel Movement

alities and particularities of these cases in light of the factors we are working with in this chapter. In terms of social structure, dependent development, once set in motion, cannot be done away with overnight: each government ran into the constraints this posed even as reforms brought about some gains. Three of the four governments ruled democratically, and the fourth, Bishop's in Grenada, was widely popular and likely could have won elections in the period of its rule. Progressive political cultures thrived, and made dramatic deepenings in Guatemala and Grenada, but at the same time, internal right-wing oppositions grew and society polarized politically. Conjunctural factors also worked against the new regimes: all experienced economic difficulties as the programs they put in place dislocated previous production and distribution systems, and all faced serious overt or covert intervention from the United States, designed to create counterrevolutionary governments. This was the outcome in all four cases, through violent CIA-sponsored coups in Guatemala and Chile, direct military intervention in Grenada, and the election of Edward Seaga's Labour Party in Jamaica. In some sense, then, the same factors that brought revolutionaries to power worked in reverse to unseat them.

Interpreted in Boolean terms, we may express the patterns of coming to power and falling in the following ways, drawing on Table 9.1 (recall that "A" signifies the presence of factor A, "a" its absence).

Coming to Power

Guatemala	ABCDE
Chile	AbCDE
Jamaica	AbCDE
Grenada	ABCDE

Guatemala in 1944 and Grenada in 1979 followed the pattern ABCDE (allowing for some ambiguity regarding an economic downturn in Grenada), while Chile in 1970 and Jamaica in 1972 produce AbCDE. Thus two subtypes exist: the usual model for success in the cases of Guatemala and Grenada, and the absence of a repressive state countered by a more explicitly organized left-wing party culture of opposition in Chile and Jamaica. These two types can be "reduced" in Boolean terms to the single path ACDE,[33] suggesting that dependent development, effective political cultures of opposition, an internal downturn, and a favorable world-systemic opportunity represent the overarching fundamental pattern in this set of cases.

The pattern for falling from power appears to be AbcDe, with all cases continuing to be subject to dependent development, more democratic politically than previously, increasingly polarized in terms of political cultures ("1–" in Table 9.1 has been converted to a small "c" to denote this problem), experiencing an economic downturn, and witnessing the closing of a favorable world-systemic opening. These last three factors – cDe – suggest a possible theory for reversals of revolution: revolutionaries fall from power when political fragmentation and polarization, economic difficulties, and outside intervention occur together.

The cases of reversed revolutions, in their coming to power phase, then, bear out the theory of social revolutions in the main, taking into account the exceptionalism of democratic paths to power in Chile and Jamaica, and the arguably slightly reduced role played by political cultures of opposition in Grenada and Guatemala at the time of the regime changes.

Type Four: attempted social revolutions

We shift now to three types of "failure," in the sense that social revolutions did not occur in conditions where we might otherwise expect them to. These three types include attempted social revolutions, political revolutions, and non-attempts. Of these, attempted social revolutions are the clearest example of a contrasting case for our model of success, for the goal of the revolutionaries was the same as in the successful cases. Note that there is a definitional problem here, for in the absence of success, how do we know that what was attempted was a *social* revolution? Here, we must rely on our judgments of the intentions of the revolutionaries and nature of the movements, and I believe that most close observers of each of the four struggles discussed here would agree that social revolutions were indeed on the agenda of the actors involved. The guiding principle of my analysis of these cases – El Salvador in the 1980s, Guatemala between the 1960s and 1980s, the Philippines in the mid- to late 1980s, and Peru since the 1980s – is that they should exhibit substantial similarities to the successful cases already studied (to explain the seriousness of the attempt), but also equally significant differences in some of the factors at work (to account for their failure). In Table 9.1, therefore, on some key indices these cases are coded "1–" to indicate the presence of the factor, with some important reservations. We shall see how this shapes the causal patterns in Boolean terms at the end of this section. Table 9.5 presents the cases.

El Salvador from 1979 to 1992 underwent perhaps the most intense revolutionary experience in human history that failed to come to power.[34] Dependent development, a repressive state, vigorous oppositional cultures, and economic difficulties helped produce a very serious popular armed challenge by 1979. Yet in the 1980s, the army and the rebels fought to a standstill, eventually concluding a peace settlement in 1992 that brought an end to the civil war with the promise of reforms but no social revolution. The key analytical reasons for this, in terms of the model, seem to lie in the *collective* nature of military rule in El Salvador, which created a broad base of elite support for the regime, coupled with the expansion of political participation in the course of the civil war to include the centrist Christian Democrats in the electoral game, thus siphoning off some middle-class and even rural worker support from the rebels as well. This polarization into two camps,

Table 9.5 Attempted social revolutions

	Social structure	State	Political cultures	Conjunctural factors	Outcome
El Salvador 1979–92	Adversely impacted and diversified by dependent development	Collective military rule with broad elite support	Marxism-Leninism, liberation theology, but polarized	Carter-Reagan intervention/ "Stable" crisis, 1970s–1980s?	Prolonged civil war – Negotiated settlement
Guatemala 1960s–1980s	Adversely impacted and diversified by dependent development	Collective military rule with broad elite support	Mostly Marxist-Leninist	USA supports government off and on/ "Stable" crisis?	Prolonged guerrilla war – Government repression
Peru 1980s–90s	Stagnant dependent development	Democratic in 1980s/Fujimori auto-golpe	Sendero Luminoso's extreme Maoism	US support/ Stable or improving	Prolonged guerrilla war – Rebels weakened
Philippines 1986–	Stagnant dependent development	Democratic under Aquino	Mostly Marxist	US support/ "Stable" crisis?	Guerrilla struggles without success

with a wavering middle in between them, was solidified by the political culture of the FMLN rebels too, for although it was extremely well articulated, and inflected by liberation theology as well, it differed from this combination of secular and religious radicalisms in Nicaragua, in that El Salvador's revolutionaries articulated a largely Marxist-Leninist discourse of acute class war not calculated to appeal to many in the middle classes. Finally, the world-systemic opening that appeared in 1979 under Jimmy Carter's human rights-oriented foreign policy and facilitated revolutionary successes in Iran and neighboring Nicaragua, began to close even in the last year of the Carter presidency as US Democrats balked at allowing *another* Third World revolution, and closed entirely in the Reagan years, during which the USA intervened massively to prop up the regime in El Salvador. These unfavorable factors produced a costly, brutal civil war that could end only with a negotiated settlement.

Guatemala produced similar, if less vigorous, guerrilla struggles for almost thirty years, beginning in the 1960s as the opposition regrouped from the 1954 defeat. At no time did all five factors come into a favorable conjuncture for success: as in El Salvador, the military found institutional rather than dictatorial means to control the political game, and increasingly opened it in the 1980s to the center, while the rebels tended to embrace uncompromising Marxist-Leninist stands in opposition, with the same lack of success in mobilizing a broad, multi-class coalition. The United States at times provided significant training and support to the army and government (especially before 1975 and again in the 1980s), or was alternately defied by the regime when it could tap other international sources of arms and support in places like Argentina and Israel. The economy through this period, while remaining very skewed and unequal, lived through an arguably "stable" process of crisis, rather than a sudden or discernible worsening of the already bad conditions. The result has been a three-decade-long civil war of varying intensity, successfully contained by the repressive arm of the governments that have ruled Guatemala.[35]

Another extremely strong Latin American insurgency has occurred in Peru, where the *sui generis* quasi-Maoist Marxists of Sendero Luminoso have threatened to seize power since the mid-1980s or earlier, spreading from their rural Andean birthplace into the shantytowns of Lima. The savagery of the guerrillas" assault on civil society, ideologically and with intense physical violence, has produced both fervent adherents and, as in El Salvador and Guatemala, few middle- and upper-class supporters. It has also alienated significant portions of the rural population as well. Nor has the regime proven vulnerable in the classic sense: Peru maintained a functioning democracy in the 1980s under the left-oriented government of Alán García, and while Alberto Fujimori later dissolved Congress, he was careful to obtain military and a surprising amount of popular support, buoyed by the *absence* of an economic downturn as his neo-monetarist economic plan restored a stable pattern of dependent development. The fortuitous 1992 capture of Sendero's mastermind Abimael Guzmán further weakened the movement's cause, as if these structural factors were not enough on their own.[36]

A final, non-Latin American case of attempted social revolution to consider is that of the Philippines after Cory Aquino replaced Ferdinand Marcos as president in 1986. The Philippines is unique in constituting a case of, first, a successful political revolution (the fall of Marcos to the People's Power movement), and then, or concurrently, the failure of a more radical project for social change led by the left-wing labor and communist movement. In this sense, we must approach it as we did China earlier, in two phases, although in the Philippines, the two are telescoped chronologically and the social revolutionary project did not succeed. We will look at the preliminary, political revolution in more detail below; here, the following brief indicators may suggest the reasons for the failure of social transformation. The reasoning is broadly similar to the cases of El Salvador, Guatemala, and Peru: Aquino represented the most democratic, and hence unassailable, government of them all, an image enhanced by the contrast with the Marcos dictatorship that had just been overthrown. The radicals, meanwhile, while enormously energetic in organizing many sectors of society in both town and village, and across gender lines, still suffered from the ability of their critics to label their political culture communist, thereby reducing its cross-class appeal. Finally, US support for Aquino was very strong, again, as in El Salvador, given the threat from the left. The result has been a difficult economic conjuncture but a relatively stable political consolidation without social transformation.[37]

In attempting to chart the patterns presented by these cases of attempted social revolution in Boolean terms, some strategic decisions must be made about interpreting the coding "1–" that occurs and recurs in Table 9.1. Boolean truth tables require yes or no answers to generate their 1's and 0's for presence or absence of relevant factors. In these cases, many of the factors are present, *but only up to a point.* We thus find repressive but collective, well-institutionalized military regimes in El Salvador and Guatemala, strong but flawed political cultures of opposition in all four cases, poor economic conditions which may have been all-too-stable, and, in the case of Peru and the Philippines, stagnant dependent development at best. If we code all cases of "1–" as instances of *presence*, however partial or qualified, of the factors in question, we may have a plausible explanation of how and why social revolutions were attempted at all in these places at these points in time. The patterns look like this:

El Salvador, 1979–92	ABCDe
Guatemala, 1960s–80s	ABCDe
Peru, 1980s–90s	AbCDe
Philippines, 1986–90s	AbCDe

Using Boolean minimization procedures, the type of state drops out of the expression, since both open and exclusionary regimes possessed otherwise similar features in all the other factors. Thus the pattern ACDe covers all four attempts: the dislocations of dependent development, elaboration of oppositional cultures, and economic downturns touched off attempts at social revolution, regardless of the type of state and in the absence of a favorable world-systemic opportunity.

Now taking the opposite tack and emphasizing the partial, flawed effectivity of the factors coded "1–" and considering them absent, we have the following patterns:

El Salvador, 1979–92	Abcde
Guatemala, 1960s–80s	Abcde
Peru, 1980s–90s	abcde
Philippines, 1986–90s	abcde

These two variations can be reduced similarly with respect to dependent development, which drops out of the reduced expression of the pattern to yield the formula bcde as an explanation for the movements" failures: rebels could not succeed when the states they faced were not repressive, exclusionary dictatorships, their political cultures did not facilitate broad cross-class alliances, the economy did not worsen perceptibly, and outside powers supported rather than abandoned incumbent regimes. These factors cluster together logically as well, for regimes that allow some political participation make it difficult for cross-class alliances to coalesce and can often attract outside military and economic support, which is even more likely to be forthcoming from the United States when the oppositional culture is, or can be labeled, Marxist-Leninist. This set of cases, then, both broadly confirms the theory of success insofar as revolutionary attempts possess almost all of the characteristics of successful cases, and gives us a working theory of failure, in that these same characteristics are crucially limited in scope or depth.

Type Five: political revolutions

Political revolutions are another important variant on our theme in that as these are revolutions made by mass-mobilizing movements and resulting in significant political change, but where the social and economic transformations that we associate with social revolutions do not accompany these changes. They thus meet only two of Skocpol's three criteria for a social revolution. The theoretical issue at stake is whether our model can point to relevant factors both enabling such revolutions to occur and yet preventing them from becoming full-fledged social revolutions. A definitional problem exists here, too: *How much* "social transformation" is required to qualify a process as a social revolution? The four cases chosen for study here seem clear enough to avoid this problem: the fall of the Manchu dynasty in 1911

251

led to social revolution only thirty-eight years later; the People's Power movement toppled Marcos in the Philippines in 1986 but led to little economic change; the same can be said of the fall of the Duvalier dictatorship in Haiti. Bolivia is often considered to have experienced a social revolution in 1952 but by the end of the decade there, too, little seems to have changed for the majority of the population. Table 9.6 orients our discussion of these cases. Let us look at each in turn.

The fall of the dynasty in China in 1911 has already been sketched in the first part of this chapter, and the appropriate contrasts drawn with the social revolution led by Mao a generation later: the two situations show clear differences in terms of the degree of dependent development and the evolution of effective political cultures of opposition, with perhaps less of an economic crisis in 1911 China than the model usually expects (and a marked downturn after World War II). This case suggests that the process of dependent development must be advanced to the point where the social structure is dislocated enough to crystallize a broad cross-class coalition for change, one which moreover is cemented by a vigorous and flexible oppositional political culture.

Haiti toward the end of the twentieth century, so different in size, and distant in time and space, seems to offer a similar pattern of political but not social revolutionary change.[38] In development terms, the island is a more classic case of dependency than dependent development, as it has ranked at the very bottom of all countries in the Americas on most indices of development and social welfare. The state, on the other hand, under the Duvaliers, *père et fils*, was a classic case of a repressive, exclusionary, personalistic police regime, with rule guaranteed by the feared paramilitary known as the *tontons macoutes*. Under these conditions, the opposition had little chance to organize more than a very rudimentary resistance culture, which, such as it was, drew on liberal democratic and liberation theology currents. Crisis economic conditions forced largely unorganized street demonstrations against Jean-Claude Duvalier between 1984 and 1986, and the regime's crackdown led the United States to withhold further aid and to encourage conspirators in the army to stage the February 6, 1986 *coup* that ended the Duvalier dynasty. The outcome, however, has been a new elite–military alliance that has stymied further attempts at reforms, radical or otherwise, symbolized in the stalemate between elected (and then exiled) president Jean-Bertrand Aristide and the army that ran the country until the mid-1990s.

A variant on this pattern presents itself in the case of the Bolivian revolution of 1952. Bolivia is similar to China and Haiti in the relative degree of underdevelopment, here marked by an enclave tin-mining economy in a largely poor, rural countryside.[39] The difference resides in the nature of the regime that was overthrown, which was a conservative, elite-led and military-supported alliance rather than the usual vulnerable dictatorship. Under these conditions, a strong oppositional culture evolved in the 1940s

Table 9.6 Political revolutions

	Social structure	State	Political cultures	Conjunctural factors	Outcome
China 1911	Proto-dependent development/ Stagnation	Nanchu dynasty	Mascent liberal-democratic currents	Foreign pressures/ Economic difficulties	Manchus fall but no social revolution
Bolivia 1952	Proto-dependent development	Military conservative rule	Nationalist, radical, and trade union currents	No intervention/ Economic difficulties	Sudden popular uprising – MNR seizes power
Philippines 1986	Limited dependent development	Marcos dictatorship	Nationalist, democratic, socialist currents	USA withdraws support for Marcos/ Economic difficulties	People's Power topples Marcos
Haiti 1986	Very limited dependent development	Duvalier dictatorship	Nascent oppositional currents	USA withdraws support for Duvalier/ Economic difficulties	Duvalier falls, military stays

with roots both in the working and middle classes, cohering around demands for nationalization of the mines, land reforms for the indigenous majority, and a consolidation of democratic norms. This combination of state and opposition is somewhat reminiscent of that of Chile and Jamaica, where radicals won power through the ballot box. The middle-class progressives of the National Revolutionary Movement (MNR) won the 1951 elections but were not allowed to take office; in April 1952 they found it fairly easy to stage a small-scale but well-coordinated urban and provincial uprising amid declining living standards and no international interference in the events. The next six years saw a substantial land reform that offered the promise of a true social revolution (and has earned the events this title in part of the literature), followed by a turn by the ruling MNR to the right under the pressures of the international financial community. The result, in the end, bears more resemblance to a political revolution than a mere coup or a proper social revolution.

Our final case, the Philippines between 1983 and 1986, as mentioned in the previous section, produced a political revolution that toppled the dictatorship of Ferdinand Marcos but brought to power the moderate reformer Corazón Aquino, rather than a revolutionary party or movement. It parallels turn-of-the-century China and 1980s Haiti in many respects: a somewhat more advanced but still very limited degree of dependent development since the 1950s, a repressive, personalist, and quite exclusionary dictatorship, and a series of economic difficulties (including unemployment and drops in incomes, low growth, and debt) that grew after the assassination of opposition figure Benigno Aquino in 1983. At the crucial moment, when reform-minded officers within the armed forces rebelled in February 1986 and found thousands of moderate and left-wing supporters among the urban population, the United States played a positive role in easing Marcos from power (Reagan offered Marcos asylum, and Senator Paul Laxalt advised Marcos to "Cut and cut cleanly. The time has come").[40] The opposition forces that underpinned this event ranged from the 1,500 officers of the Reform the Armed Forces Now Movement (RAM), the liberal middle-class opposition symbolized by eventual president Cory Aquino, and the radical nationalist and socialist forces in the National Democratic Front (NDF), the political wing of the revolutionary New People's Army. While the latter would prove too exclusive a basis to mobilize a cross-class coalition for social revolution in 1986 and after, all these forces came to together to contribute to the ouster of the Marcos dictatorship.

In searching for the paths to political revolution, we should repeat the procedure used in understanding attempted social revolutions. Thus, coding factors judged "1−" in Table 9.1 as present, we find that all four cases here produce the pattern ABCDE, which we interpret as an account of why a revolution of any type occurred, as this is identical to the model for social revolution. In emphasizing the limits to these factors by coding all cases of

"1–" as absent, we find three distinct patterns to account for the political, rather than social, outcomes of these events:

China, 1911	aBcde
Bolivia, 1952	abCde
Philippines, 1986	aBCDe
Haiti, 1986	aBcde

China and Haiti present the same pattern, with vulnerable states, but only limited degrees of all the other variables. Bolivia, in this reading, had only vigorous political cultures of opposition operating in 1952. The Philippines actually possesses three of the five factors – a vulnerable state and economy, and a strong oppositional culture – but lacked dependent development or a favorable international conjuncture. All four cases lack *both* a full-blown dependent development or a permissive world context, suggesting that these two factors – both political-economic, in differing ways – are powerful deflectors of revolutionary movements and brakes on social transformation after they take power. To this base is joined in three of the four cases (all but the Philippines) a less severe economic downturn, and in two less elaborated oppositional cultures (China and Haiti). These cases thus nuance further the theory of successful social revolutions by showing how the partial existence of some of the key factors produces instead a political transformation alone.

Type Six: no attempt at revolution

Brief consideration of a sampling of the large number of cases where no revolution has been attempted in the Third World will close this comparative survey. I have chosen the nine cases (and eight countries, counting Argentina twice) that form type six of Table 9.1 on the basis of their special significance as major Third World powers and/or to illustrate the significance of one or more of the factors specified in the theory. Here, only a few comments will be made on each case, with no corresponding tabular account and minimal footnotes, to suggest some points about the non-occurrence of revolutions.[41]

South Korea and Taiwan since the 1970s represent the undisputed economic powerhouses of the Third World. They have industrialized and thrived in a competitive world economy to the point where "dependent development" barely covers their experience of growth (hence, they are coded "1+" in Table 9.1). Their states, while exclusionary and repressive under the military in South Korea and Chiang Kai-shek's KMT in Taiwan, have progressively opened themselves to greater participation since the late 1970s. In terms of political cultures, there has been a vigorous student and labor movement in South Korea that forced state reforms, but it was not calculated to enlist the growing middle class in a revolutionary project; in Taiwan there has been little visible opposition. Nor has the conjuncture been conducive to revolution in either case at any point since the mid-1970s: both have been too dynamic economically, and both have enjoyed extensive superpower support from both the United States and Japan. Thus, sustained economic growth has created more prosperous middle and working classes who have succeeded in wresting democratic reforms from the state rather than revolutions.[42]

The Latin American counterparts of East Asia's dragon economies are Argentina, Brazil, and Mexico. All experienced a pronounced form of dependent development after the 1960s, with Argentina lagging behind the other two since the mid-1980s. Each has also experienced serious economic downturns, sometimes repeatedly, at various points since the mid-1970s. Argentina had a very repressive military regime in the 1970s that was nevertheless more institutional than personalist (Argentina's Montoneros did attempt an urban uprising, but of arguably limited scope in retrospect, suggesting that a guerrilla movement is not the same thing as an attempted social revolution). The factors conducive for revolution end here, however. Mexico's ruling party, while holding onto power for over sixty years through sometimes fraudulent means, has been quite astute at claiming to represent the major interest groups in the polity, while Argentina's transition to democracy after the débâcle of the Malvinas/Falklands war in 1983 has done away with military rule. Political cultures, except for the Mexican left's 1988 electoral challenge under Cuauhtémoc Cárdenas, have not been particularly strong in these cases: the courage of the mothers of the disappeared in Argentina is undeniable, but theirs was not a revolutionary movement, while the return to democracy in Brazil was not a result of a mass political mobilization, and the Mexican left has proven unable to consolidate any kind of popular gains at the polls. Nor can one find much of a vulnerable international conjuncture in any of these cases: Mexico and Brazil have enjoyed close relations with the United States, as has Argentina since the return of democracy. Since 1994, the dramatic emergence of the Zapatistas in Mexico shifts the country out of the category of no attempt into that of attempted social revolution. Simple inspection of the analysis here for the 1980s – with four of the five factors at least partially operative – suggests that Mexico was prerevolutionary at that point.[43]

If we turn to the Middle East, the two countries of major economic and demographic weight aside from Iran are Egypt and Turkey. Turkey has exhibited a vigorous enough growth to warrant the label of dependent development, while Egypt is much more ambiguous since the 1980s but does possess significant indices of development from earlier spurts under Nasser and Sadat. Economic downturns have occurred at various times in both, and seem almost chronic in Egypt. But both states have been only partly exclusionary: the military has seized power in Turkey in 1971 and 1980, only to return power to civilians in a carefully controlled system, and Egypt has maintained a thin veneer of democratic legality under Hosni Mubarak. And the oppositions have been particularly limited in scope in Turkey and in unity in Egypt, where secular and religious radicals have vied for hegemony. Nor, as close American allies, has either government suffered international pressure or neglect. The results are stalemated political economies with little sign of revolution on the horizon, although Egypt in particular bears watching.

A final case to consider is Zaire in central Africa. There the government of Mobutu Sese Seko has presided since 1965 over a process of growing deterioration and poverty. An exclusionary state and economic downturns, particularly since 1993, would seem to favor Mobutu's ouster. And while this could indeed come at any time, it is not likely to be the result of a social revolution, given the limited development and unity of the opposition. Here is one case where political culture, coupled perhaps with sheer underdevelopment, may preclude a revolution where we might otherwise expect one to occur.[44]

The patterns underlying this cursory survey of select Third World non-revolutionary situations can be discerned in various ways. If we code "1+," "1−," and "1/0" (indicating the factor was present at some times in the period under question, but absent at others) from Table 9.1 as instances of *presence* of the factors, we get the following, most generous expressions of their potential for revolution:

South Korea, 1970s to the present	ABCde
Taiwan, 1970s to the present	ABcde
Brazil, 1970s to the present	ABcDe
Argentina, 1970s	ABcDe
Argentina, 1983 to the present	AbcDe
Mexico, 1980s to 1994	ABCDe
Turkey, 1970s to the present	ABcDe
Egypt, 1970s to the present	ABCDe
Zaire, 1970s to the present	aBcDE

It is obvious that no case possesses all five factors posited by the theory. This by itself is a case for the combinatorial nature of the model. In an ideal test of the theory, we would find cases where four of the five were present, and one absent; this would imply the necessity of that factor for the theory of revolution. History does not provide such cases, however. The closest here are those of Mexico and Egypt. The former in the 1980s lacked only a favorable world-systemic opportunity (and in 1994 produced the Zapatista challenge to the state). The latter also witnessed the rise of a strong Islamist challenge as the 1980s wore on, one which has engaged the state in armed actions without igniting a revolution. Interestingly, eight of the nine cases lack this factor (international pressure on Mobutu in Zaire recently being the partial exception). Five of the nine cases possess three of the five factors: the pattern ABcDe occurs in Brazil, Argentina in the 1970s, and Turkey, pointing to the

257

additional importance of political cultures of opposition; ABCde in South Korea points to the significance of the absence of an economic downturn; and Zaire's aBcDE suggests that the absence of dependent development affects the possibility of revolutions negatively. Of the nine cases, we have eight cases of A, B, and e, seven of D, and six of c. If we take these as the most common situations, we get the pattern ABcDe that actually occurs in three of the cases, again suggesting the necessity of political culture and a world-systemic opening for revolutions to occur, even in the presence of other favorable factors.[45] If we use Boolean minimization procedures, including the prime implicant rule,[46] we can reduce the nine cases to the following formula for failure:

$$\text{Non-revolution} = ABe + AcDe + aBcDE$$

This suggests that three paths lead to the absence of revolution: (1) the combination of dependent development, a repressive state, and no world-systemic opening (in South Korea, Taiwan, Brazil, Argentina in the 1970s, Mexico, Turkey, and Egypt); (2) the presence of dependent development and an economic downturn coupled with a lack of oppositional culture and absent world-systemic opening (in Brazil, Argentina in both periods, and Turkey); and (3) the unique pattern presented by Zaire of no dependent development or unified opposition despite the presence of an exclusionary state, economic downturn, and a world-systemic opening.

If we take the most restrictive interpretation of the cases, coding "1+," "1–," and "1/0" as *absences* of the factors in question, the cases look like this:

South Korea, 1970s to the present	abcde
Taiwan, 1970s to the present	abcde
Brazil, 1970s to the present	Abcde
Argentina, 1970s	ABcDe
Argentina, 1983 to the present	abcDe
Mexico, 1980s to 1994	Abcde
Turkey, 1970s to the present	Abcde
Egypt, 1970s to the present	abcDe
Zaire, 1970s to the present	aBcDe

These patterns reveal far more absences of the relevant factors: South Korea, Taiwan, and Egypt lack all five; Brazil, Argentina since 1983, Mexico and Turkey are missing four; Zaire three; and Argentina in the 1970s two. In modal terms, we have five cases of a, seven cases of b, nine cases of c, six cases of d, and nine cases of e. The most common pattern then is bcde (since a/A is about evenly split, it drops out).[47] This suggests that revolutions do not occur when states are relatively open, political cultures are underdeveloped, economic downturns are not severe or chronic, and the international conjuncture is unfavorable. Following strict Boolean minimization procedures, the final formula becomes:

Non-revolution = bcde + abce + BcDe + acDe

Here, the key obstacles to revolution appear to be problematic political cultures of opposition and the world-systemic setting.

CONCLUSIONS

We have now completed our long, comparative tour of Third World revolutions. This chapter has constituted a preliminary, extended test of a model of the origins of Third World social revolutions, and a reflection on the question of "Why do so few revolutions succeed, while most fail (or do not even occur)?" The procedures of Boolean analysis have yielded the following sets of patterns:

Type One: Successful Social Revolutions (cases 1–5)

Success = ABCDE

Type Two: Anti-Colonial (Social) Revolutions (cases 6–10)

Success = ABCDE

Type Three: Reversed Social Revolutions (cases 11–14)

Coming to Power = ACDE
Falling from Power = AbcDe

Type Four: Attempted Social Revolutions (cases 15–18)

Attempt = ACDe
Failure = bcde

Type Five: Political Revolutions (cases 19–22)

Attempt = ABCDE
Political Revolution = aBcde + abCde + aBCDe

Type Six: No Attempt at Revolution (cases 23–31)

No attempt = bcde + abce + BcDe + acDe

If we attempt to summarize the model of success, we can look at the first fourteen cases, and find that two routes to power obtained: the presence of all five factors in the five classic cases of success (Mexico, China, Cuba, Nicaragua, and Iran), the five anti-colonial revolutions (Algeria, Vietnam, Angola, Mozambique, and Zimbabwe), and in two of the reversed social revolutions (Guatemala 1944 and Grenada). In two cases – Chile and Jamaica – social revolutions were made with only four of the factors (in both cases, revolutionaries did not face an exclusionary, personalist regime and came to power through elections). The answer to the question of why these dozen or so cases succeeded lies in the combination of dependent development, repressive state, oppositional political cultures, economic downturn, and world-systemic opportunity posited by the model.

To the question, why do most attempts fail, or not result in social revolutions, or not occur at all, we have found several answers. The reversed social revolutions in Guatemala, Chile, Grenada, and Jamaica suggested that the continued effects of dependent development and an economic downturn, coupled with schisms in the unity of the opposition (at least in part due to political cultures), the vulnerability of relatively democratic revolutionary regimes, and external pressures have combined to overturn revolutions in progress. This is a contribution to a theory of revolutionary outcomes, for it identifies those factors which have impeded revolutionaries even where they have obtained a hold on power.

The pattern of attempted revolutions in El Salvador, Peru, Guatemala, and the Philippines provides a further answer to the question of why many revolutions fail: in these cases, revolutionaries profited from the effects of dependent development and economic downturns and elaborated political cultures to rally the opposition. Revolutionary struggles broke out in unfavorable international contexts, however, and regardless of the type of state faced. The causes of failure included the strength of the relatively inclusive regimes the rebels fought, the limits of the political cultures elaborated, the relative stability and "normality" of economic difficulties, and the outside aid to the governments.

Political revolutions resulted in China (1911), Bolivia, the Philippines (1986), and Haiti when all five factors posited by the model came into play up to a degree. But up to a degree only: three patterns forced these movements to stop short of social transformation. In China and Haiti, relative economic and political cultural underdevelopment, lack of economic crisis, and outside pressures moderated the outcome despite the presence of a repressive state; in Bolivia, political cultures were stronger, but all other factors limited; and in the Philippines three factors – the state, political cultures, and economic downturn – were favorable, but dependent development and the international conjuncture were not. The analysis of these four cases may suggest – but by no means fully demonstrates – a future theory of the causes of political revolutions.

Finally, we have looked at a number of cases which possess some of the factors tending toward revolutionary mobilization but in which no revolution in fact was even attempted. We have traced this to the absence or limits of the key factors, in several combinations. If we look at all the combinations which did not produce successful social revolutions, we find eight distinctive routes to failure in cases 11 through 31:

$$AbcDe + bcde + aBcde + abCde + aBCDe + abce + BcDe + acDe$$

It will be noted that in each pattern the international conjuncture was unfavorable, a finding which is not surprising given the world-system imbalances in which the Third World finds itself. If we focus only on the absent factors in each of these patterns, we have failure or non-occurrence produced by

$$bce + bcde + acde + abde + ae + ce + ace$$

This suggests that in the actual historical cases at our disposal, it took the absence of at least two factors to block or prevent a social revolution. This does not imply, however, that cases with only one missing factor would produce a revolution (although this did happen in Chile and Jamaica, where the states were democratic rather than repressive and revolutionaries came to power through elections, a not impossible "anomaly").

In the end, what this all means is subject to further theoretical reflection and empirical testing. More work still needs to be done on the precise mechanisms by which factors such as dependent development, political cultures of opposition, economic downturns, and the world-system acquire their efficacy as well as their precise relations to each other. That is to say, as my critics have pointed out, that such factors require further empirical specification and theoretical elaboration. I agree with them on this, but suspect that their "measures" will prove complex. It would be desirable too to study each of the cases sketched here in greater detail, which might change our interpretation of one or another factor's presence and again, could help us understand how they interact to produce their effects. Still other cases could be studied as well: China in 1989 and Algeria in the 1990s, or Mexico since 1994, for example, as attempted revolutions, social or political.[48] And finally, one wonders what modifications would need to be introduced to take on that much smaller set of non-Third World social revolutions offered by history in the case of the English Civil War, the French and Russian Revolutions, and the events of 1989 in Eastern Europe. This chapter has hinted at ways to do this, I hope, at the same time as it has extended the range of our understanding of the comparative-historical sociology of Third World revolutions.

ACKNOWLEDGEMENTS

I would like to acknowledge the critical feedback of a number of individuals who read and commented on this chapter, including Richard Appelbaum, Kate Bruhn, Rani Bush, Eve Darien-Smith, Fernando Lopez-Alves, Chris McAuley, Becky Overmyer-Velazquez, Charles Ragin, Rich Snyder, and Tim Wickham-Crowley. I am also indebted to students in a number of classes, and to my research assistants Jackie Cabuay, Tanya Tabon, and Jen Wu, for help on the Chinese, Philippines, and Haitian cases, respectively.

I have not been able fully to address their many excellent questions in this chapter; I shall do my best in future extensions of this work!

NOTES

1. I here follow the definition of social revolutions provided by Theda Skocpol, as "rapid, basic transformations of a society's state and class structure . . . accompanied and in part carried through by class-based revolts from below': Theda Skocpol, *States and Social Revolutions: A Comparative Analysis of France, Russia, and China* (Cambridge: Cambridge University Press, 1979), 4. This is not always an easy definition to operationalize, and readers of this chapter have asked me where such cases as Ethiopia or Cambodia in the mid-1970s fit. My first reaction is that the "movement" which toppled Haile Selassie was not mass-based (much like the Afghan revolution of 1978), while the horrific events in Cambodia, while leading to great – and tragic – social transformation, were likewise limited in participatory scope. Others may well disagree. Nor do I pretend here to cover the entire universe of relevant cases, although I do believe I have touched on most of them.

2. As we shall see, China is an ambiguous case, borrowing in some respects the characteristics of an anti-colonial, and in other respects, a social revolution. My argument shall be in any case that these two types bear a close resemblance in causal terms.

3. Charles C. Ragin, *The Comparative Method: Moving Beyond Qualitative and Quantitative Strategies* (Berkeley, Los Angeles, and London: University of California Press, 1987); Timothy P. Wickham-Crowley, *Guerrillas and Revolution in Latin America: A Comparative Study of Insurgents and Regimes Since 1956* (Princeton: Princeton University Press, 1992).

4. Walter L. Goldfrank, "Theories of Revolution and Revolution Without Theory: The Case of Mexico," pp. 135–65 in *Theory and Society*, volume 7 (1979); John Walton, *Reluctant Rebels: Comparative Studies of Revolution and Underdevelopment* (New York: Columbia University Press, 1984); Jeff Goodwin and Theda Skocpol, "Explaining Revolutions in the Contemporary Third World," pp. 489–509 in *Politics & Society*, volume 17, number 4 (December 1989); Farideh Farhi, *States and Urban-Based Revolutions: Iran and Nicaragua* (Urbana and Chicago: University of Illinois Press, 1990); Wickham-Crowley, *Guerrillas and Revolution*; Jack A. Goldstone, Ted Robert Gurr, and Farrokh Moshiri, editors, *Revolutions of the Late Twentieth Century* (Boulder: Westview Press, 1991). For a critical evaluation of much of this work, see John Foran, "Theories of Revolution Revisited: Toward a Fourth Generation?" pp. 1–20 in *Sociological Theory*, volume 11, number 1 (March 1993), and "Revolutionizing Theory/Revising Revolution: State, Culture, and Society in Recent Works on Revolution," pp. 65–88 in *Contention: Debates in Society, Culture and Science*, volume 2, number 2 (Winter 1993).

5. John Foran, "A Theory of Third World Social Revolutions: Iran, Nicaragua, and El Salvador Compared," pp. 3–27 in *Critical Sociology*, volume 19, number 2 (1992), *Fragile Resistance: Social Transformation in Iran from 1500 to the Revolution* (Boulder, San Francisco, Oxford: Westview Press, 1993), and "The Causes of Latin American Social Revolutions: Searching for Patterns in Mexico, Cuba, and Nicaragua," pp. 209–44 in Peter Lengyel and Volker Bornschier, editors, *World Society Studies*, volume 3: *Conflicts and New Departures in World Society* (New Brunswick: Transaction, 1993). A theory of failures and non-occurrences is suggested in the present chapter, and further explained in my essay, "The Future

of Revolutions in a Globalizing World," Working Paper No. 26, Advanced Study Center 1995–96, International Institute, University of Michigan (March 1996).

6. See Fernando Henrique Cardoso and Enzo Faletto, *Dependency and Development in Latin America*, translated from the Spanish by Marjory Mattingly Urquidi (Berkeley: University of California Press, 1979); and John Foran, "An Historical-Sociological Framework for the Study of Long-Term Transformations in the Third World," pp. 330–49 in *Humanity and Society*, volume 16, number 3 (August 1992).

7. The vulnerabilities of this type of state are now widely agreed upon in the literature on revolutions; all that varies is the terminology used to characterize it. Thus, in Wickham-Crowley's colorful language, it is a "mafiacracy"; for Farhi, "personalist authoritarian"; for Goldstone, a "neopatrimonial" state; for Matthew Shugart, a "sultanistic regime": see Wickham-Crowley, *Guerrillas and Revolution*, 9; Farhi, *States and Urban-Based Revolutions*; Jack Goldstone, "Revolutions and Superpowers," pp. 38–48 in J. R. Adelman, editor, *Superpowers and Revolution* (New York: Praeger, 1986); and Matthew Soberg Shugart, "Patterns of Revolution," pp. 249–71 in *Theory and Society*, volume 18, number 2 (March 1989). Robert Dix probably first identified the weaknesses of this type of state in "Why Revolutions Succeed and Fail," pp. 423–46 in *Polity*, volume XVI, number 3 (Summer 1984).

8. See John Foran, *Fragile Resistance*, "A Theory of Third World Social Revolutions", and Chapter 8 in the present volume. As I make clear in that chapter, this concept draws on the work of A. Sivanandan, James Scott, Farideh Farhi, Stuart Hall, and Antonio Gramsci, among many others.

9. Alexis de Tocqueville, *The Old Regime and the French Revolution*, translated by Stuart Gilbert (Garden City, NY: Doubleday, 1955 [1856]); and James C. Davies, "Toward a Theory of Revolution," pp. 5–19 in *American Sociological Review*, volume 27 (1962).

10. On Iran, for example, see Mansoor Moaddel, *Class, Politics, and Ideology in the Iranian Revolution* (New York: Columbia University Press, 1993).

11. This notion was pioneered in 1979 by Walter Goldfrank, who refers to it as a "permissive world context': "Theories of Revolution and Revolution Without Theory." It turns somewhat on its head Skocpol's attention to international *pressures* as the cause of revolution in the case of the powerful agrarian empires she studied.

12. See Foran, "A Theory of Third World Social Revolutions," and "The Causes of Latin American Social Revolutions."

13. The standard accounts on the Mexican Revolution are by John Mason Hart, *Revolutionary Mexico: The Coming and Process of the Mexican Revolution* (Berkeley, Los Angeles, London: University of California Press, 1987), and Alan Knight, *The Mexican Revolution*, volume one: *Porfirians, Liberals and Peasants*, and volume two: *Counter-revolution and Reconstruction* (Lincoln and London: University of Nebraska Press, 1986). I have assessed the revolution in several essays: "The Causes of Latin American Social Revolutions"; "Reinventing the Mexican Revolution: The Competing Paradigms of Alan Knight and John Mason Hart," pp. 115–31 in *Latin American Perspectives* (Fall 1996); and "Race, Class, and Gender in the Making of the Mexican Revolution," pp. 139–56 in *Revue internationale de sociologie*, volume 6, number 1 (1996).

14. Wickham-Crowley judges it "one of the four or five most developed nations in Latin America, and the most developed tropical nation in the entire world," but its economy was largely American-owned: *Guerrillas and Revolution*, 166.

Meanwhile, "More Cadillacs were sold in Havana than any other city in the world in 1954," while the poorest 20 percent of the population received only 2–6 percent of the national income: Medea Benjamin, Joseph Collins, and Michael Scott, *No Free Lunch: Food and Revolution in Cuba Today* (New York and San Francisco: Food First and Grove Press, 1986), 5. These contradictory indices are a good example of what I mean by dependent development.

15. For theoretical interpretations of the revolution, see Wickham-Crowley, *Guerrillas and Revolution*, and Foran, "The Causes of Latin American Social Revolutions." The standard history is still Hugh Thomas, *Cuba: The Pursuit of Freedom* (New York: Harper & Row, 1971). Rich Snyder makes the useful point that Batista's decision to use US-supplied weapons to suppress the Cienfuegos mutiny was just as much the result of human agency as the economic downturn created by the rebels, thereby drawing our attention to the general lesson that all actors have agency, something which students of revolution as agency must heed: personal communication, June 19, 1994.

16. I realize the risk of tautology in using the term "effective" in connection with political cultures of resistance, and try to meet this objection in Chapter 8 of this volume. Like all complex concepts, this one needs further work.

17. I discuss each case in "A Theory of Third World Revolutions." Among many full-length works on Iran, see Nikki Keddie, *Roots of Revolution: An Interpretive History of Modern Iran* (New Haven and London: Yale University Press, 1981), and Ervand Abrahamian, *Iran Between Two Revolutions* (Princeton: Princeton University Press, 1982). On Nicaragua: George Black, *Triumph of the People: The Sandinista Revolution in Nicaragua* (London: Zed, 1981); John A. Booth, *The End and the Beginning: The Nicaraguan Revolution* (second edition, Boulder: Westview Press, 1985); and Carlos M. Vilas, *The Sandinista Revolution: National Liberation and Social Transformation in Central America* (New York: Monthly Review Press, 1986).

18. Jonathan D. Spence, *The Search for Modern China* (New York: W. W. Norton, 1990), 499–504. For this discussion of China, I have drawn on Spence; Skocpol, *States and Social Revolutions*; and Eric R. Wolf, *Peasant Wars of the Twentieth Century* (New York: Harper Colophon Books, 1969).

19. On this point, see Val Moghadam's Chapter 6 in this volume.

20. Basic works on Algeria include Wolf, *Peasant Wars of the Twentieth Century*; Alistair Horne, *A Savage War of Peace: Algeria 1954–1962* (London: Macmillan, 1977); William B. Quandt, *Revolution and Political Leadership: Algeria, 1954–1968* (Cambridge, MA: MIT Press, 1969); Rachid Tlemcani, *State and Revolution in Algeria* (London: Zed, 1986); and Mahfoud Bennoune, *The Making of Contemporary Algeria, 1830–1989: Colonial Upheavals and Post-Independence Development* (Cambridge: Cambridge University Press, 1988). I have learned a great deal from one of my undergraduate students, Markus McMillin, "The Dynamics of an Anti-Colonialist Social Revolution: A Study of French Algeria," honors thesis, Department of Political Science, University of California, Santa Barbara (1991). In particular, he alerted me to the significance of the *timing* of the economic downturn, and its making by rebels.

21. This quote comes from a US major in February 1968, referring to Ben Tre, a provincial capital of 35,000 people in the Mekong Delta, as reported for the AP by Peter Arnet: Peter Braestrup, *Big Story: How the American Press and Television Reported and Interpreted the Crisis of Tet 1968 in Vietnam and Washington*, abridged version (New Haven: Yale University Press, 1977), 193.

22. Key works on aspects of the Vietnamese Revolution include Wolf, *Peasant Wars of the Twentieth Century*; Martin J. Murray, *The Development of Capitalism in Colonial*

Indochina (1870–1940) (Berkeley: University of California Press, 1980); Ken Post, *Revolution, Socialism, and Nationalism in Vietnam*, four volumes (Aldershot, UK: Dartmouth, 1989); and H. John LeVan, "Vietnam: Revolution of Postcolonial Consolidation," pp. 52–87 in Goldstone *et al.*, editors, *Revolutions of the Late Twentieth Century*.

23. On Zimbabwe, see Colin Stoneman and Lionel Cliffe, *Zimbabwe: Politics, Economics and Society* (London: Pinter, 1988); Christine Sylvester, *Zimbabwe: The Terrain of Contradictory Development* (Boulder: Westview Press, 1992); and Michael Charlton, *The Last Colony in Africa: Diplomacy and the Independence of Rhodesia* (Oxford: Blackwell, 1990).

24. Key texts include Catherine V. Scott and Gus B. Cochran, "Revolution in the Periphery: Angola, Cuba, Mozambique, and Nicaragua," pp. 43–58 in Terry Boswell, editor, *Revolution in the World-System* (New York: Greenwood Press, 1989); Allen Isaacman and Barbara Isaacman, *Mozambique: From Colonialism to Revolution, 1900–1982* (Boulder: Westview Press, 1983); Barry Munslow, *Mozambique: the Revolution and its Origins* (London: Longman, 1983); and F. W. Heimer, "The Decolonization Conflict in Angola, 1974–76: An Essay in Political Sociology," in *International Studies on Contemporary Africa* (1979).

25. Iran's oil nationalization process under Muhammad Mussadegh from 1951 to 1953 could be added to this list, as indeed, the fall of the Sandinistas from power in 1990 after eleven years in power. The question this latter case raises is how long is "a relatively brief period of revolutionary rule'?

26. For accounts of these events, I have consulted Benjamin Keen, *A History of Latin America*, fifth edition (Boston: Houghton Mifflin, 1995); Jim Handy, *Revolution in the Countryside: Rural Conflict and Agrarian Reform in Guatemala, 1944–1954* (Chapel Hill: University of North Carolina Press, 1994); Stephen Schlesinger and Stephen Kinzer, *Bitter Fruit: The Untold Story of the American Coup in Guatemala* (New York: Doubleday, 1984 edition); and Edwin Lopez, "Ten Years of Spring, In a Land of Eternal Tyranny: Guatemala's 1944–1954 Era Revisited," unpublished paper, Department of Sociology, University of California, Santa Barbara (1994).

27. My sources on Chile include Keen, *A History of Latin America*; Barbara Stallings, *Class Conflict and Economic Development in Chile, 1958–1973* (Stanford: Stanford University Press, 1978); Manuel A. Garretón and Tomás Moulian, *La Unidad Popular y el conflicto político en Chile* (Santiago: Ediciones Minga, 1983); Arturo Valenzuela, *The Breakdown of Democratic Regimes: Chile* (Baltimore: Johns Hopkins, 1979); and Mark Falcoff, *Modern Chile, 1970–1989: A Critical History* (New Brunswick: Transaction, 1993).

28. Key works on Jamaica include Evelyne Huber Stephens and John D. Stephens, *Democratic Socialism in Jamaica: The Political Movement and Social Transformation in Dependent Capitalism* (Princeton: Princeton University Press, 1986); Michael Manley, *Jamaica: Struggle in the Periphery* (London: Third World Media, 1982); Michael Kaufman, *Jamaica under Manley: Dilemmas of Socialism and Democracy* (London: Zed, 1985); and Nelson W. Keith and Novella Z. Keith, *The Social Origins of Democratic Socialism in Jamaica* (Philadelphia: Temple University Press, 1992.

29. Anita M. Waters, *Race, Class, and Political Symbols: Rastafari and Reggae in Jamaican Politics* (New Brunswick: Transaction, 1985).

30. On Grenada, see Hugh O'Shaughnessy, *Grenada: Revolution, Invasion, and Aftermath* (London: Hamish Hamilton, 1984); Kai P. Schoenhals and Richard A. Melanson, *Revolution and Intervention in Grenada: The New Jewel Movement, the United States, and the Caribbean* (Boulder: Westview Press, 1985); Gordon K. Lewis, *Grenada: The Jewel Despoiled* (Baltimore: Johns Hopkins, 1987); and Jorge Heine,

editor, *A Revolution Aborted: The Lessons of Grenada* (Pittsburgh: University of Pittsburgh Press, 1990).

31. See Heine, "Introduction," in *A Revolution Aborted*, 14.

32. A theory of *outcomes* is elaborated in John Foran and Jeff Goodwin, "Revolutionary Outcomes in Iran and Nicaragua: Coalition Fragmentation, War, and the Limits of Social Transformation," pp. 209–47 in *Theory and Society*, volume 22, number 2 (April 1993).

33. See Ragin, *The Comparative Method*, on this procedure. Basically, if the absence or presence of a given variable (in this case, *B*, an exclusionary state) can bring about the same result, the variable may be dropped from the final expression.

34. I discuss this case in more detail in "A Theory of Third World Social Revolutions." The key secondary accounts include: Robert Armstrong and Janet Shenk, *El Salvador: The Face of Revolution* (Boston: South End Press, 1982); James Dunkerley, *The Long War: Dictatorship and Revolution in El Salvador* (London: Verso, 1982); idem, *Power in the Isthmus: A Political History of Modern Central America* (London: Verso, 1988); and Tommy Sue Montgomery, *Revolution in El Salvador: Origins and Evolution* (Boulder: Westview Press, 1982).

35. For analyses of Guatemala, see Wickham-Crowley, *Guerrillas and Revolution*; Dunkerley, *Power in the Isthmus*; Susanne Jonas, *The Battle for Guatemala: Rebels, Death Squads, and U.S. Power* (Boulder: Westview Press, 1991); and Jim Handy, *Gift of the Devil: A History of Guatemala* (Boston: South End Press, 1984). In early 1997, after this chapter was written, a negotiated settlement to the war took effect.

36. On Peru and Sendero, one may consult David Scott Palmer, "Rebellion in Rural Peru: The Origins and Evolution of Sendero Luminoso," pp. 127–46 in *Comparative Politics*, volume 18 (January 1986); "Fatal Attraction: Peru's Shining Path," in *NACLA (North American Congress on Latin America) Report*, volume XXIV, number 4 (December 1990/January 1991); Ilan Stavans, "Two Peruvians," pp. 18–39 in *Transition*, issue 61 (1993); and Deborah Poole and Gerardo Renique, *Peru: Time of Fear* (London: Latin American Bureau, 1992). I analyse this case somewhat further in "The Future of Revolutions."

37. On the Philippines, I have benefited greatly from an exchange of letters with Kim Scipes, Department of Sociology, University of Wisconsin, Madison. Basic works on the subject include: James Goodno, *The Philippines: Land of Broken Promises* (London: Zed, 1991); Benjamin Pimentel, *Rebolusyon! A Generation of Struggle in the Philippines* (New York: Monthly Review Press, 1990); and Daniel B. Schirmer and Stephen R. Shalom, editors, *The Philippines Reader: A History of Colonialism, Neocolonialism, Dictatorship, and Resistance* (Boston: South End Press, 1987).

38. My sources on Haiti include Michel-Rolph Trouillot, *Haiti, State Against Nation: The Origins and Legacy of Duvalierism* (New York: Monthly Review Press, 1990); James Ferguson, *Papa Doc, Baby Doc: Haiti and the Duvaliers* (Oxford: Basil Blackwell, 1987); and Alex Dupuy, *Haiti in the World Economy: Class, Race, and Underdevelopment Since 1700* (Boulder: Westview Press, 1989). A very helpful theoretical interpretation of regime transitions that includes the cases of Haiti and the Philippines, among others studied in this chapter, is provided in Richard Snyder, "Combining Structural and Voluntarist Explanatory Perspectives: Paths out of Sultanistic Regimes," in H. E. Chehabi and Juan J. Linz, editors, *Sultanistic Regimes* (Baltimore: Johns Hopkins University Press, 1997).

39. For the case of Bolivia, I have relied on Keen, *A History of Latin America*, and James Dunkerley, *Rebellion in the Veins: Political Struggle in Bolivia, 1952–1982* (London: Verso, 1984).

40. Laxalt is quoted in Raymond Bonner, *Waltzing with a Dictator: The Marcoses and the Making of American Policy* (New York: Times Books, 1987), 445, cited by Snyder, "Combining Structural and Voluntarist Explanatory Perspectives." In addition to the sources on the Philippines mentioned already in discussing the failure of social revolution, see the article by Snyder, as well as Robert L. Youngblood, *Marcos Against the Church: Economic Development and Political Repression in the Philippines* (Ithaca: Cornell University Press, 1990); Gary Hawes, *The Philippines State and the Marcos Regime: The Politics of Export* (Ithaca: Cornell University Press, 1987); James K. Boyce, *The Philippines: The Political Economy of Growth and Impoverishment in the Marcos Era* (Honolulu: University of Hawaii Press, 1993); and Stanley Karnow, *In Our Image: America's Empire in the Philippines* (New York: Random House, 1989). I have benefited from the work of research assistant Jackie Cabuay on the Philippines, particularly with respect to the economic downturn of the early to mid-1980s.

41. I take up these themes and add other cases in "The Future of Revolutions in a Globalizing World." Much work remains to be done on each of these cases.

42. A vast literature now exists on these cases. One good comparative study of their political economies is found in Walden Bello and Stephanie Rosenfeld, *Dragons in Distress: Asia's Miracle Economies in Crisis* (San Francisco: The Institute for Food and Development Policy, 1990).

43. I do a preliminary analysis of the Zapatista movement in "The Future of Revolutions."

44. Zaire is discussed in Snyder, "Combining Structural and Voluntarist Explanatory Perspectives." Some of the disarray of the opposition is conveyed by John Darnton, "Zaire Drifts Into Anarchy as Authority Collapses," *New York Times* (May 24, 1994). Since this chapter was written, the state has disintegrated further and rebel groups have appeared in the provinces.

45. Note that this is *not* the procedure advocated by Boolean analysis, which treats patterns as *combinations* (i.e., one should not take the factors out of the context of the patterns in which they appear).

46. See Ragin, *The Comparative Method*, 95–8, for the procedures used to arrive at this result.

47. Again this violates Boolean assumptions, although this partial pattern actually appears in seven of the cases.

48. I begin to look at each of these in "The Future of Revolutions."

BIBLIOGRAPHY

Abadan-Unat, Nermin. "Social Change and Turkish Women." Pp. 5–31 in *Women in Turkish Society*, edited by Nermin Abadan-Unat. Leiden: E. J. Brill, 1981.

Abdel-Malek, Anouar. *Social Dialectics*. Two volumes. Albany: State University of New York Press, 1981.

Abel, Wilhelm. *Agricultural Fluctuations in Europe*. New York: St. Martin's Press, 1980.

Abrahamian, Ervand. *Iran Between Two Revolutions*. Princeton: Princeton University Press, 1982.

——. "The Guerrilla Movement in Iran, 1963–1977." Pp. 149–74 in *Iran: Revolution in Turmoil*, edited by Haleh Afshar. Albany: State University of New York Press, 1985.

——. *The Iranian Mojehedin*. New Haven: Yale University Press, 1989.

——. *Khomeinism: Essays on the Islamic Republic*. Berkeley: University of California Press, 1993.

Ahmad, Aijaz. *In Theory: Classes, Nations, Literatures*. London: Verso, 1992.

Alexander, Jeffrey C. *Theoretical Logic in Sociology*. Four volumes. Berkeley: University of California Press, 1983.

——. *Twenty Lectures: Sociological Theory Since World War II*. New York: Columbia University Press, 1987.

Allen, Robert C. *Enclosure and the Yeoman*. Oxford: Clarendon Press, 1992.

Almond, Gabriel and Sidney Verba. *The Civic Culture*. Princeton: Princeton University Press, 1963.

Alonso, Ana Maria. "The Effects of Truth: Re-Presentation of the Past and the Imagining of Community." *Journal of Historical Sociology* 1 (1) (March 1988): 32–57.

Andean Oral History Workshop (THOA)/Silvia Rivera Cusicanqui. "Indigenous Women and Community Resistance: History and Memory." Pp. 151–83 in *Woman and Social Change in Latin America*, edited by Elizabeth Jelin. London: Zed, 1990.

Anderson, Benedict. *Imagined Communities: Reflections on the Origin and Spread of Nationalism*. London: Verso, 1983.

Anderson, Leslie and Mitchell A. Seligson. "Reformism and Radicalism among Peasants: An Empirical Test of Paige's Agrarian Revolution." *American Journal of Political Science* 38 (4) (November 1994): 944–72.

Anderson, Perry. *Lineages of the Absolutist State*. London: Verso, 1974.

Applewhite, Harriet and Darline G. Levy, editors. *Women and Politics in the Age of the Democratic Revolution*. Ann Arbor: University of Michigan Press, 1990.

Archer, Margaret. *Culture and Agency: The Place of Culture in Social Theory*. Cambridge: Cambridge University Press, 1988.

Armstrong, Robert and Janet Shenk. *El Salvador: The Face of Revolution*. Boston: South End Press, 1982.

Ash, Timothy Garton. "Eastern Europe: The Year of Truth." *The New York Review of Books* (February 15, 1990): 17–22.

——. *The Magic Lantern: The Revolution of '89 Witnessed in Warsaw, Budapest, Berlin, and Prague*. New York: Random House, 1990.

Baker, Keith Michael. *Inventing the French Revolution: Essays on French Political Culture in the Eighteenth Century*. Cambridge: Cambridge University Press, 1990.

——. "On the Problem of the Ideological Origins of the French Revolution." Pp. 197–219 in *Modern European Intellectual History: Reappraisals and New Perspectives*, edited by Dominick LaCapra and Steven L. Kaplan. Ithaca: Cornell University Press, 1982.

——, editor. *The French Revolution and the Creation of Modern Political Culture*, volume one: *The Political Culture of the Old Regime*. Oxford: Pergamon Press, 1987.

Bayo, Alberto. *150 Questions for a Guerilla Fighter*. Boulder: Paladin, 1963.

Bearman, Peter. *Relations into Rhetoric: Local Elite Social Structure in Norfolk, England, 1540–1640*. New Brunswick: Rutgers University Press, 1993.

Beik, William. *Absolutism and Society in Seventeenth-Century France: State Power and Provincial Aristocracy in Languedoc*. Cambridge: Cambridge University Press, 1985.

Bello, Walden and Stephanie Rosenfeld. *Dragons in Distress: Asia's Miracle Economies in Crisis*. San Francisco: Institute for Food and Development Policy, 1990.

Bendix, Reinhard. *Nation-Building and Citizenship*. Berkeley and Los Angeles: University of California Press, 1977.

Benjamin, Jules R. *The United States and the Origins of the Cuban Revolution: An Empire of Liberty in an Age of National Liberation*. Princeton: Princeton University Press, 1990.

Benjamin, Medea, Joseph Collins, and Michael Scott. *No Free Lunch: Food and Revolution in Cuba Today*. New York and San Francisco: Food First and Grove Press, 1986.

Bennoune, Mahfoud. *The Making of Contemporary Algeria, 1830–1989: Colonial Upheavals and Post-Independence Development*. Cambridge: Cambridge University Press, 1988.

Berenson, Edward. "The Social Interpretation of the French Revolution." *Contention: Debates in Society, Culture, and Science* 3 (2) (Winter 1994): 55–81.

Beverley, John and Jose Oviedo, editors. *The Postmodernism Debate in Latin America*. Special issue of *Boundary 2* 20 (3) (Fall 1993).

Birnbaum, Pierre. *States and Collective Action: The European Experience*. Cambridge: Cambridge University Press, 1988.

Black, George. *Triumph of the People: The Sandinista Revolution in Nicaragua*. London: Zed, 1981.

Bois, Guy. *The Crisis of Feudalism: Economy and Society in Eastern Normandy ca. 1300–1550*. Cambridge: Cambridge University Press, 1984 [1976].

Bonachea, Ramón L., and Marta San Martín. *The Cuban Insurrection, 1952–1959*. New Brunswick: Transaction, 1974.

Bonner, Raymond. *Waltzing with a Dictator: The Marcoses and the Making of American Policy*. New York: Times Books, 1987.

Bonney, Richard. *Political Change in France Under Richelieu and Mazarin, 1624–1661*. Oxford: Oxford University Press, 1978.

——. *The King's Debts: Finance and Politics in France, 1589–1661*. Oxford: Oxford University Press, 1981.

Booth, John A. *The End and the Beginning: The Nicaraguan Revolution*. Second edition. Boulder: Westview Press, 1985.

Booth, John A., and Thomas W. Walker. *Understanding Central America*. Second edition. Boulder: Westview Press, 1993.

Bosher, J. F. *French Finances 1770–1795, From Business to Bureaucracy*. Cambridge: Cambridge University Press, 1970.

Bouatta, Cherifa. "Feminine Militancy: Algerian Moudjahidates During and After the War." Pp. 18–39 in *Gender and National Identity: Women and Politics in Muslim Societies*, edited by Valentine M. Moghadam. London: Zed, 1994.

Bouatta, Cherifa and Doria Cherifati-Merabtine. "The Social Representation of Women in Algeria's Islamist Movement." Pp. 183–201 in *Identity Politics and Women: Cultural Reassertions and Feminisms in International Perspective*, edited by Valentine M. Moghadam. Boulder: Westview Press, 1994.

Bourgois, Philippe. "Nicaragua's Ethnic Minorities in the Revolution." Pp. 459–72 in *Nicaragua: Unfinished Revolution*, edited by Peter Rosset and John Vandermeer. New York: Grove Press, 1986.

Boyce, James K. *The Philippines: The Political Economy of Growth and Impoverishment in the Marcos Era*. Honolulu: University of Hawaii Press, 1993.

Braestrup, Peter. *Big Story: How the American Press and Television Reported and Interpreted the Crisis of Tet 1968 in Vietnam and Washington*. Abridged version. New Haven: Yale University Press, 1977.

Brenner, Robert. "Agrarian Class Structure and Economic Development in Pre-Industrial Europe." *Past and Present* 70 (1976): 30–75.

——. *Merchants and Revolution: Commercial Change, Political Conflict, and London's Overseas Traders, 1550–1653*. Cambridge: Cambridge University Press, 1993.

Brinton, Crane. *The Anatomy of Revolution*. Revised and expanded edition. New York: Vintage, 1965.

Brucker, Gene. *Florentine Politics and Society, 1343–1378*. Princeton: Princeton University Press, 1962.

——. *The Civic World of Early Renaissance Florence*. Princeton: Princeton University Press, 1977.

Brysk, Alison. "'Hearts and Minds:' Bringing Symbolic Politics Back In." *Polity* 27 (4) (Summer 1995): 559–85.

Burawoy, Michael and Pavel Krotov. "The Soviet Transition From Socialism to Capitalism: Worker Control and Economic Bargaining in the Wood Industry." *American Sociological Review* 57 (1992): 16–38.

Burke, Peter. *Popular Culture in Early Modern Europe*. New York: Harper & Row, 1978.

Burns, Gene. "Ideology, Culture, and Ambiguity: The Revolutionary Process in Iran." *Theory and Society* 25 (3) (June 1996).

Bush, Diane Mitsch and Stephen P. Mumme. "Gender and the Mexican Revolution: The Intersection of Gender, State, and Church." Pp. 343–65 in *Women and Revolutions in Africa, Asia, and the New World*, edited by Mary Ann Tétreault. Columbia: University of South Carolina Press, 1994.

Callinicos, Alex. *Althusser's Marxism*. London: Pluto Press, 1976.

——. *The Revenge of History: Marxism and the East European Revolutions*. University Park: Pennsylvania State University Press, 1991.

Cammack, Paul. "Bringing the State Back In?" *British Journal of Political Science* 19 (1989): 261–90.

Cannon, Terence. *Revolutionary Cuba*. New York: Thomas Y. Crowell, 1981.

Cardoso, Fernando Henrique and Enzo Faletto. *Dependency and Development in Latin America*, translated from the Spanish by Marjory Mattingly Urquidi. Berkeley: University of California Press, 1979.

Castro, Vanessa and Gary Prevost, editors. *The 1990 Elections in Nicaragua and Their Aftermath*. Lanham: Rowman & Littlefield, 1992.

Cayasso, Bassette. "Afro-Nicaraguans Before and After the Sandinista Revolution." Pp. 163–98 in *African Presence in the Americas*, edited by Carlos Moore, Tanya R. Sanders, and Shawna Moore. Trenton: Africa World Press, 1995.

Charlesworth, Andrew. *An Atlas of Rural Protest in Britain, 1548–1900*. Philadelphia: University of Pennsylvania Press, 1983.

Charlton, Michael. *The Last Colony in Africa: Diplomacy and the Independence of Rhodesia*. Oxford: Blackwell, 1990.

Chartier, Roger. *The Cultural Origins of the French Revolution*, translated by Lydia G. Cochrane. Durham and London: Duke University Press, 1991.

Chehabi, H. E. *Iranian Politics and Religious Modernism: The Liberation Movement of Iran under the Shah and Khomeini*. Ithaca: Cornell University Press, 1990.

Cherifati-Merabtine, Doria. "Algeria at a Crossroads: National Liberation, Islamization, and Women." Pp. 40–62 in *Gender and National Identity: Women and Politics in Muslim Societies*, edited by Valentine M. Moghadam. London: Zed, 1994.

Chevalier, François. "The Ejido and Political Stability in Mexico." Pp. 158–91 in *The Politics of Conformity in Latin America*, edited by Claudio Veliz. London: Oxford University Press, 1967.

Chinchilla, Norma. "Revolutionary Popular Feminism in Nicaragua: Articulating Class, Gender, and National Sovereignty." *Gender & Society* 4 (3) (1990): 370–97.

Chorley, Katharine. *Armies and the Art of Revolution*. Boston: Beacon Press, 1973 [1943].

Christian, Shirley. *Nicaragua: Revolution in the Family*. New York: Vintage, 1986.

Cockcroft, James. *Mexico: Class Formation, Capital Accumulation, and the State*. New York: Monthly Review Press, 1983.

Cohen, Jean L., and Andrew Arato. *Civil Society and Political Theory*. Cambridge, MA: MIT Press, 1992.

Cohen, Youssef. *Radicals, Reformers, and Reactionaries: The Prisoner's Dilemma and the Collapse of Democracy in Latin America*. Chicago: University of Chicago Press, 1994.

Cohn, Samuel Kline. *The Laboring Classes in Renaissance Florence*. New York: Academic Press, 1980.

Colburn, Forrest D. *The Vogue of Revolution in Poor Countries*. Princeton: Princeton University Press, 1994.

Collins, Randall. "The Romanticism of Agency/Structure Versus the Analysis of Micro/Macro." *Current Sociology* 40 (1992): 77–97.

——. "Maturation of the State-Centered Theory of Revolution and Ideology." *Sociological Theory* 11 (1) (March 1993): 117–28.

——. "Prediction in Macrosociology: The Case of the Soviet Collapse." *American Journal of Sociology* 100 (1995):1552–93.

Comninel, George. *Rethinking the French Revolution: Marxism and the Revisionist Challenge*. London: Verso, 1987.

Conroy, Michael E. "The Political Economy of the 1990 Nicaraguan Elections." *International Journal of Political Economy* 20 (3) (Fall 1990): 5–33.

Cox, Oliver. *Caste, Class, and Race*. New York: Monthly Review Press, 1970.

Cuenca, Alejandro Martínez. *Sandinista Economics in Practice*. Boston: South End Press, 1992.

Dabashi, Hamid. *Theology of Discontent: The Ideological Formation of the Islamic Revolution in Iran*. New York: New York University Press, 1993.

Darnton, Robert. "What Was Revolutionary about the French Revolution?" *New York Review of Books* (19 January 1989).

Davies, James C. "Toward a Theory of Revolution." *American Sociological Review* 27 (1) (February 1962): 5–19.

Davies, Miranda, editor. *Third World/Second Sex*. London: Zed, 1983.

Dessert, Daniel. *Argent, Pouvoir et Société au Grand Siècle*. Paris: Fayard, 1984.

Dewald, Jonathan. *The Formation of a Provincial Nobility: The Magistrates of the Parlement of Rouen, 1499–1610*. Princeton: Princeton University Press, 1980.

Dix, Robert. "Why Revolutions Succeed and Fail." *Polity* 16 (3) (Summer 1984): 423–46.

Dobbin, Frank. *Forging Industrial Policy: The United States, Britain, and France in the Railway Age*. New York: Cambridge University Press, 1994.

Dodson, Michael and Laura Nuzzi O'Shaugnessy. *Nicaragua's Other Revolution: Religious Faith and Political Struggle*. Chapel Hill: University of North Carolina Press, 1990.

Dogramaci, Emel. *The Status of Women in Turkey*. Ankara: Meteksan, 1984.

DuBois, William. *Black Reconstruction in America*. New York: Atheneum, 1983.

———. *The Suppression of the Atlantic Slave Trade*. In *Writings*. New York: The Library of America, 1986.

Dunkerley, James. *The Long War: Dictatorship and Revolution in El Salvador*. London: Verso, 1982.

———. *Rebellion in the Veins: Political Struggle in Bolivia, 1952–1982*. London: Verso, 1984.

———. *Power in the Isthmus: A Political History of Modern Central America*. London: Verso, 1988.

Dunn, John. *Modern Revolutions*. New York: Cambridge University Press, 1972.

Dupuy, Alex. *Haiti in the World Economy: Class, Race, and Underdevelopment Since 1700*. Boulder: Westview Press, 1989.

Durkheim, Emile. *Selected Writings*, edited and with an introduction by Anthony Giddens. Cambridge: Cambridge University Press, 1972.

Eckstein, Susan. "Comment on 'Revolution and the Rebirth of Inequality,' by Kelley and Klein." *American Journal of Sociology* 84 (3) (November 1978): 724–7.

———. "Capitalist Constraints on Cuban Economic Development." *Comparative Politics* 12 (3) (April 1980): 253–74.

———. "The Impact of Revolution on Social Welfare in Latin America." *Theory and Society* 11 (1982): 43–94.

———. "The Impact of the Cuban Revolution: A Comparative Perspective." *Comparative Studies in Society and History* 28 (July 1986): 503–34.

Einhorn, Barbara. "Democratization and Women's Movements in Central and Eastern Europe: Concepts of Women's Rights." Pp. 48–74 in *Democratic Reform and the Position of Women in Transitional Economies*, edited by Valentine M. Moghadam. Oxford: Clarendon Press, 1993.

Eisenstadt, S. N. "Frameworks of the Great Revolutions: Culture, Social Structure, History and Human Agency." *International Social Science Journal* 133 (August 1992): 385–401.

Emirbayer, Mustafa, and Jeff Goodwin. "Network Analysis, Culture, and the Problem of Agency." *American Journal of Sociology* 99 (1994): 1411–54.

———. "Symbols, Positions, Objects: Rethinking Network Analysis." Paper presented at the International Conference on Social Networks, London (1995).

———. "Symbols, Positions, Objects: Toward a New Theory of Revolution and Collective Action." Working Paper No. 223. New School for Social Research (1995).

Enríquez, Laura J. *Social Transformation in Latin America: Tensions Between Agroexport Production and Agrarian Reform in Contemporary Nicaragua*. Chapel Hill: University of North Carolina Press, 1991.

Evans, Peter. *Embedded Autonomy: States and Industrial Transformation*. Princeton: Princeton University Press, 1995.

Falcoff, Mark. *Modern Chile, 1970–1989: A Critical History*. New Brunswick: Transaction, 1993.

Farhi, Farideh. "State Disintegration and Urban-Based Revolutionary Crises: A Comparative Analysis of Iran and Nicaragua." *Comparative Political Studies* 21 (2) (July 1988): 231–56.

——. *States and Urban-Based Revolutions: Iran and Nicaragua.* Urbana and Chicago: University of Illinois Press, 1990.

Farsoun, Samih K. and Mehrdad Mashayekhi, editors. *Political Culture in the Islamic Republic.* London: Routledge, 1992.

"Fatal Attraction: Peru's Shining Path." *NACLA (North American Congress on Latin America) Report* XXIV (4) (December 1990/January 1991).

Ferguson, James. *Papa Doc, Baby Doc: Haiti and the Duvalier.* Oxford: Basil Blackwell, 1987.

Fischer, David Hackett. *Historians' Fallacies: Toward a Logic of Historical Thought.* New York: Harper & Row, 1970.

Foner, Philip. *A History of Cuba and its Relations with the United States.* Two volumes. New York: International Publishers, 1962, 1963.

——. *History of Black Americans.* Volume one. Westport, CT: Greenwood Press, 1975.

Foran, John. "An Historical-Sociological Framework for the Study of Long-Term Transformations in the Third World." *Humanity and Society* 16 (3) (August 1992): 330–49.

——. "A Theory of Third World Social Revolutions: Iran, Nicaragua, and El Salvador Compared." *Critical Sociology* 19 (2) (1992): 3–27.

——. *Fragile Resistance: Social Transformation in Iran from 1500 to the Revolution.* Boulder: Westview Press, 1993.

——. "Revolutionizing Theory/Revising Revolution: State, Culture, and Society in Recent Works on Revolution." *Contention: Debates in Society, Culture and Science* 2 (2) (Winter 1993): 65–88.

——. "Theories of Revolution Revisited: Toward a Fourth Generation?" *Sociological Theory* 11 (1) (March 1993): 1–20.

——. "The Causes of Latin American Social Revolutions: Searching for Patterns in Mexico, Cuba, and Nicaragua." Pp. 209–44 *World Society Studies*, volume three: *Conflicts and New Departures in World Society*, edited by Peter Lengyel and Volker Bornschier. New Brunswick: Transaction, 1994.

——. "The Iranian Revolution and the Study of Discourses: A Comment on Moaddel." *Critique: Journal of Critical Studies of Iran & the Middle East* 4 (Spring 1994): 51–63.

——. "The Future of Revolutions in a Globalizing World." Working Paper No. 26. Advanced Study Center 1995–96. International Institute, University of Michigan (March 1996).

——. "Race, Class, and Gender in the Making of the Mexican Revolution." *Revue internationale de sociologie* 6 (1) (1996): 139–56.

——. "Reinventing the Mexican Revolution: The Competing Paradigms of Alan Knight and John Mason Hart." *Latin American Perspectives* (Fall 1996): 115–31.

Foran, John, and Jeff Goodwin. "Revolutionary Outcomes in Iran and Nicaragua: Coalition Fragmentation, War, and the Limits of Social Transformation." *Theory and Society* 22 (2) (April 1993): 209–47.

Foran, John, Linda Klouzal, and Jean-Pierre Rivera. "Who Makes Revolutions? Class, Gender, and Race in the Mexican, Cuban, and Nicaraguan Revolutions." *Research in Social Movements, Conflicts and Change* (1997).

Foucault, Michel. *Discipline and Punish: The Birth of the Prison.* New York: Vintage, 1979.

——. *The History of Sexuality*, volume one: *An Introduction.* New York: Vintage, 1990.

Friedland, Roger, and Robert R. Alford. "Bringing Society Back In: Symbols, Practices, and Institutional Contradictions." Pp. 232–63 in *The New Institutionalism in Organizational Analysis*, edited by Walter W. Powell and Paul J. DiMaggio. Chicago: University of Chicago Press, 1991.

De la Fuente, Alejandro. "Race and Inequality in Cuba, 1899–1981." *Journal of Contemporary History* 30 (1995): 131–68.

Furet, François. *Interpreting the French Revolution*. Cambridge: Cambridge University Press, 1981.

Garretón, Manuel A. and Tomás Moulian. *La Unidad Popular y el conflicto politico en Chile*. Santiago: Ediciones Minga, 1983.

Geertz, Clifford. *The Interpretation of Cultures*. New York: Basic Books, 1973.

Gellner, Ernest. *Postmodernism, Reason, and Religion*. London: Routledge, 1992.

Gilbert, Jorge. *Cuba: From Primitive Accumulation of Capital to Socialism*. Toronto: Two Thirds Editions, 1981.

Girvan, Norman. "Aspects of the Political Economy of Race and in the Caribbean and the Americas." Working Paper No. 7. Kingston: Institute of Social and Economic Research, University of the West Indies, 1975.

Goffman, Erving. *Frame Analysis: An Essay on the Organization of Experience*. New York: Harper & Row, 1974.

Goldfield, Michael. "Worker Insurgency, Radical Organization, and New Deal Labor Legislation." *American Political Science Review* 83 (1989): 1257–82.

Goldfrank, Walter L. "Theories of Revolution and Revolution Without Theory: The Case of Mexico." *Theory and Society* 7 (1979): 135–65.

Goldman, Wendy Zeva. "Women, the Family, and the New Revolutionary Order in the Soviet Union." Pp. 59–81 in *Promissory Notes: Women in the Transition to Socialism*, edited by Sonia Kruks, Rayna Rapp, and Marilyn B. Young. New York: Monthly Review Press, 1989.

Goldstone, Jack A. "Theories of Revolution: The Third Generation." *World Politics* 32 (3) (April 1980): 425–53.

——. "The Comparative and Historical Study of Revolutions." *Annual Review of Sociology* 8 (1982): 187–207.

——. "Revolutions and Superpowers." Pp. 34–48 in *Superpowers and Revolutions*, edited by Jonathan R. Adelman. New York: Praeger, 1986.

——. *Revolution and Rebellion in the Early Modern World*. Berkeley and Los Angeles: University of California Press, 1991.

——, editor. *Revolutions: Theoretical, Comparative, and Historical Studies*. Second edition. San Diego: Harcourt Brace Jovanovich, 1993.

——. "Analyzing Revolutions and Rebellions: A Reply to Critics." Pp. 178–99 in *Debating Revolutions*, edited by Nikki R. Keddie. New York: New York University Press, 1995.

——. "Predicting Revolutions: Why We Could (and Should) Have Foreseen the Revolutions of 1989–1991 in the U.S.S.R. and Eastern Europe." Pp. 39–64 in *Debating Revolutions*, edited by Nikki R. Keddie. New York: New York University Press, 1995.

Goldstone, Jack A., Ted Robert Gurr, and Farrokh Moshiri, editors. *Revolutions of the Late Twentieth Century*. Boulder: Westview Press, 1991.

Goldthwaite, Richard A. *The Building of Renaissance Florence: An Economic and Social History*. Baltimore: Johns Hopkins University Press, 1980.

Goodno, James. *The Philippines: Land of Broken Promises*. London: Zed, 1991.

Goodwin, Jeff. "States and Revolutions in the Third World: A Comparative Analysis." Ph.D. dissertation, Harvard University (1988).

——. "Colonialism and Revolution in Southeast Asia: A Comparative Analysis." Pp. 59–78 in *Revolution in the World-System*, edited by Terry Boswell. Westport: Greenwood Press, 1989.

——. "Why Guerrilla Insurgencies Persist, or the Perversity of Indiscriminate State Violence." Paper presented at the annual meetings of the American Sociological Association, Miami Beach (1993).

——. "Old Regimes and Revolutions in the Second and Third Worlds: A Comparative Perspective." *Social Science History* (4) 18 (Winter 1994): 575–604.

——. "Toward a New Sociology of Revolutions." *Theory and Society* 23 (6) (December 1994): 731–66.

——. *State and Revolution, 1945–91.* Cambridge: Cambridge University Press, 1998.

Goodwin, Jeff and Mustafa Emirbayer. "Symbols, Positions, Objects: Toward a New Theory of Revolutions and Collective Action." Working Paper No. 223. New York: New School for Social Research Center for Studies of Social Change (1995).

Goodwin, Jeff, and Theda Skocpol. "Explaining Revolutions in the Contemporary Third World." *Politics and Society* 17 (4) (December 1989): 489–507.

Gosse, Van. *Where the Boys Are: Cuba, Cold War America and the Making of a New Left.* London: Verso, 1993.

Goubert, Pierre. *L'Ancien Régime.* Two volumes. Paris: A. Colin, 1969.

Gould, Jeffery. *To Lead As Equals: Rural Protest and Political Consciousness in Chinandega, Nicaragua, 1912–1979.* Chapel Hill: University of North Carolina Press, 1990.

——. "Notes on Peasant Consciousness and Revolutionary Politics in Nicaragua, 1955–1990." *Radical History Review* 48 (1990): 65–87.

Gould, Roger V. "Multiple Networks and Mobilization in the Paris Commune, 1871." *American Sociological Review* 56 (1991): 716–29.

Gouldner, Alvin W. *The Future of Intellectuals and The Rise of the New Class.* New York: Continuum, 1978.

Griswold, Wendy. *Cultures and Societies in a Changing World.* Thousand Oaks, London, New Delhi: Pine Forge Press, 1994.

Guevara, Carlos Rangel. *The Latin Americans: Their Love–Hate Relationship with the United States.* New York: Harcourt Brace Jovanovich, 1977.

Guha, Ranajit and Gayatri Chakravorty Spivak, editors. *Selected Subaltern Studies.* New York: Oxford University Press, 1988.

Gulhati, Kaval and Lisa M. Bates. "Developing Countries and the International Population Debate: Politics and Pragmatism." Pp. 47–77 in *Population and Development: Old Debates, New Conclusions*, edited by Robert Cassen *et al.* New Brunswick: Transaction, 1994.

Gurr, Ted Robert. *Why Men Rebel.* Princeton: Princeton University Press, 1970.

——. "Persisting Patterns of Repression and Rebellion: Foundations for a General Theory of Political Coercion." Pp. 149–68 in *Persistent Patterns and Emergent Structures in a Waning Century*, edited by Margaret P. Karns. New York: Praeger, 1986.

Hale, Charles R. *Resistance and Contradiction: Miskitu Indians and the Nicaraguan State, 1894–1987.* Stanford: Stanford University Press, 1994.

Hale, J. R. *Florence and the Medici.* New York: Thames & Hudson, 1977.

Hall, Peter A. *Governing the Economy: The Politics of State Intervention in Britain and France.* New York: Oxford University Press, 1986.

Hall, Stuart. "Pluralism, Race, and Class in Caribbean Society." Pp. 150–82 in *Race and Class in Post-Colonial Society: A Study of Ethnic Group Relations in the English-speaking Caribbean, Bolivia, Chile and Mexico.* Paris: UNESCO, 1977.

——. "Marxism and Culture." *Radical History Review* 18 (1978): 5–14.

——. "Cultural Studies: Two Paradigms." *Media, Culture and Society* 2 (1980).

——. "Race, Articulation and Societies Structured in Dominance," Pp. 305–45 in *Sociological Theories: Race and Colonialism*. Paris: UNESCO, 1980.

——. "Signification, Representation, Ideology: Althusser and the Post-Structuralist Debates." *Critical Studies in Mass Communication* 2 (2) (1985): 91–114.

——. "The Problem of Ideology: Marxism Without Guarantees." *Journal of Communication Inquiry* 10 (2) (1986): 28–44.

——. "Clinging to the Wreckage: A Conversation with Frederick Jameson." *Marxism Today* (September 1990): 28–31.

——. "Cultural Studies and Its Theoretical Legacies." Pp. 277–94 in *Cultural Studies*, edited by Lawrence Grossberg, Cary Nelson, and Paula A. Treichler. London: Routledge, 1992.

Hall, Stuart, John Clarke, Tony Jefferson, and Brian Roberts. "Subcultures, Cultures and Class: A Theoretical Overview." *Working Papers in Cultural Studies* 7/8 (Summer 1975): 9–74.

Hall, Stuart, Bob Lumley and Gregor McLennan. "Politics and Ideology: Gramsci." Pp. 45–76 in *On Ideology*, edited by Stuart Hall, B. Lumley, and G. McLennan. London: Hutchinson, 1978.

Hammond, Thomas. *Red Flag Over Afghanistan*. Boulder: Westview Press, 1984.

Handy, Jim. *Gift of the Devil: A History of Guatemala*. Boston: South End Press, 1984.

——. *Revolution in the Countryside: Rural Conflict and Agrarian Reform in Guatemala, 1944–1954*. Chapel Hill: University of North Carolina Press, 1994.

Hanson, Brad. "The 'Westoxication' of Iran: Depictions and Reactions of Behrangi, Al-e Ahmad, and Shari'ati." *International Journal of Middle East Studies* 15 (1) (February 1983): 1–23.

Hart, John Mason. *Revolutionary Mexico: The Coming and Process of the Mexican Revolution*. Berkeley, Los Angeles, London: University of California Press, 1987.

Hawes, Gary. *The Philippines State and the Marcos Regime: The Politics of Export*. Ithaca: Cornell University Press, 1987.

Heimer, F. W. "The Decolonization Conflict in Angola, 1974–76: An Essay in Political Sociology." *International Studies on Contemporary Africa* (1979).

Heine, Jorge, editor. *A Revolution Aborted: The Lessons of Grenada*. Pittsburgh: University of Pittsburgh Press, 1990.

Helg, Aline. *Our Rightful Share: The Afro-Cuban Struggle for Equality, 1886–1912*. Chapel Hill: University of North Carolina Press, 1995.

Hill, Christopher. "The Norman Yoke." Pp. 50–122 in *Puritanism and Revolution*. London: Mercury Books, 1962.

——. *God's Englishman: Oliver Cromwell and the English Revolution*. New York: Harper & Row, 1972.

——. *The World Turned Upside Down*. Harmondsworth: Penguin, 1972.

Hintze, Otto. *The Historical Essays of Otto Hintze*, edited by Felix Gilbert. New York: Oxford University Press, 1975.

Hodges, Donald. *Intellectual Foundations of the Nicaraguan Revolution*. Austin: University of Texas Press, 1986.

Holmes, George. *Florence, Rome and the Origins of the Renaissance*. Oxford: Clarendon Press, 1986.

Homans, George C. "Bringing Men Back In." *American Sociological Review* 29 (5) (December 1964): 809–18.

Horne, Alistair. *A Savage War of Peace: Algeria 1954–1962*. London: Macmillan, 1977.

Hornik, Richard. "Bursting China's Bubble." *Foreign Affairs* 73 (1994): 28–42.

Hunt, Lynn. *Politics, Culture, and Class in the French Revolution*. Berkeley: University of California Press, 1984.

——. *The Family Romance of the French Revolution*. Berkeley: University of California Press, 1992.

Huntington, Samuel P. *Political Order in Changing Societies*. New Haven: Yale University Press, 1968.

Hyde, J. K. *Society and Politics in Medieval Italy: The Evolution of Civil Life, 1000–1350*. London: Macmillan, 1973.

Isaacman, Allen and Barbara Isaacman. *Mozambique: From Colonialism to Revolution, 1900–1982*. Boulder: Westview Press, 1983.

James, Cyril. *The Black Jacobins*. New York: Vintage, 1963.

Jameson, Fredric. "Third World Literature in the Age of Multinational Capital" *Social Text* (Fall 1986): 65–88.

Jasper, James M. *Nuclear Politics: Energy and the State in the United States, Sweden, and France*. Princeton: Princeton University Press, 1990.

Jayawardena, Kumari. *Feminism and Nationalism in the Third World*. New York: Monthly Review Press, 1986.

Jelin, Elizabeth. "The Politics of Memory: The Human Rights Movement and the Construction of Democracy in Argentina." *Latin American Perspectives* 21 (2) (Spring 1994): 38–58.

Johansen, Bruce. *Forgotten Founders*. Boston: Harvard Common Press, 1982.

Jonas, Susanne. *The Battle for Guatemala: Rebels, Death Squads, and U.S. Power*. Boulder: Westview Press, 1991.

Kandiyoti, Deniz. "Women and the Turkish State: Political Actors or Symbolic Pawns?" Pp. 126–49 in *Women-Nation-State*, edited by Nira Yuval-Davis and Floya Anthias. London: Macmillan 1989.

Kaplonski, Christopher. "Collective Memory and Chingunjav's Rebellion." *History and Anthropology* 6 (2–3) (1993): 235–59.

Karnow, Stanley. *In Our Image: America's Empire in the Philippines*. New York: Random House, 1989.

Katz, Friedrich. *The Secret War in Mexico: Europe, the United States, and the Mexican Revolution*. Chicago: University of Chicago Press, 1981.

Katznelson, Ira. "Working-Class Formation and the State: Nineteenth-Century England in American Perspective." Pp. 257–84 in *Bringing the State Back In*, edited by Peter B. Evans, Dietrich Rueschemeyer, and Theda Skocpol. Cambridge: Cambridge University Press, 1985.

Kaufman, Michael. *Jamaica under Manley: Dilemmas of Socialism and Democracy*. London: Zed, 1985.

Keddie, Nikki. *Roots of Revolution: An Interpretive History of Modern Iran*. New Haven and London: Yale University Press, 1981.

——, editor. *Debating Revolutions*. New York: New York University Press, 1995.

Keen, Benjamin. *A History of Latin America*. Fifth edition. Boston: Houghton Mifflin, 1995.

Keith, Nelson W. and Novella Z. Keith. *The Social Origins of Democratic Socialism in Jamaica*. Philadelphia: Temple University Press, 1992.

Kelly, Linda. *Women of the French Revolution*. London: Hamish Hamilton, 1987.

Kennedy, Paul. *The Rise and Fall of the Great Powers: Economic Change and Military Conflict from 1500 to 2000*. New York: Random House, 1987.

Kennedy, Roger. *Orders From France*. New York: Alfred A. Knopf, 1988.

Kent, Dale. *The Rise of the Medici: Faction in Florence 1426–1434*. Oxford: Oxford University Press, 1978.

Kerkvliet, Benedict J. *The Huk Rebellion: A Study of Peasant Revolt in the Philippines*. Berkeley and Los Angeles: University of California Press, 1977.

Kettering, Sharon. *Judicial Politics And Urban Revolt in Seventeenth-Century France: The Parlement of Aix, 1629–1659*. Princeton: Princeton University Press, 1978.

——. "The Causes of the Judicial Frondes." *Canadian Journal of History* 17 (1982): 275–306.

Keyder, Çaglar. "The Political Economy of Turkish Democracy." *New Left Review* 115 (May–June 1979): 3–44.

Khomeini, Imam. *Islam and Revolution: Writings and Declarations of the Imam Khomeini*, translated and annotated by Hamid Algar. Berkeley: Mizan, 1981.

Kimmel, Michael S. *Revolution: A Sociological Interpretation*. Philadelphia: Temple University Press, 1990.

Kirk, John M. *Politics and the Catholic Church in Nicaragua*. Gainesville: University Press of Florida, 1992.

Kitschelt, Herbert P. "Political Opportunity Structures and Political Protest: Anti-Nuclear Movements in Four Democracies." *British Journal of Political Science* 16 (1986): 57–85.

Klima, Arnost. "Agrarian Class Structure and Economic Development in Pre-Industrial Bohemia." *Past and Present* 85 (1979): 49–67.

K'Meyer, Tracy. "Shared Memory in Community." Paper presented at the International Oral History Conference, Columbia University (October 1994).

Knauss, Peter. *The Persistence of Patriarchy: Class, Gender and Ideology in Twentieth Century Algeria*. Boulder: Westview Press, 1987.

Knight, Alan. *The Mexican Revolution*, volume one: *Porfirians, Liberals and Peasants*. Lincoln and London: University of Nebraska Press, 1986.

——. *The Mexican Revolution*, volume two: *Counter-revolution and Reconstruction*. Lincoln and London: University of Nebraska Press, 1986.

——. "Racism, Revolution, and Indigenismo: Mexico, 1910–1940." Pp. 71–113 in *The Idea of Race in Latin America, 1870–1940*, edited by Richard Graham. Austin: University of Texas Press, 1990.

Kohli, Atul, and Vivienne Shue. "State Power and Social Forces: On Political Contention and Accomodation in the Third World." Pp. 293–326 in *State Power and Social Forces: Domination and Transformation in the Third World*, edited by Joel S. Migdal, Atul Kohli, and Vivienne Shue. Cambridge: Cambridge University Press, 1994.

Kowalewski, David. "Periphery Revolutions in World-System Perspective." *Comparative Political Studies* 24 (1) (April 1991): 76–99.

Kurzman, Charles. "Historiography of the Iranian Revolutionary Movement, 1977–79." *Iranian Studies* 28 (1–2) (Winter 1995): 25–38.

Lachmann, Richard. "Feudal Elite Conflict and the Origins of English Capitalism." *Politics and Society* 14 (3) (1985): 349–78.

——. *From Manor to Market: Structural Change in England, 1536–1640*. Madison: University of Wisconsin Press, 1987.

——. "Origins of Capitalism in Western Europe: Economic and Political Aspects." *Annual Review of Sociology* 15 (1989): 47–72.

——. "Class Formation Without Class Struggle: An Elite Theory of the Transition to Capitalism." *American Sociological Review* 55 (1990): 398–414.

——. *Capitalists in Spite of Themselves*. Oxford: Oxford University Press, 1997.

Lamont, Michele. *Money, Morals, and Manners: The Culture of the French and American Upper-Middle Classes*. Chicago: Chicago University Press, 1992.

Lefebvre, Georges. *The Great Fear of 1789*. New York: Vintage, 1973 [1932].

Lehman, David. *Signs of the Times: Deconstruction and the Fall of Paul de Man*. New York: Poseidon, 1991.

Lenin, Vladimir Il'ich. "The Dual Power." Pp. 301–4 in *The Lenin Anthology*, edited by Robert C. Tucker. New York: Norton, 1975 [1917].

LeVan, H. John. "Vietnam: Revolution of Postcolonial Consolidation." Pp. 52–87 in *Revolutions of the Late Twentieth Century*, edited by Jack A. Goldstone, Ted Robert Gurr, and Farrokh Moshiri. Boulder: Westview Press, 1991.

Levi, Margaret. *Of Rule and Revenue*. Berkeley and Los Angeles: University of California Press, 1988.

Lewis, Gordon K. *Puerto Rico*. New York: Monthly Review Press, 1963.

——. *Grenada: The Jewel Despoiled*. Baltimore: Johns Hopkins, 1987.

Lipset, Seymour Martin. *Political Man: The Social Bases of Politics*. Second edition. Baltimore: Johns Hopkins, 1981.

——. "Radicalism or Reformism: The Sources of Working-Class Politics." *American Political Science Review* 77 (1983): 1–18.

Liss, Sheldon B. *Radical Thought in Central America*. Boulder: Westview Press, 1991.

——. *Fidel! Castro's Political and Social Thought*. Boulder: Westview Press, 1994.

Litchfield, R. Burr. *Emergence of a Bureaucracy: The Florentine Patricians, 1530–1790*. Princeton: Princeton University Press, 1986.

Lobao, Linda. "Women in Revolutionary Movements: Changing Patterns of Latin American Guerilla Struggles." Pp. 180–204 in *Women and Social Protest*, edited by Guida West and Rhoda Lois Blumberg. New York and Oxford: Oxford University Press, 1990.

Lopez, Edwin. "Ten Years of Spring, In a Land of Eternal Tyranny: Guatemala's 1944–1954 Era Revisited." Unpublished paper, Department of Sociology, University of California, Santa Barbara (1994).

Lot, Ferdinand and Robert Fawtier, editors. *Histoire des institutions irançaises au moyen age*, volume one: *Institutions seigneuriales*. Paris: Presses Universitaires de France, 1957.

Lucas, Colin, editor. *The French Revolution and the Creation of Modern Political Culture*, volume two: *The Political Culture of the French Revolution*. Oxford: Pergamon Press, 1988.

Lynch, John. *The Latin American Revolutions: 1808–1826*. New York: W. W. Norton, 1973.

McAdam, Doug. *Political Process and the Development of Black Insurgency, 1930–1970*. Chicago: University of Chicago Press, 1982.

——. "Recruitment to High-Risk Activism: The Case of Freedom Summer." *American Journal of Sociology* 92 (1986): 64–90.

McCarthy, John D., and Mayer N. Zald. "Resource Mobilization and Social Movements: A Partial Theory." *American Journal of Sociology* 82 (1977): 1212–41.

McClintock, Anne. "The Angel of Progress: Pitfalls of the Term Post-Colonialism." *Social Text* 31/32 (Summer 1992): 84–98.

McDaniel, Tim. *Autocracy, Modernization, and Revolution in Russia and Iran*. Princeton: Princeton University Press, 1991.

McGarrity, Gayle and Osvaldo Cardenas. "Cuba." Pp. 77–107 in *No Longer Invisible: Afro-Latin Americans Today*, edited by Minority Rights Group. London: Minority Rights Publications, 1995.

McMillin, Markus. "The Dynamics of an Anti-Colonialist Social Revolution: A Study of French Algeria." Honors thesis, Department of Political Science, University of California, Santa Barbara (1991).

Magagna, Victor V. *Communities of Grain: Rural Rebellion in Comparative Perspective*. Ithaca: Cornell University Press, 1991.

Mahoney, James. "Social Structure and Political Culture in the Explanation of Third World Social Revolutions: Iran and Cuba Compared." Unpublished paper. Department of Political Science, Berkeley (1993).

Major, J. Russell. *Representative Government in Early Modern France*. New Haven: Yale University Press, 1980.

Manley, Michael. *Jamaica: Struggle in the Periphery*. London: Third World Media, 1982.

Mann, Michael. *The Sources of Social Power*, volume two: *The Rise of Classes and Nation-States, 1760–1914*. Cambridge: Cambridge University Press, 1993.

Mannheim, Karl. *Ideology and Utopia*. New York: Harcourt, Brace & World, 1936.

——. *Essays in the Sociology of Knowledge*, edited by Paul Kecskemeti. London: Routledge & Kegan Paul, 1952.

Marx, Karl and Friedrich Engels. *The Marx-Engels Reader*. Second edition, edited by Robert C. Tucker. New York: W. W. Norton, 1978.

Mason, T. David, and Dale A. Krane. "The Political Economy of Death Squads: Toward a Theory of the Impact of State-Sanctioned Terror." *International Studies Quarterly* 33 (1989): 175–98.

Massell, Gregory. *The Surrogate Proletariat*. Princeton: Princeton University Press, 1974.

Matthews, George Tennyson. *The Royal General Farms in Eighteenth-Century France*. New York: Columbia University Press, 1958.

Merton, Robert K. "Insiders and Outsiders: A Chapter in the Sociology of Knowledge." *American Journal of Sociology* 78 (1) (July 1972): 9–47.

——. "Three Fragments from a Sociologist's Notebooks: Establishing the Phenomenon, Specified Ignorance, and Strategic Research Materials." *Annual Review of Sociology* 13 (1987): 1–28.

Meyer, Alfred. *Leninism*. Boulder: Westview Press, 1986.

Mies, Maria. *Patriarchy and Accumulation on a World Scale*. London: Zed, 1986.

Migdal, Joel S. *Strong Societies and Weak States: State–Society Relations and State Capabilities in the Third World*. Princeton: Princeton University Press, 1988.

——. "The State in Society: An Approach to Struggles for Domination." Pp. 7–34 in *State Power and Social Forces: Domination and Transformation in the Third World*, edited by Joel S. Migdal, Atul Kohli, and Vivienne Shue. Cambridge: Cambridge University Press, 1994.

Migdal, Joel S., Atul Kohli, and Vivienne Shue. "Introduction: Developing a State-in-Society Perspective." Pp. 1–4 in *State Power and Social Forces: Domination and Transformation in the Third World*, edited by Joel S. Migdal, Atul Kohli, and Vivienne Shue. Cambridge: Cambridge University Press, 1994.

Mills, C. Wright. *The Marxists*. New York: Dell, 1962.

Mitchell, Timothy. "The Limits of the State: Beyond Statist Approaches and Their Critics." *American Political Science Review* 85 (1991): 77–96.

Moaddel, Mansoor. "State Autonomy and Class Conflict in the Reformation." *American Sociological Review* 54 (3) (June 1989): 472–4.

——. *Class, Politics, and Ideology in the Iranian Revolution*. New York: Columbia University Press, 1993.

——. "The Significance of Discourse in the Iranian Revolution: A Reply to Foran." *Critique: Journal of Critical Studies of Iran & the Middle East* 4 (Spring 1994): 65–72.

Moghadam, Valentine M. "The Left and the Revolution in Iran: A Critical Analysis." Pp. 23–40 in *Post-Revolutionary Iran*, edited by Hooshang Amirahmadi and Manoucher Parvin. Boulder: Westview Press, 1988.

——. "Populist Revolution and the Islamic States in Iran." Pp. 147–63 *Revolution in the World-System*, edited by Terry Boswell. Westport: Greenwood Press, 1989.

——. "Gender and Restructuring: Perestroika, the 1989 Revolutions, and Women." UNU/WIDER Working Paper No. 87. Helsinki: UNU/WIDER, 1990.

——. "Islamic Populism, Class, and Gender in Postrevolutionary Iran." Pp. 189–222 in *A Century of Revolution: Social Movements in Iran*, edited by John Foran. Minneapolis: University of Minnesota Press, 1994.

Mohlo, Anthony. *Florentine Public Finances in the Early Renaissance, 1400–1433*. Cambridge, MA: Harvard University Press, 1971.

Molyneux, Maxine. "Socialist Societies: Progress towards Women's Emancipation?" *Monthly Review* 34 (3) (1982): 56–100.

——. "Mobilization Without Emancipation? Women's Interests, the State, and Revolution in Nicaragua." *Feminist Studies* 11 (2) (1985): 227–54.

——. "The Politics of Abortion in Nicaragua: Revolutionary Pragmatism – or Feminism in the Realm of Necessity?" *Feminist Review* 29 (1988): 114–32.

——. "Legal Reform and Socialist Revolution in South Yemen: Women and the Family." Pp. 193–214 in *Promissory Notes: Women in the Transition to Socialism*, edited by Sonia Kruks, Rayna Rapp, and Marilyn B. Young. New York: Monthly Review Press, 1989.

——. "Women's Role in the Nicaraguan Revolutionary Process: The Early Years." Pp. 127–47 in *Promissory Notes: Women in the Transition to Socialism*, edited by Sonia Kruks, Rayna Rapp, and Marilyn B. Young. New York: Monthly Review Press, 1989.

Montgomery, Tommie Sue. *Revolution in El Salvador: From Civil Strife to Civil Peace*. Boulder: Westview Press, 1994.

Moore, Barrington, Jr. *Social Origins of Dictatorship and Democracy: Lord and Peasant in the Making of the Modern World*. Boston: Beacon Press, 1966.

——. *Injustice: The Social Bases of Obedience and Revolt*. White Plains: M. E. Sharpe, 1978.

Moore, Carlos. *Castro, the Blacks, and Cuba*. Los Angeles: Center for Afro-American Studies, UCLA, 1988.

——. "Afro-Cubans and the Communist Revolution." Pp. 199–239 in *African Presence in the Americas*, edited by Carlos Moore, Tanya R. Sanders, and Shawna Moore. Trenton: Africa World Press, 1995.

Moote, A. Lloyd. *The Revolt of the Judges: The Parlement of Paris and the Fronde, 1643–1652*. Princeton: Princeton University Press, 1971.

Morgan, Lewis. *League of the Iroquois*. New York: Citadel, 1962.

Mornet, Daniel. *Les Origines intellectuelles de la Révolution française 1715–1787*. Paris: Armand Colin, 1933, 1967.

Morrill, John. *The Nature of the English Revolution*. London: Longman, 1993.

Mukerji, Chandra and Michael Schudson. "Introduction: Rethinking Popular Culture." Pp. 1–61 in *Rethinking Popular Culture: Contemporary Perspectives in Cultural Studies*, edited by Chandra Mukerji and Michael Schudson. Berkeley: University of California Press, 1991.

Munslow, Barry. *Mozambique: the Revolution and its Origins*. London: Longman, 1983.

Murray, Martin J. *The Development of Capitalism in Colonial Indochina (1870–1940)*. Berkeley: University of California Press, 1980.

Najemy, John M. *Corporatism and Consensus in Florentine Electoral Politics, 1280–1400*. Chapel Hill: University of North Carolina Press, 1982.

Najmabadi, Afsaneh. "Power, Morality and the New Muslim Womanhood." Pp. 366–89 in *The Politics of Social Transformation in Afghanistan, Iran, and Pakistan*, edited by Myron Weiner and Ali Banuazizi. Syracuse: Syracuse University Press, 1994.

National Network in Solidarity with the Nicaraguan People. "Atlantic Coast: Miskitu Crisis and Counterrevolution." Pp. 83–90 in *The Nicaragua Reader*, edited by Peter Rosset and John Vandermeer. New York: Grove Press, 1983.

Neveux, Hugues. "Déclin et réprise: la fluctuation biseculaire." Pp. 11–173 in *Histoire de la France rurale*, volume 2: *L'Age classique des paysans 1340–1789*, edited by Emmanuel Le Roy Laduric. Paris: Seuil, 1975.

Olson, Mancur. *The Logic of Collective Action*. Cambridge, MA: Harvard University Press, 1965.

Oppenheimer, Andres. *Castro's Final Hour*. New York: Simon & Schuster, 1992.

O'Shaughnessy, Hugh. *Grenada: Revolution, Invasion, and Aftermath*. London: Hamish Hamilton, 1984.

Padgett, John F. and Christopher K. Ansell. "Robust Action and the Rise of the Medici, 1400–1434." *American Journal of Sociology* 98 (6) (1993): 1259–319.

Paige, Jeffery M. *Agrarian Revolution: Social Movements and Export Agriculture in the Underdeveloped World*. New York: Free Press, 1975.

———. "Social Theory and Peasant Revolution in Vietnam and Guatemala." *Theory and Society* 12 (6) (November 1983): 699–737.

Palmer, David Scott. "Rebellion in Rural Peru: The Origins and Evolution of Sendero Luminoso." *Comparative Politics* 18 (January 1986): 127–46.

Papanek, Hanna. "The Ideal Woman and the Ideal Society: Control and Autonomy in the Construction of Identity." Pp. 42–75 in *Identity Politics and Women: Cultural Reassertions and Feminisms in International Perspective*, edited by Valentine M. Moghadam. Boulder: Westview Press, 1994.

Park, Kyung Ae. "Women and Revolution in China: The Sources of Constraint on Women's Emancipation." Pp. 137–60 in *Women and Revolutions in Africa, Asia, and the New World*, edited by Mary Ann Tétreault. Columbia: University of South Carolina Press, 1994.

Parker, David. *La Rochelle and the French Monarchy: Conflict and Order in Seventeenth-Century France*. London: Royal Historical Society, 1980.

———. *The Making of French Absolutism*. London: Edward Arnold, 1983.

Pateman, Carol. *The Sexual Contract*. Cambridge: Polity, 1988.

Paz, Octavio. *The Labyrinth of Solitude*. New York: Grove Press, 1985.

Pearce, Jenny. *Promised Land: Peasant Rebellion in Chalatenango, El Salvador*. London: Latin America Bureau, 1985.

Pérez, Luis A., Jr. *Cuba: Between Reform and Revolution*. New York: Oxford University Press, 1988.

Pérez-Stable, Marifeli. *The Cuban Revolution: Origins, Course, and Legacy*. New York: Oxford University Press, 1993.

Perlman, Selig. *A Theory of the Labor Movement*. Philadelphia: Porcupine Press, 1979 [1928].

Pimentel, Benjamin. *Rebolusyon! A Generation of Struggle in the Philippines*. New York: Monthly Review Press, 1990.

Polanyi, Karl. *The Great Transformation*. Boston: Beacon Press, 1944.

Poole, Deborah, and Gerardo Renique. *Peru: Time of Fear*. London: Latin American Bureau, 1992.

Popkin, Samuel L. *The Rational Peasant: The Political Economy of Rural Society in Vietnam*. Berkeley and Los Angeles: University of California Press, 1979.

Post, Ken. *Revolution, Socialism, and Nationalism in Vietnam*. Four volumes. Aldershot, UK: Dartmouth, 1989.

Pullan, Brian. *A History of Early Renaissance Italy: From the Mid-Thirteenth to the Mid-Fifteenth Century*. New York: St. Martin's Press, 1972.

BIBLIOGRAPHY

Putnam, Robert D. *Making Democracy Work: Civic Traditions in Modern Italy*. Princeton: Princeton University Press, 1993.

Pye, Lucian and Sidney Verba, editors. *Political Culture and Political Development*. Princeton: Princeton University Press, 1965.

Quandt, William B. *Revolution and Political Leadership: Algeria, 1954–1968*. Cambridge, MA: MIT Press, 1969.

Quarles, Benjamin. "Lord Dunmore as Liberator." Pp. 35–47 in *Black Mosaic: Essays in Afro-American History and Historiography*. Amherst: University of Massachusetts Press, 1988.

———. "The Revolutionary War as a Black Declaration of Independence." Pp. 48–64 in *Black Mosaic*. Amherst: University of Massachusetts Press, 1988.

Ragin, Charles C. *The Comparative Method: Moving Beyond Qualitative and Quantitative Strategies*. Berkeley, Los Angeles, and London: University of California Press, 1987.

Randall, Margaret. *Gathering Rage: The Failure of Twentieth Century Revolutions to Develop a Feminist Agenda*. New York: Monthly Review Press, 1993.

Reed, John. *Insurgent Mexico*. New York: International Publishers, 1969.

Reynolds, Siân. "Marianne's Citizens? Women, the Republic, and Universal Suffrage in France." Pp. 101–22 in *Women, State and Revolution: Essays on Power and Gender in Europe since 1789*, edited by Siân Reynolds. Amherst: University of Massachusetts Press, 1987.

———, editor. *Women, State and Revolution: Essays on Power and Gender in Europe since 1789*. Amherst: University of Massachusetts Press, 1987.

Rivera, Jean Pierre. "Agency and Political Consciousness in the Nicaraguan Revolution." MA thesis, Department of Sociology, University of California, Santa Barbara (1993).

Roediger, David. *The Wages of Whiteness*. New York: Verso, 1991.

Rosenau, Pauline Marie. *Post-Modernism and the Social Sciences*. Princeton: Princeton University Press, 1992.

Rowbotham, Sheila. *Women, Resistance, and Revolution*. London: Allen Lane, 1972.

Rudé, George. *Ideology and Popular Protest*. New York: Pantheon, 1980.

Ruiz, Ramon. *The Great Rebellion: Mexico 1905–1924*. New York: W. W. Norton, 1980.

———. *Triumphs and Tragedy: A History of the Mexican People*. New York: W. W. Norton, 1992.

Said, Edward. *Orientalism*. New York: Vintage, 1978.

———. *Culture and Imperialism*. New York: Vintage, 1993.

Schama, Simon. *Citizens*. New York: Knopf, 1989.

Schirmer, Daniel B. and Stephen R. Shalom, editors. *The Philippines Reader: A History of Colonialism, Neocolonialism, Dictatorship, and Resistance*. Boston: South End Press, 1987.

Schlesinger, Stephen and Stephen Kinzer. *Bitter Fruit: The Untold Story of the American Coup in Guatemala*. New York: Doubleday, 1984.

Schoenhals, Kai P. and Richard A. Melanson. *Revolution and Intervention in Grenada: The New Jewel Movement, the United States, and the Caribbean*. Boulder: Westview Press, 1985.

Scott, Catherine V. and Gus B. Cochran. "Revolution in the Periphery: Angola, Cuba, Mozambique, and Nicaragua." Pp. 43–58 in *Revolution in the World-System*, edited by Terry Boswell. New York: Greenwood Press, 1989.

Scott, James. *The Moral Economy of the Peasant*. New Haven: Yale University Press, 1976.

———. "Hegemony and the Peasantry." *Politics and Society* 7 (3) (1977): 267–96.

———. *Domination and the Arts of Resistance: Hidden Transcripts*. New Haven: Yale University Press, 1990.

Selbin, Eric. *Modern Latin American Revolutions*. Boulder: Westview Press, 1993.

——. "Socio-cultural Origins of Revolution and Rebellion in Latin America and the Caribbean." Paper presented at the meetings of the Latin American Studies Association, Washington, DC (1995).

Sewell, William H. Jr. *Work and Revolution in France: The Language of Labor from the Old Regime to 1848*. Cambridge: Cambridge University Press, 1980.

——. "Ideologies and Social Revolutions: Reflections on the French Case." *Journal of Modern History* 57 (1) (March 1985): 57–85.

Shayne, Julia Denise. "Salvadorean Women Revolutionaries and the Birth of Their Women's Movement." MA thesis, Department of Women's Studies, San Francisco State University, April 1995.

Sherwood, Steven Jay, Philip Smith, Jeffrey C. Alexander. "The British Are Coming . . . Again! The Hidden Agenda of 'Cultural Studies'." *Contemporary Sociology* 22 (3) (May 1993): 370–5.

Shohat, Ella. "Notes on the Post-Colonial." *Social Text* 31/32 (Summer 1992): 99–113.

Shugart, Matthew Soberg. "Patterns of Revolution." *Theory and Society* 18 (2) (March 1989): 249–71.

Siavoshi, Sussan. *Liberal Nationalism in Iran: The Failure of a Movement*. Boulder: Westview Press, 1990.

Simon, Julian. *The Ultimate Resource*. Princeton: Princeton University Press, 1981.

Simon, Julian and Herman Kahn, editors. *The Resourceful Earth: A Response to Global 200*. Oxford: Basil Blackwell, 1984.

Sivanandan, A. "Imperialism in the Silicon Age." *Monthly Review* 32 (3) (July–August 1980): 24–42.

Skocpol, Theda. "Old Regime Legacies and Communist Revolutions in Russia and China." *Social Forces* 55 (2) (December 1976): 284–315.

——. *States and Social Revolutions: A Comparative Analysis of France, Russia, and China*. Cambridge: Cambridge University Press, 1979.

——. "Rentier State and Shi'a Islam in the Iranian Revolution" (including comments by Nikki Keddie, Eqbal Ahmad and Walter Goldfrank). *Theory and Society* 11 (2) (May 1982): 265–303.

——. "What Makes Peasants Revolutionary?" *Comparative Politics* 14 (April 1982): 351–75.

——. "Bringing the State Back In: Strategies of Analysis in Current Research." Pp. 3–37 in *Bringing the State Back In*, edited by Peter B. Evans, Dietrich Rueschemeyer, and Theda Skocpol. Cambridge: Cambridge University Press, 1985.

——. "Cultural Idioms and Political Ideologies in the Revolutionary Reconstruction of State Power: A Rejoinder to Sewell." *Journal of Modern History* 57 (1) (March 1985): 89–96.

——. "Social Revolutions and Mass Military Mobilization." *World Politics* 40 (2) (January 1988): 147–68.

——. "Reconsidering the French Revolution in World-Historical Perspective." *Social Research* 56 (1) (Spring 1989): 53–70.

——. *Social Revolutions in the Modern World*. Cambridge: Cambridge University Press, 1994.

Skocpol, Theda, and Kenneth Finegold. "Explaining New Deal Labor Policy." *American Political Science Review* 84 (1990): 1297–304.

Smelser, Neil J. *Theory of Collective Behavior*. New York: Free Press, 1962.

Smil, Vaclav. *China's Environmental Crisis*. Armonk, NY: M. E. Sharpe, 1993.

Smith, Rob. "Simultaneity and Identity: The Imagining, Making, and Politics of a Transnational Mexicano Migrant Community Between the United States and Mexico." Paper presented at the International Conference on Oral Histor, Columbia University (October 20, 1994).

Snow, David A., and Robert D. Benford. "Master Frames and Cycles of Protest." Pp. 133–55 in *Frontiers of Social Movement Theory*, edited by Aldon D. Morris and Carol McClurg Mueller. New Haven: Yale University Press, 1992.

Snow, David A., E. Burke Rochford, Jr., Steven K. Worden, and Robert D. Benford. "Frame Alignment Processes, Micromobilization, and Movement Participation." *American Sociological Review* 51 (1986): 464–81.

Snow, David A., Louis A. Zurcher, Jr., and Sheldon Ekland-Olson. "Social Networks and Social Movements: A Microstructural Approach to Differential Recruitment." *American Sociological Review* 45 (1980): 787–801.

Snyder, Richard. "Explaining Transitions from Neopatrimonial Dictatorships." *Comparative Politics* 24 (1992): 379–99.

———. "Combining Structural and Voluntarist Explanatory Perspectives: Paths out of Sultanistic Regimes." In *Sultanistic Regimes*, edited by H. E. Chehabi and Juan J. Linz. Baltimore: Johns Hopkins University Press, 1997.

Soboul, Albert. *The French Revolution, 1787–1799*. London: New Left Books, 1974 [1962].

Somers, Margaret and Walter Goldfrank. "The Limits of Agronomic Determinism: A Critique of Paige's *Agrarian Revolution*." *Comparative Studies in Society and History* 21 (July 1979): 443–58.

Spence, Jonathan D. *The Search for Modern China*. New York: W. W. Norton, 1990.

Spillman, Lyn. "Culture, Social Structures, and Discursive Fields." *Current Perspectives in Social Theory* 15 (1995): 129–54.

Stallings, Barbara. *Class Conflict and Economic Development in Chile, 1958–1973*. Stanford: Stanford University Press, 1978.

Stavans, Ilan. "Two Peruvians." *Transition* 61 (1993): 18–39.

Stephens, Evelyne Huber and John D. Stephens. *Democratic Socialism in Jamaica: The Political Movement and Social Transformation in Dependent Capitalism*. Princeton: Princeton University Press, 1986.

Stevens, Beth. "Women in Nicaragua." *Monthly Review* 40 (4) (September 1988): 1–18.

Stoneman, Colin and Lionel Cliffe. *Zimbabwe: Politics, Economics and Society*. London: Pinter, 1988.

Swidler, Ann. "Culture in Action: Symbols and Strategies." *American Sociological Review* 51 (2) (April 1986): 273–86.

Sylvester, Christine. *Zimbabwe: The Terrain of Contradictory Development*. Boulder: Westview Press, 1992.

"Symposium on Prediction in the Social Sciences." *American Journal of Sociology* 100, (6) (May 1995): 1520–626.

Taheri, Amir. *The Spirit of Allah: Khomeini and the Iranian Revolution*. Bethesda: Adler & Adler, 1986.

Tait, Richard. "The King's Lieutenants in Guyenne, 1580–1610: A Study in the Relations Between the Crown and the Great Nobility." Ph.D. dissertation, Oxford University (1977).

Tapper, Nancy. "Causes and Consequences of the Abolition of Bride-Price in Afghanistan." Pp. 291–305 in *Rebellions and Revolutions in Afghanistan*, edited by Nazif Shahrani and Robert Canfield. Berkeley: University of California Press, 1984.

Tarrow, Sidney. *Power in Movement: Social Movements, Collective Action and Politics*. Cambridge: Cambridge University Press, 1994.

Tétreault, Mary Ann, editor. *Women and Revolution in Africa, Asia, and the New World.* Columbia: University of South Carolina Press, 1994.

Thomas, Hugh. "Middle-Class Politics and the Cuban Revolution." Pp. 249–77 in *The Politics of Conformity in Latin America,* edited by Claudio Veliz. London: Oxford University Press, 1967.

———. *Cuba: The Pursuit of Freedom.* New York: Harper & Row, 1971.

Thompson, E. P. *The Making of the English Working Class.* New York: Vintage Books, 1966 [1963].

———. "The Moral Economy of the English Crowd in the Eighteenth Century." *Past and Present* 50 (February 1971): 76–136.

Tilly, Charles. *The Vendée.* Cambridge, MA: Harvard University Press, 1964.

———. *From Mobilization to Revolution.* Reading, MA: Addison-Wesley, 1978.

———. "War Making and State Making as Organized Crime." Pp. 169–91 in *Bringing the State Back In,* edited by Peter B. Evans, Dietrich Rueschemeyer, and Theda Skocpol. Cambridge: Cambridge University Press, 1985.

———. "Domination, Resistance, Compliance . . . Discourse." *Sociological Forum* 6 (3) (September 1991).

———. *Coercion, Capital, and European States, AD 990–1992.* Revised edition. Cambridge: Blackwell, 1992.

———. "The Bourgeois Gentilshommes of Revolutionary Theory." *Contention* 2 (2) (Winter 1993): 153–8.

———. *European Revolutions, 1492–1992.* Oxford: Blackwell, 1993.

———. "In Search of Revolution." *Theory and Society* 23 (6) (December 1994): 799–803.

Tlemcani, Rachid. *State and Revolution in Algeria.* London: Zed, 1986.

de Tocqueville, Alexis. *The Old Regime and the French Revolution.* Translated by Stuart Gilbert. New York: Doubleday, 1955 [1856].

———. *Democracy in America.* New York: Modern Library, 1981.

Tohidi, Nayereh. "Modernity, Islamization, and Women in Iran." Pp. 110–47 in *Gender and National Identity: Women and Politics in Muslim Societies,* edited by Valentine M. Moghadam. London: Zed, 1994.

Traugott, Mark. *Armies of the Poor: Determinants of Working-Class Participation in the Parisian Insurrection of June 1848.* Princeton: Princeton University Press, 1985.

———. "Capital Cities and Revolution." *Social Science History* 19 (1995): 147–68.

Trimberger, Ellen Kay. *Revolution from Above: Military Bureaucrats and Development in Japan, Turkey, Egypt, and Peru.* New Brunswick: Transaction, 1978.

———. "E. P. Thompson: Understanding the Process of History." Pp. 211–43 in *Vision and Method in Historical Sociology,* edited by Theda Skocpol. Cambridge: Cambridge University Press, 1984.

Trotsky, Leon. *The History of the Russian Revolution.* London: Pluto Press, 1977.

Trouillot, Michel-Rolph. *Haiti, State Against Nation: The Origins and Legacy of Duvalierism.* New York: Monthly Review, 1990.

Underdown, David. *Revel, Riot, and Rebellion: Popular Politics and Culture in England 1603–1660.* Oxford: Clarendon Press, 1985.

Urdang, Stephanie. *And Still They Dance: Women, War and the Struggle for Change in Mozambique.* New York: Monthly Review Press, 1989.

Valenzuela, Arturo. *The Breakdown of Democratic Regimes: Chile.* Baltimore: Johns Hopkins, 1979.

Vanden, Harry. "Ideology of the Nicaraguan Revolution." *Monthly Review* 34 (2) (1982): 25–39.

Vilas, Carlos M. *The Sandinista Revolution: National Liberation and Social Transformation in Central America*. Translated by Judy Butler. New York: Monthly Review Press, 1986.

——. *State, Class, and Ethnicity in Nicaragua: Capitalist Modernization and Revolutionary Change on the Atlantic Coast*, translated by Susan Norwood. Boulder and London: Lynne Rienner, 1989.

Wallerstein, Immanuel. *The Modern World-System*, volume three: *The Second Era of Great Expansion of the Capitalist World-System, 1730–1840s*. New York: Academic Press, 1989.

Walton, John. *Reluctant Rebels: Comparative Studies of Revolution and Underdevelopment*. New York: Columbia University Press, 1984.

Warman, Arturo. "The Historical Framework of Inter-Ethnic Relations." Pp. 341–54 in *Race and Class in Post-Colonial Society: A Study of Ethnic Group Relations in the English-speaking Caribbean, Bolivia, Chile and Mexico*. Paris: UNESCO, 1977.

Waters, Anita M. *Race, Class, and Political Symbols: Rastafari and Reggae in Jamaican Politics*. New Brunswick: Transaction, 1985.

Waters, Elizabeth. "In the Shadow of the Comintern: The Communist Women's Movement, 1920–1943." Pp. 29–56 in *Promissory Notes: Women in the Transition to Socialism*, edited by Sonia Kruks, Rayna Rapp, and Marilyn B. Young. New York: Monthly Review Press, 1989.

Watson, D. "Can *Memory* Survive the *Storm*?" *New Internationalist* 247 (September 1993): 14–16.

Weber, Max. *The Methodology of the Social Sciences*. Translated and edited by Edward A. Shils and Henry A. Finch. New York: Free Press, 1949.

Welch, S. H. *Communities of Resistance and Solidarity: A Feminist Theology of Liberation*. New York: Orbis Books, 1985.

West, Guida and Rhoda Lois Blumberg, editors. *Women and Social Protest*. New York and Oxford: Oxford University Press, 1990.

Wickham-Crowley, Timothy P. *Exploring Revolution: Essays on Latin American Insurgency and Revolutionary Theory*. Armonk, NY: M. E. Sharpe, 1991.

——. *Guerrillas and Revolution in Latin America: A Comparative Study of Insurgents and Regimes Since 1956*. Princeton: Princeton University Press, 1992.

——. "States and Societies in Revolution: Two Steps Forward, Perhaps One Step Back?" *Theory and Society* 23 (6) (1994): 777–83.

Williams, Raymond. *Culture and Society, 1780–195*. New York: Columbia University Press, 1960.

——. *Politics and Letters: Interviews with New Left Review*. London: Verso, 1979.

——. *Culture*. Cambridge: Fontana, 1981.

Wolf, Eric R. *Peasant Wars of the Twentieth Century*. New York: Harper & Row, 1969.

Womack, John. *Zapata and the Mexican Revolution*. New York: Vintage, 1968.

The Woman Question: Selections from the Writings of Karl Marx, Frederick Engels, V. I. Lenin, Clara Zetkin, Joseph Stalin. New York: International Publishers, 1977.

Wunder, Heide. "Peasant Organization and Class Conflict in East and West Germany." *Past and Present* 78 (1978): 47–55.

Wuthnow, Robert. "State Structures and Ideological Outcomes." *American Sociological Review* 50 (1985): 799–821.

——. "State Structures and Class Conflict in the Rete Structures and Class Conflict in the Reformation (A Reply to Moaddel)." *American Sociological Review* 54 (3) (June 1989): 474–6.

——. *Communities of Discourse: Ideology and Social Structure in the Reformation, the Enlightenment, and European Socialism*. Cambridge, MA: Harvard University Press, 1989.

Youngblood, Robert L. *Marcos Against the Church: Economic Development and Political Repression in the Philippines*. Ithaca: Cornell University Press, 1990.

Zagorin, Perez. *Rebels and Rulers*, volume one. Cambridge: Cambridge University Press, 1982.

INDEX